Transcending Reason

New Heidegger Research

Series Editors: Gregory Fried, Professor of Philosophy, Boston College, USA; Richard Polt, Professor of Philosophy, Xavier University, USA

The *New Heidegger Research* series promotes informed and critical dialogue that breaks new philosophical ground by taking into account the full range of Heidegger's thought, as well as the enduring questions raised by his work.

Titles in the Series
After Heidegger?, edited by Gregory Fried and Richard Polt
Correspondence 1949–1975, Martin Heidegger, Ernst Jünger, translated
 by Timothy Quinn
Existential Medicine, edited by Kevin Aho
Heidegger and Jewish Thought, edited by Micha Brumlik and Elad Lapidot
Heidegger and the Environment, Casey Rentmeester
Heidegger and the Global Age, edited by Antonio Cerella and Louiza Odysseos
Heidegger Becoming Phenomenological: Preferring Dilthey to Husserl, 1916–1925,
 Robert C. Schaff
Heidegger in Russia and Eastern Europe, edited by Jeff Love
Heidegger's Gods: An Ecofeminist Perspective, Susanne Claxton
Making Sense of Heidegger, Thomas Sheehan
Proto-Phenomenology and the Nature of Language, Lawrence J. Hatab
Heidegger in the Islamicate World, edited by Kata Moser, Urs Gösken,
 and Josh Hayes
Time and Trauma: Thinking through Heidegger in the Thirties, Richard Polt
Contexts of Suffering: A Heideggerian Approach to Psychopathology, Kevin Aho
Heidegger's Phenomenology of Perception: An Introduction, Volume I,
 David Kleinberg-Levin
Confronting Heidegger: A Critical Dialogue on Politics and Philosophy,
 edited by Gregory Fried
*Proto-Phenomenology, Language Acquisition, Orality, and Literacy:
 Dwelling in Speech II*, Lawrence J. Hatab
Transcending Reason: Heidegger on Rationality, edited by Matthew Burch and
 Irene McMullin

Transcending Reason

Heidegger on Rationality

Edited by
Matthew Burch and Irene McMullin

ROWMAN &
LITTLEFIELD
INTERNATIONAL

London • New York

Published by Rowman & Littlefield International Ltd.
6 Tinworth Street, London, SE11 5AL, UK
www.rowmaninternational.com

Rowman & Littlefield International Ltd. is an affiliate of Rowman & Littlefield
4501 Forbes Boulevard, Suite 200, Lanham, Maryland 20706, USA
With additional offices in Boulder, New York, Toronto (Canada), and Plymouth (UK)
www.rowman.com

Copyright © Matthew Burch and Irene McMullin, 2020
Copyright in individual chapters is held by the respective chapter authors.

All rights reserved. No part of this book may be reproduced in any form or by any electronic or mechanical means, including information storage and retrieval systems, without written permission from the publisher, except by a reviewer who may quote passages in a review.

British Library Cataloguing in Publication Data
A catalogue record for this book is available from the British Library

ISBN: HB 978-1-78660-958-8

Library of Congress Cataloging-in-Publication Data

Library of Congress Control Number: 2020940245

ISBN: 978-1-78660-958-8 (cloth)
ISBN: 978-1-5381-4820-4 (pbk)
ISBN: 978-1-78660-959-5 (electronic)

Contents

Acknowledgments	vii
Abbreviations of Heidegger's Works	ix
Introduction: Transcending Reason—Heidegger on Rationality	1

PART I: NORMATIVITY AND REASONS   **15**

1 Transcending Reason Heidegger's Way   17
Steven Crowell

2 Freedom and Justification: Heidegger on the Essence of Ground   53
Daniel O. Dahlstrom

3 What Does It Mean to "Act in the Light of" a Norm? Heidegger and Kant on Commitments and Critique   79
Sacha Golob

4 Giving a Damn about Getting It Right: Heideggerian Constitutivism and Our Reasons to Be Authentic   99
Matthew Burch

PART II: PRACTICAL DELIBERATION AND THE UNITY OF AGENCY   **123**

5 Heidegger and Aristotle on Reason, Choice, and Self-Expression: On Decisionists, Nihilists, and Pluralists   125
Denis McManus

6 Heidegger on Deliberation 151
   Patrick Londen

7 Grice and Heidegger on the Logic of Conversation 171
   Chad Engelland

8 Rational Ideals and the Unity of Practical Agency:
   Kant's Postulates of Practical Reason and Their
   Heideggerian Reconceptualization 187
   Irene McMullin

PART III: METHOD 211

9 What Did Edmund Husserl's Phenomenology Want
   to Accomplish? And What Now? 213
   Burt C. Hopkins

10 "Die angebliche Frage nach dem 'Sein des Seienden'":
   An Unknown Husserlian Response to Heidegger's
   "Question of Being" 237
   Jered Janes and Sebastian Luft

11 Phenomenology Rediviva 259
   Thomas Sheehan

12 Heidegger's Philosophy of Science 277
   Ingo Farin and Jeff Malpas

Index 299

About the Authors 305

Acknowledgments

The editors would like to thank Rowman & Littlefield, especially Richard Polt and Gregory Fried for believing in the project, and Rebecca Anastasi for seeing it through. They would also like to thank the intellectual community at the School of Philosophy and Art History at the University of Essex for providing such a vital and congenial philosophical environment to do the kind of philosophy they care about. The editors also thank Jack Marsh for his role in initiating this project, the volume's contributors for their thought-provoking work, and Steve Crowell for twenty years of conversation, inspiration, and friendship. Last but not least, they thank their daughters, Lucy and Mary, for their patience, snuggles, and joyful presence.

Abbreviations of Heidegger's Works

GERMAN TEXTS

References are to the *Gesamtausgabe* edition (Frankfurt: Klostermann, 1975–; abbreviated as GA), with the exception of several texts.

SZ	*Sein und Zeit*. Tübingen: Niemeyer, 1957.
GA1	*Frühe Schriften*. Friedrich-Wilhelm von Herrmann, ed., 1978.
GA2	*Sein und Zeit*. Friedrich-Wilhelm von Herrmann, ed., 1977; first edition 1927.
GA3	*Kant und das Problem der Metaphysik*. Friedrich-Wilhelm von Herrmann, ed., 1991.
GA4	*Erläuterungen zu Hölderlins Dichtung*. Friedrich-Wilhelm von Herrmann, ed., 1996.
GA5	*Holzwege*. Friedrich-Wilhelm von Herrmann, ed., 2003.
GA6	*Nietzsche Vol. I*. Brigitte Schillbach, ed., 1996.
GA7	*Vorträge und Aufsätze*. Friedrich-Wilhelm von Herrmann, ed., 2000.
GA8	*Was heißt Denken*. Paola-Ludovika Coriando, ed., 2002.
GA9	*Wegmarken*. Friedrich-Wilhelm von Herrmann, ed., 2004.
GA10	*Der Satz vom Grund*. Petra Jaeger, ed., 1997.
GA11	*Identität und Differenz*. Friedrich-Wilhelm von Herrmann, ed., 2006.
GA12	*Unterwegs zur Sprache*. Friedrich-Wilhelm von Herrmann, ed., 1985.
GA13	*Aus der Erfahrung des Denkens*. Hermann Heidegger, ed., 2002.
GA14	*Zur Sache des Denkens*. Friedrich-Wilhelm von Herrmann, ed., 2007.

GA15	*Seminare.* Curd Ochwadt, ed., 1986.
GA16	*Reden und andere Zeugnisse eines Lebensweges.* Hermann Heidegger, ed., 2000.
GA18	*Grundbegriffe der aristotelischen Philosophie.* Mark Michalski, ed., 2002.
GA19	*Platon: Sophistes.* Ingeborg Schüßler, ed., 1992.
GA20	*Prolegomena zur Geschichte des Zeitbegriffs.* Petra Jaeger, ed., 1979.
GA21	*Logik. Die Frage nach der Wahrheit.* Walter Biemel, ed., 1976.
GA22	*Die Grundbegriffe der antiken Philosophie.* Franz-Karl Blust, ed., 1993.
GA24	*Die Grundprobleme der Phänomenologie.* Friedrich-Wilhelm von Herrmann, ed., 1975.
GA26	*Metaphysische Anfangsgründe der Logik im Ausgang von Leibniz.* Klaus Held, ed., 1978.
GA27	*Einleitung in die Philosophie.* Otto Saame & Ina Saame-Speidel, ed., 2001.
GA29/30	*Die Grundbegriffe der Metaphysik: Welt—Endlichket—Einsamkeit,* Friedrich-Wilhelm von Herrmann, ed., 1983.
GA31	*Vom Wesen der menschlichen Freiheit. Einleitung in die Philosophie.* Hartmut Tietjen, ed., 1982.
GA34	*Vom Wesen der Wahrheit. Zu Platons Höhlengleichnis und Theätet.* Hermann Mörchen, ed., 1997.
GA38	*Logik als die Frage nach dem Wesen der Sprache.* Günter Seubold, ed., 1998.
GA40	*Einführung in die Metaphysik.* Petra Jaeger, ed., 1983.
GA41	*Die Frage nach dem Ding. Zu Kants Lehre von den transzendentalen Grundsätzen.* Petra Jaeger, ed., 1984.
GA45	*Grundfragen der Philosophie. Ausgewählte "Probleme" der "Logik."* Friedrich-Wilhelm von Herrmann, ed., 1984.
GA49	*Die Metaphysik des deutschen Idealismus. Zur erneuten Auslegung von Schelling: Philosophische Untersuchungen über das Wesen der menschlichen Freiheit und die damit zusammenhängenden Gegenstände (1809).* Günter Seubold, ed., 1991.
GA54	*Parmenides.* Manfred S. Krings, ed., 1982.
GA56/57	*Zur Bestimmung der Philosophie.* Bernd Heimbüchel, ed., 1987.
GA58	*Grundprobleme der Phänomenlogie (1919/20).* Hans-Helmuth Gander, ed., 2010.
GA59	*Phänomenologie der Anschauung und des Ausdrucks.* Claudius Strube, ed., 2007.

GA60	*Phänomenologie des religiösen Lebens.* Matthias Jung, Thomas Regehly, and Claudius Strube, eds., 1995.
GA61	*Phänomenologische Interpretationen zu Aristoteles. Einführung in die phänomenologische Forschung.* Walter Bröcker and Käte Bröcker-Oltmanns, eds., 1985.
GA62	*Phänomenologische Interpretationen ausgewählter Abhandlungen des Aristoteles zur Ontologie und Logik.* Günther Neumann, ed., 2005.
GA63	*Ontologie. Hermeneutik der Faktizität.* Käte Bröcker-Oltmanns, ed., 1988.
GA64	*Der Begriff der Zeit.* Friedrich-Wilhelm von Herrmann, ed., 2004.
GA65	*Beiträge zur Philosophie (Vom Ereignis).* Friedrich-Wilhelm von Herrmann, ed., 1989.
GA66	*Besinnung.* Friedrich-Wilhelm von Herrmann, ed., 1997.
GA70	*Über den Anfang.* Paola-Ludovika Coriando, ed., 2005.
GA71	*Das Ereignis.* Friedrich-Wilhelm von Herrmann, ed., 2009.
GA73	*Zum Ereignis-Denken.* Peter Trawny, ed., 2013.
GA75	*Zu Hölderlin. Griechenlandreisen.* Curd Ochwadt, ed., 2000.
GA76	*Leitgedanken zur Entstehung der Metaphysik, der neuzeitlichen Wissenschaft und der modernen Technik.* Claudius Strube, ed., 2009.
GA77	*Feldweg-Gespräche 1944/45.* Ingrid Schüssler, ed., 2007.
GA94	*Überlegungen II–VI (Schwarze Hefte 1931–1938).* Peter Trawny, ed., 2014.
GA98	*Anmerkungen VI–IX.* Peter Trawny, ed., 2018.
US	*Unterwegs zur Sprache.* Pfullingen: Neske, 1959.
WHD	*Was Heißt Denken?* Tübingen: Max Niemeyer Verlag, 1954.

ENGLISH TRANSLATIONS

BCArP	*Basic Concepts of Aristotelian Philosophy.* Robert Metcalf & Mark Tanzer, trans. Bloomington: Indiana University Press, 2009.
BP	*The Basic Problems of Phenomenology.* Albert Hofstadter, trans. Bloomington: Indiana University Press, 1982.
BT	*Being and Time.* John Macquarrie and Edward Robinson, trans. New York: Harper & Row, 1962.
BW	*Basic Writings.* David Farrell Krell, ed., trans. San Francisco: HarperSanFrancisco, 1992.

CTR	*The Concept of Time*. William McNeill, trans. New York: John Wiley & Sons, 1992.
EG	"On the Essence of Ground." In *Pathmarks*. William McNeill, trans., ed., 97–135. Cambridge: Cambridge University Press, 1998.
FCM	*The Fundamental Concepts of Metaphysics*. William McNeill and Nicholas Walker, trans. Bloomington: Indiana University Press, 1995.
HCT	*History of the Concept of Time: Prolegomena*. Theodore Kisiel, trans. Bloomington: Indiana University Press, 1985.
IPR	*Introduction to Phenomenological Research*. Daniel O. Dahlstrom, trans. Bloomington: Indiana University Press, 2005.
L	"Logos (Heraclitus, Fragment B 50)." In *Early Greek Thinking: The Dawn of Western Philosophy*. David Farrell Krell and Frank A. Capuzzi, trans., 59–78. San Francisco: HarperCollins Publishers, 1975.
OET	"On the Essence of Truth." In *Pathmarks*. William McNeill, ed., 136–154. Cambridge: Cambridge University Press, 1998.
MFL	*The Metaphysical Foundations of Logic*. Michael Heim, trans. Bloomington: Indiana University Press, 1984.
MWP	"My Way to Phenomenology." In *On Time and Being*. Joan Stambaugh, trans., 74–82. New York: Harper & Row, 1972.
PIA	*Phenomenological Interpretations of Aristotle*. Richard Rojcewicz, trans. Bloomington: Indiana University Press, 2001.
PLT	*Poetry, Language, Thought*. Albert Hofstadter, trans. New York: Harper & Row, 1971.
PM	*Pathmarks*. William McNeill, ed., Cambridge: Cambridge University Press, 1998.
PR	*The Principle of Reason*. Reginald Lilly, trans. Bloomington: Indiana University Press, 1991.
PRL	*The Phenomenology of Religious Life*. Matthias Fritsch and Jennifer Anna Gosetti-Ferencei, trans. Bloomington: Indiana University Press, 2004.
PS	*Plato's Sophist*. Richard Rojcewicz and Andre Schuwer, trans. Bloomington: Indiana University Press, 2003.
WDR	"Wilhelm Dilthey's Research and the Struggle for a Historical Worldview." In *Supplements*. C. Bambach, trans., J. van Buren, ed. Albany: State University of New York Press, 2002.

WM	"What Is Metaphysics?" In *Pathmarks*. William McNeill, ed., 82–96. Cambridge: Cambridge University Press, 1998.
WN	"The Word of Nietzsche: 'God Is Dead.'" In *The Question Concerning Technology and Other Essays*. William Lovitt, trans., 53–112. New York: Harper & Row.
WCT	*What Is Called Thinking?* J. Glenn Gray, trans. New York: Harper & Row, 1968.

Introduction

Transcending Reason—Heidegger on Rationality

This volume's title is ambiguous by design, playing on two notions of "transcendence." On the one hand, transcending can mean a going beyond that leaves behind. That Heidegger transcends reason in this sense represents the received view of his work: namely, that it leaves no place for the traditional philosophical ideal of reason. On this reading, Heidegger does not simply dismiss particular representatives of the ideal of reason; rather, he rejects *any* substantive philosophical ideal of reason as a misbegotten by-product of the errant history of metaphysics. As a result, this well-known interpretation continues, and Heidegger effectively cuts us off from any robust sources of normativity, painting a picture of epistemic and practical agents without access to substantive reasons by which to justify their beliefs and actions. In short, the interpretation casts Heidegger as an enemy of reason.

In contrast, this book explores other possibilities for understanding the place of reason in Heidegger's thought, and it does so in a way that reflects the second meaning of "transcending reason": namely, it rethinks reason in terms of what Heidegger calls "the *transcendence* of Dasein" (GA9: 135)—the capacity to occupy the world as a space of normatively structured meanings in which we navigate our striving to be. On this reading, Heidegger doesn't reject reason; rather, he offers a new conception of reason's nature and function by showing how it emerges from Dasein's care-driven striving to be and the norm-responsiveness to which that striving gives rise. Properly understood, reason is the orientation toward measure of an agent situated in the normative landscape of her own everyday existence. In his widely read presidential address to the American Philosophical Association, Hubert Dreyfus claimed that Heidegger "made a start" at answering the question of "how our conceptual capacities grow out of our nonconceptual ones" (2005: 61). According to this second interpretation of Heidegger's philosophical legacy, he did much more than make a start; in fact, his work offers an extended phenomenological analysis of the manner in which the space of reasons emerges from Dasein's normatively ordered, pretheoretical transcendence.

This introduction sets the stage for the volume's exploration of this second interpretation of "transcending reason." We begin by expanding on the first interpretation—the idea that Heidegger transcends reason by leaving it behind—as this helps clarify why so many eminent philosophers consider Heidegger an irrationalist. We then briefly indicate how the chapters in this volume contribute to a relatively new but growing body of literature that challenges the first interpretation and advances the claim that Heidegger *does* leave room for reason in his philosophy.

TRANSCENDING REASON I: HEIDEGGER AS AN ENEMY OF REASON

I appeal to the philosophers of all countries to unite and never again mention Heidegger or talk to another philosopher who defends Heidegger. This man was a devil.

—Sir Karl Popper on his ninetieth birthday
(Quoted in Yue-Ching Ho 1992)

The list of illustrious philosophers who denounce Heidegger as an irrationalist is too long to canvass here, but at the top of any such list we find two of Heidegger's earliest eminent students, Karl Löwith and Herbert Marcuse. Both men were initially drawn to Heidegger's work, excited by what they saw as its revolutionary potential, but soon declared it a philosophical dead end.[1] For example, in 1929, Marcuse had high hopes that Heideggerian phenomenology would breathe new life into Marxism, writing that *Being and Time* "seemed to mark a turning point in the history of philosophy" that would clear "the way for a new 'concrete' science" (cited in Abromeit 2004: 132). By 1933, however, he saw Heidegger as a Nazi shill, and viewed his core existential concepts such as "authenticity" and "resoluteness" as little more than vacuous fascist fodder, affording nothing that might advance "the rational aims of society" (Marcuse 2004: 69).

Similarly, Ernst Tugendhat inveighs against the putative irrationalism at work in Heidegger's claim that "truth, in the most primordial sense, is Dasein's disclosedness" (BT: 265). This claim, Tugendhat argues, plunges Heidegger into an indefensible relativism, because it implies that "any truth-assertion about inner-worldly beings is relative to the historical horizon of our understanding" (1993: 237). If everything we say about inner-worldly entities is relative to the "world" horizon of Dasein's disclosedness, then truth loses its normative dimension—the idea of getting the thing right *as it is in itself* drops out, and gets replaced by describing the thing *as it appears to me (in this particular world horizon)*. Moreover, Tugendhat argues, Heidegger sees different world horizons as fundamentally incommensurable, and so leaves us without a common measure in light of which we might claim that one is better than the other. In this way, Tugendhat claims, the notion that Dasein's disclosedness is the truth in the most "primordial sense" amounts to a "renunciation of the idea of critical consciousness" (1993: 238).

In *Self-Consciousness and Self-Determination*, Tugendhat explores what he takes to be the implications of this account of truth for Heidegger's practical philosophy. On traditional accounts of practical reason, he notes, deliberation aims at "an objectively justified choice" (1986: 212) in light of considerations about what is "good, better, the best" (ibid.: 171). In other words, to aim at an objectively justified choice in light of what is best, I have to try to get things right. But, as we just saw, for a relativist like Heidegger—at least, as Tugendhat sees him—there are no objective material criteria for deliberation to draw upon. Authentic choice, it seems, is a decision for decision's sake, an empty "decisionism" that makes no appeal to reasons or considerations about what's best.

This assessment of Heidegger's practical philosophy reverberates throughout subsequent criticisms of his work. To take a prominent example, in *The Philosophical Discourse of Modernity*, Habermas (1987) sums up Heidegger's philosophical project in *Being and Time* as "a decisionism of empty resoluteness" (141). Heidegger's magnum opus, Habermas claims, denigrates rational public discourse, disparaging the giving and taking of reasons as "inauthentic" "idle talk." Moreover, he continues, Heidegger suggests that the only way to rise above the "levelling" mediocrity of the public sphere is to take a blind leap of faith, "choosing to choose" oneself, without recourse to the publicly available reasons of *"das Man."*

Eminent French philosophers raise similar criticisms. In *Totality and Infinity*, Emmanuel Levinas argues that "Heideggerian ontology, which subordinates the relationship with the Other to the relation with Being in general, remains under the obedience to the anonymous, and lends inevitably to another power, to imperialist domination, to tyranny" (1969: 46f). Elsewhere he ties Heidegger's philosophy even more directly to fascism, claiming that the "source of the bloody barbarism of National Socialism" is "inscribed within the ontology of a being concerned with being—a being, to use the Heideggerian expression, 'which in its own being is concerned with that being'" (1990: 63). In short, the problem, according to Levinas, is that Heidegger's philosophy seems to allow no room for an external check on the self—for whom all meaning is circumscribed by the horizon of its projects and its place in the history of Being. Paul Ricoeur echoes Levinas and

Tugendhat. Like Levinas, he argues in *Oneself as Another* that by making "being-guilty" the ontological foundation of morality, Heidegger abolishes "the primacy of ethics" and proffers "a moral situationism destined to fill the silence of an indeterminate call" (1994: 350–51). And like Tugendhat, Ricoeur describes Heidegger's practical philosophy in starkly "decisionistic" terms in his *Memory, History, Forgetting*:

> What is termed authenticity . . . lacks any criterion of intelligibility: the authenticity speaks for itself and allows itself to be recognized as such by whomever is drawn into it. It is a self-referential term in the discourse of *Being and Time*. Its impreciseness is unequalled, except for that striking other term of the Heideggerian vocabulary: resoluteness, a term singularly associated with "being ahead of oneself" and which contains no determination, no preferential mark concerning any project of accomplishment whatsoever; conscience as a summons of the self to itself without any indication relative to good or evil, to what is permitted or forbidden, to obligation or interdiction. From start to finish, the philosophical act, permeated with *angst*, emerges from nothingness and is dispersed in the shadows. (2004: 349)

Important American commentators draw broadly similar conclusions. Robert Pippin (1997), for instance, argues that Heidegger's philosophy provides an inadequate account of normativity and the critical potential of reason. To highlight this putative shortcoming, Pippin compares Hegel's and Heidegger's respective accounts of the social origin of meaning. For Hegel, Pippin argues, that origin is "inherently 'rational'" and "governed by norms that are actively and in some sense self-consciously sustained by a community"; Heidegger, on the other hand, is "deeply suspicious" of any claim about the inherent rationality of human sociality (1997: 377). And that suspicion, Pippin continues, leaves Heidegger unable to account for rational social critique: Heidegger can describe "the way we go on, the way we *follow* social norms without 'representations,'" but he cannot explain "my 'distance,' as it were, *from* the norm, my not merely responding and initiating appropriately, but in the *light of*, and so with some possible alteration or rejection of, such presumed shared sense of appropriateness" (ibid.: 387, original emphasis). Pippin acknowledges that the discussion of "anxiety, guilt, the call of conscience, authenticity, and resoluteness" in Division II are meant to provide that normative leverage, but, like Tugendhat and Ricoeur, he thinks the account lacks critical bite (ibid.: 386). The breakdown of the self in the face of "existential death," he claims, represents a kind of "indeterminate negation" of the social self (ibid.); but it offers no resources that might justify reason's critical authority. Thus, according to Pippin, Heidegger explains our tendency toward social conformism, but he says nothing substantive about our capacity for rational social critique.

Finally, in another important American interpretation, Hubert Dreyfus and Jane Rubin argue that the "call of conscience" discloses "Dasein's essential structural nullity" (1991: 312), with the implication that "all possibilities [for being a self] are generic and contingent, equally meaningful and therefore equally meaningless" (ibid.: 323). Dreyfus and Rubin put a positive spin on this revelation—calling it "an exciting manifestation of Dasein's finitude" (ibid.: 317)—but, by our lights, the interpretation harbors an unsettling nihilism: in its encounter with death, resolute Dasein discovers no orientation toward the good to fall back on; instead, it comes face to face with the sheer, irremediable meaninglessness of human existence. Although Dreyfus and Rubin do not count themselves among Heidegger's critics, then, some may find their interpretation reads like damning praise, dovetailing with the portrait of Heidegger as a decisionistic nihilist.

TRANSCENDING REASON II: SITUATING REASON IN DASEIN'S TRANSCENDENCE

To summarize the previous section, we can say that Heidegger's critics bring three major charges against him: (1) his conception of truth commits him to a critically toothless relativism, (2) he offers no resources for an ethics, and (3) he has nothing substantive to say about reasons, the good, or the sources of normativity. Recent Heidegger scholarship has mounted defenses against all three charges. Limiting ourselves to English-language publications, there are excellent interpretations of Heidegger's theory of truth that challenge the charge of relativism (Guignon 1983; Richardson 1986; Crowell 2001; Dahlstrom 2001; Carman 2003; Martin 2006; Smith 2007; Cerbone 2008; Thomson 2011; Wrathall 2010; McManus 2012; Haugeland 2000, 2013; Sheehan 2015; and Golob forthcoming). There is a growing body of work that suggests that Heidegger does in fact offer the grounds for an ethics (Vogel 1994; Hodge 1995; Olafson 1998; Young 1997; Hatab 2000; Lewis 2005; McMullin 2013; Smith 2013; Crowell 2013, 2015; Farin and Malpas 2016; Sikka 2017; Fried and Polt 2017; and Reid 2018). Finally, in the last decade, philosophers have also begun to challenge the idea that Heidegger has nothing substantive to say about reasons, the good, and the sources of normativity (Burch 2010; Braver 2012; Crowell 2001, 2013, 2017a, 2017b, 2019; Golob 2014; McManus 2015a, forthcoming; and McMullin 2013, 2018).

The response to the third charge remains the least developed; and it's the area of scholarship to which the present volume most significantly contributes. How does Heidegger conceive of reason and our orientation toward the good? What, according to Heidegger, are the sources of normativity? Why should we strive to think and act in light of what's best? How does Heidegger account for the centrality of practical deliberation and the practice of giving and asking for reasons in human life? This volume attempts to answer these and other related questions in three distinct but deeply connected sections.

PART I: NORMATIVITY AND REASONS

The first section explores Heidegger's attempt to rethink reason in terms of Dasein's "transcendence." The section opens with a chapter by Steven Crowell, a leader in this area of research. In *Husserl, Heidegger, and the Space of Meaning* (2001), Crowell began to explore how, for Heidegger, the space of reasons emerges from the pretheoretical space of meaning thematized by phenomenological reflection. Since then, he has continued to research Heidegger's account of the "existential sources of normativity" (i.e., the manner in which our normative capacities, especially our reasons-responsiveness, are rooted in the fundamental structures of being-in-the-world). Such issues take center stage in the later chapters of his *Normativity and Phenomenology in Husserl and Heidegger* (2013), which is essential reading for anyone interested in the issues explored in this volume. Crowell deepens his work in this vein with his chapter in this volume entitled "Transcending Reason Heidegger's Way." In it, he offers an exposition of the volume's guiding motif, along with a philologically rich and philosophically rigorous discussion of the way Heidegger's stance on reason evolved over the course of his career. It is the perfect chapter to open this particular volume.

In the next chapter, Daniel O. Dahlstrom offers an illuminating, fine-grained reading of Heidegger's 1928 essay "On the Essence of Ground." As Dahlstrom notes, with the exception of a handful of authors (e.g., see Crowell 2013 and Golob 2014), scholars have largely ignored this early essay, and Dahlstrom does an excellent job showing why this is a mistake, drawing out the essay's originality and philosophical significance. In *Heidegger's Concept of Truth* (2001), Dahlstrom offered a major response to critics of Heidegger's so-called relativism; here he advances our understanding of Heidegger's efforts to anchor reason and reason-giving in Dasein's transcendence.

The next chapter in this section is by Sacha Golob. Like Crowell, Golob has already made a major contribution to this area of research with his *Heidegger on Concepts, Freedom and Normativity* (2014), wherein he argues that "the task which *SZ* sets us is to give a new account of normativity" (Golob 2014: 254). In the third chapter of this volume, he further develops his views on these matters by exploring Kant's and Heidegger's respective approaches to what it means to act *in light of* a norm. In part, Golob's chapter can be read as a response to Pippin's worry that Heidegger can't account for our critical distance *from* the norms to which we are responsive. Golob explains how this is possible in Heidegger by way of comparison with Kant's view, and along the way raises a number of fascinating issues for future research in this area, in particular questions about the tools Heidegger makes available for social critique.

Finally, Matthew Burch adds the last chapter to this section. Elsewhere, Burch (2010) challenges what he calls the "Decisionism Critique" of Heidegger's practical philosophy (i.e., the first interpretation of "transcending reason" discussed above) and argues that Heidegger in fact offers rich resources for thinking about both ordinary and deep varieties of practical deliberation. In chapter 4 of this volume, he identifies striking parallels between Heidegger's position—especially as interpreted by Haugeland (2000) and Crowell (2013)—and contemporary work on "constitutivism," a family of meta-normative views that grounds normativity and reasons in the constitutive features of agency. While Burch challenges certain aspects of Crowell's view, he also builds on resources from Crowell's work to offer his own Heidegger-inspired constitutivist argument. That argument concludes that simply in virtue of being agents we face a categorical normative demand to get our existence right (i.e., to think and act in light of what's best).

PART II: PRACTICAL DELIBERATION AND THE UNITY OF AGENCY

Burch's chapter segues naturally into the second section, which focuses on Heideggerian approaches to deliberation and the unity of practical agency. The section opens with a chapter by Denis McManus. Like Dahlstrom, McManus made an important contribution to debates about Heidegger's alleged relativism in *Heidegger and the Measure of Truth* (2012). In his more recent work, he has developed a novel interpretation of Heidegger's concept of authenticity that challenges the third charge brought by Heidegger's critics (McManus 2015a, 2015b, forthcoming). In chapter 5 of this volume, he refines that position further, rejecting the decisionistic reading of Heidegger as misguided and developing a fascinating analysis of Heidegger's Aristotle-inspired approach to *phronesis* and deliberation. Specifically, he argues that Heidegger, in his 1920s lectures on Aristotle, "sets out an account of something one could naturally call 'authenticity,' understood as a readiness to bring to bear one's own judgment on how to act best in situations in which one finds oneself" (129).

The sixth chapter by Patrick Londen pairs well with McManus's contribution. The chapter opens by noting the common criticism—mentioned above—that Heidegger offers no account of deliberation. Londen debunks this claim by discussing the passages on deliberation in *Being and Time*, before turning, as McManus does, to the account of deliberation Heidegger developed in his 1920s Aristotle lectures. Although McManus and Londen draw on similar source material, each accentuates different aspects of Heidegger's account of deliberation, taking it in an entirely original direction. By Londen's lights, Heidegger's approach breaks significantly with traditional conceptions of deliberation. For Heidegger, he argues, we don't deliberate to reach an explicit judgment about the right course of action; rather, deliberation is a "process of figuring out what to do that consists in seeing the world in a way that is conducive to one's projects" (152). Thus, Londen offers an account that is novel as an interpretation of Heidegger and as a conception of deliberation.

Deliberation, however, is not just about carefully considering what to do on my own; it's also a collaborative enterprise in which we talk things over with others. In chapter 7, Chad Engelland shifts things in this direction by developing a Heideggerian approach to the logic of conversation. Engelland takes Paul Grice's classic analysis of conversation as a starting point, expanding the Gricean framework in light of a Heideggerian analysis of being-in-the-world. At the heart of his fascinating analysis, Engelland raises the question of when one interlocutor is justified in challenging the contribution of another. To answer this question, he turns to Heidegger's analysis of discourse "as governed by the normativity of care for self and for another" (172), and he argues that it is an agent's orientation toward the good of the interlocutor, in conjunction with an intention to occasion a new insight, that warrants challenging that interlocutor's contribution.

In chapter 8, Irene McMullin brings this section of the book to a close by considering a meta-deliberative problem that hovers in the background of the other three chapters. If, as we see in the other chapters in this section, deliberation tends to take place *in* a particular situation and *from* the standpoint of a particular "practical identity" or "form of life," when and how does an agent address the wider question of the overall unity of practical agency? In other words, I might get it right each time I deliberate as a parent or a teacher or a spouse in the relevant context, but I'm also living a life in which I need to balance the claims of all those identities over time. This chapter puts Heidegger in dialogue with Kant to think through a possible solution to this problem.

PART III: METHOD

The question of method ties in to the themes of the volume, because Heidegger's stance on the phenomenological method not only speaks to his views on rationality, evidence, and justification, but it also raises anew the specter of irrationalism. Many scholars accept a narrative about the history of phenomenology in which Heidegger jettisons Husserl's notion of "presuppositionless" description, because "all description involves *interpretation*," and so all description must be "situated inside a radically historicized hermeneutics" (Moran 2000: 20). This widely accepted view reintroduces worries about Heidegger's so-called relativism, but at the methodological level. If all phenomenological claims are made within a radically historicized hermeneutics, then it seems that phenomenology can make no claims to universal truth. Moreover, the historicist interpretation of Heidegger seems to undercut any hopes that his method can support something like a "research program" (Crowell 2002: 420). To sustain a research program, a philosophical enterprise needs more than just a shared set of founding texts; it also requires shared methodological norms that make it "clear how to go on and do what the 'founding' texts did" (D'Amico 1999: 254; cited by Crowell 2002: 423). If what Heidegger offers is a "radically historicized hermeneutics" of meaning, however, it's hard to see how those who come after him can be understood as using the same tools to pursue a shared aim. What seems possible, rather, is a series of historically relative acts of interpretation. In other words, his method leaves us with no shared truths and no shared research program.

As Burt Hopkins points out in chapter 9, many phenomenologists have taken this historicist interpretation of Heidegger as grounds for rejecting Husserl's transcendental criterion of purity and his foundational aspirations for phenomenological research. The historicist turn suggests that Husserl's phenomenological analysis of objectivity is in fact guided by a "historically dated derivative meaning of Being" (216). Crowell's (2013) recent work challenges this picture by suggesting that Heidegger in fact preserves Husserl's foundational aspirations—shifting away from Husserl's emphasis on transcendental subjectivity toward the first-personal authority and existential self-responsibility called forth by the experience of anxiety. Hopkins argues that Crowell thereby presents an important corrective to contemporary approaches, defending phenomenology's claim to provide epistemic warrant for its analyses. However, deepening a line of thought from his *The Origin of the Logic of Symbolic Mathematics* (2011), Hopkins argues that it's still unclear whether Dasein's experience of "Being-guilty" can outstrip its history. As such, he claims that the historicist challenge remains a concern.

In chapter 10, Sebastian Luft and Jered Janes take another look at the tension between Husserl and Heidegger due to the latter's reformulation of phenomenology. The chapter opens by noting that in the time leading up to Husserl's 1931 lectures at the Kant Societies in Berlin, Halle, and Frankfurt, Husserl was planning to write an article against Heidegger. However, no overt criticism of Heidegger appears in those lectures, leaving scholars to wonder what became of Husserl's plan to challenge Heidegger directly. Through careful philological work, Luft and Janes argue that Husserl's outline of an article against Heidegger was in fact published in *Husserliana* XXXIV 2002. They unpack the argument of that text, explain how it constitutes a criticism of Heidegger's position, and consider a potential Heideggerian response thereto. Husserl's argument speaks directly to the issues Hopkins raises in chapter 9: against the notion that Husserl's transcendental method must be situated in a radically historicized hermeneutics, Husserl argues that Heidegger's own *Seinsfrage* presupposes a return to the phenomenological reduction and the transcendental subject.

In chapter 11, Thomas Sheehan weighs in on the same set of issues. He opens the chapter by arguing that the standard view of the history of phenomenology—that Heidegger ditched Husserl's reduction in favor of a historicized hermeneutics—is deeply mistaken. Against the grain of that standard narrative, Sheehan suggests that Heidegger scholars take a cue from works like *Transcendental Heidegger* (Crowell and Malpas 2007) and *Normativity and Phenomenology in Husserl and Heidegger* (Crowell 2013), which maintain that Heidegger did not reject Husserl's transcendental method but rather drew inspiration from it, adding to the phenomenological research program rather than creating something completely discontinuous with it. Sheehan then goes on to elaborate his own compelling take on Heidegger's approach to the reduction. Building on his work in *Making Sense of Heidegger* (2015), he demonstrates that the correlational method of phenomenology and its emphasis on the constitution of meaningful experience is essential to appreciating the nature and significance of Heidegger's phenomenology.

In the volume's final chapter, Ingo Farin and Jeff Malpas take a fascinating look at Heidegger's approach to the question of science, arguing that his philosophy of science is not simply an application or branch of his philosophy but rather an integral part of his philosophy itself. In this vein, they argue that, for Heidegger, science cannot be grasped as a set of context-transcendent, true propositions; rather, it must be understood as rooted in Dasein's transcendence: "Leaving to one side the 'logical' construction of scientific theory, Heidegger focuses on the 'existential concept of science,' which thematizes science from the perspective of the theorizing human being, and according to which scientific theorizing is a specific 'mode of being-in-the world'" (SZ: 472; cited by Farin and Malpas: 282–283). By developing this line of thought, Malpas and Farin resist the familiar and facile assimilation of Heidegger's thinking on science to Thomas Kuhn's notion of "paradigms" and Michel Foucault's "epistemes," and demonstrate the originality of Heidegger's philosophy of science as an integral aspect of his larger philosophical project. The rational project of science, then, is ultimately grounded in Dasein's transcending freedom—but a freedom, as we see throughout this volume, that is oriented toward measure.

This introduction only scratches the surface of what our contributors offer in the pages that follow. We hope we have made it clear, however, that this volume poses a significant challenge to the charge that Heidegger set himself against the philosophical ideal of reason and endorsed relativism, decisionism, nihilism, and any other "-ism" associated with the outright rejection of reason. Taking Heidegger's claim that reason is the "stiff-necked adversary of thought" (WN: 112) too literally has obscured the fact that, for Heidegger, Dasein occupies a space of meaning that is not a neutral collection of facts but a normatively polarized arena of practical engagement. To be Dasein is to care about being Dasein well, and as such we find reason-responsiveness in many different domains: practical, moral, theoretical, etc. Traditional approaches to Heidegger's thought are right to challenge the overly cognitivist interpretation of the human agent's distance from the given and the corresponding capacity to assess it in terms of better and worse. But this should not lead us to dismiss the notion that Heidegger offers us resources to think about our orientation toward the good, how and why we act on reasons, and the sources of normativity.

NOTE

1. For helpful accounts of their respective encounters with Heidegger, see Löwith 1995 and Marcuse 2004.

BIBLIOGRAPHY

Abromeit, John. 2004. "Marcuse's Critical Encounter with Heidegger." In *Herbert Marcuse: A Critical Reader*, edited by John Abromeit and Mark Cobb, 131–51. London: Routledge.
Bourdieu, Pierre. 1991. *The Political Ontology of Martin Heidegger*. Translated by Peter Collier. Cambridge: Polity Press.
Braver, Lee. 2012. *Groundless Grounds: A Study of Wittgenstein and Heidegger*. Cambridge, MA: MIT Press.
Burch, Matthew. 2010. "Death and Deliberation: Overcoming the Decisionism Critique of Heidegger's Practical Philosophy." *Inquiry* 53, no. 3: 211–34.
Carman, Taylor. 2003. *Heidegger's Analytic: Interpretation, Discourse, and Authenticity in* Being and Time. Cambridge: Cambridge University Press.
Cerbone, David R. 2008. *Heidegger: A Guide for the Perplexed*. London: Continuum.
Crowell, Steven Galt. 2001. *Husserl, Heidegger, and the Space of Meaning: Paths Toward Transcendental Phenomenology*. Evanston, IL: Northwestern University Press.
———. 2002. "Is There a Phenomenological Research Program?" *Synthese* 131, no. 3: 419–44.

———. 2013. *Normativity and Phenomenology in Husserl and Heidegger*. Cambridge: Cambridge University Press.
———. 2015. "Second-Person Phenomenology." In *The Phenomenology of Sociality: Discovering the "We,"* edited by Thomas Szanto and Dermot Moran, 70–92. London: Routledge.
———. 2017a. "Competence over Being as Existing: The Indispensability of Haugeland's Heidegger." In *Giving a Damn: Essays in Dialogue with John Haugeland*, edited by Zed Adams and Jacob Browning, 73–102. Cambridge, MA: MIT Press.
———. 2017b. "Exemplary Necessity: Heidegger, Pragmatism and Reason." In *Pragmatic Perspectives in Phenomenology*, edited by Ondrej Svec and Jakub Capek, 242–56. London: Routledge.
———. 2019. "A Philosophy of Mind: Phenomenology, Normativity, and Meaning." In *Normativity, Meaning, and the Promise of Phenomenology*, edited by Matthew Burch, Jack Marsh, and Irene McMullin, 329–54. London: Routledge.
Crowell, Steven Galt, and Jeff Malpas. 2007. *Transcendental Heidegger*. Stanford, CA: Stanford University Press.
Dahlstrom, Daniel O. 2001. *Heidegger's Concept of Truth*. Cambridge: Cambridge University Press.
D'Amico, Robert. 1999. *Contemporary Continental Philosophy*. Boulder, CO: Westview Press.
Dreyfus, Hubert L. 1991. *Being-in-the-World: A Commentary on Heidegger's Being and Time, Division I*. Cambridge, MA: MIT Press.
———. 2005. "Overcoming the Myth of the Mental: How Philosophers Can Profit from the Phenomenology of Everyday Expertise." *Proceedings and Addresses of the American Philosophical Association* 79, no. 2: 47–65. American Philosophical Association.
Dreyfus, Hubert L., and Jane Rubin. 1991. "Appendix: Kierkegaard, Division II, and Later Heidegger." In *Being-in-the-World: A Commentary on Heidegger's Being and Time, Division 1*, edited by Hubert L. Dreyfus, 283–340. Cambridge, MA: MIT Press.
Farin, Ingo, and Jeff Malpas, eds. 2016. *Reading Heidegger's Black Notebooks 1931–1941*. Cambridge, MA: MIT Press.
Fried, Gregory, and Richard Polt, eds. 2017. *After Heidegger?* London: Rowman & Littlefield International.
Golob, Sacha. 2014. *Heidegger on Concepts, Freedom and Normativity*. Cambridge: Cambridge University Press.
———. Forthcoming. "Was Heidegger a Relativist?" In *The Emergence of Modern Relativism: The German Debates from the 1770s to the 1930s*, edited by K. Kinzel, M. Kusch, J. Steizinger, and N. Wildschut. London: Routledge.
Guignon, Charles B. 1983. *Heidegger and the Problem of Knowledge*. Indianapolis: Hackett Publishing.
Habermas, Jürgen. 1987. "The Undermining of Western Rationalism through the Critique of Metaphysics: Martin Heidegger." In *The Philosophical Discourse of*

Modernity: Twelve Lectures, 131–48. Translated by Frederick Lawrence. Cambridge, MA: MIT Press.

Hatab, Lawrence J. 2000. *Ethics and Finitude: Heideggerian Contributions to Moral Philosophy*. New York: Rowman & Littlefield.

Haugeland, John. 2000. "Truth and Finitude: Heidegger's Transcendental Existentialism." In *Heidegger, Authenticity, and Modernity: Essays in Honor of Hubert L. Dreyfus*, Vol. 1, edited by Mark Wrathall and Jeff Malpas, 43–77. Cambridge, MA: MIT Press.

———. 2013. *Dasein Disclosed*. Cambridge, MA: Harvard University Press.

Hodge, Joanna. 1995. *Heidegger and Ethics*. New York: Routledge.

Hopkins, Burt C. 2011. *The Origin of the Logic of Symbolic Mathematics: Edmund Husserl and Jacob Klein*. Bloomington: Indiana University Press.

Levinas, Emmanuel. 1969. *Totality and Infinity: An Essay on Exteriority*. Translated by Alphonso Lingis. Pittsburgh: Duquesne.

———. 1990. "Reflections on the Philosophy of Hitlerism," translated by S. Hand. *Critical Inquiry* 17, no. 1: 62–71.

Lewis, Michael. 2005. *Heidegger and the Place of Ethics*. London: Bloomsbury.

Löwith, Karl. 1995. *Martin Heidegger and European Nihilism*, edited by Richard Wolin. New York: Columbia University Press.

Marcuse, Herbert. 2004. "German Philosophy Between 1871 and 1933." In *Herbert Marcuse: Heideggerian Marxism*, edited by Richard Wolin and John Abromeit. Lincoln: University of Nebraska Press.

Martin, Wayne. 2006. *Theories of Judgment: Psychology, Logic, Phenomenology*. Cambridge: Cambridge University Press.

McManus, Denis. 2012. *Heidegger and the Measure of Truth*. Oxford: Oxford University Press.

———. 2015a. "Anxiety, Choice and Responsibility in Heidegger's Account of Authenticity." In *Heidegger, Authenticity and the Self: Themes from Division Two of* Being and Time, edited by Denis McManus, 163–85. London: Routledge.

———. 2015b. "Being-towards-Death and Owning One's Judgment." *Philosophy and Phenomenological Research* 91: 245–72.

———. Forthcoming. "On a Judgment of One's Own: Heideggerian Authenticity, Standpoints, and All Things Considered." *Mind*. https://doi.org/10.1093/mind/fzx045.

McMullin, Irene. 2013. *Time and the Shared World: Heidegger on Social Relations*. Evanston, IL: Northwestern University Press.

———. 2018. *Existential Flourishing: A Phenomenology of the Virtues*. Cambridge: Cambridge University Press.

Moran, Dermot. 2000. *Introduction to Phenomenology*. London: Routledge.

Olafson, Frederick A. 1998. *Heidegger and the Ground of Ethics: A Study of Mitsein*. Cambridge: Cambridge University Press.

Pippin, Robert. 1997. "On Being Anti-Cartesian: Hegel, Heidegger, Subjectivity and Sociality." In *Idealism as Modernism*, 375–94. Cambridge: Cambridge University Press.

Reid, James D. 2018. *Heidegger's Moral Ontology*. Cambridge: Cambridge University Press.
Richardson, John. 1986. *Existential Epistemology: A Heideggerian Critique of the Cartesian Project*. Oxford: Oxford University Press.
Ricoeur, Paul. 1994. *Oneself as Another*. Chicago: University of Chicago Press.
———. 2004. *Memory, History, Forgetting*. Translated by Kathleen Blamey and David Pellauer. Chicago: University of Chicago Press.
Sheehan, Thomas. 2015. *Making Sense of Heidegger: A Paradigm Shift*. London: Rowman & Littlefield International.
Sikka, Sonia. 2017. *Heidegger, Morality and Politics: Questioning the Shepherd of Being*. Cambridge: Cambridge University Press.
Smith, William H. 2007. "Why Tugendhat's Critique of Heidegger's Concept of Truth Remains a Critical Problem." *Inquiry* 50, no. 2: 156–79.
———. 2013. *The Phenomenology of Moral Normativity*. London: Routledge.
Thomson, Iain D. 2011. *Heidegger, Art, and Postmodernity*. Cambridge: Cambridge University Press.
Tugendhat, Ernst. 1970. *Der Wahrheitsbegriff bei Husserl und Heidegger*. Berlin: Walter de Gruyter & Co.
———. 1986. *Self-Consciousness and Self-Determination*. Translated by Paul Stern. Cambridge, MA: MIT Press.
———. 1993. "Heidegger's Concept of Truth." In *The Heidegger Controversy: A Critical Reader*, edited by Richard Wolin, 245–63. Cambridge, MA: MIT Press.
Vogel, Lawrence. 1994. *The Fragile "We": Ethical Implications of Heidegger's Being and Time*. Evanston, IL: Northwestern University Press.
Wolin, Richard. 1992. *The Politics of Being: The Political Ontology of Martin Heidegger*. Cambridge, MA: MIT Press.
Wrathall, Mark A. 2010. *Heidegger and Unconcealment: Truth, Language, and History*. Cambridge: Cambridge University Press.
Young, Julian. 1997. *Heidegger, Philosophy, Nazism*. Cambridge: Cambridge University Press.
Yue-Ching Ho, Eugene. 1992. "At 90, and Still Dynamic: Revisiting Sir Karl Popper and Attending His Birthday Party." *Intellectus* 23: 1–5. http://www.tkpw.net/hk-ies/n23a/.

Part I

NORMATIVITY AND REASONS

Chapter 1

Transcending Reason Heidegger's Way

Steven Crowell

"Reason" is not one of Heidegger's words. It would be hard to find any passages in Heidegger's vast *Gesamtausgabe* where, in *propria persona*, he uses the German *Vernunft* in an affirmative sense. Typically, reason is treated as a symptom of the *Seinsvergessenheit* that infects philosophy as metaphysics, a "stiff-necked adversary of thought" (WN: 112) that demands a "theoretical" attitude toward everything and enables the calculated world of technological *Verwahrlosung* (PR: 30). There is, then, an important sense in which Heidegger's *Denkweg* involves transcending reason as the measure of philosophy's commitment to truth. This is fully on display in *Being and Time*, which recasts the *animale rationale* as care: that being "in whose very being, that being is an issue for it" (BT: 32). Little wonder, then, that many have dismissed *Being and Time* as "irrationalism," with all the skepticism, relativism, and nihilism this is supposed to entail.[1]

Such a judgment is not universally shared, of course. Some who have found in Heidegger a powerful way of raising philosophical questions and identifying overlooked phenomena (among whom I count myself) have pushed back against the charge of irrationalism by questioning the assumptions underlying the way reason is ritually invoked as an *unhintergehbar* philosophical criterion. Understandably, most of these efforts focus on defending Heidegger's demotion of reason from the "law of the World" (Hegel) to a tool we rely on when things go badly (practical deliberation) or need to bring order to our empirical observations (theory).[2] Such efforts have demonstrated how Heidegger can contribute productively to debates within analytic philosophy and other contemporary philosophical approaches, but by and large they embrace the negative sense of "transcending reason" introduced above. Less frequently explored has been the question of whether Heidegger's ontology of Dasein might include an understanding of reason as belonging to the care-structure itself. The explanation might seem obvious: among the categories that make up the care-structure, reason is not to be found. However, if, although unnamed, it could be shown to be there, "transcending reason" might be heard in an affirmative way: reason belongs to transcendence. Only such an understanding of reason could undermine the charge of irrationalism from the ground up.

In previous publications I have argued that if we attend to the *phenomenological* character of Heidegger's thinking from first to last, focusing on his appropriation of Husserl's concept of meaning (*Sinn*) as *veritas transcendentalis*, we find an affirmative conception of reason, and not only in *Being and Time*. Of course, this is only *one* way of approaching Heidegger, and it cannot capture everything that is of philosophical interest in his work. But if it is not an imposition on that work, and if it yields a phenomenological concept of reason unburdened by traditional disputes between rationalism and empiricism, dogmatism and skepticism, this approach would seem to be of some philosophical interest.

What is novel about Heidegger's way of transcending reason can be captured in a slogan: the phenomenology of meaning requires a normativity-first approach to reason rather than a traditional reasons-first approach to normativity: reason is possible thanks to our orientation toward a "measure" whose normativity is not grounded in reason. In what follows, I propose to map this path through Heidegger's thinking, with the aim of clarifying the essential features of Heidegger's normativity-first approach to reason.

A map cannot include everything of course, but it must not focus too narrowly either, and so I will say something about how the idea plays out across three stages of Heidegger's *Denkweg*. The path is marked by an etymological and conceptual point to which Heidegger frequently returns: the term "reason" (*Vernunft*) embodies the dual heritage of the Greek *noein* (*nous*) and *legein* (*logos*). Although this heritage is immensely complicated, here it is enough to note that it requires taking a stand on the relations between two capacities associated with our cognitive and practical life: "intuition" or seeing and "discursivity" or speaking. With this in mind, the map of Heidegger's affirmative conception of reason represents three territories, which correspond to the Early Heidegger (1912–1925), the *Being and Time* period (1925–1934), and Later Heidegger (post-1935). These are distinguished by three different ways of understanding the relation between *noein* and *legein*. In the first, *legein* is the target sense of "reason" and *noein* is subordinated to it, slowly emerging as the main topic; in the second, *legein* is subordinated to *noein*; in the third, Heidegger identifies "thinking" as the "unity" of *noein* and *legein*. In what follows, I will devote a section to each, although only the second will receive detailed treatment.

First, in publications and lecture courses from his student years up to *Being and Time*, Heidegger is concerned primarily with *legein* in the form of logic. Embracing Husserl's focus on intentionality while also criticizing its presuppositions, Heidegger pursues a phenomenological account of meaning (*Sinn*) as the bearer of validity (*Geltung*) in scientific cognition. Here meaning proves irreducible to traditional ontological categories, whether ontic (*ousia*, Aristotle) or transcendental (*synthesis*, Kant). But Heidegger tries to "bring Aristotle and Kant as close together as possible" (GA1: 33)[3] through a phenomenological interpretation of meaning as "being in the sense of truth" (*on hos alethes, ens tanquam verum*), a move that will define his thinking to the very end.[4] More specifically, Heidegger's reflection on the logical structure of meaning yields the pivot of his thinking: the "ontological difference" between beings (*Seiendes*) of any sort and the being (*Sein*) of those beings, what they in truth are, what it *means* for them to be.

Second, in publications and lectures from *Being and Time* through roughly the *Rektoratsrede*, Heidegger's ontological phenomenology of meaning and intentionality decisively subordinates *legein* to *noein*. In unpacking the conditions of possibility of Dasein's understanding of being—our capacity for encountering things *as* they in truth are—Heidegger shows how assertion (and with it reason as *logos*, logic) is grounded in Dasein's transcendence.[5] Transcendence has the character of *noein* in two respects: First, it gives "sight" to our encounters with things, our ability to circumnavigate the world as a totality of significance. Second, this ability is grounded phenomenologically in a "moment of vision" (*Augenblick*) arising from Dasein's "ownmost" ability: being answerable for the normativity that constitutes meaning. Such answerability transcends reason (*logos*) but is also beholden to reason (*noein*): there is no Dasein—and so no meaning, and so no "being" (BT: 272)—without "taking over *being* a ground [*Grund*, reason]" (BT: 330). Since this is a *transcendental* or categorial point, Heidegger devotes much effort during this period to specifying the relation between Dasein (transcendence) and the human being, who can no longer simply be called a rational animal.

When Heidegger abandons this project, the third territory on our map opens up, where transcendence is reconfigured as "thinking" or the unity (*Gefüge*) of *noein* and *legein*. Here as elsewhere, Heidegger does not outline a positive role for reason; indeed, his remarks about reason are now at their most dismissive. However, the *way* thinking incorporates *noein* and *legein* depends on key elements Heidegger introduced in his account of transcendence—a "phenomenological residue" in Heidegger's late work which otherwise seems to (and nominally does) abandon his transcendental approach to the meaning of being. When abstracted from its contextualization in Heidegger's history of being as metaphysics, this residue preserves the affirmative meaning of "transcending reason" found in *Being and Time*.

With this map in mind, then, we turn first to Heidegger's confrontation with transcendental logic, where the roots of his critical stance toward reason as *logos* are found.

LOGIC AND THE PHENOMENOLOGY OF MEANING

Heidegger's dissertation and *Habilitationsschrift* thematize reason in its theoretical capacity as logic, the "form" of thinking that makes scientific knowledge possible. Heidegger mentions Russell and Whitehead's mathematical logic, or "logistics" (GA1: 40–42), but the logical calculus does not interest him. Instead, he aims to make logic philosophical again, taking his start from the traditional division of logic into theories of Concept, Judgment, and Inference.[6]

What does it mean to make logic philosophical again? For many philosophers of the period, including Heidegger, it meant rejecting psychologism, the idea that logic is a branch of psychology.[7] But for Heidegger, following Emil Lask, it also meant that philosophical logic requires a logic *of philosophy*. These two aspects converge on the phenomenon of meaning (*Sinn*). As a key term in the critique of psychologism, meaning, the "object of logic," is neither a psychic nor a physical entity, nor any combination thereof. It thus poses the philosophical problem of clarifying how meaning can be cognized, a theory of categories ("logic") of philosophical cognition. In this sense, meaning "has never been given its due [. . .] in the entire history of philosophy" (GA1: 24), and Heidegger's collected works are an extended attempt to address this lacuna.

Heidegger's earliest publications focus primarily on the theory of judgment, the locus of truth (GA1: 64). For psychologism, judging is a psychic occurrence that combines representations in the mind which then get expressed in the grammar of natural language. This seems to preclude a principled relation between judgment and truth, however, since it is quite obscure how a psychic occurrence, or a combination of mental representations, or a string of vocal or written signs, can have any relation to other entities at all, beyond the "causal" ones available to psychology (GA1: 162–64). If the judgment is supposed to be assessable in terms of truth, then its relation to an object must be of an "intentional" sort, that is, it must mean its object in a way that intentionally implicates its *normative* assessability. For Heidegger, then, the element of judgment that concerns logic is the proposition (*Satz*): neither the psychic act nor the grammatical form, but the "ideal meaning" that either does or does not "hold" of the object of cognition. Logic is a science of meaning, not thinking. "But what, then, is meaning?" (GA1: 170).

Answering this question demands a logic of philosophy that clarifies the categorial conditions that enable philosophical cognition of meaning. Here Heidegger follows Lotze and Lask: there is a categorial distinction between everything that "is" (physical, psychological, super-sensible *entities*) and what "holds" or is "valid" (*gilt*) "without having to be" (Lask 2003: 5). This is the decisive yield of Kant's "critical" turn from cognition of objects to reflection on the conditions of possibility of such cognition, but Heidegger agrees with Lask that Kant himself did not escape psychologism. As Lask put it, Kant leaves "the world of the logical [. . .] entirely homeless" because he provides "no place for the categorial forms" or "logical conditions of his own critique of reason" (2003: 214, 216). The distinction between *Seiendes* and *Geltendes* suggests where this home is to be found: "valid meaning" belongs neither to the domain of substance, nor to that of subjectivity, but to "the realm of truth" (2003: 30), *on hos alethes*.[8] Philosophical cognition of what logical meaning *is* requires bringing Aristotle and Kant as close to one another as possible: there is a necessary connection between beings and truth, the measure of judgment (Aristotle), but this connection is unintelligible without reference to a subject categorially defined by its attunement to the *normativity* of such a measure (Kant). The wellspring of Heidegger's "fundamental" ontology lies here: the phenomenology of logically valid meaning transcends reason (as *logos*) because the meaning it cognizes as the condition of all cognition (including its own) presupposes a subject whose attunement to the normative makes it answerable *for* the measure, truth, upon which logic depends.

Heidegger's phenomenological approach contrasts with the two main strands of neo-Kantianism, which also employ the distinction between "ideal validity" and what "is." For the Marburg school, preserving the apriority and ideality of logic requires eliminating any consideration of "'subjective logic'" (GA1: 404). Starting with the "fact" of scientific cognition, Natorp's (neo-Hegelian) transcendental logic grounds cognition by "constructing" a system of categories that explains the possibility of cognitive validity.[9] For the Fichte-inspired Baden school, on the other hand, the normativity of truth is central. Truth is an ideal "ought" (*Sollen*), and "being" (*valid* meaning) is defined as what ought to be judged by a subject in cognitive contexts.[10] Against both views, Heidegger embraces Husserl's position: truth is not an ought but an ideal relation between the meaning-content of judgment and its "fulfillment" by the object meant; logic is a "theoretical," not a "normative" (practical) discipline.[11] But neither is truth captured by a logical construction; the way meaning holds of an object must be traced to *pre*theoretical capacities of the subject for whom, before any explicit cognition, meaning is already there. As Lask put it, "the most elemental problems of logic only show themselves to those [. . .] who take 'pre-scientific' cognition" into account (2003: 154). Here Heidegger's focus on logic (reason as *legein*) runs up against the second strand in the concept of reason: intuition or *noein*. A brief contrast with Lask will help clarify Heidegger's position.

One thing that Heidegger finds attractive in Lask's doctrine of categories is its recognition that judgment-meaning is an "artificial structural complication" of a more original meaning-unity, the thing itself, the object as the primitive unity (*Urbild*) of category and categorial material. But while this original meaning is not a thing-in-itself of which we have no experience, for Lask it is *only* experienced; it is not *cognized* in that experience (2003: 191). Pretheoretical life "lives in the truth"—*on hos alethes*—but for cognition such truth is a "lost paradise" (2003: 192, 361).

Lask calls the primary relation of the subject to such original meaning *Hingabe*, submission (2003: 190), which he understands as a kind of *noein*, an unmediated intuition of what subsequently becomes discursively articulated. We are familiar with this original meaning—Lask argues that without it, the logical form of the judgment would be without the measure of a referent, empty in principle—but *legein* is cut off from noetic submission by the "original sin of cognition" (2003: 361), the "incursion" of subjectivity, the *reflective* character of knowledge. Lask's logic of philosophy is thus aporetic: If the object "untouched by all subjectivity" (2003: 360) is the "paradigmatic meaning" present in noetic submission, then categories drawn from a *logic* of valid meaning will leave the subject, for whom alone there can be such meaning, categorially homeless. Heidegger addresses this aporia by grounding reason as *legein* in a phenomenological investigation of noetic submission itself, explicating the categorial structure of a subject for whom the world can be immediately there as meaningful.

In lecture courses from the early 1920s Heidegger transcends reason through a "hermeneutics of facticity" which attempts to identify the "categories of factic life." While still concerned with valid meaning, a *hermeneutics* of factic life makes explicit that meaning is first of all a correlate of understanding, not cognition.[12] Understanding is neither submission nor objectification; meaning is neither experienced as an objective "given" nor *aufgegeben* (Natorp) as a cognitive task. But neither is the facticity of meaning a lost paradise in Lask's sense. Phenomenologically, meaning belongs to the *unity* of factic life, a unity constituted by a shifting list of categories.[13] Because *legein*—the way life "expresses itself"—arises from this original meaning, reason (as *logos*, logic) presupposes, but does not constitute, *Reluzenz*, the *noein* that belongs to life (GA61: 119).

Heidegger thus replaces the logic of philosophy with a hermeneutics of facticity, but the cognitive status of his categories of factic life still yields an aporia similar to Lask's. On the one hand, because life is movement—flowing, temporal, historical—reflection on life, "objectifying" it, always "stills the stream" (GA56/57: 101). Thus no logic is adequate to it. On the other hand, philosophy is not simply a "repetition" of life's own movement; it "goes along with" life, "speaking out" about it for the sake of elucidating its categorial structure (GA56/57: 117). In doing so, philosophy cultivates "hermeneutic intuition," an "understanding intuition or intuitive understanding" (GA56/57: 117, 126).

The "understanding" element of philosophical thinking is expressed in what Heidegger calls "formal-indicating concepts."[14] Categories of factic life are not cognitive elements in a logical construction of life; they serve the *methodological* function of leading the philosopher back to the factic "evidence-situation" from which they have been drawn (GA61: 35). And it is this evidence-situation that supplies the "intuitive" element. Formal-indicating concepts are the tools required in order to phenomenologically "see" what factic life *is*, and the normative success conditions for such intuitive understanding—which distinguish it from simply living a life—are provided by one's acting for the sake of being a (philosophical) logician.

I have deliberately phrased this account, anachronistically, in the language of *Being and Time* because I want to argue that Heidegger's hermeneutics of factic life is hobbled by an *over*-reaction to logicism in the phenomenology of meaning. Formal-indicating concepts provide an understanding (*legein*) of how original meaning can be there in factic life by getting us to see (*noein*) how life and meaning belong together, thus obviating Lask's aporia of submission and reflection. But Heidegger, like Lask, still denies that philosophy can attain *knowledge* of this belonging—the reason, in Heidegger's case, being that life cannot be made into an object and so is in principle unknowable. But Heidegger came to reject this logicist conception of knowledge, and so, while many of the categories of factic life have analogues in *Being and Time*, and while the notion of formal-indication is retained there,[15] they serve a very different project.

In the mid-1920s, as Kisiel (1993: 409–15) details, Heidegger developed a new reading of Kant that drew on the resources of Husserl's *transcendental phenomenology*—specifically, on the latter's noetic-noematic elucidation of the concept of transcendence. For Husserl, transcendental cognition of categories is achieved not through Kantian deduction or neo-Kantian construction but through reflective *clarification* of how the meaning of what is transcendent (i.e., intended as real) is constituted in the noetic-noematic correlation of experience.[16] Heidegger does not follow Husserl in all particulars, of course, but he embraces enough of this approach to argue that philosophy cannot begin with the concept of life (Dilthey), since life is a particular *region* of being, a particular transcendent domain whose meaning must itself be elucidated transcendentally. The problems of "subjective logic" that led Heidegger to the hermeneutics of factic life must be approached in an ontically neutral way, without appeal to such regions.

So while Heidegger rejects Husserl's conception of transcendental philosophy as grounded in "absolute consciousness" (HCT: 110), he follows Husserl in refusing to identify transcendental subjectivity by any sortal predicate drawn from the world. "Dasein"—a *"reiner Seinsausdruck"*—is that being in whose "very being, that being is an issue for it" (BT: 33, 32). In *Being and Time*, then, phenomenological ontology is prior to any anthropology, including philosophical anthropology. And while *Being and Time* is still concerned with Dasein's pretheoretical experience, the latter is no longer a cognitive surd, since its own practical "sighting" of itself is internally categorially articulated. Thus *Being and Time* is *legein*, theoretical discourse about conditions of possibility, but those conditions entail the priority of *noein*.[17] Phenomenology is *legein*—*letting* something be seen—but also, and more fundamentally, *noein*, seen "from itself." This correlation is transcendental truth: *veritas transcendentalis* (BT: 62).

THE PRIORITY OF *NOEIN* IN *BEING AND TIME'S* NORMATIVITY-FIRST APPROACH TO REASON

Heidegger's hermeneutics of facticity aims to displace logic as the privileged philosophical approach to meaning, a project he continues in *Being and Time*. It thus might seem—as is dramatically expressed in "What is Metaphysics?"—that "the idea of 'logic' itself disintegrates in the turbulence of a more original questioning" (WM: 92). This negative sense of "transcending reason" is firmly established in the Heidegger literature, and it *seems* reinforced by Heidegger's treatment of *noein*. For instance, while Heidegger allows that in ancient philosophy the primary sense of truth is not *legein*, "judgment," but *"noein*, [the] simple awareness of something [. . .] in its sheer presence at hand" (BT: 48), he argues that the ancient approach already misses the ontological boat because *noein* is understood as a matter of cognition, "knowing the world" (BT: 85). In Husserl, for instance, *noein* is reconfigured as *Wesensschau*, an intuition in which the "being"—categorial constitution—of beings is "given" in its ideality.[18] Since Heidegger is committed to the idea that, whatever might be said about the beings that are known, the meaning presupposed in cognition cannot be approached this way, his position might seem to call for transcending reason not only in its logical sense but in its "noetic" sense as well.

However, focusing exclusively on Heidegger's rejection of the tradition's identification of *noein* with *theoria* and cognition risks missing his phenomenological "retrieval" of *noein* and the role it plays in the existential analytic of Dasein.[19] Logic is certainly demoted to derivative status in *Being and Time*, but this derivation involves an appeal to "sight" (*noein*), whose relation to reason is captured in the German term *Vernehmen*.[20] As we shall see, this polysemous term allows both for phenomenological clarification of how discourse and meaning belong together, and for retrieving reason in a normativity-first way: not as logic but as measure-taking and reason-giving (*logon didonai*).

If Heidegger's early reflections on logic begin by acknowledging the distinctive ontological status of propositional meaning—that it holds (*gilt*) without having to be—he now calls this whole approach "opaque" (BT: 198) and cautions that the phenomenon of meaning cannot be understood in these terms (see also BP: 218–22). As critical as Heidegger is of the concept of *Geltung*, however, he remains attentive to the reason it became a *Zauberwort* in the first place—namely, that it highlights meaning's *normative* structure. If the approach through *logos* (reason as logical validity) fails, then another must be found. On the standard reading of *Being and Time*, Heidegger's alternative involves grounding the normativity of meaning in our embedded and embodied practical experience. Correct as far as it goes, we will miss the point of this turn to practices unless we see that it succeeds only by retrieving reason as *noein*. If meaning—both in the early works and in *Being and Time*—is the phenomenological synonym for *on hos alethes*,[21] Heidegger's early work approaches meaning through judgment (*legein*) while *Being and Time* approaches it through comportment (*noein*).

We can see this already in Heidegger's explication of what *logos* means in the term "phenomenology." Heidegger argues that the primary sense of *legein* is "pointing out" or letting something be seen. Interpreting Aristotle's notion of *apophainesthai* ("letting be seen *from* itself"), apophantic *logos* (assertion) is said to involve two moments: making what is talked about "accessible to the other [person]," and "letting something be seen in its *togetherness* with something" (BT: 56). In contrast to Heidegger's earlier logical approach, assertion is neither a relation—a "binding [. . .] together of representations"—nor the valid determination of an object. It is letting something "be seen *as* something" (BT: 56). Although the "as" still seems tied exclusively to *legein* here, not *noein*—meaning is not seeing something, but seeing it discursively in its togetherness *with* something—this is not the whole story: the "as" signifies being in the sense of *truth*, and assertion is not the "primary 'locus' of truth" (BT: 57, 269).

Truth is the *measure* of assertion. To say that an assertion can be true *or* false is to say that no assertion measures itself. If the success of an assertion lies in letting something "show itself *just as* it is in itself" (BT: 261),[22] then its failure lies in concealing that about which it speaks. If truth is the measure of this success or failure, then *on hos alethes* is the thing itself *as* it in truth is.

But if the thing itself is to measure the assertion, it must be available to play such a role. As Heidegger reads Aristotle, this availability is accomplished in "the direct [*schlichtes*] *Vernehmen* of something," achieved in both *aisthesis* and *noein* (BT: 57). While the former makes the sensible world present, the latter includes "the direct observing [*hinsehende*] *Vernehmen* of the most elementary ontological determinations of the entity as such." Both are "true in the primary sense" since they "can never cover up," can "never be false" but "at worst remain *Unvernehmen*, *agnoein*, not sufficing for straightforward and appropriate access" (BT: 57).

Two things must be noted here: one positive, one negative. On the positive side, because *logos* primarily means "*Vernehmen*-lassen des Seienden," it can "signify reason [*Vernunft*]" (BT: 58). The rationality of apophantic *logos* lies in the possibility that it can let something be perceived as it is, a "letting" measured by that very thing. This guarantees a connection between thinking and being, one that is not eliminated in skeptical modernity but only made more complicated. On the negative side, however, when *noein* is traditionally understood as "'beholding' [*Anschauung*] in the widest sense," and "thinking (*dianoein*)" is oriented toward that kind of access to things, *noein* seems ill-suited to measure the assertion (BT: 129).[23] What we need is not merely access, openness to the world, but access to something that has a structure suitable for measuring what we say about it.[24] If meaning is only possible where there is an as-structure, and if the "as" is the specialty of apophantic discourse—which "lets something be seen *as* something" by "harking back to something else to which it points" (BT: 57)—then *noein*, the pure intuiting of what is, lacks the structure of meaning and so cannot measure apophantic discourse.

Here we encounter a version of Lask's *Hingabe* problem: original truth is experienced in pure submission, but such "paradigmatic meaning" is a lost paradise, since it does not possess the "structural complication" that characterizes judgment-meaning as the vehicle of cognition. However, in *Being and Time* Heidegger tackles this problem head-on by rejecting the traditional conception of *noein* as intuition, using Husserl's phenomenology as his primary foil. Such a conception, Heidegger argues, is not neutral but entails an ontological commitment: traditionally, *noein* is "direct *Vernehmen* of something *present at hand*" (BT: 25).

Uncovering such commitments is part of Heidegger's strategy for getting Dasein's categorial structure phenomenologically into view by "de-structing" the history of ontology, one chapter of which is devoted to showing how cognition is a "founded mode" of being-in-the-world (BT: 86–90). Against Husserl, for instance, he argues that primary "access" to Dasein is not achieved through "direct *vernehmende* reflection" (BT: 151), an intuitive, en-presenting grasp of consciousness and its structure. Dasein *cannot* be accessed that way, since its kind of being is not presence-at-hand.²⁵ To discharge the demand left open in Heidegger's early work—addressing the problems of "subjective logic" through a categorial account of the "subjectivity of the subject" (BT: 24)—phenomenology must start with *pre*theoretical experience. Cognitive comportment—*vernehmendes Erkennen*—presupposes the access to things enabled by our practical dealing with them, "which manipulates things and puts them to use" (BT: 67).

But we must be clear about the philosophical point here: the turn to practices is important because it enables a retrieval of *noein*. While Heidegger is indeed interested in the kind of "knowledge" (Heidegger's scare-quotes) found in practices, he does not offer a pragmatic epistemology that grounds cognition in practical reason, the technical rules that might be drawn from skillful coping or the practical principles that govern deliberation.²⁶ Instead, his concern is exclusively with the kind of *access* to entities that practices involve, since through such access, and *absent* any apophantic *logos*, entities are experienced as meaningful—i.e., as *normatively* appropriate or inappropriate (BT: 97). Division I of *Being and Time* thus represents the first stage in Heidegger's retrieval of *noein*; it will be followed, in Division II, by a second and decisive stage, one not tied to practices but everywhere presupposed in the first: determining the kind of access Dasein has to its *own* kind of being.

The first stage runs like this: In our everyday concerns, things are there for us *as* something—hammers, nails, lumber—but we cannot encounter hammers, nails, and lumber in an observing intuition. The hammer shows itself as a hammer (i.e., as it is "in itself") only when it "disappears" into its use (BT: 106). This is because what it is *to be* a hammer, its meaning, lies in its being appropriate or inappropriate for the task at hand, a normative significance determined *in* the practice.²⁷ The subject of such meaningful experience, then, cannot be a disengaged intuiter but must be attuned to the normativity in question (how the hammer is *supposed* to be) and exquisitely responsive to the most various kinds of failure, not just when the hammer breaks. This attunement is what Heidegger calls "circumspection" (*Umsicht*), a kind of "sight" that is neither pure intuiting nor categorially restricted to what is accessible in visual (or other sensory) perception. Circumspection is a kind of access granted by Dasein's pretheoretical, but norm-responsive, "understanding" (BT: 98).

That "sight" is Heidegger's gloss on *noein* is evident from his claim that "'seeing' does not mean just perceiving with the bodily eyes [*aisthesis*], but neither does it mean pure non-sensory awareness of something present at hand in its presence at hand [*noein*]" (BT: 187). In *Being and Time* "sight" is a formal-indicating concept: An aspect of our ordinary notion of seeing— that it "lets entities that are accessible to it be encountered unconcealedly in themselves"—is "formalized" into "access in general," a "universal term for characterizing any access to entities or to being" (BT: 147). "Sight" is a *methodological* term that leads phenomenology back to the evidence-situations, however various they may be, in which we have access to beings as they in truth are.

Heidegger thematizes three evidence-situations formally-indicated by three kinds of sight:[28] "circumspection," in which the paraphernalia of our tasks show up meaningfully in the instrumentally normative evidence-situation of "concern" (*Besorgen*); "considerateness" (*Rücksicht*), in which other Dasein show up meaningfully in an evidence-situation normatively constituted by "solicitude" (*Fürsorge*); and finally "transparency" (*Durchsichtigkeit*), the "sight directed upon the being itself for the sake of which Dasein in each case is as it is" (BT: 146).[29] Because Dasein is being-in-the-world, transparency is not "inspecting a point called the 'self'" but is transparency "in the constitutive moments of existence" and so extends to one's "being-alongside the world and [one's] being-with others" (BT: 146). The evidence-situation for such access to oneself is normatively structured by *Selbst-sorge*,[30] which is ontologically fundamental because the understanding that belongs to it grounds the understanding of *being* and so access to beings as such and as a whole.

Here we must note an important point for understanding Heidegger's retrieval of *noein*: not every access to entities is also access to their being. Sight lets the entities "that are accessible to" living beings "be encountered," but not all entities *are* accessible to every living being through vision or other senses (*aisthesis*).[31] Heidegger's definition of sight as "any access to entities *or to being*" removes this restriction: as Dasein, the human being's practical involvements include access to the *being* of entities. Arguably, many living beings are able to use something in order to bring about something else. But in Dasein, this ability involves an "understanding of being" (*noein*), a capacity that does not belong to life *qua* life, but to care. Why? Clarifying the evidence-situation in which this distinction is phenomenologically grounded will be the task of Division II, the second, and decisive, stage of Heidegger's retrieval of *noein*.

If all sight is grounded in understanding, what sort of understanding belongs to *Selbst-sorge*, without which there is no understanding of being, no meaning? In Division I, Heidegger defines it as acting for the sake (*Umwillen*) of *being* something. Understanding myself as a teacher, for instance, grounds the circumspection in which the paraphernalia of teaching show up. This is not because I know how such things should be used—although such know-how cannot be altogether absent[32]—but because what it *means* to be a teacher is at issue for me as that for the sake of which I am acting. Trying to be a teacher, a form of *praxis*, is itself norm-guided, although not in the way that a tool's appropriateness is determined by the work to be done. Although more or less explicit norms of teaching are always available—one typically acts in conformity to what is publicly expected of teachers—their meaning is always at issue *in* that trying. If anything fixes the meaning in practical contexts, it is my care (*Selbst-sorge*) about whether I succeed or fail, the transparency of my commitment to teaching. If I don't care about succeeding as a teacher, then *whatever* I do within the instrumental framework of teaching will be normatively under-determined: the norms that make *this* chalkboard or *this* grade appropriate will lack normative ("intelligible," internal or motivational) force, and so such things will lack meaning—that is, I will not be able to encounter them in their being.

In this sense, then, understanding is not originally a matter of interpreting "the text of the world"; nor does it align with the traditional distinction between "explanation" and "understanding." As a transcendental-phenomenological concept it indicates the evidence-situation in which access to my own being is noetically accomplished. And because what it means for me to be is at issue in everything I do—in all cognitive and practical comportment—understanding is prior to any meaning determined by cognitive or practical norms, including rational norms.

If transparency belongs to Heidegger's retrieval of *noein*, and if understanding of being depends on transparency with regard to one's commitments, we can see how *Being and Time* subordinates reason as logic (*legein*) to *noein*. The logical meaning of assertion, the proposition, is a "structural complication" (the "binding and separating" thematized in *Geltungslogik*) of a prior *normative* order. But because Heidegger nowhere links this sense of *noein* explicitly to reason, the charge of irrationalism might still seem warranted.

Indeed, one might think that Heidegger remains caught in Lask's *Hingabe* problem: if the meaning of being is always *at issue* in whatever we are trying to be, isn't this just to say that, while we might experience such meaning in pure submission, our acting cuts us off from it no less than Lask's "original sin of cognition," since acting involves an incursion of commitment into the world's normative order?[33] To address the charge of irrationalism from the ground up it must be shown that commitment's "incursion" into being is what makes *on hos alethes*—normative beholdenness to the way things are—*possible*, and that such beholdenness is a kind of *reason*.

Being and Time does not address this challenge directly, but the second stage of Heidegger's retrieval of *noein*, his phenomenology of the *breakdown* of Dasein's everyday being-in-the-world, suggests a response. First, transparency—the sight that gives Dasein access to itself—is a kind of *hearing*.[34] As hearing, *noein* cannot be pure submission because it involves an internal "structural complication," a kind of *address* that lies in the domain of second-person phenomenology.[35] And second, this hearing is *prior* to any acting for the sake of some particular ability-to-be: Dasein originally "hears" when it does not act at all but, in "the blink of an eye" (*Augenblick*),[36] understands its ownmost possibility, its *being*-possible (BT: 232).[37] Since the evidence-situation in which Dasein attains transparent access to itself—*noein* as "*verstandnismässiges Vernehmen*" (BT: 131)—is thus modally determined from within, it brings with it (as I shall now argue) a demand for reasons (*logon didonai*).

Consider, first, hearing. If "sight" means access in general, and if, for Dasein, access is *verstandnismässiges Vernehmen*, then that to which Dasein gains access has the character of meaning.[38] Absorbed in our practical affairs, we do not see colors and shapes but tables and chairs; nor do we hear "noises or complexes of sounds" but rather "the creaking wagon, the motor-cycle" (BT: 207). If *Vernehmen* is translated as "perception," then neither visual nor acoustic perception can be understood as intuition since we do not *intuit* meaning, we *get* it, understand it in a familiar way. "Dasein hears [and sees] because it understands" (BT: 206). Hence we are not simply submitted to something that would represent a lost paradise for any explicit interpretation we might offer. Rather, "behind" the meaning that is seen or heard in our encounter with entities—the "phenomena of phenomenology"—there is "essentially nothing else" (BT: 60).[39]

The difference between intuiting meaning and getting it grounds Heidegger's approach to *legein* (discourse). Discourse is *intrinsically* connected to understanding: it "articulates" (speaks out) the "intelligibility" in understanding (BT: 204). The idea is that there are many ways in which discourse articulates intelligibility, none of which can be conceived as cutting us off, by the very *fact* of articulation, from some original meaning. Thus, if assertion is *Vernehmen-lassen*, it is not originally a letting something be perceived (intuited) but a *letting be heard*, a "giving to understand" (BT: 316). "Both talking and hearing are based on understanding" (BT: 208). Because the "apophantic as" is grounded in this "hermeneutic as" (BT: 201), the structure of the proposition (logic) is not a universally normative constraint on meaning. In Heidegger's retrieval of *noein* as hearing, then, his earlier search for a "pure logical grammar" is displaced by the demand to "liberat[e] grammar from logic" (BT: 209).

Admittedly, this displacement seems to separate meaning from reason even more radically than does the traditional account of *noein* as *vernehmendes Hinsehen*. But when Heidegger turns to the way hearing characterizes Dasein's access to its own being, he shows that this separation is only apparent.

Transparency, the "sight which is related primarily and on the whole to existence," extends to being-in-the-world as a whole: one's "being-alongside the world and [one's] being-with others" (BT: 146). Although such transparency (*noein*) can never be absent, it can be occluded (*agnoein, Unvernehmen*) in various ways. "Authentic" transparency is characterized as "resoluteness," which transforms the circumstances in which I find myself ("general situation," *Lage*) into the "situation" (*Situation*), where I "take action" as I myself (BT: 346–47). In the literature, this moment of taking action—the *Augenblick* (BT: 376)—is often seen as a decisionistic leap,[40] but this ignores the evidence-situation that provides its phenomenological context: it is not in resoluteness as such that Dasein gains primary access to itself, but in the *breakdown* of the everyday *agnoein* access in which Dasein "fails to hear" (*überhört*) itself.

Just as the breakdown of the hammer is the evidence-situation that allows us, as phenomenologists, to "catch sight of " (BT: 105) the being of the tool and the normative structure of "world" to which it belongs, so the breakdown of Dasein's everyday acting for the sake of what it is trying to be allows us to catch sight of the categories that determine Dasein's being.[41] But the sight at issue here, the *noein* in which Dasein is given to understand itself, is a kind of *hearing*: "hearing constitutes the primary and authentic way in which Dasein is open for its ownmost possibility [ability-to-be, *Seinkönnen*]" (BT: 206). This means that Dasein "knows itself" originally as the addressee of a "call"—as "*Hören-können*"—and so as *modally* determined in its response (i.e., *free*) (BT: 207). Heidegger's phenomenological analysis of breakdown—a formal-indicating discourse that enables us to "get" the ontological structure evidenced therein—articulates the ontological ground of meaning and so transcends his earlier misguided (Hegel-inspired) idea of a "logic" of philosophy. But it does not transcend reason altogether. In the phenomenology of conscience as the ground of meaning, Heidegger retrieves an affirmative sense of "transcending reason."

Conscience is a call, the hearing of which contrasts "in every way" with how Dasein, absorbed in its practical affairs, "hears" itself (BT: 317). First, in everyday life Dasein "knows" (Heidegger's scare quotes) what it is up to and what it is capable of; that is, it acts for the sake of some ability-to-be and so is capable of getting on with the various tasks at hand (BT: 315). For the most part, however, this self-understanding is *agnoein* because it *necessarily* takes place in a world whose meanings have been standardized and anonymized by the way things are publicly interpreted: "*Das 'Man'* itself articulates the referential context of significance" (BT: 167), and so Dasein "fails to hear [*überhört*] itself" because it "listens away to *das Man*" (BT: 316).[42] In contrast, the call of conscience lacks such "mediation," and so also the "ambiguity" that clings to the way that terms like "teacher" denote a social-normative status that can apply to anyone and everyone. Transparent *Vernehmen* bypasses any such role to reach Dasein "unmistakably and unequivocally."[43] The "I" who hears in this noetic way, *I-myself*, "simply cannot be mistaken for anything else." So too, what is heard must be "silent" (no *aisthesis*) but "lose nothing of its *Vernehmbarkeit*." The "vocalization" of what is heard is not a sound but a "giving to understand." Nevertheless, it delivers no "information," and so is not a form of apophantic *logos*. Instead, what is heard in the call has the character of a *command* or "summons" (BT: 316–22).

These contrasts suggest how Heidegger's retrieval of *noein* as hearing avoids the problem of construing noetic reason as pure intuition (submission, *theorein*). As hearing the call, *Vernehmen* simply *cannot* be a direct intuition of something present at hand because what it discloses, the self, is already the *addressee* of a call that gives it to understand itself as having to respond. Dasein understands itself as *at issue*. For this reason, too, the "hearing that genuinely corresponds [*entspricht*] to the call"—"authentic self-understanding" (BT: 324)—is not a counter-discourse that engages the caller in a debate about what is to be done.[44]

But if what the call gives to understand takes the form of an imperative or summons, Dasein's primary access to itself is as the *you-accusative*, an addressee who, by the very structure of address, is situated in normative space.[45] This is expressed in Heidegger's formal-indication of what is "said in the call," namely "guilty" (*schuldig*). Although "guilt" is formalized so that it is not "tied to any law or ought,"[46] it still captures the normative orientation belonging to the illocutionary force of an imperative: "[you] *must* take over *being* a ground" (BT: 330). In understanding guilt as "a predicate for the 'I am'" (BT: 326)—or better, the "you are" (i.e., one that articulates what it is to *be* Dasein)—I know myself as "answerable [*verantwortlich*]" (BT: 334). I am answerable both for myself and to the others with whom I am. But if I-myself am answerable for being a ground, for what am I answerable to the *other*?

In *Being and Time* Heidegger does not explain what taking over being a ground means, nor does he explicitly link the answerability of the you-accusative to reason-giving. He does distinguish two poles between which *how* I take over being a ground moves: an inauthentic taking over, in which my answerability is more or less occluded (*agnoein*), and an authentic or transparent version. But since both are modes of acting, and since "all action is necessarily 'conscienceless'" (BT: 334), they presuppose answerability without contributing to its elucidation. Elsewhere,[47] I have argued that conscience discloses my answerability for taking over my factic "grounds" (*Gründe*)—the givens of the "general situation" (*Lage*), over which I have no control—as possible *Gründe* in the sense of possibly justifying reasons, reasons in the normative sense. One might think of this as the difference between *having* reasons in some objective sense that does not require uptake of them, and their being *my* reasons in an internal or motivational sense. But Heidegger's deeper ontological point is that talk of "objective" reasons only makes sense in the context of Dasein's answerability. Answerability is what *being* a ground means, and it is presupposed in any acting for the sake of being something. Because Dasein "is" (without further qualification—i.e., basically, originally, intrinsically) a you-accusative, it "must" treat factic grounds as normatively at issue in a choice about which of the reasons I have—inclinations, public mores, moral principles—are to be endorsed as *my* reasons for what I do or say. Answerability is thus a stand on what I think/feel is best in regard to how to go on.[48] In decision, the *Lage* becomes a *Situation*, a "centered" normative order for which now some particular *one*—I myself—am answerable: not for the norms themselves (their normativity), but for their normative *force* as my *reasons*.

Further, I have argued that this interpretation is supported by *Vom Wesen des Grundes* (1928), where Heidegger designates the entire care-structure, evidenced phenomenologically in the call of conscience, as "freedom" (transcendence). This text preserves the ambiguity in the term *Grund*: "The originary relation of freedom to ground" is "grounding," and grounding involves three forms: *Stiften, Boden-nehmen,* and *Begründen* (EG: 127). The latter is another name for reason-giving (*Rechtfertigung*; EG: 131: *logon didonai*). The key point is that freedom ("the origin of ground," taking over being a ground) gives rise to the "why-question," and so freedom "*must* account for itself," give reasons (EG: 129–30).

Reason thus belongs to transcendence, not as its ground but as its intrinsic answerability. Here "transcending reason" is reason that arises from and goes along with transcendence. This is not to say that Dasein is a rational animal. The traditional definition, while "not 'false' [. . .], covers up the phenomenal basis" from which it is drawn (BT: 208). To put it another way: *whatever* theory one might hold about the rationality of values and norms (e.g., realism, prescriptivism, conventionalism), there is no understanding them *as* norms (i.e., they have no "being," no practice-guiding meaning) except for a being who can be answerable for their normative force. And if answerability is Dasein's being (care) noetically accessed in conscience, then care is the phenomenological origin of reason because reason is an *intentional implication* of answerability.

Heidegger's phenomenology of conscience thus yields a normativity-first account of reason, but the link between being a ground (*noein*; answerability) and reason-*giving* (*logon didonai*) remains obscure in one important respect. Since *legein* is subordinated to *noein*, it might seem that logical reason could float altogether free from noetic reason—that the "as what" I take a thing to be in taking over being a ground could be altogether independent of what that thing "is." To complete the mapping of this territory, then, we must turn to *Fundamental Concepts of Metaphysics* (1929–1930), where Heidegger addresses this potential lacuna between *is* and *as*.

Heidegger informs us that the apparent lacuna arises from an "illusion" besetting the approach to assertion in *Being and Time*, so that now he must "deviate essentially and decisively" from that approach without, however, "really invalidat[ing]" what was said there (FCM: 337). The illusion consists in taking the "positive and true" form of assertion as basic for explaining other forms such as the negative or false assertion; the deviation, in turn, consists in emphasizing the irreducibly modal character of assertion, the *possibility* that it can be either true *or* false. Inquiring into the ground of the modal essence of assertion, Heidegger is again led back to the as-structure—that is, to *noein* as the *Vernehmen* of "something as something" (FCM: 311)—but the deviation requires that the normative structure of *noein* be made explicit. Heidegger thereby provides a concept that was missing in *Being and Time*'s normativity-first approach to reason: answerability is *measure*-taking.

For Heidegger, the "is" of assertion is neither a formal logical operator nor a relation; it has a "manifold meaning" that can become evident only if one treats its formal relational character as an indication of the "task" of grasping the "proper dimension [. . .] within which the relevant relation can be what it is" (FCM: 293).[49] This dimension is what we have been calling the phenomenological evidence-situation. As a formal-indication, the "is" of assertion does not "express or intend" what it refers to; rather, it indicates that "anyone who seeks to understand is called upon" to exercise their "free ability to hearken [*freien Aufhorchenkönnen*] to things" (FCM: 299). As a first pass at showing what this ability to hearken to things consists in, Heidegger notes that the "propositional content" of the "a is b" could not mean what it does without emerging from an underlying experience of the "a as b"—that is, from the "originary dimension of the as" (FCM: 301–2).[50]

Heidegger finds an anticipation of this in Aristotle's approach to language (*legein*, discourse) as "utterances [. . .] that have a meaning." We do not attach meaning to words; rather, because "our essence is to understand," our utterances mean something (FCM: 307). We have already encountered this idea: If Dasein's essence is to understand, this is because, in contrast to living beings, its "being open for. . . has the character of apprehending *something as something*," an openness that here, as in *Being and Time*, Heidegger terms "comportment," acting for the sake of something (FCM: 306). Because Dasein "holds itself together with something" insofar as it "holds itself in a *comportment* toward other beings," it is able to "refer to these other beings *as* such [i.e., *as beings*]" (FCM: 308). This tells us nothing about what comportment holds itself together *with*, and so how comportment yields the as-structure. But just here the deviation from *Being and Time* comes into play.

The essence of assertion is the *possibility* of being true *or* false. Following Aristotle, the structure of assertion—a putting together (*sunthesis*) that takes apart (*dihairesis*)—can either reveal or conceal the entity because it rests on a prior "assembling (a taking together) of the *Vernommenen*" that "forms something like a unity." This forming is a "*Ver-nehmen* [ap-perception] of a belonging together" (FCM: 313–14).⁵¹ Thus "the *logos* is grounded in a *Vernehmen, noesis, nous,* [. . .]—or rather *logos,* according to its essence, *is* such *Vernehmen*" (FCM: 314). This last—rather surprising—claim drawn from Aristotle's analysis of assertion reflects the aforementioned deviation: rather than focus on the logical or grammatical form of assertion, Heidegger emphasizes its *necessary* connection to comportment (FCM: 316). At the syntactic level, the assertion "a is b" both separates a from b and joins them. But as belonging to comportment, assertion presupposes an ap-perception that already joins and separates what is *vernommen* (a *as* b), one that yields a "structured phenomenon"—the "as-structure"—whose "unity" is "the essence of *nous*" (FCM: 317).

The "as" does not signify a bringing together of subject and predicate (or, *de rei,* the belonging of an ontic property to something present at hand). Rather, the unity achieved in the comportment to which assertion, as "pointing out," belongs "[lets] what is at hand be seen *as such*" (i.e., in its "presence" *as being*) (FCM: 319). Because assertion is understood modally, and because such "possibility" depends on "a comportment toward, i.e., a relation toward beings as such at one's disposal," the "is" of assertion "contains being as manifest" but in a way that is "not originary" (FCM: 338). Rather, the copula *formally-indicates* the dimension of the "as," and so means the "undifferentiated manifold of what-being, that-being, and being-true" (FCM: 326f).⁵²

The phenomenological payoff of Heidegger's deviation from *Being and Time,* then, is that it provides "insight into [being's] manifold *structure,*" the "dimension of the as" (FCM, 334). By grounding the modal character of assertion in *noein* (that is, by approaching *legein* as a comportment), Heidegger demonstrates that "'being' [the copula]" and "the 'as' *point to the same origin*" (FCM: 333). Comportment is the origin of—i.e., makes possible (FCM: 335)—the ontological difference between beings and being (*on hos alethes*).

If comportment (*noein* as ap-perception) is the "originary synthesis" in which the "as and the as-structure is grounded," then the "manifestness of beings *as such* and *as a whole*"—the normative space of meaning Heidegger calls "world" (FCM: 338)—is grounded in *nous*. Hence, the possible truth of assertion, its normative orientation toward the measure of conformity with things (*adequatio rei et intellectus*), depends on whatever it is about comportment that makes the experience of such a measure possible. To clarify what that is, Heidegger introduces the idea of a *"fundamental* comportment" (FCM: 343).

In a few dense pages toward the end of *Fundamental Concepts of Metaphysics*—pages that reverberate in countless ways in his subsequent writings—Heidegger supplies the missing link between comportment as acting for the sake of being something, the call to take over being a ground, and reasons. Here we can only touch on the points most relevant for understanding the relation between *legein* and *noein* in the concept of *Vernunft*.

There are countless comportment-types, but each one phenomenologically entails a fundamental comportment, *freedom*, a synonym for transcendence. Assertion belongs to a kind of comportment—let's call it acting for the sake of being a truth-teller—that grounds the ability of assertion to be either true or false.[53] What links acting for the sake of being a truth-teller to the modal character of assertion is that conformity (*adaequatio*) with beings is *at issue* in it. Such comportment, then, cannot be mere submission to beings; it requires that beings be "announced" in their "*binding* character." That is, beings must be *vernommen* as normative for this comportment: *logos* must "already [have] the possibility [...] of *measuring* [...] whether it suitably conforms to those beings." This possibility belongs to freedom as fundamental comportment: "only where there is freedom do we find the possibility of something having a *binding* character" (FCM: 339).

Acting for the sake of being a truth-teller is possible because its measure (*adaequatio*) is entailed by freedom's *intrinsic* openness to "beings as such"—that is, *as beings*. The binding character of beings is thus *introduced* through freedom because freedom, ap-perception, is intrinsically "structurally articulated" by the distinction between a being and what it is/means to be that being (FCM: 339). Further, the structure of freedom, "for its part, articulates" a *Spielraum* that belongs to "the human being" as Da-sein: a normatively attuned space where an interplay between what things *in truth* are and what we take them to be (the "as") is *at issue*.

But *why* is freedom intrinsically open to beings as beings? Because it is measure-*taking*. If any comportment—say, acting for the sake of being a teacher—involves caring about whether one succeeds or fails at it, then such trying is necessarily oriented toward a measure or norm. We earlier expressed this in language foreign to *Being and Time*: the comportment of teaching (trying to be a teacher) is trying to do what is *best* in the matter of teaching. *Fundamental Concepts of Metaphysics* confirms this interpretation, since comportment takes the measure of being a teacher.

Measure-taking (*Maß-nehmen*) is Heidegger's term for acting for the sake of being something: teacher, parent, truth-teller. The measure is what is *at issue* in such comportment.[54] In fundamental comportment—"being free in an originary sense" (FCM: 343)—the measure at issue is what it is/means to be the you-accusative addressed in the call of conscience, which summons Dasein to take over being a ground.[55] "Taking over" is measure-taking—i.e., standing toward factic grounds in light of measure, thus as *claims* to the normative status of reasons. This categorial structure can be found in *all* comportment, including that of being a truth-teller.

"[B]eing open for beings themselves" (*noein*), which grounds the modal character of assertion (*legein*), is not a *vernehmendes Hinsehen* or intuition; it must "from the very outset"—i.e., necessarily—be "a free *holding oneself toward*" those beings. Free holding oneself toward is "letting *oneself* be bound" (FCM: 342): commitment. Letting oneself be bound distinguishes comportment from the "behavior" of living beings, in which "we never find any letting oneself be bound by something binding" (i.e., by any *measure*). In one's commitment to the measure of truth-telling, this "measure is transferred to beings *in advance*" so that "conformity or non-conformity is *regulated by beings*" (FCM: 342). In measuring myself by what it means to be a truth-teller, I "let" beings "be," and so I am bound to them, normatively beholden to them, as what they are.[56] This transferal of measure to beings, such that beings serve as measures to which I am beholden, is answerability for the measure, *being* a ground for whom that measure is at issue. Freedom is answerability for measure, and this attunement to the normative provides the *Spielraum* to "decide concerning the conformity or non-conformity" of our comportment toward whatever is binding (FCM: 339)—for instance, what is best in the matter of truth-telling, what I *ought* to assert.

This completes Heidegger's normativity-first account of reason. Letting oneself be bound (commitment) is measure-taking, a "bringing toward itself in advance and *as* something that can be binding"—i.e., as normative— "whatever is to provide the measure." If logic (reason as *logos*) is to be such a measure, bind us in any way, then it cannot be the ground of normativity but must originate in measure-taking as taking over being a ground.

Heidegger's subordination of *legein* to *noein* in this period thus provides something like an affirmative understanding of reason. First, because comportment is measure-taking, and because our fundamental comportment is taking over being a ground, then whether I act authentically or inauthentically, I measure myself by what is best in what I am trying to be. But to act in light of what is best is to act for reasons. In acting, the actor formally exemplifies the Socratic definition of a reason: because I think it is best to go on this way. Second, letting oneself be bound, commitment, is not an irrational decisionism, since it gives rise to the *demand* for reasons: I am responsible for how I go on, but I am also answerable to the others with whom I am. I *owe* them reasons, good or bad. The logical structure of reasons does not impose itself on us as a *sui generis* norm; *there are* reasons because I must take over being a ground. Third, this means that commitment is not an "incursion" into a meaning "untouched by all subjectivity," a lost paradise from which we are cut off by our very presence; rather, it makes *possible* the normatively structured space of meaning (*on hos alethes*) at issue in our comportments: the "phenomena of phenomenology" behind which "there is essentially nothing else."

THE UNITY OF *NOEIN* AND *LEGEIN*: THINKING

In the third stage of Heidegger's *Denkweg*, the third territory on our map, it is just this claim that seems to be denied. There *is* something behind the "phenomena of phenomenology" or the being of beings, namely "being as such." This suggests that reason must be transcended in order that what calls for thinking can be heard: transcendental thought is merely the preparation for a "leap" (PR: 78) in which thinking responds to a call that *speaks* in the demand for reasons (*logon didonai*) but that has been obscured in the history of philosophy as metaphysics. Metaphysics is understood as the fateful working-out of the principle of sufficient reason as nihilism, the way that "calculation" robs human beings—"mortals," in Heidegger's later vocabulary—of their "roots" (*Boden*) and transforms the world into a technological desert (PR: 30). The relentless pursuit of reasons—*ratio, rechnen*, calculation—has its basis in "anxiety in the face of thinking" (L: 78). But what, then, is it to think? And in what sense *can* reason be transcended?

Heidegger's own attempt to think in such a situation turns to "topological" concepts that seem to leave phenomenological correlationism behind in favor of minding (*Besinnung*) the place of mortals in the space of meaning, or the truth of being as such.[57] In my view, there is a lot more phenomenology in Heidegger's later work than meets the eye, but this is not the place to argue for that. Instead, as a kind of coda to the territories explored so far, I want to mention a few places in Heidegger's third territory where now-familiar phenomenological tropes remain in play as he attempts to steer philosophy from a concern with the being of beings to a concern with being as such.[58] For the rest, I will make no judgment on the plausibility of Heidegger's history of being as metaphysics.[59]

If *Being and Time*'s normativity-first approach to reasons aimed to show how reason originates in the call to take over being a ground, with its demand to give reasons, Heidegger's later work is focused on the origin of this call. Heidegger now swerves from his earlier claim—that the caller is Dasein itself—to a position closer to the one I have defended, namely, that the caller cannot be identified. I say "closer" because Heidegger does *nominalize* the caller, "being as such," but he also argues that this nominalization is precisely the "matter" for thinking, what is at issue, in play for mortal thinking, and must remain so. Being as such, then, is not a ground in the sense of a reason; it is the *"measure"* (PR: 111) that puts mortals into play (i.e., "leads them into their essence," the *"fitting"*) (PR: 68).[60] In contrast, a concern with identifying the addresser is what defines metaphysical thinking, governed by the principle of sufficient reason, *der Satz vom Grund*.

As Heidegger first interprets the Leibnizian version of this principle—"nothing is without reason"—it is a demand that a reason be given for every being, including the highest being, which must therefore be *self*-grounding (PR: 28). Traditionally, this being is God, but in modernity its place has been occupied by the subject, the human being who represents all beings to itself in terms of calculative reason, *ratio*, logic. For Heidegger, this identification of the caller who demands that reasons be given for every being is a product of metaphysical philosophy, whose history originates in pre-Socratic thinking, the "first beginning." Heraclitus names this originary moment in the following fragment:

Οὐκ ἐμοῦ ἀλλὰ τοῦ Λόγου ἀκούσαντας ὁμολογεῖν σοφόν ἐστιν Ἓν Πάντα
"Listening not to me but to the Logos it is wise to agree that all things are one."

which Heidegger couples with another (L: 72):[61]

Ἓν τὸ Σοφὸν μοῦνον λέγεσθαι οὐκ ἐθέλει καὶ ἐθέλει Ζηνὸς ὄνομα
"One thing, the only truly wise, does not and does consent to be called by the name of Zeus."

That the "does not" appears first means, for Heidegger, that the source of the call cannot be captured in the metaphysical thinking that emerged from the way *logos* was interpreted in classical Greek philosophy.

This means that metaphysics has failed to hear the principle of reason; or rather, it has heard only one of the two "tonalities" in which it can be understood (PR: 39). Metaphysics understands the principle as a claim about *beings*: "*nothing* is *without* [sufficient] reason." But hearing it in the second tonality, as a claim about *being*—"nothing *is* without ground"—prepares us to recognize the ambiguity in the term *Grund* such that we can ask about the relation between reason and ground as such (PR: 44–45).[62] That is: if metaphysics understands grounds as reasons and subjects all beings to this principle, thinking that hears in the second tonality can recognize the metaphysical understanding as *one* possibility for responding to the claim of ground, while holding itself open for another understanding, namely, that the being of beings is subject to the demand for reasons because being as such is heard as *Grund*.

Heidegger introduces this distinction between "ground" and "reason" by commenting on a saying by Angelus Silesius (a contemporary of Leibniz): "the rose is without why; it blooms because it blooms" (PR: 36). The difference between why (reason) and because (ground), for Heidegger, lies in the "attention" to grounds that speaks in the why. In the "because," an "attention to grounds does not insert itself in between [the rose's] blooming and the ground for blooming," an attention thanks to which alone "grounds could first be *as* grounds" (PR: 37). It is the lot of mortals that they "must pay attention to what grounds are determinative for them" (PR: 37). Why? Because for them, unlike the rose, their own "ground" has a "demand-character" that requires "the rendering of ground" (i.e., giving reasons) (PR: 38). But if this demand stems from a call that has been *überhört*, perhaps it can eventually be heard differently.

Silesius's saying suggests that "humans, in the concealed ground of their essential being, first truly are when, in their own way, they are like the rose—without why" (PR: 38). In its second tonality, the principle of reason "does not speak by the force of a demand for a why"—it is a "call" that calls the human being into what is fitting for it, the essential. Nevertheless, "we *must* ask: why? For we cannot leap out of the present age" (PR: 128). Giving reasons, then, does not belong to our essence, as it does in *Being and Time*, but it remains at issue for mortals—both in the sense that it belongs to our "destiny" (*Geschick*) and in the sense that such destiny is itself a "destining" of being: not a fate that compels but one that allows for hearing, and perhaps hearing otherwise.

In the third stage of Heidegger's thinking about *noein* and *legein*, then, mortal hearing retains its essential role, but what is at stake is no longer the demand to give reasons (now understood as just one *possible* response to the call), but the demand to think that which "gives measure" for mortal dwelling—"ground" in the sense of what is fitting for living otherwise than under the sway of the principle that reasons must be rendered. In "thinking," as in the call of conscience, we are "acquainted with an experience" in which "we find ourselves expressly addressed by that which lays claim to us in our essence" (PR: 68). Thinking "is a listening that brings something into view," a "hearing and a seeing" (PR: 47), a unity of *noein* and *legein*. But what "speaks to us" (the claim) "only becomes perceivable through our response" (PR: 48). Meaning, *on hos alethes*, the truth of being, depends on thinking ("needs us" [PR: 68]), since we alone, as mortals "capable of death *as* death,"[63] are put into play, in question, by hearing the claim as a demand (PR: 111–12).

What, then, is it to think, once we have "transcended reason" in the sense laid out in *Der Satz vom Grund*? Let us begin by recalling the rather surprising statement from *Fundamental Concepts of Metaphysics* that "*logos* is grounded in a *Vernehmen, noesis, nous*, [. . .]; or rather, according to its essence, *is* such *Vernehmen*" (FCM: 316). Here the defining feature of the second territory—the subordination of *legein* to *noein*—gives way to the defining feature of the third: the unity, or identity-in-difference (*Gefüge*), of *noein* and *legein*.

This unity emerges from Heidegger's lengthy meditation on Parmenides's fragment:

Χρὴ τὸ λέγειν τε νοεῖν τ' ἐὸν ἔμμεναι
"That which can be spoken and thought needs must be"[64]

Here Heidegger remarks that "we may not give 'thinking' as the translation of either *legein* taken by itself, or *noein* taken by itself"—neither *dialegesthai* nor *dianoeisthai*. Rather, "both, in their community, constitute that from which the nature of thinking first begins to emerge" (WCT: 197). In Heidegger's gloss on the term *chre*, there is a residue of his earlier phenomenological approach: first, *chre* (*es brauchet*; it is useful) suggests the point, made in *Being and Time*, that "the user lets the used thing enter into the propriety of its own nature, and there preserves it"; and second, *chre* involves "a command, a calling [*Heissen*]" that opens up the realm in which "all mortal doing belongs" (WCT: 196). It is this "call which was first to summon *legein* and *noein* to that essence"—their unity or *Gefüge*—"which was subsequently restricted in a way ruled by the decree [*Entscheid*] that logic is the essence of thinking" (WCT: 197; translation modified). These phenomenological traces—the fact that meaning ("all mortal doing") belongs in a "realm" opened up by the mortal's response to a command, an address—suggest that we are in the province of a normativity-first account of reason. This is confirmed by the way Heidegger "translates" *legein* and *noein* in the fragment.

The peculiar unity of *noein* and *legein* involves a crossing of activity and passivity. As Heidegger understands it, *legein* is active in the sense of *legen*, "laying"; but such action depends on something *vor-liegende* that it "lets lie before us" (i.e., "makes it appear"). *Noein*, in contrast, *Vernehmen*, perceiving, is a kind of "receiving," but one that is no "passive acceptance." Rather, the perceived "concerns us" such that we "take it up" (*vornehmen*) by "taking it to heart" (*in Acht nehmen*) (WCT: 202–3). Taking to heart, in turn, leaves what is taken to heart "exactly as it is," "keeping" it at heart. In this way *noein* and *legein* do not stand side by side but "each enters into [*fügt sich*] the other," and this *Gefüge* achieves "what later, and only for a short time, is specifically called *aletheuein*: to disclose and keep disclosed what is unconcealed": the truth of being (WCT: 208–9).

Now, a disclosing that does not "make" but "lets lie" or "appear," and a "keeping disclosed" that is no passive acceptance but a "concern," have the structure of something *at issue*, meaning (*Sinn*). *Noein* "perceives beforehand" (*vor-nimmt*) by "taking to heart," a kind of "wakeful watch that takes what lies before us into the true [*in die Wahr nimmt*]." This taking up, in turn, requires the "safekeeping" (*Verwahrung*) accomplished "in *legein* as gathering" that lets lie before us: in speaking. Thinking is *Besinnung*, "a minding [*Sinnen*] that has something in mind [*im Sinn hat*] and takes it to heart." That is, it is "on the scent" of something; "presages" (*Ahnen*) an "arrival" of something: "Genuine presaging is the manner through which what is essential appears [*ankommt*] to us and gives itself to the heart so that we may keep it therein" (WCT: 207). Presaging—the appearance of the essential—is measure-taking.

What is essential is the measure, the "being" of beings, what it is/means to be. For mortals, this measure is never a possession but always at issue in a way that calls them into their essence as thinking things. Human speaking—*legein* as discourse—receives its own measure (i.e., is what it is) in the response to this call.

What is it, then, to hear such a call? Heidegger's answer begins by reflecting on the fragment from Heraclitus we introduced above:

Οὐκ ἐμοῦ ἀλλὰ τοῦ Λόγου ἀκούσαντας ὁμολογεῖν σοφόν ἐστιν Ἓν Πάντα

If we think what the Greeks did not—namely, that "the saying and talking of mortals comes to pass [. . .] as *legein*, laying [*Legen*]" (L: 63)—we are attending to the "mystery" that language takes place out of the unconcealedness of beings, the dispensation (*Schickung*) of the *being* of beings (L: 64). This, according to Heidegger, is what speaks in Heraclitus's invocation of *logos*: "Listening not to me, but to the *logos*." Mortals hear not by registering sounds; such hearing "goes in one ear and out the other." Mortal hearing must be "gathered to what is addressed [*Zugesprochene*]"—namely, "that which lies before us, *as* gathered and laid before us" (L: 65). Indeed, hearing *is* "this gathering of oneself that pulls itself together on hearing the claim [*Anspruch*] and address [*Zuspruch*]" (L: 65; translation modified). Hearing is hearkening to an address that claims it, promising a measure. That measure-taking is at issue here is suggested when Heidegger asserts that mortal hearing is such that it can fail to hear, or "catch," the essential (L: 65). "We have heard when we belong [*gehören*] to the address" (i.e., are *homologein* with what lies before us "gathered in its entirety") (L: 66). This *homologein* establishes what lies before us *as* lying before us (i.e., "*as* itself"). *Logos*, then, can come to be understood as "meaning and reason" only if mortal hearing has already heard the *logos* in the sense of belonging to it, *necessarily* addressed by it (L: 66).

By "it"?

As with the caller of conscience, the nominalized *logos* can deflect us from recognizing the phenomenon being described, the address itself. Heraclitus warns us against this danger by saying "listening not to me"—that is, to someone or something—"but to the *logos*," a listening that Heidegger has now glossed as "maintaining [oneself] in hearkening attunement [*horchsamen Gehören*]" (L: 67). *Logos* is the address, not the addressor. Because "genuine hearing belongs to [*gehört*] the *logos*" it too is a kind of *legein*: *homologein*. Here *sophon* "comes to pass," a "having seen [*Gesehenhaben*]" (L: 68) that, like hearing itself, is not a mere grasping but an understanding, "a comportment [*Verhalten*]" (L: 68). Such comportment is *geschicklich* (skillful, fateful) when, as Heraclitus says, it hears *hen panta*.

Now, mention of understanding here, and *hen panta*, points toward the concept—the one-in-many or many-in-one—that is, toward reason (Hegel).

But Heidegger hears something else in it. Insofar as *logos* "lets what lies before us lie before us *as such*, it discloses [*entbirgt*] what is present *in* its presence," and thus, since "disclosure is *aletheia* [truth]," *logos* is truth (L: 70). *Logos* is *aletheuein* of what is fitting/fateful. But because "mortal *legein* as *homologein* sends itself [*sich schickt*] into the fitting," it is "in its own way fitting" (L: 72; translation modified). To be fated into the fitting is to be toward measure. What measure?

Heraclitus provides a hint: all that is present is steered into presence by the "flash of lightning" (*Blitz*). Such "steering" allots to everything *in advance* its "designated, essential place" (L: 72). As an *attribute* of Zeus, the lightning flash, as Heraclitus says, "does not and does consent to be called by the name of Zeus." For Heidegger, the "does not" takes priority: *hen panta*, the "one" that steers and directs in all, is not itself something present. What measures, allots place, steers into what is fitting: this is neither some highest entity nor an authoritative addresser. The *hen* must be *vernommen* from *logos* itself (i.e., properly heard). Failing that—and the history of *logos* as reason, *ratio*, logic, is the history of this failure—the "totality of beings" will be seen as under the directive of a "highest present being" (L: 74). If, in contrast, *logos* is the address, not the addresser, then *hen panta* names the *measure* of what is fitting.

Metaphysics, then, with its demanding principle of reason, is what happens when mortals fail to hear what speaks as *logos*: an address of being as such that grants a certain "beingness"—the calculable, the rational—to beings. But let us conclude by considering an objection to the late Heidegger's attempt to transcend reason, one he himself raises: *hen panta* is supposed to provide a hint of how *logos* prevails as *legein* (L: 70). But isn't all *legein*, "whether gathering or saying," always "only a kind of mortal comportment"? Haven't we just "elevated and carried over" a mortal mode of being to *logos*, so that our own *legein* then appears as a "copy" of gathering and saying (L: 74)? And does this not invite a Feuerbachian-anthropological deconstruction of the whole thing? Heidegger's answer, it seems, is a kind of "yes and no."

If we conceive *logos* as reason (*Grund*) and ground as a highest entity, this objection has a certain justification. But Heidegger thinks that the situation requires us to see beyond such an "either/or," since asking in this way never reaches what is at stake in the inquiry (L: 74–75). If that is so, then "neither can *logos* be the transcending [*Übersteigerung*] of mortal *legein*, nor can the latter be only a copying of the measure-giving *logos*" (L: 75). Mortal speaking and the *legein* of *logos* have their "more originary origin [*anfänglichere Herkunft*] in the simple middle region between both." And in this direction, Heidegger asks, might one find "a path for mortal thinking" (L: 75)?

Having come this far, what can we say about transcending reason Heidegger's way? Our brief foray into the thicket of Heidegger's late thinking has taught us a couple of things. First, thinking is not reasoning. Whatever else it is, the unity of *noein* and *legein* responds to a call that is to be heard in a manner that altogether contrasts with the way metaphysics hears it—that is, as a call to provide reasons for every being, and so also to be answerable, in the sense of accountable, for oneself. And yet, while Heidegger believes that our most pressing task is to cultivate an attunement to such a call in order that we might live somewhat closer to the manner of the rose, "without why," he also recognizes that we *must* ask why, must offer grounds, since we cannot simply exit our historical situation. And if that *is* our situation, then, in the language of *Being and Time*, we must be prepared to take it up in light of what addresses us and take over our being as belonging to what addresses us. This seems to explain Heidegger's approach to the historical situation: he provides plenty of reasons for why he interprets figures in the history of philosophy the way that he does, and these reasons are supposed to reflect his anticipation or presaging of what is really the "matter for thought," a matter to which he thus makes himself answerable as his measure. Whether those reasons convince us or not is another question, to which each must provide an answer for themselves. In a sense, then, even Heidegger's late thinking rests upon a phenomenological basis that is thoroughly consistent with his analysis in *Being and Time*.

And what if his reasons are *not* convincing and his historicizing of the transcendental-phenomenological approach is rejected in one way or another? Then on one interpretation—the one I would like to defend—the most important thing is to understand reason in a normativity-first way, as phenomenologically delineated in *Being and Time*. An answer to the why-question, on such a view, does not entail logical completeness—i.e., it is independent of the principle of sufficient reason because the *origin* of reason-giving lies in the measure-taking that, always at issue, takes the measure of what is best in whatever it is that I am trying to be.

Such measure-taking is not the sign of a finitude that would measure itself against the pure "intelligibility" of the concept (Hegel). It is a finitude whose orientation toward measure yields "the phenomena of phenomenology," the world of meaning, *on hos alethes*, being in the sense of truth. As Heidegger argued from his very first publications on, reason as logic *depends* on such meaning but does not *govern* it. Thus, whether or not we are convinced by Heidegger's late account of the history of being as metaphysics, we must—at least for now—be answerable in the sense of giving reasons. In such a situation, the virtue of *Being and Time*'s normativity-first account of reason-giving is that it offers an affirmative sense of "transcending reason"—reason belongs to transcendence—that suggests *both* why the "reign of logic" can be called into question ("transcended" in the negative sense), *and* why doing so, getting over it, may not be the last word about the place of reason in our lives.

NOTES

1. Beginning, perhaps, with Husserl, whose remarks in the *Crisis* about how philosophy threatens to succumb to "skepticism, irrationalism, and mysticism" (Husserl 1970a: 3) are often thought to be aimed at Heidegger. More recent versions of the charge can be found in Habermas (1987), Wolin (1990), Rockmore (1992), and Fritsche (1999).
2. See, for instance, Gethmann (1974), Guignon (1983), Richardson (1986), Olafson (1987), Dreyfus (1991), Blattner (1999), Polt (1999), Lafont (2000), Carman (2003), McManus (2012), and Haugeland (2013).
3. Heidegger is here speaking of Lask, but he embraces this project as his own. See Crowell (2001).
4. The thread from *on hos alethes* to Heidegger's later idea of the "truth of being" has been extensively explored in Sheehan (2015).
5. In *Being and Time* care is constituted by facticity (thrownness) and transcendence (projection), but around 1928 Heidegger begins to use the term "transcendence" for the whole care-structure. The reasons for this shift are complicated, but see Pöggeler (1987), Tengelyi (2014), Schmidt (2016), and Crowell (2018).
6. On the neo-Kantian context in which Heidegger's early work stands, see Köhnke (1991), Crowell (2001), and Beiser (2014).
7. On psychologism see Kusch (1995); on judgment see Martin (2006); for a recent look at Heidegger's early arguments against psychologism, see MacAvoy (2019).
8. Lask (2003: 36) calls this "truth in the paradigmatic [*urbildlich*] sense": meaning is *identical* to the object itself as the primitive unity (*Gefüge*) of categorial form and categorial material. My Aristotelian shorthand, "being in the sense of truth," is meant to capture this paradigmatic sense and its transformation in Heidegger's thinking. See Crowell (2001).
9. In addition to the works on neo-Kantianism mentioned above, see Luft (2015), which offers a new approach to the Marburg tradition.
10. An interpretation of phenomenology's relation to the Baden school is found in Staiti (2010).
11. Husserl argues this point in (1970b: 74–89); Heidegger reproduces parts of it in his critique of Heinrich Maier (GA1: 103–14).
12. Robert Scharff (2018) shows in detail how this period in Heidegger's thinking is framed by Heidegger's reading of Dilthey as a foil to Husserl's phenomenology.
13. For instance, *Bewegtheit, Ruinanz, Jeweiligkeit, Bekümmering, Reluzenz*, and many others. This fluctuation testifies to the distance between Heidegger's phenomenological approach and a Hegelian "system" of categories.
14. For an analysis of the phenomenological provenance of this notion, see Crowell (2001: ch. 7).
15. See Burch (2013).
16. Early on, J. N. Mohanty (1985) explicated this difference, followed by Crowell (2001). It has some connections with the position Charles Taylor advances (1995), but we cannot explore these here.
17. In *Basic Problems of Philosophy* Heidegger goes so far as to say that "ontology," or "transcendental science," is "the objectification of being as Temporal" (BP

327). John van Buren (1994) treats this whole period of Heidegger's thinking as a regrettable swerve from the "deconstructive" tendency of Heidegger's thought as a whole, but our concern here is exclusively with the *phenomenological* aspects of Heidegger's way of transcending reason, and this is independent of claims about whether the "Kantian" framework of *Being and Time* is an aberration.

18. Heidegger does not dismiss *Wesensschau* altogether. It lets "the entity be seen in its objectivity," and this "actually presents the entity more truly in its 'being-in-itself'" (HCT: 70–71). Much later, he will say that "categorial intuition" showed him the way toward the manifold senses of being (MWP 78).

19. Such "retrieval" belongs to the task of "de-structing" the history of ontology and means securing "access" to the "primordial 'sources' from which [traditional] categories and concepts [. . .] have been in part quite genuinely drawn," in order to "preserve the force of the most elemental words in which Dasein expresses itself" (BT: 43, 262).

20. In what follows I will generally leave this term untranslated. It is often translated as "perception," but as we shall see, this conceals the central philosophical point at issue for Heidegger. *Vernehmen* is etymologically connected to *Vernunft* (reason), although we cannot explore the details here.

21. "Being (not entities) is something which 'there is' only insofar as truth is. And truth *is* only insofar as and so long as Dasein is. Being and truth 'are' equiprimordially" (BT: 272). Truth is a "transcendental" in the medieval sense.

22. There is, of course, a long-standing debate, going back to Tugendhat (1970), about whether Heidegger's own account of truth can do justice to this claim. On this point, see Dahlstrom (2001), Smith (2007), and Wrathall (2011).

23. Heidegger makes this point in his discussion of Descartes: when *noein* is understood as intuiting what a thing really is, then that thing is reduced to what intuiting can access, that is, what is "mathematical" in things (BT: 129). The issue deserves closer attention than can be given in a mere map of the territory.

24. This was the role "categorial intuition" played for Husserl, and something like it seems to be called for in recent discussions within analytic metaphysics about how to discern "structure" in the world (Sider 2011) or how to know when we have concepts that "carve nature at the joints."

25. We will unpack this claim below, but we should note here that Heidegger admits that *something* can be accessed in such reflection: a "formal phenomenology of consciousness" (BT: 151). This might well be important for some philosophical purposes, even if those are not Heidegger's.

26. This does not mean that a pragmatic interpretation of *Being and Time* (e.g., Okrent 1988) has nothing to teach us. On the contrary, it has a great deal to teach us about the *implications* of Heidegger's approach to ontology.

27. Of course, we can recognize hammers without using them. But recognition in this sense—which is based on the public character of language and, more generally, on the fact that "everyday" Dasein inhabits a socially typified world—does not count as "encountering" them in Heidegger's sense.

28. Irene McMullin (2019) provides a lucid analysis of these evidence-situations as distinct sources of normativity, irreducible "normative domains" tied to first-,

second-, and third-person perspectives on ourselves. Further, she shows how these domains yield three different sorts of reason.

29. "Sicht auf das Sein als solches, umwillen dessen das Dasein je ist, wie es ist." The sentence shows that "Sein als solches" here does not mean some vision of "being as such" but rather Dasein's orientation toward what it means to be whatever it is trying to be: existentiell understanding.

30. Heidegger does not employ this term, since "care [*Sorge*] already harbors within itself the phenomenon of the self," so that "the expression *Selbstsorge* would be tautological" if used in parallel with the other two (BT: 366). I resurrect it here to emphasize its *distinct* evidence-situation.

31. This point marks a divide—extensively pursued in *Fundamental Concepts of Metaphysics*—between the transcendental-phenomenological approach to ontology in *Being and Time* and the "metaphysical" approach that Heidegger pursues between 1928 and 1934. As a living being, the human being does not have access to *das Seiende als solches und im Ganzen*; as Dasein, it does. See the discussion in Crowell (2017).

32. There must be *some* level of "skillful coping" at work—as Dreyfus (1991) forcefully argues—if we are to be able to say that one is actually *doing* something, as opposed (say) to just learning it, or just playing around.

33. Where Lask claims that we "live in the truth," Heidegger claims that "Dasein is already both in truth and in untruth" (BT: 265).

34. In German, *vernehmen*, unlike *wahrnehmen*, is tightly connected to hearing, although it certainly can be used for "perception" of other kinds. To say that Dasein's access to itself (*Durchsicht*) is a mode of hearing, coupled with the previously established point that both seeing and hearing are grounded in Dasein's understanding, indicates that the other modes of "sight" (*noein* as access in general)—*Umsicht, Rücksicht*—are themselves modes of hearing, that is, provide access to beings in their being, as *meaningful*. The phenomenological connection between *noein* as hearing and meaning as *on hos alethes* is what is at issue in Heidegger's analysis of Dasein's mode of access to its own being in breakdown.

35. See Crowell (2016) and Waldenfels (1994).

36. William McNeill (1999) provides a penetrating and wide-ranging treatment of Heidegger's *Denkweg* centered upon transformations in the notions of seeing, *theoria*, and the *Augenblick*.

37. On various senses of possibility in Heidegger see Blattner (1999: 37–39); on the relation between ontological possibility and these other senses, see Haugeland (2013: 187–220); on being-possible as "possibilizing," see Crowell (2013: 208–10).

38. The "meaningless" is an *abstraction*: "It requires a very artificial and complicated frame of mind to 'hear' a 'pure noise'" (BT: 207). Because Dasein is originally sense-making (Sheehan 2015), even the "abyss of meaninglessness" becomes "accessible only as meaning" (BT: 194).

39. Dan Zahavi (2017) arrives at the same point from a Husserlian perspective in his attempt to spell out the connection between transcendental phenomenology and metaphysics.

40. For a discussion, with references, see Burch (2010).

41. Here I must forgo an account of the methodological role of angst and the intimate phenomenological relation between angst, death, and conscience it entails, but see Crowell (2013: Part III).

42. Dreyfus (1991), via Wittgenstein, shows us the positive *necessity* for such public intelligibility, but as Heidegger notes, it also "deprives the particular Dasein of its answerability" (BT: 165).

43. "Not to what Dasein counts for, can do, or concerns itself with in being with one another publicly, nor to what it has taken hold of, set about, or let itself be carried along with" (BT: 317). The call thus reaches Dasein *as* nothing (of this sort).

44. Nor does such *entsprechen* require that the *addresser* of the call be identified; indeed, from the ontological (phenomenological) point of view, the addresser *cannot* be identified. Heidegger rightly notes that "the caller is definable in a 'worldly' way by nothing at all" (BT: 321), but when he goes on to claim that the caller is "Dasein itself" he goes beyond what is attested in this evidence-situation—as do those who identify the addresser with God. I cannot argue this point here, but as we shall see, Heidegger himself embraces it in the third stage of his thinking about *noein* and *legein*.

45. This phenomenological point plays a central role for both Korsgaard (1996) and Darwall (2006).

46. That is, it excludes reasons for guilt of the form "I am guilty *because*. . . ." Heidegger seems to provide such a reason: because I can only choose one possibility at a time (BT: 331). But here, as in the case of his identification of the caller as Dasein, the phenomenology of conscience does not authorize such a reason. Only by insisting on this point will we understand the importance of Heidegger's interpretation of what is said in the call—the "must" of taking over being a ground—for retrieving reason in *Being and Time*.

47. Crowell (2013: Part III).

48. The slash in the think/feel construction stands in for the complicated interplay of *Befindlichkeit* and *Verstehen* in the context of action. A full account of Heidegger's moral psychology would require unpacking this interplay in more detail than the present context allows.

49. It would be interesting to consider—in another context—how all this relates to the idea of "quantifier pluralism" (McDaniel 2017). Treating the copula as a formal-*indication* might suggest what McDaniel calls the "derivative" character of the "universal" meaning of existential quantification. For some problems with this view, see McManus (2013).

50. For a keen discussion of this point, see Golob (2014: ch. 3).

51. I translate *Ver-nehmen* here as "ap-perception" to bring out the positive relation to Leibniz's thinking that informs Heidegger's own in the period around FCM. See Crowell (2018) for a brief discussion. Heidegger's thinking about Leibniz on reason and apperception undergoes a significant change after 1935.

52. These manifold senses of being require more discussion, but here we need only note that *one* such sense, being-true, references the key concept of Heidegger's thinking, *on hos alethes*.

53. Heidegger anticipates this move in *Being and Time* but does not develop it: the fact that "entities in themselves can be *binding* for every possible assertion"

presupposes that Dasein can "free" them, and this it can do because truth is "something for the sake of which Dasein *is*" (BT: 270).

54. A fuller account here would require phenomenological analysis of the relation between *Vor-bild* (exemplar) and transcendence as *Welt-bildend*. See Golob (2014: 123–55) and Crowell (2008).

55. Or, as Heidegger puts it during this period: fundamental measure-taking is how the "human being" is transformed into "the Da-sein in us." For some problems with this, see Crowell (2017); for an alternative reading, see Engelland (2015).

56. See Haugeland, "Truth and Finitude" (2013: 187–220). I would only add that letting oneself be bound—commitment (*Bindung, Entschlossenheit*)—is what it means to take over being a ground.

57. The topographical character of Heidegger's later work has been extensively explored in Malpas (2006).

58. Chad Engelland (2017) traces this transcendental-phenomenological residue—which he calls "Heidegger's shadow"—throughout Heidegger's *Denkweg*, although he draws somewhat different conclusions from it than I do.

59. This move from the *Leitfrage* to the *Grundfrage* in Heidegger's *Kehre* is cogently analyzed in Keiling (2015).

60. Here I translate *das Schickliche* as "the fitting," which raises a difficult issue in translating the later Heidegger, who uses various forms derived from the word *schicken* (to send) in ways that often turn on two central but quite different meanings related to "fate/destiny" on the one hand, and to "fitting, skillful, appropriate" on the other. In the present chapter I cannot deal with these matters in detail, so I will translate these various uses as I believe the philosophical context warrants, although in doing so I will occasionally alter existing translations without being able to give full justification for such changes.

61. The translations here, and of the fragment from Parmenides below, are from Kirk and Raven (1969: 188, 204). Needless to say, Heidegger will translate them otherwise.

62. Here Heidegger notes his swerve from his approach to these issues in *Vom Wesen des Grundes*.

63. Here I take the phrase "capable of death *as* death" as shorthand for the entire phenomenological structure of Angst-Death-Conscience as presented in *Being and Time*, which is anchored in the existential concept of death as Dasein's ownmost ability-to-be. Justifying this shorthand must wait for another occasion.

64. Kirk and Raven (1969: 270).

BIBLIOGRAPHY

Beiser, Frederick. 2014. *The Genesis of Neo-Kantianism, 1796–1880*. Oxford: Oxford University Press.

Blattner, William. 1999. *Heidegger's Temporal Idealism*. Cambridge: Cambridge University Press.

Burch, Matthew. 2010. "Death and Deliberation: Overcoming the Decisionism Critique of Heidegger's Practical Philosophy." *Inquiry* 53, no. 3: 211–34.

———. 2013. "The Existential Sources of Phenomenology: Heidegger on Formal Indication." *European Journal of Philosophy* 21, no. 2: 258–78.
Carman, Taylor. 2003. *Heidegger's Analytic: Interpretation, Discourse, and Authenticity in Being and Time*. Cambridge: Cambridge University Press.
Crowell, Steven. 2001. *Husserl, Heidegger, and the Space of Meaning: Paths Toward Transcendental Phenomenology*. Evanston, IL: Northwestern University Press.
———. 2008. "Measure-Taking: Meaning and Normativity in Heidegger's Philosophy." *Continental Philosophy Review* 41, no. 3: 261–76.
———. 2013. *Normativity and Phenomenology in Husserl and Heidegger*. Cambridge: Cambridge University Press.
———. 2016. "Second-Person Phenomenology." In *The Phenomenology of Sociality: Discovering the "We,"* (70–89), edited by Thomas Szanto and Dermot Moran. London: Routledge.
———. 2017. "We Have Never Been Animals: Heidegger's Posthumanism." *Études phénoménologiques / Phenomenological Studies* 1, 217–40.
———. 2018. "The Middle Heidegger's Phenomenological Metaphysics." In *The Oxford Handbook of the History of Phenomenology* (229–50), edited by Dan Zahavi. Oxford: Oxford University Press.
Dahlstrom, Daniel. 2001. *Heidegger's Concept of Truth*. Cambridge: Cambridge University Press.
Darwall, Stephen. 2006. *The Second-Person Standpoint: Morality, Respect, and Accountability*. Cambridge: Cambridge University Press.
Dreyfus, Hubert. 1991. *Being-in-the-World. A Commentary on Heidegger's Being and Time, Division I*. Cambridge, MA: MIT Press.
Engelland, Chad. 2015. "Heidegger and the Human Difference." *Journal of the American Philosophical Association* 1, no. 1: 175–93.
———. 2017. *Heidegger's Shadow: Kant, Husserl, and the Transcendental Turn*. New York: Routledge.
Fritsche, Johannes. 1999. *Historical Destiny and National Socialism in Heidegger's Being and Time*. Berkeley: University of California Press.
Gethmann, Carl Friedrich. 1974. *Verstehen und Auslegung: Das Methodenproblem in der Philosophie Martin Heideggers*. Bonn: Bouvier Verlag.
Golob, Sacha. 2014. *Heidegger on Concepts, Freedom and Normativity*. Cambridge: Cambridge University Press.
Guignon, Charles. 1983. *Heidegger and the Problem of Knowledge*. Indianapolis: Hackett.
Habermas, Jürgen. 1987. *The Philosophical Discourse of Modernity*, tr. Frederick Lawrence. Cambridge, MA: MIT Press.
Haugeland, John. 2013. *Dasein Disclosed*, ed. Joseph Rouse. Cambridge, MA: Harvard University Press.
Husserl, Edmund. 1970a. *The Crisis of European Sciences and Transcendental Phenomenology*, tr. David Carr. Evanston, IL: Northwestern University Press.
———. 1970b. *Logical Investigations*, Vol. I, tr. J. N. Findlay. London: Routledge & Kegan Paul.
Keiling, Tobias. 2015. *Seinsgeschichte und phänomenologischer Realismus: Eine Interpretation und Kritik der Spätphilosophie Heideggers*. Tübingen: Mohr Siebeck.

Kirk, G. S. and J. E. Raven. 1969. *The Presocratic Philosophers*. Cambridge: Cambridge University Press.
Kisiel, Theodore. 1993. *The Genesis of Heidegger's* Being and Time. Berkeley: University of California Press.
Köhnke, Klaus Christian. 1991. *The Rise of Neo-Kantianism: German Academic Philosophy Between Idealism and Positivism*, tr. R. J. Hollingdale. Cambridge: Cambridge University Press.
Korsgaard, Christine. 1996. *The Sources of Normativity*. Cambridge: Cambridge University Press.
Kusch, Martin. 1995. *Psychologism: A Case Study in the Sociology of Philosophical Knowledge*. London: Routledge.
Lafont, Cristina. 2000. *Heidegger, Language, and World-Disclosure*. Cambridge: Cambridge University Press.
Lask, Emil. 2003. *Die Logik der Philosophie* and *Die Lehre vom Urteil*. Jena: Dietrich Scheglmann Reprintverlag.
Luft, Sebastian. 2015. *The Space of Culture*. Oxford: Oxford University Press.
MacAvoy, Leslie. 2019. "The Space of Meaning, Phenomenology, and the Normative Turn." In *Normativity, Meaning, and the Promise of Phenomenology* (29–46), edited by Matthew Burch, Jack Marsh, and Irene McMullin. London: Routledge.
Malpas, Jeff. 2006. *Heidegger's Topology: Being, Place, World*. Cambridge, MA: MIT Press.
Martin, Wayne. 2006. *Theories of Judgment*. Cambridge: Cambridge University Press.
McDaniel, Kris. 2017. *The Fragmentation of Being*. Oxford: Oxford University Press.
McManus, Denis. 2012. *Heidegger and the Measure of Truth*. Oxford: Oxford University Press.
———. 2013. "Ontological Pluralism and the *Being and Time* Project." *Journal of the History of Philosophy* 51, no. 1: 651–73.
McMullin, Irene. 2019. *Existential Flourishing: A Phenomenology of the Virtues*. Cambridge: Cambridge University Press.
McNeill, William. 1999. *The Glance of the Eye: Heidegger, Aristotle, and the Ends of Theory*. Albany: SUNY Press.
Mohanty, J. N. 1985. *The Possibility of Transcendental Philosophy*. The Hague: Martinus Nijhoff.
Okrent, Mark. 1988. *Heidegger's Pragmatism: Understanding, Being, and the Critique of Metaphysics*. Ithaca, NY: Cornell University Press.
Olafson, Frederick. 1987. *Heidegger and the Philosophy of Mind*. New Haven, CT: Yale University Press.
Pöggeler, Otto. 1987. *Martin Heidegger's Path of Thinking*, tr. Daniel Magurshak and Sigmund Barber. Atlantic Highlands: Humanities Press.
Polt, Richard. 1999. *Heidegger: An Introduction*. Ithaca, NY: Cornell University Press.
Richardson, John. 1986. *Existential Epistemology. A Heideggerian Critique of the Cartesian Project*. Oxford: Clarendon Press.
Rockmore, Tom. 1992. *On Heidegger's Nazism and Philosophy*. Berkeley: University of California Press.

Scharff, Robert. 2018. *Heidegger Becoming Phenomenological: Interpreting Husserl Through Dilthey, 1916–1925*. London: Rowman & Littlefield.
Schmidt, Stefan. 2016. *Grund und Freiheit. Eine phänomenologische Untersuchung des Freiheitsbegriffs Heideggers*. Dordrecht: Springer.
Sheehan, Thomas. 2015. *Making Sense of Heidegger: A Paradigm Shift*. London: Rowman & Littlefield.
Sider, Theodore. 2011. *Writing the Book of the World*. Oxford: Oxford University Press.
Smith, William H. 2007. "Why Tugendhat's Critique of Heidegger's Theory of Truth Remains a Critical Problem." *Inquiry* 50, no. 2: 156–79.
Staiti, Andrea. 2010. *Geistigkeit, Leben und geschichtliche Welt in der Transzendentalphänomenologie Husserls*. Würzburg: Ergon Verlag.
Taylor, Charles. 1995. "The Validity of Transcendental Arguments." In *Philosophical Arguments* (20–33). Cambridge, MA: Harvard University Press.
Tengelyi, László. 2014. *Welt und Unendlichkeit. Zum Problem phänomenologischer Metaphysik*. Freiburg: Alber.
Tugendhat, Ernst. 1970. *Der Wahrheitsbegriff bei Husserl und Heidegger*. Berlin: Walter de Gruyter & Co.
Van Buren, John. 1994. *The Young Heidegger: Rumor of the Hidden King*. Bloomington: Indiana University Press.
Waldenfels, Bernhard. 1994. *Antwortregister*. Frankfurt: Suhrkamp.
Wolin, Richard. 1990. *The Politics of Being: The Political Thought of Martin Heidegger*. New York: Columbia University Press.
Wrathall, Mark. 2011. *Heidegger and Unconcealment: Truth, Language, and History*. Cambridge: Cambridge University Press.
Zahavi, Dan. 2017. *Husserl's Legacy: Phenomenology, Metaphysics, and Transcendental Philosophy*. Oxford: Oxford University Press.

Chapter 2

Freedom and Justification
Heidegger on the Essence of Ground
Daniel O. Dahlstrom

Based upon its reception, Heidegger's 1928 essay "On the Essence of Ground" can hardly be considered an important work in his oeuvre. Although Heidegger saw fit to publish a stand-alone edition in 1931 and again in 1949 and to have it included in *Wegmarken* in 1967, the essay has been repeatedly omitted from anthologies and typically passed over or neglected in surveys and studies of Heidegger's thought.[1] Some responsibility for the neglect can no doubt be traced to a subject matter so elusive that a recondite recourse to trope after trope is often Heidegger's only means of shedding any light on it.[2] Moreover, much like Husserl's reference to time-analysis in *Ideas I*, Heidegger alludes to a deeper level of consideration, involving care and temporality, that he forgoes in the essay (GA9: 171).

But along with the obscurity of the essay's basic theme and argument, its place in Heidegger's thought and his own expression of reservations in later years about its contents may explain the weak reception of it. While the Heidegger of the *Beiträge* rejects any invocation of concepts of subjectivity and transcendence, the argument for the essence of ground in the 1928 essay turns on these very themes.[3] In a later edition he also makes it clear that it is a transitional text, "still conducted completely in the framework of traditional metaphysics and in simple . . . correspondence to the truth of beings and unveiledness of beingness." Although the third part opens up one path to overturning ontology as such, "the overturning is not conducted and erected originally from the standpoint of what is attained" (GA9: 126n). In his 1957 lectures *Satz vom Grund* he criticizes the earlier essay's often misleading way of treating the principle of sufficient reason as a statement about beings and not being.[4]

Neglect of the essay is nonetheless hardly warranted. Coming on the heels of *Sein und Zeit* (SZ), the essay continues to focus on being-in-the-world but by addressing themes like freedom and justification in ways that were only implicit at best in SZ. In addition to introducing in print significant new terminology (e.g., "ontological difference," "ontic truth," and "ontological truth"), the essay surveys meanings historically assigned to the "world" that complement the account of it in SZ. Nor should it be overlooked that the essay, written for a 1929 festschrift for Husserl, offers an explanation of intentionality. Last but perhaps not least, the essay is invaluable for any effort to unpack Heidegger's retrospective on where his thinking suffers from its metaphysical trappings during this period.[5]

The aim of this chapter is to clarify and question the transcendental account Heidegger gives of the essence of ground in the 1928 essay as it pertains, in particular, to what are typically understood to be issues of theoretical and practical reason. Heidegger's prefatory remarks and the first two parts of the essay set the stage for the essay's main argument, while providing vital clues to the operative senses of "essence" and "transcendence" at work in the argument. Following glosses on this preliminary material, the chapter focuses on the main argument that the essence of ground is a kind of freedom that transcendentally grounds other sorts of grounds, including the grounds provided by intentional experiences. While I hope to make clear the trenchancy of this argument (despite certain ambiguities), I call into question certain implications for theoretical and practical reason that Heidegger purports to draw from it.[6]

SETTING THE WORLD-STAGE

Drawing on Aristotle's accounts of different sorts of grounds, Heidegger's opening remarks provide the readers with intimations of the meaning of "essence." He then devotes the first part of the essay to demonstrating the problem presented by Leibniz's identity-based account of the ground (i.e., the limitations and insightfulness of his principle of sufficient reason). In the second part of the essay he locates the transcendental region in which the question of ground is to be posed: the world. The first segment of the present chapter charts these three moves.

INTIMATIONS OF AN ESSENCE

Heidegger introduces his essay by noting how Aristotle's analysis of the notion of ground (*arche*), including its division into four causes (*aitia*), illustrates that "ground" is said in many ways, thereby raising the question of whether there is some essence of ground, interconnecting those ways in some principled, not merely verbal manner (i.e., common use of a term). To be sure, even though Aristotle's account of the connection among the four causes moves toward "an original illumination of ground in general," he fails to articulate that "inner connection" because the "original character of transcendental grounds" (over against the supreme ontic grounds) allegedly remains hidden from him (GA9: 124f, 171).

Despite their critical tone, these remarks indicate that Heidegger takes his bearings here, as elsewhere, from Aristotle. The essence of ground should explain how certain different yet preeminent sorts of grounds (e.g., the ground for being what something is, the reason that it is at all, or something's causal grounds) are internally connected. The reference to an inner connection (*inneren Zusammenhang*) entails some non-contingent usage of "ground," "cause," or "reason"; it is "inner" in the sense that the connection is not based upon an arbitrary, external assignment of the meanings of the terms. Heidegger will argue that the essence of grounds, so construed, is to be found in freedom, understood transcendentally.

THE PROBLEM PRESENTED BY THE PRINCIPLE OF SUFFICIENT REASON

Leibniz's principle of sufficient reason—*Satz vom Grund* (principle of the ground)—suffers in Heidegger's estimation from presupposing that the meaning of "ground" (*ratio*) is self-evident. At the same time the account has the virtue of deriving the principle from a conception of truth as the identity (*idem esse*) that grounds the propositional ascription of a predicate to a subject. While Leibniz fails, Heidegger submits, to recognize that the truth grounding the proposition is not the same as the proposition itself, Leibniz's recognition of such a grounding truth is nonetheless the clue or guiding thread (*Leitfaden*) that Heidegger purports to find for unpacking the problem of the ground. Truths refer to something *on the basis of which* [*auf Grund wovon*] what is expressed by the subject and the predicate are in accord with one another, an agreement that "announces itself" in their identity. In other words, the relation to a ground demonstrates that propositional truth is derivative, grounded in a more originary truth, "the pre-predicative manifestness *of entities* that is called *ontic truth*" (GA9: 130).

In a clear challenge to Husserl's phenomenology, Heidegger rejects the notion that this manifestness is experienced in an intuition. Rehearsing but also amplifying points made in SZ, he gives two reasons for this rejection. The first reason is the fact that the manifestation occurs as "a manner of finding ourselves [*Sichbefinden*] amid beings, that is beset by drives and accords with moods" and in "comportments toward entities that are co-grounded therein, in keeping with what is striven for and willed" (GA9: 131). (This characterization of finding ourselves, beset by drives, in the midst of beings and its juxtaposition with talk of "comportments" raises questions regarding intentionality to be discussed later in this chapter.) The second reason (for rejecting the appeal to intuition) is that these ways of behaving toward things (beings) would be incapable of making them accessible in themselves "if their manifesting were not . . . guided in advance by an understanding of the being (constitution of being: being-what and being-how) of beings" (GA9: 131).[7] Heidegger introduces the term "ontological truth" to characterize this unveiledness of being that first enables the manifestness of beings. As in SZ, he is quick to add that, far from constituting a full-blown ontology in the narrow sense, the understanding of being is "pre-ontological or ontological in the broader sense" (GA9: 132).

While the difference between ontic truth and ontological truth concerns the difference between "beings *in* their being" and "the being *of* beings," they essentially belong together on the basis of their relation to the ontological difference (being and beings). What characterizes Dasein is precisely its way of relating to entities by way of understanding being (i.e., moving beyond entities as it were to being). Heidegger accordingly calls "this ground of the ontological difference the *transcendence* of Dasein" (GA9: 135).[8]

In sum, Leibniz's account of the principle of sufficient reason proves to be usefully problematic since it invokes a truth—the manifestness of beings (ontic truth)—that requires a grounding in both the unveiledness of being (ontological truth) and the distinctive manner of being of the entity—Dasein—to whom those beings are manifest (by virtue of transcending them through its understanding of being). Since transcendence is Dasein's distinctive manner of being, "the question of the essence of ground becomes the problem of transcendence" (GA9: 135).

THE WORLD AS THE TRANSCENDENTAL REGION OF THE QUESTION

"Transcendence" designates Dasein's "basic constitution, occurring prior to all behaving [comportment, *Verhalten*]" (GA9: 137). Notwithstanding some misleading connotations of Heidegger's metaphors for transcendence—an apparatus or overpass (*Überstieg*) extending over a barrier or space, the process of climbing over (*übersteigen*) it—transcendence is something that is happening (*Geschehen*), a directional movement but not an intermittent one. Nor is there any immanent sphere that Dasein must move out from and no gap, separating it from objects, which it must pass over. What is transcended is instead precisely any entity that can be present to Dasein, not hidden from it, including nature and Dasein itself. Dasein only comes to itself, that is, it only exists as itself "in and as transcendence" and only as such "can it relate 'itself' to entities that have necessarily been surpassed" (GA9: 138f).

Yet it comes to itself precisely as a being-in-the-world where the world is what transcendence is directed at. What this means, Heidegger immediately adds, depends upon how the world is conceived (i.e., whether it is conceived in an ordinary, pre-philosophical or transcendental manner). On the ordinary conception, "world" stands for the totality of beings on hand, a unity that embraces everything, albeit in no determinate respect. Such a conception is incompatible with the notion of a world in the transcendental sense peculiar to Dasein, since every being, including Dasein, is transcendent in the trivial sense of being on hand with other beings in this totality (the world, as ordinarily conceived).

But what then is the world, transcendentally conceived, that is, as inherent to the transcendence that is distinctive of Dasein? What light does it specifically shed on the argument for the essence of ground? Heidegger sets the stage for answering this question by reviewing prominent past conceptions of the world, all of which allegedly point to the fact that the meaning of the "world" concerns "the interpretation of human existence *in its relation to beings as a whole*" (GA9: 156). The review is meant to demonstrate that conceiving the world as inherently related to the structure of Dasein is hardly "arbitrary."

Not itself an entity, the world in the transcendental sense is Dasein's entire ensemble (*Ganzheit*) of possibilities and accordingly the vantage point from which (*das, aus dem*) it is able to relate meaningfully to any entity and to do so in the manner it does. By way of elucidation, Heidegger adds:

> In coming-to-itself in this way from the world [*in diesem Auf-es-zukommen aus der Welt*], Dasein comes about [*zeitigt sich*] as a *self*, as a being entrusted with having *to be*. In the being of this entity, *what matters is its potential-to-be*. Dasein is such that it exists *for the sake of itself*. (GA9: 157)

Some of the language here is familiar to readers from the existential analysis in SZ. Having to be is essential to existing as a self but it is a completely worldly experience. What "Dasein" means coincides with the process of having to be and, indeed, be oneself. This process turns on existing for its own sake, with its own unique potential-to-be, even as it has been thrown into a situation not of its choosing and while it is caught up in a world of possibilities that it has always already projected. In this whirr of chosen and unchosen possibilities, it remains in some sense up to Dasein what potential it actualizes (herein lies one of the senses of "freedom" that allegedly grounds being-here). The possibilities projected by Dasein make up its world. Dasein exists as a self inasmuch as it more or less explicitly comes to itself from this world of possibilities that exist for its sake.

Selfhood coincides with having to be in our respective worlds—i.e., with having a sense of our worldly possibilities, possibilities that in one way or another we are always already projecting (e.g., breathing and running, hammering and experimenting, reading and writing). It is useful here to distinguish the implicitness of always already projecting possibilities for oneself from more or less explicitly coming back to oneself from those possibilities. I come to myself from this world of possibilities (i.e., the entire ensemble of possibilities that is my world, existing for the sake of myself). Existing for the sake of oneself in this way, Heidegger is quick to add, cannot be understood solipsistically or egoistically; to the contrary, an "I" as a self can only relate to a "you" that is a self and, indeed, always discloses itself only in the other because Dasein is determined by selfhood (GA9: 157).[9]

Transcending entities, Dasein aims at its world because its world is what matters to it (what it *cares* about), coinciding with the self for the sake of which Dasein exists.[10] Again, since being a self is equivalent to "having to be" in the sense of projecting possibilities and existing for the sake of them, it is also equivalent to having a world, as the entirety of those possibilities.[11] A homely example may help illuminate the point. When my aunt goes fishing, she projects an entire array of possibilities as she gets the gear together, looks for a likely spot, casts in a certain direction, decides on live bait or lures, hopes that the fish are biting, and so on. She projects the possibility of finding but also missing gear, locating but also failing to locate a spot where the fish are biting, casting to where she wanted but also casting in the wrong direction, and so on. She has an entire world before her, but it is clearly no single entity or even the full set of entities involved. Instead, the world is the ensemble of possibilities that she projects—hence, the label "world-projection" (*Weltentwurf*)—and for the sake of which, in the respective moments, she exists as an angler. Because she is always already projecting these possibilities, she comes to herself—as an angler—on the basis of them. In the final analysis, she is the one who projects these possibilities so that they make up *her* world, even though their description includes tokens of types inherited and handed down (e.g., from the northern pike (*Esox lucius*) pursued to the circa 1960 brand of lure she still uses ["Daredevil"]).

Employing yet another metaphor, Heidegger notes that the world-projection acts like a throwover (*Überwurf*) that enables entities to manifest themselves and Dasein to relate to them. (Think of how a pillow's contours show up when a blanket has been thrown over it.) Entities, nature in the broadest sense, could not be manifest without the occasion of entering into a world, something that happens with the existence of Dasein "that transcends as existing." After observing that "the happening [*Geschehen*] of this projecting throwover" is being-in-the-world, Heidegger refers to that event of transcendence as the "primal history" (*Urgeschichte*) (GA9: 158f). To say that "Dasein transcends" is to say that it is "in the essence of its being, *world-forming*," where "forming" is polyvalent, signifying the process of "letting a world happen, giving itself with the world an original view (picture) that is not explicitly grasped, functioning precisely as the proto-type [*Vor-bild*] for every being that can reveal itself"—including the respective Dasein itself (GA9: 158).[12]

Left somewhat ambiguous in Heidegger's account here is the relation between the understanding of being and the projection of the world.[13] To be sure, his review of the history of conceptions of the world underscored that it typically concerns "the interpretation of human existence *in its relation to beings as a whole*," a relation that arguably entails an understanding of being and the different modes of being as such. As it is thrown over things, as noted in the last paragraph, a blanketing that ironically allows them to manifest themselves, the world-projection functions like an understanding of being. Particularly since he describes the "projection of being" as the "primal action [*Urhandlung*] of human existence in which all existing amid beings must be rooted," he appears to conceive them (the understanding of being and the projection of the world) as, if not identical, then at least as coinciding or co-constituting the same happening. The central point seems to be that Dasein transcends beings, moving beyond them to the world (the entire ensemble of possibilities it projects for its own sake), but in such a way that it returns to those beings with an understanding of being that makes it possible to relate to them as beings.

FREEDOM AS THE ESSENCE OF GROUND

The grounding of the principle of sufficient reason as a principle about beings (ontic truth) in an understanding of being (ontological truth) effectively refers the problem of ground—such is the argument of the first part of the essay (I. "Freedom, Transcendence, and Obligation")—to the region of transcendence that has been determined—in part two (II. "Freedom, Justification, and Intentionality")—through analysis of the concept of the world. The task of the final part is to bring to light the essence of ground by demonstrating its origin in this transcendence, conceived as a kind of freedom.

I. FREEDOM, TRANSCENDENCE, AND OBLIGATION

Regardless of the time or the place, we find ourselves in the midst of things with others. But the way in which we are amid things and with others is nothing like a mere juxtaposition of ourselves with them. To the contrary, as noted above, the way we find ourselves amid things and others is "beset by drives and accords with moods." (Driven by certain needs, my joy in the presence of someone, like my sadness at her absence, colors how I am in the midst of things and others generally.) At the same time, we are connected with things and others by virtue of projecting certain possible ways of relating to them that preclude other possible means of doing so. These possibilities also determine what we take things to be and who we take others and ourselves to be. All these possibilities are tokens of types of possibilities that have been handed down to us (we can read or not, vote or not) or that have landed in our laps, based upon our biology and DNA (we can impregnate or be impregnated). Taken as a whole, these projected possibilities—including the way that they preclude other possibilities—make up a world. But the way they make it up is structured by the fact that each Dasein projects those possibilities for the sake of itself.

Dasein's understanding of being coincides with its process of climbing over itself (*sich übersteigen*) in the direction of the world; this transcending is a constant movement that it undertakes for its own sake, moving beyond where it is and has been toward where it *wants*—and in a sense *wills*—to be. "The process of passing over [surpassing] this or that for the sake of something [*Der umwillentliche Überstieg*] occurs only in a 'will' that as such projects itself onto possibilities of itself" (GA9: 163).[14] It is not, however, an act of willing (*Willensakt*) alongside other comportments since all comportments are rooted in this transcendence. "Freedom" is Heidegger's term for this will that, "as and in surpassing [itself and other entities toward the world]," forms the "for-the-sake-of-which" (GA9: 163). It is the will that, in projecting possibilities and projecting itself onto them, sets forth (*entwerfend vorwirft*) the for-the-sake-of in general, but not as some occasional achievement. Heidegger identifies freedom with this will directed at the world and forming what it is for but doing so in a transcendental sense, as a condition for reflective, willful action.[15]

The for-the-sake-of-which, Heidegger iterates, is not something that the transcendence as freedom happens to hit upon, as though it were some value or purpose on hand. "Instead freedom maintains itself—*and to be sure as freedom*—opposite [*entgegen*] the for-the-sake-of" (GA9: 164). Thus, this freedom not only wills possibilities but also maintains itself opposite the possibilities (its own possibilities) for-the-sake-of which it exists. This talk of freedom opposite its possibilities is no doubt meant to flag the fact that some of these possibilities include potential but abandonable commitments, thereby setting the stage for the imminent introduction of obligatoriness.[16]

> In this process of holding itself opposite [*entgegen*] the for-the-sake-of, Dasein occurs in the human being, such that in the essence of its existence it can be

obligated to itself [*sich verpflichtet*], i.e., can be a free self. At the same time, however, freedom reveals itself herein as the enabling of something binding and obligatoriness [*Bindung und Verbindlichkeit*] in general. *Freedom alone can let a world hold sway and world* [*welten*]. (GA9: 164)

Heidegger hardly prepares his readers for this remarkable if somewhat opaque passage, pointing in several directions at once. The passage introduces a difference if not of two levels, then at least of two respects, namely, (1) the transcendent movement constitutive of Dasein, now conceived in terms of transcendental notions of willing and freedom, and (2) how this transcendence happens in human beings. The passage indicates further that this transcendence happens in a human being by enabling a duty to oneself as well as a binding character and obligations generally. The general point here is that someone can have a duty or something can be binding for her only if it is possible for her and yet she is not necessitated by it. In other words, someone can have duties or obligations only if she transcends them, maintaining her freedom opposite them as possibilities. While Heidegger is no doubt tapping into the traditional distinction between ethical duties to oneself and others,[17] he speaks here of obligations generally, presumably ranging over every sort of obligation (ethical, contractual, legal, social, political, and so on). His point is simply—even trivially—that whatever is binding is made possible, in the final analysis, by the freedom that consists in Dasein projecting its world (the entirety of its possibilities) but also maintaining itself over against it.[18]

In contrast to what is necessary in the sense of what must happen, what is binding supposes different possibilities, including the possibilities of being fulfilled or not. As such, obligatoriness presupposes the projection of possibilities that coincides with Dasein's freedom, its transcendence of itself toward the world. The possibilities are not free-floating but structured in the sense of constituting what Dasein exists for the sake of, namely, itself as being-in-the-world that also entails being with others and existing in some sense for them.[19] Thus, to take a mundane example, in traffic I have an obligation to myself and others to signal to oncoming drivers that I intend to turn left, precisely in view of the possibilities I project for-the-sake of all of us in the world we share. One of the possibilities, on which the concept of obligation turns, is precisely noncompliance with it.

This example is, of course, only meant to illustrate how obligatoriness fits structurally into the grounding role assigned to freedom in the grounding, transcendental sense. Freedom, so construed, is not a kind of spontaneity, as though it were an occurrence that "begins of itself" (*von-selbst-anfangen*) as an unconditioned causal condition. Such an interpretation construes freedom as an occurrence that begins indiscriminately (i.e., without regard for the specific sort of being of the entity in question, namely, Dasein). If a concept of spontaneity is to be used here, then it is necessary first, Heidegger submits, to clarify ontologically both the selfhood in play in talk of "beginning of itself" and the character of an occurrence in regard to a self (in order to be able to determine the manner of movement of this beginning).

Concluding his brief gloss on spontaneity, he reaffirms the connection between transcendence and selfhood (not to be confused with egohood):

> *But the selfhood of the self already underlying all spontaneity lies in transcendence.* Letting the world hold sway and doing so by way of projecting and throwing-over [*entwerfend-überwerfend*] is freedom. Only because this freedom makes up transcendence can it give notice of itself in the existing Dasein as an extraordinary sort of causality. (GA9: 164)

While explaining talk of an extraordinary sort of causality (likely referring to Kant's account of spontaneity), freedom in the sense of transcendence is not to be understood as a form of causality. As Heidegger rightly points out, to interpret freedom as causality is to work with a specific understanding of ground, whereas freedom as transcendence is, he is attempting to show, not only one sort of ground but the origin of ground in general.

In sum, Heidegger initially glosses freedom in the transcendental sense of enabling and sustaining something binding. Freedom in this sense makes what is binding possible by projecting possibilities yet maintaining itself opposite them.

II. FREEDOM, JUSTIFICATION, AND INTENTIONALITY

Heidegger moves closer to establishing that the essence of ground is freedom in the transcendental sense, by elaborating three manners of "grounding," his term for "the original relation of freedom to ground" (GA9: 165). The three manners of grounding are *founding, occupying,* and *justifying*.[20] In this contribution to a festschrift for Husserl, Heidegger uses his account of the third manner of grounding to explain intentionality, a concept central to Husserl's phenomenology.

The first two manners of grounding belong—much like the future and the past—to *one* temporal unfolding, co-constituting it.[21] With this reference to temporality Heidegger is undoubtedly amplifying a central contention of SZ, namely, that temporality is the sense of Dasein's being (existence), defined by the basic existentials and their equiprimordiality. The founding sort of grounding corresponds to Dasein's futurity—i.e., its projection of possibilities (the world) and of itself as what those possibilities are for the sake of. This projection entails that Dasein "in and through the surpassing" comes back to entities as such. The projected *for-the-sake-of* points back, moreover, to all the entities that can be revealed in the world horizon, including Dasein and entities other than Dasein. Yet the entities are not apparent or manifest in the projection itself, nor could they be if Dasein did not already find itself in the midst of entities. This alreadiness corresponds to the past that, constitutionally, Dasein never sheds. Finding itself in a throng of entities, attuned to them and captivated (literally, "taken in," *eingenommen*) by them, is not a way of explicitly relating (comporting oneself) to them. But it is a way of—as it were—occupying a parcel of land or taking root (literally, "soil," that is, *Boden nehmen*) and, in that sense, acquiring a ground.

This second sort of grounding corresponds to the first basic existential in SZ, namely, disposedness (*Befindlichkeit*), just as the first sort of grounding corresponds to the second basic existential, understanding. As in SZ, Heidegger stresses their underlying unity (*befindliches Verstehen*). Thus, Dasein would lack the leeway to be variously captivated, permeated, and absorbed by entities in this second sort of grounding (grounding qua occupying) without some dawning of the world, however dim or opaque—i.e., without the projection of the world in the first sort of grounding (grounding as founding). But, again, this projection is hardly *ex nihilo*; Dasein projects possibilities from where it already finds itself and that means, too, in terms of the things it finds itself amid and the others it is with. "Dasein grounds (founds) a world only by grounding itself in the midst of entities" (GA9: 167).

In the founding sort of grounding—related to projection and Dasein's originary futurity—Dasein overshoots (or swings beyond, *überschwingt*) itself since the possibilities it projects exceed the possibilities it possesses by virtue of its facticity (given the ground it occupies). At the same time, the possibilities it projects eliminate other possibilities. This withdrawal of possibilities brings "Dasein *face to face [entgegen]* with the possibilities of the world-projection that can 'actually' be seized upon." Driving home the point, he observes:

> The withdrawal [of certain possibilities] fashions, precisely for the binding character of the projected project that remains [*verbleibenden entworfenen Vorwurfs*], the power behind the way it [that binding character] prevails in the region of Dasein's existence. (GA9: 167)

While Heidegger is making this point rather abstractly, it is simple but hardly trivial. In the course of moving to a new town, for example, I project possibilities that "overshoot" or "swing past" my current possibilities, while at the same time closing off certain possibilities. This withdrawal of possibilities opens up, indeed, *mandates* others (hence, their *binding* character). The fact that the respectively overshooting projection of a world becomes powerful and comes to be possessed only in the withdrawal of possibilities "transcendentally documents," Heidegger adds, the finitude of Dasein's freedom.[22]

At this pivotal juncture he reintroduces the concept of intentionality, construed in a broad sense as a way of relating to entities or, more precisely, behaving/comporting oneself toward them (*Verhalten zum Seienden*).[23] The fact that we find ourselves captivated by the entities around us and attuned to them (singing their tune, as it were, in a way that is always accompanied by a revelation of the world) is not the same as taking up a stance (*Halt*) toward them. The experience of a mood is not a form of intentionality, so construed.[24] Moreover, since Dasein's transcendence is directed at the world and the world is not itself an entity, the usual equation of the essence of transcendence with intentionality is mistaken.

But this mistake does not, in Heidegger's view, absolve him from explaining how intentional behavior (*intentionales Verhalten*) is possible. As noted above, the first two forms of grounding—the grounding that *founds* and the grounding that *occupies*—correspond respectively to the first two basic existentials discussed in SZ, the thrown projection—i.e., the way Dasein finds itself thrown into the midst of things while projecting a world (of possibilities). Yet, while neither of these basic components of human existence by itself constitutes an intentional relation toward entities, together they transcendentally enable intentionality by "temporally co-yielding" (*mitzeitigen*) a third form, namely, grounding as *justifying* (*be-gründen*). In this third form of grounding, the transcendence of Dasein (an ontological truth) enables ontic truth, the manifestation of entities in themselves.

Just as the other forms of grounding correspond to the future and the past that make up Dasein's being (its projection of possibilities and finding itself among them), so this third form corresponds in some sense to Dasein's present (presenting things). But particularly with regard to the explanation of intentional behavior that Heidegger is offering, it is necessary to distinguish ontological and ontic levels, the former transcending and the latter transcended. The presenting that corresponds to the ground that is ultimately justifying is at once transcendental and ontological, passing beyond whatever else determines particular beings and construing them as being. This temporally structured understanding of being is what enables intentionality, the capacity to behave, in different ways, toward entities as entities.[25]

In German philosophical discourse, *begründen* typically has the sense of proving theoretical propositions. In ordinary discourse, it can be used to justify some behavior or to corroborate something.[26] As Heidegger often does, he piggybacks on these various senses even as he looks to establish "a fundamentally original meaning," relative to which justifying in the theoretical sense of a proof or demonstration is narrow and derivative. Whereas we prove a conclusion in order to establish why it holds, the meaning of "justification" in the original sense *"makes the question of why possible at all"* (GA9: 168).

As already noted, Heidegger depicts this third sort of grounding as emerging from the other two. More specifically, he traces it to a tension between them that gives rise to the why-question. The world-projection (i.e., the founding grounding) yields a surfeit of possibilities, while Dasein's experience of its thrown facticity (i.e., the grounding by way of occupying) is an experience of being enmeshed in actual things. The contrast of possibilities and actualities gives rise to the questions: "Why *this way* and not otherwise? Why this entity and not that? *Why something at all and not nothing?*" (GA9: 169). But however these why-questions are posed, they presuppose a "preconceptual, foregoing understanding of being-what, being-a-certain way, and being (nothing) in general" and "this understanding of being first enables the why" (GA9: 169).[27]

Particularly noteworthy in this account is Heidegger's construal of the second form of grounding, corresponding to the experience of finding oneself always already amid entities, as a *nonintentional* experience and nonetheless an experience of actualities. Pushback from the Husserlian phenomenologist in particular is bound to find traction here, given the foundational role that intentionality plays in Husserl's phenomenology.[28] To be sure, Husserl lacks Heidegger's specific notion of finding oneself, together with the moods and attunements that come with it. Nonetheless, horizons in Husserl's account have a parallel function of contributing significantly to enabling straightforwardly intentional experiences like perception and yet doing so by virtue of sporting more or less determinate levels of their own distinctively intentional character.[29] From this Husserlian vantage point, Heidegger's account of being amid entities, captivated by them—and, indeed, as actualities in contrast to possibilities projected—seems to smuggle, if not modes of perception (filled intentions), then at least the intentional awareness of horizons of perception into the account. For ease of reference, I refer to this charge subsequently as the "intentionality criticism."

How might Heidegger respond to this criticism? One avenue of response would be for him to "double-down" on the overriding purposiveness of experience. Without denying actualities and our experiences of them, he might stress how the possibilities of being for-the-sake-of overdetermine any actuality or intentional experience of it. Thus, the projection of possibilities undoubtedly entails certain perceptions and actions but always and tendentiously in view of the projection for Dasein's sake. So, too, the actuality of perceptions (all of which are intentional in nature) as well as actions can be construed as subordinate to the ways in which they are possibilities. Thus, insofar as a perception or action is not completed, it remains a possibility just as it remains an open question (possibility) whether or how it contributes to achieving its end (that for-the-sake-of which it is done).[30] Moreover and more to the point of the criticism, Heidegger's allusion to how drives shape our ways of finding ourselves amid things arguably rules out intentional experiences of things as they are rather than how they conform or not to our drives. Accordingly, in the experience of being amid entities, absorbed into them, there neither is, nor can there be, any intentional experience, least of all one of unveiling present actualities for what they are. The moods we have by being thrown in the midst of things, together with the possibilities we project, first give rise to intentional experiences but the reverse does not hold. That is to say, there is no meaningful way to assert that intentional experiences likewise determine those projections or those moods.[31]

Yet just as the present, while not independent of the past and future, is not reducible to them, so it would seem that intentional experiences and their ground in justification, while transcendentally grounded in the other forms of grounding, are not reducible to them. Moreover, the experience of a perception (a paradigmatic intentional experience) giving rise to projections of possibilities and to moods seems commonplace enough to cast doubt on this first avenue of response, even if we acknowledge Heidegger's insight that any form of presenting (*gegenwärtigen*) also looks to the future on the basis of a past.[32] Doesn't projecting possibilities exemplify intentionality?

These considerations suggest a second avenue of response that Heidegger might make to the "intentionality criticism" raised above—i.e., the criticism that being amid entities (grounding as occupying) entails intentional experiences of some sort (even if the experience is horizonal in one of Husserl's senses of horizon)—a fact that Heidegger's view fails to accommodate. Heidegger might mount this second avenue of response by insisting that, despite his use of ordinals, all three forms of grounding, roughly like the basic existentials and temporal ecstases, are equiprimordial. Indeed, his use of the term *mitzeitigen*—translated "co-yielding" above—can be read in this way, particularly given his insistence that the first two forms of grounding together make up one temporal unfolding (*Zeitigung*) (GA9: 166). To be sure, he introduces grounding as justification (and thereby the grounding of intentionality) on the heels of accounts of the other sorts of grounding but this order of presentation (even if it coincides with the order of knowing) should not be confused with the ways these sorts of grounds are ordered to one another.[33]

What further speaks for this second avenue of response is the fact that Heidegger construes them as "inseparable" and refers to the "equiprimordiality of the transcendental origin of the threefold grounding" despite the fact that the grounding is "strewn" among them in a way that rules out identification of a common genus (GA9: 171). In view of this characterization, Heidegger would presumably have no problem with allowing the presence of actual things to Dasein to be matters of intentional experiences like perception (or even imagination) that are distinct but inseparable from projects and moods (corresponding respectively to the first and second forms of grounding).

An interpretation of Heidegger's account of grounding along the lines of this second line of response to the intentionality criticism must still contend with the fact that Heidegger explains how the first two manners of grounding give rise to the third without offering an account of how one or both of them depend upon the third.[34] Still, this interpretation has the distinct advantage of securing the irreducibility yet transcendental unity of each of the three manners of grounding. On this interpretation, his insistence on characterizing the second manner of grounding—i.e., being amid beings, without recourse to intentional experiences of them, by no means rules out the inseparability of that grounding from the third manner of grounding and its understanding of being that justifies such experiences. Above all, this interpretation preserves Heidegger's explanation of the essence of ground on the basis of the threefold grounding: *"The essence of the ground is the threefold grounding, transcendentally springing forth, in a world-projection, absorption in beings, and ontological justification of them"* (original italics, GA9: 171).

JUSTIFICATION AND CORROBORATION: CAUSES AND LEGITIMATION

As noted earlier, Heidegger observes that the meaning of grounding as justification includes an understanding of being that makes the question why in general possible at all. The observation is unobjectionable; certainly the question why there is something rather than nothing supposes some understanding of being. The understanding of being is, as he puts it, the first and last, primordial answer (*die erst-letzte Urantwort*) for all questioning. That is to say, the answer to any line of questioning must take into account what is, and it can only do so by presupposing an understanding of being. Inasmuch as it provides the answer that lies in advance of any other (*vorgängigste Antwort*), that understanding is the first and last justification.

The understanding of being coincides with Dasein's transcendence of itself in the direction of the world, allowing it to come back to itself and to entities as such (i.e., to countenance them as being). The notion of grounding as justification captures this coincidence: "In it [the understanding of being] transcendence is as such justifying. Because being and the constitution of being are unveiled therein [in transcendence], transcendental justification is deemed the *ontological truth*" (GA9: 169). In order to appreciate the significance of this passage, it bears recalling that transcendence—in contrast to intentionality, to ways of behaving toward beings generally—is Dasein's move beyond itself and any other beings toward the world. Returning from this move with an understanding of being, Dasein is able to relate to itself and any other entity *as* being, *as* something that is.

By the same token, beings identify themselves—i.e., they present themselves for what they are and how they are (ontic truth), because Dasein has an understanding of being, an understanding that transcends beings and, in the ultimate sense of the term, justifies them (ontological truth). No intentional experience can take the place of this understanding as the ultimate or transcendental justification (ground) in the sense of justifying whatever else may be said or known of anything. Both notions—"ultimate justification" and "ontological truth"—signify a grounding of other justifications and truths, albeit not in the sense of justification typical of logical or theoretical argumentation.

Having made the claim that the understanding of entities as beings (ontic truth) presupposes the transcendental grounding as justification (ontological truth), Heidegger makes the further, more radical claim that this third sense of grounding (ontological truth) entails the form that ontic truths take. Thanks to the transcendental grounding (again, the ultimate justification that comes with the understanding of being), every way that an entity manifests itself must be a form of justification of its own, pointing out or corroborating (establishing, identifying) what and how it is. The phrase "point out" literally translates the operative German verb here, *ausweisen*, a term that is also used in connection with corroborating. For example, the verb is used in the sense of identifying someone or establishing a person's identity (*Ausweis* is the German term for a person's form of identification—e.g., passport).

> But now because every case of an entity becoming manifest (ontic truth) is transcendentally pervaded from the outset by the *justifying* [*Begründen*] that we have just characterized, every ontic uncovering and disclosing must be in its way "justifying," i.e., the entity must corroborate itself [identify itself or, literally, point itself out, *sich ausweisen*].[35] In the corroboration [*Ausweisung*], *an entity is introduced* that is demanded by what and how the entities in question are and the *sort of unveiling* (truth) proper to them, an entity that gives notice of itself as, for example, "cause" or as "motivation" (motive) for an already manifest connection among entities. (GA9: 169f)

This complex passage contains two levels of entailment, neither of which is obvious, particularly given the fact that what is entailed in the first case is something necessary (entities "must" corroborate—i.e., provide some evidence, some demonstration or even explanation of who or what they are) and, in the second case, with the corroboration comes a "demand" for a cause or motive. Although Heidegger alluded earlier to causation and, at least indirectly, to motivation (in the reference to what is binding), he hardly prepares his readers for these references to corroboration (identification or demonstration), to causes and motives, let alone for their supposedly necessary grounding in an ontologically foundational sense of justification.

To be sure, Heidegger iterates that Dasein's transcendence justifies insofar as, projecting possibilities and finding itself among entities, it forms an understanding of being. The understanding of being is justifying in the sense, as noted above, that it provides the ultimate answer to every question why, the grounding reason or justification of any justification. Why, in the end, do we know that water freezes at a certain temperature? We know it because it manifests this very property (i.e., because it shows this aspect of it). At the same time, this ontic truth supposes the ontological truth, the understanding of being at all, namely, that to be is convertible with being present in some respect, absent in others so as to *justify itself*.[36]

Each form of grounding, it bears emphasizing, is "equiprimordial" (i.e., on a par with the others, making a claim on Dasein that is irreducible to the other forms even as it implicates them). Because justification as the ultimate form of grounding takes place equiprimordially with the two other forms in the unity of transcendence (springing, in effect, from Dasein's finite freedom), it is possible for Dasein to spurn grounds in its factical corroborations and justifications (*faktischen Ausweisungen und Rechtfertigungen*), to suppress the claim to them, to pervert them and cover them up. So, too, as a consequence of the origin of justifying and its equiprimordiality with the other manners of grounding, it is left to the freedom of Dasein how far it pursues corroboration. Thus, for example, Dasein is free to pursue that corroboration to the point that it understands "the unveiling of its transcendental possibility."[37] "Freedom" in the justifying manner of grounding signifies that Dasein issues the constraints of theoretical and practical reason, corroboration and legitimation, but by the same token is not bound by them (herein lies a further dimension of the sense of Heidegger's remark, cited earlier, about freedom maintaining itself "opposite" the very possibilities it projects).

Still, the fact that Dasein is free, that it may or may not heed what is corroborated or legitimate does not by itself explain why such corroborations and legitimations have to obtain. It also fails to explain why reference to causes and motives is required. When it comes to these requirements, Heidegger plainly overreaches. That is, his account lacks the resources to explain why one thing rather than another is the case (corroborated or caused) or, analogously, why some actions are binding and others are not.[38]

Instead of shedding any light on these requirements, Heidegger is content to rehearse the different ways that transcendence is revealed. The point he does make is nonetheless phenomenologically crucial; instead of giving us a "just so" story or a rationale for conditions that are not evident but theoretically called for, he is in effect telling us how transcendence and, with it, grounding is experienced. In this regard he registers three points.

(1) While being is always revealed in transcendence, no conceptual grasp of it is required and transcendence as such can, he acknowledges, be hidden to a degree. In such a case we may be familiar with it only in an "indirect" interpretation.
(2) Yet even then, Heidegger submits, it is revealed in a sense, precisely by virtue of allowing for something to come forth in the basic constitution of being-in-the-world. (Again, by way of analogy, the angler's understanding of her sport, together with the projection of possibilities attending it, hardly needs to be conceptual for something to enter into the world—understandably, meaningfully—as a lure or rod or for there to be some corroboration of the presence of fish in the part of the lake where she finds herself.) Heidegger adds that "the self-revelation of transcendence announces itself" in the basic constitution of being-in-the-world. In other words, to the extent that entities enter our world, transcendence is presumably revealed pre-conceptually as what enables them to do so.
(3) But transcendence also reveals itself explicitly as the origin of grounding when this grounding is brought into view as springing forth in its threefold way, namely, projecting possibilities, occupying a certain piece of land, and corroborating what there is. In an originally unifying manner, these grounds produce the whole in which Dasein should, respectively, be able to exist.

FREEDOM AND THE ABYSS

Heidegger's terms for the different manners of grounding (founding, occupying, justifying) unmistakably echo ordinary senses of them. By way of bringing the present chapter to a close, I attempt to identify how these different manners of grounding similarly exemplify different ordinary senses of "freedom" or conditions of those senses.[39] "Freedom," as invoked by Heidegger in his study, stands principally for the transcendence that constitutes Dasein's being-in-the-world, its manner of moving past entities (including itself) to the world and returning to them with the understanding of being that its world-projection entails. Freedom in this transcendental sense grounds (1) by *founding* a world in projecting possibilities, (2) by *occupying* the place where it finds itself amid things, and (3) by *justifying* what there is and how it is.

The first manner of grounding constitutes the freedom of not being tied down to specific actualities or some finished state of things. The process of projecting certain possibilities opens up further possibilities but also forecloses others, while the projected possibilities themselves present it with certain constraints and obligations. Yet, testifying to the nimbleness of Dasein's freedom, to the fact that its founding of a world is not a one-and-done affair, the fact that it founds the world entails that it continues to maintain itself freely vis-à-vis worldly bonds and obligations. They are binding only because we have allowed them to oblige but not compel us.

Dasein's freedom would not be possible without the second manner of grounding (i.e., without having, as it were, the home base of its operations, from which it ventures in founding its world). In short, Dasein can only project possibilities for itself from the place it finds itself. Thanks to the ground it occupies (the factical world it has been thrown into), its freedom is finite but also capable of being authentic—"authentic" in the sense of being grounded and hence both free for and constrained by the possibilities of the ground it occupies.

The third manner of grounding (grounding as justifying) is the freedom of corroborating what there is in the world and how it is, a corroboration that somehow entails the causes of things and the motivations of actions. The constitution of the respective being of beings is transcendentally binding but precisely because it is rooted in Dasein's freedom. For the same reason, Dasein also has the freedom to abide or not by what is corroborated or right and so, too, the freedom to look for the ultimate justification (ground). As the transcendental origin of ground in the three irreducible but united senses, "freedom is the essence of ground" (GA9: 165, 170, 173).[40]

Is there a ground of Dasein's grounding, its freedom? The question is obviously a kind of category mistake, given the transcendental character of the grounding. Heidegger characterizes freedom accordingly as "the ground of ground"—not as another manner of grounding leading to a regress—but as "the grounding unity of the transcendental dispersal of grounding," adding that "as *this* ground, freedom is the abyss [*Ab-grund*] of Dasein" (GA9: 174). With this last notion, Heidegger aims to underscore that Dasein's freedom, far from being groundless, inserts it into possibilities that open up, like a chasm, "before its finite choice, i.e., in its fate" (GA9: 174). This fatefulness of the abyss corresponds to the familiar fact that Dasein, as a potential-to-be, is *"thrown as a free* potential-to-be among entities" and that "the transcendence, as the primal happening, is not in its power" (GA9: 175). And yet, Heidegger concludes, only through the distances opened up by transcending all entities does a genuine nearness to things arise in us; only being able to listen at a distance awakens a response to others with whom "Dasein can surrender its ego-hood in order to become an authentic self" (GA9: 175).

NOTES

1. The essay is omitted in prominent anthologies (Krell 2008, Figal 2009), coverage of it is missing from several collections on Heidegger's thought and particular

works (Braver 2009, Dahlstrom 2011, Davis 2010, Dreyfus and Wrathall 2005, Nelson and Raffoul 2013, Thomä 2003); not coincidentally, "ground" is not to be found in the indexes of prominent studies of Heidegger's work (Sheehan 2015, Capobianco 2010, Engelland 2017, John Richardson 2012). Notable exceptions to this trend include Braver 2012, Crowell 2013, Golob 2014, William Richardson 1963, and Tugendhat 1970.

2. Richardson characterizes the essay as "one of the hardest diamonds in all of Heidegger's ample treasury" (W. Richardson 1963: 161).

3. Heidegger qualifies but embraces the need for "a constantly renewed, ontological interpretation of the subjectivity of the subject" (GA9: 137f, 162).

4. GA10: 37, 67–73. In these 1957 lectures he admits, as the author of the earlier essay, to having failed, no less than his peers, to grasp the immense power of the principle of sufficient reason.

5. Particularly revealing in this regard are several footnotes in GA9 that contain marginal comments inserted by Heidegger into his copies of different editions of the essay. Some of these comments amplify a respective passage, while others clarify where Heidegger sees them falling short of his more mature position. Discussion of these invaluable comments must be postponed here.

6. I am very grateful to Irene McMullin for valuable, critical comments on the penultimate draft of this chapter and to James Kinkaid for similar comments on an even earlier draft. While I have by no means been able to respond to all of their worries, the chapter is better for attempting to do so.

7. One might (following a suggestion made by James Kinkaid) argue that these two considerations, far from ruling out intuition, merely explain how it is possible. While that is unquestionably often the case, Heidegger would likely respond that we also frequently fear something impending or understand a problem without, strictly speaking, intuiting it.

8. At this juncture Heidegger first introduces the theme of intentionality, conceived as any behavior toward entities. He contends that, as such, far from being identical to transcendence or making it possible, intentionality is itself grounded in transcendence. While these contentions are not immediately explained or justified, Heidegger attempts to make good on them later in the essay, as discussed below.

9. This proposition, Heidegger stresses, is structural; far from implying any "solipsistic isolation" of Dasein or "egoistic intensification of it," the proposition provides "the condition of the possibility that human beings can behave *either* 'egotistically' or 'altruistically'" (GA9: 157). This reference to "solipsistic isolation" may be a way of qualifying the talk of "existential 'solipsism'" in SZ (SZ: 188). Notably, while the *I* only and invariably discloses itself in the *you*, selfhood is never related to the *you* but is instead neutral with respect to being *I* or being *you* or being gendered, precisely because it makes all the latter possible.

10. GA9: 157: "The world has the basic character of the for-the-sake-of . . . and has it in the original sense that it first provides the inner possibility for every factically self-determining 'on your account,' 'on his account,' 'on this account,' and so on. But what Dasein exists for-the-sake-of is itself. World is inherent to selfhood; this world is essentially related to Dasein."

11. Recognizing that the characterization of the world as inherent to selfhood can be read as rendering it "something purely 'subjective,'" Heidegger makes two observations to ward off this reading. First, since the meanings of "subject" and "subjective" turn on the clarification of transcendence, enlisting them here is premature at the least. His second and more substantive point is that the world is subjective insofar as it is related to Dasein but not as an entity that collapses into "the inner spheres of a 'subjective' subject" and, for the same reason, it is not merely objective if that means that it belongs among objects (GA9: 158).

12. Heidegger ends this second part by relating Plato's conception of the transcendent *agathon* (despite its political context) to what Heidegger deems "the primal action of human existence," namely, the "unveiling-projecting of being" (GA9: 160; GA26: 237–38). After recounting how the *agathon* enables truth, understanding, and even being, Heidegger asserts that the essence of *agathon* lies in the power (*Mächtigkeit*) of itself and, "as the *for-the-sake-of* . . . , it is the source of possibility as such" (GA9: 161). For a valuable appropriation of these passages (translating *Mächtigkeit seiner selbst* as "sovereignty over itself" and linking *agathon* with authentic *Umwillen*), see Crowell 2013: 209, 223–24 and Crowell 2008: 268.

13. See W. Richardson 1963: 167n15.

14. Heidegger exploits a wordplay here that does not readily translate into English. While the expression "for-the-sake-of"—as a translation of the preposition *umwillen*—captures the latter's ordinary significance, it lacks the term *Wille* ("will") that Heidegger uses to characterize this process of transcending as kind of freedom, albeit a non-willful one. This account iterates points made in his 1928 lectures; see GA26: 238: "But a for-the-sake-of [*Umwillen*] is essentially only possible where there is a will. . . . Only where freedom [obtains], is there a for-the-sake-of and only there is there a world. In short, freedom and Dasein's transcendence are identical!"

15. The echoes of Schopenhauer, if not Nietzsche, are too stark to go unmentioned.

16. Still, it seems doubtful that Heidegger identifies *all* possibilities with such potential, albeit abandonable, commitments. For one thing, there is the question of whether freedom is itself in some sense a possibility distinct from those it maintains itself opposite. If so, then it would have to be a possibility in another sense. Secondly, Dasein can maintain itself opposite possibilities that it projects for-the-sake-of itself that entail no obligation or that require nothing of it (from relishing the taste of wine and engaging in spontaneous reveries and play to accepting certain offers of love and graciousness). Finally, as is the case for the Aristotelian *hou heneka* causation (the literal template for Heidegger's conception of "for-the-sake-of") there are no possibilities without actualities and, perhaps more to the point, there must be a reality in which they are united. Heidegger's characterization of Dasein's freedom as the essence of ground is his attempt to reaffirm that unity. Special thanks to Irene McMullin for pressing me on this point.

17. See, for example, Kant 1785: 52–53.

18. The term for something binding (*Bindung*) is typically used in an interpersonal, ethical, or loosely normative manner (e.g., bond, commitment, law) but it is possible, particularly given subsequent remarks, that Heidegger intends it in a much broader

sense to signify what is in any way binding (e.g., logically, cognitively, pragmatically, and so on).

19. Existing for others' sake, entailed by existing for one's own sake, can also be authentic or inauthentic; see Dahlstrom 2014.

20. So, too, we ground an institution by founding it, a position in line by occupying it, a contention by justifying it.

21. The three sorts of grounding springing from transcendence belong to one time because "transcendence is rooted in one temporality, albeit in its ecstatic-horizonal constitution" (GA9: 166, 166n60; see, too, GA9: 171, 171n. a).

22. Grounding by founding and grounding by occupying are inseparable, it bears underlining, in the way that future and past are inseparable in Dasein's existence, a connection Heidegger explicitly draws even as he notes that he deliberately sets aside the temporal interpretation of transcendence in the essay (GA9: 166n60).

23. Although Heidegger paints intentionality with a broad brush, it includes what Husserl deems the paradigmatically intentional experiences of perception and cognition as well as other intentional experiences like imagining, dreaming, thinking.

24. Heidegger's advice to read "On the Essence of Ground" together with "What is Metaphysics?"—the former considering the ontological difference, the latter the concept of the nothing—may be instructive here since the mood (angst) at the center of "What is Metaphysics?" takes place in the face of nothing, rather than any particular entities, a nonintentional experience complementing how Dasein transcends (passes over) beings to being. See GA9: 114: "In the bright night of the nothing of angst, the original openness of a being as such first emerges, namely, that it is a being—and not nothing"; GA9: 118: "Dasein being held out into the nothing, on the basis of the hidden angst, passes over beings as a whole: the transcendence"; GA9: 123: "The nothing is the not of beings and thus it is being, experienced from the standpoint of beings."

25. Here, too, Heidegger appears to be rehearsing the position elaborated in SZ that Dasein is among beings, co-constitutive of their presence to it, by virtue of its understanding of being. Regrettably perhaps, Heidegger does not explicitly elaborate how this understanding implicates others, despite the fundamental character that he assigns to being-with. In other words, his talk of justification does not explicitly invoke—or, better, does not explicitly claim to invoke—others. For an adaptation ("creative restructuring") of Heidegger's thinking that effectively demonstrates how answerability to others—and not merely to things and oneself—is inherent in a world-time constituted by being-with, see McMullin 2013: 4, 124 and passim.

26. It is also used to substantiate a claim as well as to explain, establish, confirm, or provide adequate evidence for something. For examples of its use in philosophy shortly before Heidegger arrives on the scene, see Lotze 1880: 198, 274 and Husserl 1900–1901: 123.

27. It is noteworthy that two of the three aspects that Heidegger includes in this understanding (corresponding to the three questions) parallel two of Aristotle's senses of *archai*, noted in the preliminary remarks to the essay; see GA9: 124 and *Metaphysics* Delta, 1, 1013a: 17–19.

28. Not all experiences are intentional for Husserl; in particular, "feeling-sensations" (*Gefühlsempfindungen*) are not (see Hua XIX/1: 405f and Dahlstrom 2015).

Nonetheless, Husserl takes the intentional character of certain basic experiences—pre-eminently experiences of perception and cognition but also thinking, imagining, signifying, and even of time's flow—as their *grounding* trait. For a Husserlian argument that intentionality is "a primitive notion," devoid of prior conditions, "pre-reflectively and non-thematically" directed at the self as subject and the world as a whole (both comprised in the experience of the temporal flow of concrete experiences), see Drummond 2019: 102–5. Whereas Crowell follows Heidegger in regarding moods as pre-intentional, Drummond adapts Husserl's contention that moods are a unity of intentional feelings (ibid.: 113f). For Crowell's response to Drummond, see Crowell 2019: 337–40.

29. On Husserl's conception of horizons, see Dahlstrom 2006. As noted earlier, Heidegger speaks of a *Welthorizont* (GA9: 166).

30. Herein lies a non-trivial sense of the mantra that the possible lies "higher" than the actual (GA9: 161).

31. For a defense of Heidegger on this score, see W. Richardson 1963: 177–79 and—perhaps—Golob 2014: 206–7.

32. Omitted here is a further essential consideration in this regard, namely, the experience of catching sight (*Augenblick*) of the present situation while authentically being here (SZ: 328, 338).

33. On the difference between *ordo exhibitendi et discendii, ordo cognoscendi,* and *ordo essendi*, see Dahlstrom 1984.

34. Here again McMullin's approach may remove the difficulty by showing that the third form of grounding coincides with the domain of intersubjective answerability in terms of which a world and, with it, the other forms of grounding are possible at all; see, for example, McMullin 2013: 158ff.

35. Here I read the "es" in "es muß sich ausweisen" as referring to *das Seiende*; another grammatically possible reading refers "es" to "alles ontische Entdecken und Erschliessen."

36. While this gloss explicitly introduces knowing into the relation between the two sorts of truth, a similar line of argument might simply ask why water freezes at a certain temperature. It does so because its molecules slow down, giving way to the intermolecular forces that bond them to one another.

37. Here I follow the 1949 edition that has *Ausweisung* in place of *Ausweitung*; see Heidegger 1949: 65–66 and GA9: 170.

38. On the issue of corroboration (*Ausweisung*), Tugendhat suggests that Heidegger missed an opportunity to explain its necessity; see Tugendhat 1970: 366–67. For a cognate point, see Golob 2014: 210–11. While Heidegger is egregiously short on details in regard to the demand for causation, he may be thinking of *hou heneka* causation as the *primus inter pares* of Aristotle's four causes—where (1) matter and (2) form necessarily cohere in a (3) production, all existing together for (4) what they are for.

39. W. Richardson 1963: 179–82; Golob 2014: 195–98.

40. In a way at least structurally paralleling Husserl's contrast between the transcendental ego and the empirical ego, the freedom that makes up Dasein's original transcendence forms the space in which factical Dasein maintains itself amid entities as a whole by projecting possibilities for itself and justifying what and how anything is.

BIBLIOGRAPHY

Braver, Lee. 2009. *Heidegger's Later Writings*. London: Continuum.
———. 2012. *Groundless Grounds: A Study of Wittgenstein and Heidegger*. Cambridge, MA: MIT Press.
Burch, Matthew, Jack Marsh, and Irene Mcmullin (eds). 2019. *Normativity, Meaning, and the Promise of Phenomenology*. New York: Routledge.
Capobianco, Richard. 2010. *Engaging Heidegger*. Toronto: University of Toronto Press.
Crowell, Steven. 2008. "Measure-Taking: Meaning and Normativity in Heidegger's Philosophy." *Continental Philosophy Review* 160: 335–54.
———. 2013. *Normativity and Phenomenology in Husserl and Heidegger*. New York: Cambridge University Press.
———. 2019. "A Philosophy of Mind: Phenomenology, Normativity, and Meaning." In Burch, Marsh, and McMullin 2019, 329–54.
Dahlstrom, Daniel. 1984. "Transzendentale Schemata, Kategorien und Erkenntnisarten." *Kant-Studien* 75. Jahrgang, Heft 1: 38–54.
———. 2006. "Lost Horizons." In *Passive Synthesis and Life-World*, edited by Alfredo Ferrarin. Pisa: Edizioni ETS, 211–31.
———, ed. 2011. *Interpreting Heidegger: Critical Essays*. Cambridge: Cambridge University Press.
———. 2014. "Existential Socialization." In *The Horizons of Authenticity in Phenomenology, Existentialism, and Moral Psychology: Essays in Honor of Charles Guignon*, edited by Hans Pedersen and Megan Altman. Amsterdam: Springer.
———. 2015. "Interoception and Self-Awareness: An Exploration in Interoceptive Phenomenology." In *Philosophy of Mind and Phenomenology: Conceptual and Empirical Approaches*, edited by D. Dahlstrom, A. Elpidorou, and W. Hopp. New York: Routledge, 2015, 141–64.
Davis, Bret W., ed. 2010. *Martin Heidegger: Key Concepts*. Durham: Acumen.
Dreyfus, Herbert L., and Mark A. Wrathall, eds. 2005. *A Companion to Heidegger*. Oxford: Blackwell.
Drummond, John. 2019. "Intentionality and (Moral) Normativity." In Burch, Marsh, and McMullin 2019, 101–19.
Engelland, Chad. 2017. *Heidegger's Shadow: Kant, Husserl, and the Transcendental Turn*. London: Rowman & Littlefield.
Figal, Günther, ed. 2009. *The Heidegger Reader*. Bloomington: Indiana University Press.
Golob, Sacha. 2014. *Heidegger on Concepts, Freedom and Normativity*. New York: Cambridge University Press.
Heidegger, Martin. 1949. *Vom Wesen des Grundes*. Frankfurt am Main: Klostermann.
Husserl, Edmund. 1900–1901. *Logische Untersuchungen*. Halle: Niemeyer.
Kant, Immanuel. 1785. *Grundlegung zur Metaphysik der Sitten*. Riga: Hartknoch.
Krell, David, ed. 2008. *Martin Heidegger: Basic Writings*. New York: HarperCollins.
Lotze, Hermann. 1880. *Logik: Drei Bücher vom Denken, vom Untersuchen und vom Erkennen*. Leipzig: Hirzel.

McManus, Denis. 2012. *Heidegger and the Measure of Truth*. Oxford: Oxford University Press.
McMullin, Irene. 2013. *Time and the Shared World: Heidegger on Social Relations*. Evanston, IL: Northwestern University Press.
Nelson, Eric S., and François Raffoul, eds. 2013. *The Bloomsbury Companion to Heidegger*. London: Bloomsbury.
Richardson, John. 2012. *Heidegger*. New York: Routledge.
Richardson, William. 1963. *Heidegger: Through Phenomenology to Thought*. The Hague: Nijhoff.
Sheehan, Thomas. 2015. *Making Sense of Heidegger: A Paradigm Shift*. London: Rowman & Littlefield.
Thomä, Dieter, ed. 2003. *Heidegger Handbuch: Leben—Werk—Wirkung*. Stuttgart: Metzler.
Tugendhat, Ernst. 1970. *Der Wahrheitsbegriff bei Husserl und Heidegger*. Berlin: de Gruyter.

Chapter 3

What Does It Mean to "Act in the Light of" a Norm?

Heidegger and Kant on Commitments and Critique

Sacha Golob

1. ACTING "IN THE LIGHT OF" OR "MERELY IN ACCORDANCE WITH" NORMS

It is natural to read post-Kantian philosophy as a series of disputes over normativity. On the one hand, these disputes concern specific sets of norms. Kantian morality, for example, is attacked as a radically inadequate fragment of some larger whole (Hegel) or as a mask for psychological and political maneuvers (Nietzsche). On the other hand, there is the underlying question of what it even means to appeal to norms when explaining behavior. Are norms rules, for example, and if so, what does it mean to say that someone follows a rule? Of particular importance is the tradition that runs from Kant through Brandom on which normativity explains the very nature of rational agency: the difference between my reliable assertion that it is raining and the lump of iron's equally reliable response of rusting (Brandom 1994: 350–51).

The present chapter focuses on this underlying question: what does it mean to act "in the light" of a norm and what are the implications for Heidegger's early work?[1] It is striking how divided Heidegger's commentators are. For Crowell, *Being and Time* illuminates the conditions that allow us "to think and act not merely in accord with norms, but *in light* of them" (Crowell 2001: 170; original emphasis). For Pippin, Heidegger failed to explain the very same thing: "my 'distance' as it were *from* the norm, my not merely responding and initiating appropriately, but in *the light of*" it (Pippin 1997: 387; original emphasis).

Both Pippin and Crowell present the point contrastively: one might act in the light of a norm, or one might act merely in accordance with it.[2] Talk of "responding to norms" is ambiguous between these options: Crowell occasionally talks of "responsiveness to the normative *as* normative" to make clear that he is using the locution in the former sense (Crowell 2013e: 24; original emphasis). The first thing I want to do is to flesh out this contrast by looking at the thinker who set the subsequent agenda: Immanuel Kant.

Kant's *Groundwork* draws a contrast between two types of being, defined in terms of their relationship to laws: "Everything in nature works in accordance with laws. Only a rational being has the capacity to act *in accordance with the representation* of laws, that is, in accordance with principles" (GM 4: 412; original emphasis). He equates the ability to act on principles with the ability to act on the basis of "ideas . . . a connection that is expressed by ought" (Prol. 4: 345). Let's unpack this. The Kantian natural world is deterministic: hence, it operates "in accordance with laws." However, a subset of beings requires a distinctive form of explanation, one that refers to what those beings *take to be* laws (i.e., what they take to be required or forbidden or permissible). As Brandom puts it, such laws are "mediated by our attitude towards" them (Brandom 1994: 31). This explains why they may fail to determine our behavior: I ought not to make inferential errors, but unlike a stone bound by the law of gravity, the laws of logic do not automatically determine what I will do.

Kant's distinction prompts some useful clarifications. One use of "norm" is merely statistical: norms in this sense, which we can treat as averages, are relatively uninteresting for Kant, and indeed for Heidegger, and are found in both the case of rational and non-rational beings. There is a norm height in this sense for humans and dogs and Audis. What is important is rather the use of norm that Kant links exclusively with rational agents. Consider the behavior of a dog. For Kant, this is governed by a deterministic pattern of input-output correlations, whose mechanisms are associative (Br. 11: 52). This allows us to train such animals: by bringing them to associate food with the bell, Pavlov exploited the biological laws governing them. Here the dog acts *in accordance* with a law, but *not* in the light of it. In explaining its obedience to biology I will undoubtedly have to talk about the way it represents the world, but the efficacy of biological laws in determining its behavior is entirely independent of the dog's (nonexistent) attitude to such laws. In contrast, to explain why someone acted morally or failed to do so, I need to reference both the law and their attitude to it—even if that attitude is one of ignorance or indifference, it needs to be cited if we are to explain why, unlike biological laws, the law failed to determine action.

From this sketch, we can see the familiar contours of the Kantian system emerging. First, unlike, say, with Dennett's intentional stance, the divide between normative and non-normative explanation is fundamentally an ontological one.³ As a rational being I demand a form of explanation that non-human animals (henceforth simply "animals") do not.

Second, it is a hard divide. Kant's views on animals have been the subject of much recent debate, but it is agreed by all that he posits two distinct philosophies of mind: animals lack apperception and understanding, for example.⁴ While they may even mimic human behavior, as a dog might be trained to get up on hearing the national anthem, the underlying mechanisms are quite different.

Third, Kant takes this divide to have far-reaching metaphysical implications. For example, he holds that natural laws necessarily underdetermine normative questions—it may be a natural law that I desire x or that I find inferential move y plausible but that does not show that I ought to act on that desire or affirm that inference. To see myself as a rational agent is to see myself as acting, at least insofar as I am responsible, on the basis of what I take myself to have reason to do. By extension, to see myself as a rational agent is to see natural laws alone as insufficient to explain my actions, insofar as they necessarily leave that normative question open (Relig. 6: 23–24). This is known as the "Incorporation Thesis": in Kantian jargon, incentives determine behavior only once incorporated into a maxim.⁵ Beyond Kant's own writings, this move is present in what one might call "neo-Kantian" philosophy of mind: as Moran puts it, in the deliberative stance, "I am not simply free to appraise [an impulse], but also free to choose whether it shall be something I act upon or not" (Moran 2001: 144–45).⁶ Kant thus interweaves a story about normativity with a theory of freedom, aimed to insulate agency from causal determination. This combination is an obvious target for naturalistic debunking, for example, by emphasizing third-person facts about "animal psychology" that allegedly show first-person deliberation to be a charade, driven by biological drives (Nietzsche 2002: §§3, 117). It is also an obvious target for Aristotelian accounts that reject the underlying picture of biology as leaving normative questions open.

Turning to Heidegger, even this rough outline of Kant has immediate echoes. First, the distinction between Dasein and other beings is self-avowedly an ontological one and the starting point for Heidegger's system, rather than an artifact of downstream notions such as an intentional stance. For a Heideggerian, talk of an "intentional stance" immediately begs the prior question of the being of the entity adopting such a stance. The exact sense in which Dasein is to be analyzed in normative terms is discussed below, but for the moment we can simply note some obvious points regarding the Heideggerian world. To see something as a hammer as opposed to a sculpture is, among other things, to see it as appropriate for certain tasks. Similarly, to see that there are things "one just doesn't talk about" is to refer to a norm, that there are certain things that *ought not* be addressed.[7] The Heideggerian world is thus suffused with an awareness of norms, an awareness he evidently thinks is not present in a rock.[8] As Heidegger himself puts it, in a deliberately Kantian idiom, for Dasein "entities are manifest in their binding character [*Verbindlichkeit*]" (GA29/30: 492)—i.e., as located within a web of obligations, prohibitions, and requirements.

Second, Heidegger is insistent that, while the behavior of animals may mimic our own, it has a fundamentally different explanatory structure. He thus lines up with Kant against naturalistic thinkers such as Hume who viewed continuity here as a "touchstone" by which one "may try every system" (Hume 1978: 1.3.16.3). This is Heidegger responding to that Humean line of thought:

> But a skillful monkey or dog can also open a door to come in and out? Certainly. The question is whether what it does when it touches and pushes something is to touch a handle, whether what it does is something like opening a door. We talk as if the dog does the same as us; but . . . there is not the slightest criterion to say that it comports itself towards the entity. (GA27: 192)

Elsewhere he denies that animals understand being or that they can encounter entities "as" something (GA27: 192; GA29/30: 397, 416, 450).[9] The normative character of the Heideggerian everyday meshes neatly with this: insofar as they cannot see something "as" a hammer, animals cannot see it as subject to the norms governing hammers. In Brandom's terms, the "as" is the point of "mediation," the point at which my attitudes to norms enter the picture.

Third, like Kant, Heidegger takes these distinctions to have far-reaching metaphysical implications. As Derrida observed, Heidegger's treatment of the animal as a function of its drives is close to traditional, deterministic, models (Derrida 2008: 159–60). Conversely, his treatment of Dasein's freedom often mirrors the Incorporation Thesis. The following could be a statement of Kant's position with only minor rephrasing:

> Conscience discloses that I am a being for whom thrown grounds can never function simply as causes: because Dasein has been "released from the ground, not through itself but to itself, so as to be as this [ground]," grounds take on the character of reasons for which I am accountable. My natural impulses are not within my power, but it is I who make them normative for me, reasons for what I do. (Crowell 2013b: 209)[10]

Crowell notes that this aspect of Heidegger's position is "close to Korsgaard's" (Crowell 2001: 453n38). In many ways, this is unsurprising: while Heidegger dislikes Kant's antinomial story (GA31: 191–92), he clearly shares the desire to remove human agency from mechanistic explanation and to locate it within a discourse of self-responsibility:

> Freedom makes Dasein in the grounds of its essence responsible [*verbindlich*] to itself, or more exactly, gives it the possibility of commitment. . . . Selfhood is free responsibility to and for itself. (GA26: 247)

The Incorporation Thesis, suitably modified as in Crowell's discussion of conscience, achieves this by reframing the debate in terms of reason, not causes.

Some of these links between Kant and Heidegger change as Heidegger ages. For example, *Being and Time* offers little challenge to the Kantian picture of the natural world: in contrast to Hegel or to the Heidegger of the 1930s, *Being and Time* aims to separate Dasein from the present-at-hand rather than to question the thinking of nature in terms of the latter concept. However, even if Heidegger's subsequent remarks on *phusis* are taken as reintroducing something like Aristotelian teleology, Dasein's distinctive place remains: it alone stands in a relation to being, a relationship that requires us to respond appropriately. On other points, Heidegger's alignment with Kant persists unchanged. For example, the first volume of the *Schwarze Hefte* returns to the "abyss" between humans and animals, an abyss founded on our relationship to being: "*Seyn*" is that which we breathe and without which we are "reduced" to "mere cattle" [*bloßen Vieh*] (GA94: 232). Given the scope of the current paper, however, I want to focus on the early work. The question is this: are the continuities sketched enough to locate Heidegger's position on normativity? To answer that, we need to press the comparison with Kant a little further.

2. PRESSING THE KANTIAN LEGACY: CONCEPTS AND PERCEPTUAL NORMATIVITY

As phenomenology has always emphasized, huge amounts of human action fall below the level of thematization and argument. Consider my fluid response to the traffic signs as I drive, or my unthinking tracking of social norms, such as those governing how close I should stand to strangers, or native speakers' responsiveness to grammatical rules that they cannot formulate, let alone deliberately endorse. All seem to be cases in which I act "in the light of the relevant norms." Yet all present a challenge for Kantians who tend to link normativity with "deliberation" and "reflection," privileging cases in which I carefully weigh my options (Korsgaard 1996: 94; Moran 2001: 144–45). Accounts such as Korsgaard's have thus been severely criticized by

Heideggerians as intellectualist and phenomenologically inadequate (Okrent 1999: 70; Crowell 2007: 321). To get to the bottom of the matter, we need to look more closely at the Kantian picture and at what exactly it offers. We will then be in a better position to address Heidegger.

The best way to approach the issue is via one of Kant's own analyses of the contrast between rational and non-rational experience. Kant couches this in terms of concepts: I discuss the significance of that below. He begins by confronting an argument of Meier's in favor of animals being ascribed such concepts:

> An ox's representation of its stall includes the clear representation of its characteristic mark of having a door; therefore, the ox has a distinct concept of its stall [this is Meier's view—SG]. It is easy to prevent the confusion here. The distinctness of a concept does not consist in the fact that that which is a characteristic mark of the thing is clearly represented, but rather in the fact that it is recognized [*erkannt*] as a characteristic mark of the thing. (SvF: 59)

The ox has a clear visual awareness of some property or "mark" of the stall, namely having a door. This clear representation underpins both differential reaction (the ox would behave differently in a stall with no door), and association (the ox becomes anxious or excited depending on past experiences with doors). The rational agent, however, is distinguished by the ability to *recognize* this mark, something that can be shared by many stalls and by many non-stalls, as a generic property. One way to express this is to say that we, unlike the ox, see the door "as" a door. For Kant, this ability to recognize generic properties or marks is the ability to employ concepts (Refl.16: 300).[11]

Why is this ability significant? The answer is that it is here that norms enter: for Kant, to conceptualize something *is* to employ a certain inferential rule in thinking about it (KrV: A126; A106). Specifically, to recognize a mark is to recognize a set of inferences as grounded in it: to recognize something as exhibiting the mark <door> is to recognize both a fact about the entity involved and certain implications for how we must understand it—for example, any door "necessitates the representation of extension" (KrV: A106). To paraphrase the title of one of Sellars's papers, concepts involve laws and are inconceivable without them (Sellars 1948). Kant argues that this basic capacity, the awareness of "oughts," transforms our experience along three dimensions.

The first is what we might call "the subjective ought." To apply a concept is to require myself either to attribute further properties in line with the relevant rules, or to revisit the initial attribution. Mark recognition thus imposes a normative order on experience, preventing it from being "haphazard" (KrV: A104). By extension, my experience can be critically assessed for coherence and accuracy: in conceptualizing something as a door, I take on a host of further commitments—commitments that may turn out to be true or false. My experience now makes *claims*; in contrast, the ox's awareness is simply a series of *events*, with one representation bringing to mind another. The second is what we might call "the objective ought." To apply a concept is to possess an awareness of some inferences as putatively grounded in the properties of the "thing," in this case the stall. By extension, it is to possess, if only tacitly, an awareness of the distinction between such inferences and ways of combining representations that are not so grounded. It is in this sense that "judgment" allows me "to say that the two representations are combined in the object," as opposed to simply associating them (KrV: B141–42). Norms, in other words, sustain the distinction between merely subjective and purportedly objective property combinations: they ground the subject/object distinction.[12] The third I label the "intersubjective ought." To apply a concept is to be aware, if only tacitly, that insofar as an inference is putatively grounded in properties of the "thing," and not merely an artifact of my own psychological history, the posited connection should hold for any other observer, "regardless of any difference in the condition of the subject" (KrV: B141–42). In short, norms establish the triangle of subjective, objective, and intersubjective.

We can now give an initial gloss on what it means to act "in the light of norms" for Kant: it refers to the presence of a certain representational capacity and an attendant *cognitive architecture*, as just outlined. None of this needs to be explicit or thematic: a glance at the door is enough to sustain a form of awareness that the ox necessarily lacks. This difference in content will almost certainly manifest itself in behavioral differences, but for Kant that is the symptom rather than the cause: even if the ox is trained to mimic my reactions, the underlying contents, the underlying representational architecture, are quite different. Hence it acts at most "in accordance with norms," for example, insofar as training establishes associationistic input-output correlations.[13]

In light of this, I want to introduce a provisional distinction between two stages in Kant's analysis of normativity. First, there is the *core* stage: this refers to the material just sketched, the basic analysis of what normative content contributes to a theory of representation. Second, there is what you might call the *elaboration* stage. This occurs insofar as he attempts to further analyze that core in terms of specific methods or mental states. For example, Kantian normativity is often elaborated in terms of reflection, construed as a particular mental state in which an agent deliberately steps back from, thematizes, and evaluates her commitments. Korsgaard offers the classic formulation: for her, this ability to "back up and . . . have a certain distance" marks the human/animal boundary and thus the domain of responsibility (Korsgaard 1996: 93). Such an elaboration is immediately suspicious from a phenomenological perspective. Reflection, so construed, seems a relatively rare and marginal occurrence: it makes poor sense of the majority of our behavior (GA24: 227; Okrent 1999; Crowell 2007).[14]

As we saw in section 1, Heidegger mirrors several aspects of the Kantian position: these range from the normative structure of human agency, to the sharp divide from animals, to a non-deterministic freedom along the lines of the Incorporation Thesis. We can now formulate a preliminary claim: Heidegger might retain what I called the *core* aspects of Kant's account, while rejecting the specific *elaborations* offered on it.

The task is to test this hypothesis and to evaluate its consequences for Heidegger's thought. After all, taking only part of the Kantian legacy may bring problems of its own. The dominant reading of early Sartre provides a cautionary tale in this regard. Sartre clearly endorses something very like the Incorporation Thesis: even under torture, it is up to me whether I take the pain as a reason to talk, and it is this gap that guarantees my freedom and my responsibility (Sartre 2003: 403). But in the absence of a priori reason, it is unclear on what basis such an agent should choose: insofar as all empirical incentives necessarily leave open what I should do, on what basis do I actually decide? The result is the standard picture of early Sartre where absolute freedom is coupled with an absurd voluntarism. My point is not that Sartre cannot respond to this line of thought, but that its prevalence stems directly from his attempt to keep some parts of the Kantian package while rejecting others. The question now is whether Heidegger is able to find any more stable a balance.

3. CROWELL, IDENTITY, AND A KANTIAN COMPROMISE?

Given the systematic place of these issues in Heidegger's thought, there are many avenues we could now take: one, following the Sartrean case, would be to examine the question of voluntarism and whether Heidegger can avoid it.[15] But rather than that kind of piecemeal approach, I want to address the most sophisticated attempt to grapple with the structure of normativity in Heidegger's work: the reading put forward by Steven Crowell.

At the heart of Crowell's picture is a displacement of reason in favor of care; it is the latter that is taken to be the true ground of normativity. As in the attack on Korsgaard, Kant is presented as overly intellectualist.

> For Heidegger, what Kant mistakenly attributes to reason has deeper roots, and though Kant may succeed in uncovering conditions for a certain kind of intentionality (the regional ontology of nature as the occurrent), this is accomplished only

by concealing those deeper roots through an aporetic approach to the "subject" as something equally occurrent. It is not reason, then—the power of combining representations into judgments, the power of subsuming under rules, or drawing inferences—that explains how entities show up for us, but rather Dasein's "transcendence," its "projection of possibilities for being its self" in light of which things can show themselves as what they are. (Crowell 2013b: 192)

The reference to judgments and rules matches §2. Elsewhere, Crowell puts the point in terms of autonomy:

[U]nlike Kant, Heidegger does not ground autonomy in rationality. Dasein is not autonomous because it is rational; rather, justifying reasons are possible at all because Dasein, as care, is autonomously responsible for its being. (Crowell 2014: 219)

More specifically, the claim is that Dasein's fundamental orientation toward the normative comes from its awareness of possibility, from its *trying to be* something. There Dasein

"understands itself in *terms* of . . . a *possibility* of itself" (GA2, p. 17/12/33), that is, it measures *itself* against a standard whose meaning is part of what is at stake in existing as that possibility. For instance, to "be" a father is for what it means to be a father to be at issue for me in trying to be one: I do not merely do certain things but commit myself to the possibility of failure. That is, for *me* being a father is a normative status. Even if I cannot define what it means to be a father, I am oriented toward that meaning as toward a measure. (Crowell 2013a: 215; original emphasis)

The result is a position that retains the characteristic Kantian links between freedom and the first person—I must decide what I make of the situation into which I am thrown—and yet where reason is displaced in favor of care. As Crowell summarizes, "Freedom is thus norm-oriented from the outset, which is not to say that it is oriented toward reason" (Crowell forthcoming: 19).[16]

Once this primitive normativity has been secured, the rest of the Heideggerian world falls into place: the pile of scripts precariously balanced on the office floor shows up for me "as for marking" just as they may show up to the cleaners "as for disposal." As Crowell nicely observes:

This holds of my affective intentional states as well, whose reason-responsiveness is tied to what I am currently trying to be. For instance, as I lecture I notice a student sleeping and I become angry. A sleeping student is not inherently a reason to get angry, but given my practical identity as a teacher it is an instance of what Heidegger might call "obtrusiveness" (SZ: 73) and constitutes a (defeasible) reason for anger. (Crowell 2014: 225)

It is thus Dasein's self-understanding that is the basis for normative grounding:

> Why is there anything such as a why and a because? Because Dasein exists . . . the for-the-sake-of-which, as the primary character of world, i.e. of transcendence, is the primal phenomenon of ground as such. (GA26: 276)

Crowell's account, developed over many years, is an immensely subtle one, and this sketch is at best an attempt to isolate some key strands. One way to respond would be direct exegesis: do the texts support his reading? My own view is that they do, but I also think, given the complexity and opacity of some of Heidegger's remarks, that is not the best way to proceed. Instead, let us assume that Crowell's story is representative of Heidegger's position, and draw out some of the philosophical and historical consequences that follow; insofar as we assume a principle of charity, these questions bear on the exegetical ones too. It is possible to raise three points.

First, the status of norms not derived directly from Dasein's for-the-sake-of-which needs clarification. Consider, for example, Levinas when he writes, contra Heidegger, of how:

> As equipment, the objects of everyday use are subordinated to enjoyment—the lighter to the cigarette one smokes, the fork to the food, the cup to the lips. Things refer to my enjoyment. (Levinas 2013: 133)

Levinas's point is that the normative web is structured around enjoyment, not identity: the reason the food is to be eaten is not because of anything I am "trying to be." There are, of course, highly complex, often gendered, norms surrounding such pleasure. But even if gender roles explain why only the boy is able to unselfconsciously relish the burger, they do not explain what makes it so tasty. Heidegger's account thus needs supplementation. But there is no obvious reason that he should be unable to do so, and one could easily argue that the pleasure of food makes sense only within an environment structured by the classic Heideggerian framework of the pots, the kitchen, the break from work, the time to relax, etc.

Second, it is striking how accounts such as Crowell's shift the locus away from what for Kant, or indeed Husserl, was the classic problem: namely, the constitution of a stable object out of a temporally disjointed set of sensations.[17] A parallel point can be made at the ontological level: from a Kantian point of view, the ability to treat entities as ready-to-hand depends upon the prior ability to represent them as causally ordered and existing unperceived, as present-at-hand in Heidegger's terms. After all, if the hammer sometimes bent, sometimes melted and sometimes vanished when I turned my back, it is hard to see how I would ever have developed a stable practice of using it "for-the-sake-of" anything. The change stems from Heidegger's very different philosophy of perception. For him the challenge is not to "constitute" entities, but to render them meaningful, to "free" them by creating a context against which the entity can show itself (Golob 2014: 81–82). This line of thought inevitably begins from a "later" point than the Kantian one: to even talk about the meaning of an entity assumes something more than the "blooming, buzzing, confusion" from which the Kantian subject begins.[18] Thus, when Heidegger employs Husserlian terminology, he quickly redefines it:

> "Constituting" does not mean producing in the sense of making and fabricating; it means letting the entity be seen in its objectivity. (GA20: 97)

Third, it is difficult to assess Heidegger's account of normativity in relation to its Kantian counterpart without the discussion expanding exponentially. For example, Crowell acutely criticizes Kant's "additive" conception of human agency, part rationality, part animality (Crowell 2007: 324). The charge is that this combination "serves to obstruct the question of the actual being of the acts, the being of the intentional" (GA24: 123). But from a Kantian point of view, Heidegger's insistence on a full separation of Dasein from animality makes things too easy. It occludes the sense in which we are physical creatures whose behavior is indeed subject to casual explanation and prediction by the various natural and social sciences. Kant's split conception of human agency is intended to recognize this fact, and it is unclear that Heidegger can offer any better story: to remain solely within the categories of Dasein risks neglecting this dimension of our existence, while to accept that we are simultaneously Dasein and present-at-hand seems as additive as Kant's position.

We can now return to the "preliminary hypothesis" of section 2. There I distinguished the core of Kant's theory from its subsequent elaboration, a distinction that paved the way for a possible compromise: Heidegger might retain the former and reject only the latter. We now have some grounds for thinking Heidegger may need to do exactly that. The basic act of taking on commitments through mark recognition, for example, is plausibly assumed by anything like Heidegger's picture: when I walk to my car "for-the-sake-of" performing all the various tasks ahead of me, I am making myriad assumptions about the behavior of the vehicle and its properties, assumptions such as the fact that it will start when I turn the key or that it will respond to gasoline in a stable fashion. One might argue that these assumptions are "non-conceptual" and the term is so vague that on some glosses some of them may well be. But they are not well analyzed by talk of my self-understanding, since they pertain essentially to the *object's* independent causal properties, nor are they typically a function of my embodiment, to take another familiar phenomenological move. Instead, they have all the hallmarks of Kant's three "oughts": subjective, intersubjective, and objective. This applies both to properties that are "occurent" or "present-at-hand" and those that are not. To see myself as a father or a hippie or a sports show host is to see myself in terms of all the qualities inferentially linked to those ideas, and to see those connections as grounded in the ideal I am trying to live up to, rather than as mere associations.

Here is another way to put the point. Heidegger's arguments typically show that *certain specific speech acts or certain specific phenomenological states*—assertion or reflection—are explanatorily derivative. But this is compatible with the idea that *propositional normativity*, in the sense sketched in Kant's reply to Meier above, might still be explanatorily basic: from a Kantian point of view, Heidegger is entirely correct that assertion occurs only in an already richly specified context (SZ: 157–58), but that context is itself at least partly a function of the kind of mark recognition defined in section 2. Of course, one may take Heidegger to have separate arguments against propositional content, perhaps hanging on the rich nature of perceptual awareness. I have discussed such moves in detail elsewhere (Golob 2014), but what I want to emphasize here is that *even if* they are granted the Heideggerian world still relies on a vast range of assumptions, that are not plausibly understood as *perceptually* "rich" in this fashion—assumptions well-handled by Kant's mark model, such as the hammer's rigidity or the car's solidity or the fact that to be a father is to take on certain duties and not others.

If this is correct, there are two opportunities for compromise between Kant and Heidegger. First, one might combine the Kantian "propositional core" with what I called an alternate "elaboration." The suggestion is that we separate self-consciousness qua phenomenological state from self-consciousness qua normative condition. What do I mean here by "normative condition"? Well, as discussed in section 2, mark recognition necessarily brings with it the idea of further commitments: to see something as <solid> *is* to commit myself to various outcomes occurring if it is struck. Concept application thus assumes a notion of "oneself" at least as a locus of such commitments. The result is the thin reading of apperception, found in Kantians such as Longuenesse:

> In referring his thoughts to "I," the thinker (perceiver, imaginer) is doing nothing more than committing himself to the unity and consistency of his thoughts, and committing himself to obtaining a unified standpoint that could be shared by all: an objective standpoint, also called by Kant "objective unity of apperception." (Longuenesse 2008: 17)

Heidegger would thus be free to oppose Kant's reliance on self-consciousness in the sense of explicit reflection or deliberation (GA24: 216), while joining with him in an acceptance of its normative centrality. Second, one might combine this Kantian "propositional core" with some distinct set of norms operative at some bodily or non-conceptual level, and lacking the kind of inferential structure found in Kantian mark recognition. The result would be two distinct models of normativity, operating hand in hand, each explicating distinct parts of the fabric of experience: on the one hand, we would act "in the light of" propositional norms, on the other, non-propositional ones.

The questions that these proposals face are partly methodological. With respect to the first option, is it possible to abstract out Kant's "core" in this way? How much sense, in other words, can we make of "mark recognition" if we refuse to elaborate it in terms of specific states such as reflection or assertion? With respect to the second, the suggested compromise abandons the hope of a single "primordial" point of explanation. There is a natural Heideggerian tendency to try to restore such primordiality by arguing the non-propositional possesses priority, with the propositional deriving from it. As I see it, the two are sufficiently interwoven to make any linear priority claim implausible: however finely my motor skills weight the hammer, my behavior makes sense only if I have a range of beliefs about how its surface will react when meeting the wood.

These potential compromises need not unjustly limit the Heideggerian's room for maneuver. They are, for example, compatible with Crowell's model: they explain what it is to understand notions such as fatherhood that I am trying to live up to. Similarly, one might develop a reading on which the primitive form of mark-recognition was necessarily a matter of intersubjective recognition. Such developments will impact the relationship between the two lines of compromise just sketched: as one approaches an elaboration such as Brandom's on which "only communities, not individuals" have "original intentionality," there will be a concomitant pressure to minimize the non-propositional in favor of the linguistic (Brandom, 1994: 61, 143). But this sort of limitation is to be welcomed; it is simply a consequence of the different lines of thought playing out.

In sum, I have outlined two lines along which Heideggerian and Kantian accounts could, and indeed should, mesh. Heidegger's position is best seen as a distinctive elaboration of a Kantian core, within which "mineness" plays a role close to thin models of apperception. Readings such as Crowell's would provide highly sophisticated ways of fleshing out this elaboration.

4. FROM THE PHILOSOPHY OF MIND TO PHILOSOPHY AS CRITIQUE

I want to close by addressing a final question. The reason for doing so is that it is also naturally framed in terms of a contrast between action "in the light of a norm" and action "merely in accordance with it." However, the meaning of that distinction is very different, and it is worth making that explicit.

Pippin gives an eloquent formulation of the problem. The difficulty, as he sees it, is that while Heidegger dismisses an account of normativity in terms of rule-following, he offers no alternative that

> could explain my "distance" as it were *from* the norm, not merely responding and initiating appropriately but *in the light of*, and so with some possible alteration or rejection, of such presumed shared sense of appropriateness. (Pippin 1997: 387; original emphasis)

Pippin acknowledges that themes such as death or anxiety are meant to supply the missing distance, but fears that they ultimately yield only a "Manichean" voluntarism (Pippin 1997: 387).

The charge of voluntarism is a familiar one, and I have addressed it elsewhere (Golob forthcoming-a). But more important is the basic conception of the problem. The issue is no longer simply human responsiveness to norms, in a way that animals lack. Rather, it is the ability to call given norms into question: for example, by altering or rejecting the dominant social standards.

One problematic feature of Heidegger's presentation is that it sometimes blurs these two questions. For it is unclear how compromised *das Man*'s relation to norms really is. Crowell sometimes suggests that inauthentic agents are no longer acting in the light of norms:

> As the one-self I have my reasons for what I do, but the one-self as such cannot really be distinguished from the carpenter ant who acts in accord with norms but not in light of them. (Crowell 2013d: 295)

Given the close links between normativity and the first-person perspective as expressed by the Incorporation Thesis, this occasionally leads him to deny that such agents really have a first-person point of view (Crowell 2001: 437). Blattner has criticized this aspect of Crowell's presentation (Blattner 2014). Yet, I think it does not well express Crowell's considered view: as he stresses elsewhere, "[t]o take over being a ground is not to pass from some prenormative ontological condition to one governed by norms" (Crowell 2013c: 249).[19] This yields a very different perspective on *das Man*, one in which it continues to act in the light of norms, but fails to establish critical distance with respect to them.

It seems to me this was Heidegger's position: many of the instances he adduces of inauthentic agents are involved in sophisticated, yet in some sense sophistical, reasoning. For example, he views scholarly exegesis of *Being and Time*'s links to Kierkegaard as a derailment device by which academics serve to distract both themselves and the public from the book's real import (GA94: 74; 39). Similarly, GA20 presents academic conferences as devices for "covering up" ideas through parroting them out (GA20: 376). Such agents are clearly "in the space of reasons": they are evaluating and offering inferences, arguments, counterpoints, etc., albeit within a deeply limited discursive framework.

What I am suggesting, to put it another way, is that *das Man*, while "deprived of its answerability," retains the structural features that, for Heidegger and for Kant, allow action in the light of norms—for example, the first-person perspective. As Heidegger puts it, "Authenticity and inauthenticity . . . are both grounded in the fact that any Dasein whatsoever is characterized by mineness" (SZ: 42–43). Thus, we have an important ambiguity in the "in the light of"/"in accordance with" distinction. In sections 2 and 3, it tracked a difference in the *philosophy of mind*: what model of intentionality do we need for humans as opposed to well-trained animals? Here in contrast, it is now a *matter of critique*: the distinction is drawn within the set of Dasein (i.e., within the class of agents responsive to norms), between those who are responding appropriately and those who are rehashing the kinds of sophistry or banality associated with *das Man*. It is only because such agents are responsive to "oughts" in the first place that they can be faulted for failing to be suitably distanced from them.

If this is right, the phenomenon of *das Man* has immediate links to the classic Enlightenment political dilemma: the problem is a group of agents who, while acting in the light of norms, are unwilling or unable to adequately challenge them (Auf. 8: 35). The point can equally be expressed in terms of authenticity: Heideggerian authenticity becomes "just the distinction between following reasons transparently and following them . . . as though they were quasi-natural 'givens'" (Crowell 2007: 326).[20] It is precisely such "quasi-natural givens" that a text such as Kant's "What Is Enlightenment?" sought to disturb.

What is striking, however, is the change in the remedial mechanism. Kant's solution, besides urging courage, is to defend the juridical and cultural space for a broader self-conception, one in which everyone sees themselves as a scholar making "public" use of reason and capable of challenging any premise—in contrast, a "private" use of reason is one in which some assumed role, such as that of a soldier, renders certain obligations off-limits to critique (Auf. 8: 37–38).[21] Such scholarship, coupled with the natural tendency of each of us "to live as an individual," will allow for an increasingly robust debate, provided the corresponding legal protections are in place. In such a debate all commitments are ultimately called for justification (Idee 8: 21).

There are two moves here: one an appeal to public debate; the other to a specific identity, the scholar, a specific "for-the-sake-of-which" in

Heideggerian terms. In the aftermath of the Enlightenment, both are widely challenged. From a Nietzschean perspective, say, they are naïve at best, and Nietzsche offers his own mechanisms, such as genealogy, designed to create the kind of distance from contemporary norms that Pippin sought. My suggestion is that rather than focusing on the well-worn debate surrounding voluntarism, we should approach Heidegger in this new context: we need to ask what distinctive *mechanisms* he makes available for critique. Seen in such a light, the key questions will be ones like these: How does Heidegger's "destruction" of the canon differ from a process such as genealogy? How does his attempt to "awaken" fundamental moods in GA29/30 work; what techniques does it use? How might Heideggerian anxiety short-circuit or circumvent the need to work off or leverage an existing set of identity commitments? The aim of this chapter has been to clarify what it means to "act in the light of norms." The task now should be to ask after the strategies and tactics by which agents improve or transform their relationship to the normative, a relationship in which as rational agents we all stand.[22]

NOTES

1. My concern is roughly with the period from 1919 to 1935: for stylistic reasons, I talk simply of "Heidegger" in what follows.

2. These options are evidently not exclusive: one might deliberately flout a norm or have no relation to it whatsoever.

3. For a detailed presentation see Dennett 1987. There are complex issues here regarding the links between the "ontological," in the Kantian, Heideggerian, and contemporary senses, and the "metaphysical." Views on which Kantian freedom is to be understood in terms of regulative conditions on agency remain ontological in the sense used here: it is because we are entities of a certain sophisticated sort that we must see ourselves in a certain way.

4. For analysis of the recent debate see Golob forthcoming-b.

5. The expression comes from Allison 1990: 51.

6. I am simplifying Moran's position, which is ultimately aimed at establishing deliberative authority: the authority to make up my own mind, as a basis for a constitutive theory of self-knowledge.

7. This remains true even in secondary cases where the speaker is talking sociologically: for example, "this group, in which I don't include myself, subscribe to the norm that. . . ."

8. Might the Heideggerian rock be subject to normative explanation in some other form, for example, via Aristotelian teleology? I touch on this at the end of the section.

9. As with Kant, there are points at which the lines blur: the animal is supposedly "poor in world," rather than lacking one entirely (GA29/30: 261). But, as with Kant,

it is unclear how to take these gestures of rapprochement—what could Heideggerian familiarity with a world, poor or otherwise, amount to in the absence of being or the "as"? Indeed, Heidegger himself retracts the move in GA40: there the animal "*hat keine Welt*" (GA40: 48).

10. Similarly:

> Taking over being-a-ground cannot mean that I create myself; my inclinations are not mine to create.
> Rather to take over the ground into which I am thrown is to see my inclinations in a normative light, that is, as "possible" rather than inevitable grounds of my behavior; it is to see them as potentially justifying reasons. In taking them over I become responsible for them either by making them my reasons or refusing to do so. Only by "understanding the call" in this sense can Dasein "be responsible [*verantwortlich*]" (GA2: 382/288/334). (Crowell 2013d: 299).

11. I develop this textual analysis in greater detail in Golob forthcoming-b.

12. Of course, I may be wrong about which properties I attribute to an object; the point concerns the underlying capacity to distinguish such attributions from facts about my own mental states.

13. One question, which I cannot address directly here, is the link between such conceptual architecture and the distinctive phenomenology of perception. Accounts such as Brandom's effectively stress the former while sidelining the latter. From a Kantian perspective, Brandomian agents resemble zombies somehow armed with sophisticated inferential abilities (for this complaint see McDowell 2010).

14. This is not the only worry: as Nagel noted in his reply to Korsgaard's original lectures it is unclear why reflection introduces normativity as opposed to simply more information (Nagel 1996: 201). Why does stepping back not just bring into view another set of *facts*, facts about events occurring within my body—how does the "ought" enter?

15. I have discussed this elsewhere—see Golob forthcoming-a.

16. I stress the Kantian aspects of the view for present purposes; as Crowell often notes, it has deeper roots still in Plato (Crowell 2001).

17. For a particularly clear treatment in a Husserlian context see Husserl 2004: 23–47; for Kant see KrV: A98–A113.

18. Thus, Heidegger's preferred metaphors are of removing barriers to sight, of letting us see what is there, rather than of producing it through the multiple processing stages characteristic of Kantian synthesis. There is a deep methodological issue here: from a Heideggerian perspective, the Kantian starting point is a myth, lacking any phenomenological warrant, whose sole purpose is to motivate an illusory demand for synthetic reconstruction.

19. Thus, despite the passage on the ants just cited, one can also find clear rejections of any equation of inauthentic agents with animals:

> But surely one cannot say that mindless coping expresses the animal teleology that would have governed me were I not a self-conscious being. When I gear unreflectively into the world, going about my daily tasks, do I really recover the Edenic garden of nature? (Crowell 2007: 328)

20. Likewise, Haugeland's reading on which Heideggerian authenticity requires a classic Kantian combination of scrutiny and choice—a role is subject to "critical scrutiny" and only then taken over "because I claim it by my own choice" (Haugeland 2013: 14–15).

21. Kant's phrasing sounds confusing to modern ears: his examples of "private," that is, limited, uses of reason are typically the holders of public roles, such as soldiers, clergy, etc. For discussion see O'Neill 1989: 123–50.

22. I am hugely indebted to all the participants at the International Society for Phenomenology meeting in Maine for their feedback, insight, and guidance. I am particularly grateful to Steven Crowell for discussion of these issues, and to the editors for their very helpful comments on a draft. The errors are, it goes without saying, all my own.

REFERENCES

Heidegger's Works

References are to the *Gesamtausgabe* edition (Frankfurt: Klostermann, 1975–; abbreviated as GA), with the exception of SZ, where I use the standard text (Tübingen: Max Niemeyer, 1957). With respect to translations, I have endeavored to stay close to the Macquarrie and Robinson version of SZ on the grounds that it is by far the best known. Where other translations exist, I have typically consulted these but often modified them.

Abbreviations to Kant's Works

References are to *Kants gesammelte Schriften* (Berlin: de Gruyter, 1900–; abbreviated as Ak.). For KrV, however, I employ the standard A/B pagination. I have consulted both the *Cambridge Edition of the Writings of Immanuel Kant* (New York: Cambridge University Press, 1992–) and Norman Kemp Smith's version of the *Critique of Pure Reason* (London: Macmillan, 1933) in translating Kant's texts.
Auf.—*Beantwortung der Frage: Was ist Aufklärung?* (Ak., vol. 8)
Idee—*Idee zu einer allgemeinen Geschichte in weltbürgerlicher Absicht* (Ak., vol. 8)
Br.—*Briefe* (Ak., vol. 11)
GMS—*Grundlegung zur Metaphysik der Sitten* (Ak., vol. 4)
KrV—*Kritik der reinen Vernunft* (Ak., vol. 4)
Prol.—*Prolegomena zu einer jeden künftigen Metaphysik* (Ak., vol. 4)
Relig.—*Die Religion innerhalb der Grenzen der bloßen Vernunft* (Ak., vol. 6)

Other References

Allison, H. 1990. *Kant's Theory of Freedom*. Cambridge: Cambridge University Press.
Blattner, W. 2014. "Essential Guilt and Transcendental Conscience." In *Heidegger, Authenticity and the Self*, edited by D. McManus. London: Routledge, 116–35.

Brandom, R. 1994. *Making It Explicit*. London: Harvard University Press.
Crowell, S. 2001. "Subjectivity: Locating the First-Person in Being and Time." *Inquiry* 44.
———. 2007. "Sorge or Selbstbewußtsein? Heidegger and Korsgaard on the Sources of Normativity." *European Journal of Philosophy* 15: 315–33.
———. 2013a. "Being Answerable." In *Normativity and Phenomenology in Husserl and Heidegger*, edited by S. Crowell. Cambridge: Cambridge University Press, 214–36.
———. 2013b. "Conscience and Reason." In *Normativity and Phenomenology in Husserl and Heidegger*, edited by S. Crowell. Cambridge: Cambridge University Press, 191–213.
———. 2013c. "The Existential Sources of Normativity." In *Normativity and Phenomenology in Husserl and Heidegger*, edited by S. Crowell. Cambridge: Cambridge University Press, 239–60.
———. 2013d. "Heidegger on Practical Reasoning, Morality and Agency." In *Normativity and Phenomenology in Husserl and Heidegger*, edited by S. Crowell. Cambridge: Cambridge University Press, 282–303.
———. 2013e. "Making Meaning Thematic." In *Normativity and Phenomenology in Husserl and Heidegger*, edited by S. Crowell. Cambridge: Cambridge University Press, 9–30.
———. 2014. "Responsibility, Autonomy, Affectivity: A Heideggerian Approach." In *Heidegger, Authenticity and the Self*, edited by D. McManus. London: Routledge, 215–42.
———. Forthcoming. *Commitment*.
Dennett, D. 1987. *The Intentional Stance*. Cambridge, MA: MIT Press.
Derrida, J. 2008. *The Animal That Therefore I Am*. Ashland, OH: Fordham University Press.
Golob, S. 2014. *Heidegger on Concepts, Freedom and Normativity*. Cambridge: Cambridge University Press.
———. Forthcoming-a. "Was Heidegger a Relativist?" In *The Emergence of Modern Relativism: The German Debates from the 1770s to the 1930s*, edited by K. Kinzel, M. Kusch, J. Steizinger, and N. Wildschut. London: Routledge.
———. Forthcoming-b. "What Do Animals See? Intentionality, Objects and Kantian Nonconceptualism." In *Kant and Animals*, edited by J. Callanan and L. Allais. Oxford: Oxford University Press.
Haugeland, J. 2013. *Dasein Disclosed*. Cambridge, MA: Harvard University Press.
Hume, D. 1978. *A Treatise of Human Nature*. Oxford: Clarendon Press.
Husserl, E. 2004. *Husserliana 34: Wahrnemung Und Aufmerksamkeit: Texte Aus Dem Nachlass (1893–1912)*. Dordrecht: Springer.
Korsgaard, C. M. 1996. *The Sources of Normativity*. Cambridge: Cambridge University Press.
Levinas, E. 2013. *Totality and Infinity: An Essay on Exteriority*. Pittsburgh, PA: Duquesne University Press.
Longuenesse, Béatrice. 2008. "Kant's 'I Think' Versus Descartes' 'I Am a Thing That Thinks.'" In *Kant and the Early Moderns*, edited by Daniel Garber and Béatrice Longuenesse. Princeton, NJ: Princeton University Press, 9–31.

McDowell, J. 2010. "Brandom on Observation." In *Reading Brandom*, edited by J. Wanderer and B. Weiss, 129–45. Oxford: Routledge.

Moran, R. 2001. *Authority and Estrangement*. Princeton, NJ: Princeton University Press.

Nagel, T. 1996. "Universality and the Reflective Self." In *The Sources of Normativity*, edited by C. Korsgaard. Cambridge: Cambridge University Press, 200–9.

Nietzsche, F. 2002. *Beyond Good and Evil*. Cambridge: Cambridge University Press.

O'Neill, O. 1989. *Constructions of Reason*. Cambridge: Cambridge University Press.

Okrent, M. 1999. "Heidegger and Korsgaard on Human Reflection." *Philosophical Topics* 27: 47–76.

Pippin, R. 1997. "On Being Anti-Cartesian: Hegel, Heidegger, Subjectivity and Sociality." In *Idealism as Modernism*. Cambridge: Cambridge University Press, 375–95.

Sartre, J.-P. 2003. *Being and Nothingness*. London: Routledge.

Sellars, W. 1948. "Concepts as Involving Laws and Inconceivable Without Them." *Philosophy of Science* 15: 287–315.

Chapter 4

Giving a Damn about Getting It Right

Heideggerian Constitutivism and Our Reasons to Be Authentic

Matthew Burch

With each step along his crooked *Denkweg*, Heidegger advanced an irrationalist philosophical program: relativism, decisionism, nihilism, you name it—if it deflates the demands of reason, he held the view. That's one popular version of his intellectual biography (see our introduction: 2–5).

No one has done more to challenge this narrative than John Haugeland and Steven Crowell. Heidegger, they contend, does not dismiss the demands of reason but rather clarifies how they get a grip on us in the first place. That is, Heidegger shows that rational agency is only possible, because, to borrow Haugeland's (1998) phrase, we "give a damn" about things (47). Crowell expresses the idea this way: for Heidegger, "care is the phenomenological origin of reason" (this volume: 33). In making a case for this reading of Heidegger, Haugeland and Crowell do more than merely interpret his writings; they also construct original lines of thought that speak to contemporary philosophical concerns. Here I aim to highlight the promise of that constructive work by building on their Heidegger-inspired approaches to normativity and reasons.

The chapter unfolds as follows. Section 1 sets the stage by introducing "constitutivism," a family of views widely discussed in recent work on normativity and reasons (e.g., Velleman 2009, Ferrero 2009, Korsgaard 2009, Katsafanas 2013, Smith 2015). Section 2 constructs a Heidegger-inspired constitutivist account of *hypothetical* normativity based on Haugeland's work; and section 3 constructs a Heidegger-inspired constitutivist account of *categorical* normativity based on Crowell's work. Sections 2 and 3 are not mere summaries; neither Haugeland nor Crowell explicitly pitches his work in terms of constitutivism. Part of my contribution, then, is to recast their views as varieties of constitutivism in order to further illuminate their work and to add to the growing list of plausible constitutivist views. Section 4 challenges a claim from Crowell's work that plays a central role in his recent writings and in my reconstruction of his constitutivism. Finally, in section 5, I draw on resources from the foregoing discussion to offer my own constitutivist account of a categorical normative demand to get our existence right; and I argue that aiming to meet that demand in turn gives us reasons to be authentic.[1]

1. CONSTITUTIVISM

The tie that binds the constitutivist family is the notion that "certain normative claims apply to us merely in virtue of the fact that we are agents" (Katsafanas 2016: 367). In other words, constitutivism grounds normativity in the constitutive features of action (or agency).

Constitutivism grounds *hypothetical* normativity in the constitutive features of actions we already have independent reason to undertake. For example, the norms of table-making aren't *intrinsically* normative; rather, such norms have normative force for me *if* I already have an independent reason to make a table. *If* I have such a reason, then I have reason to act in light of table-making norms; moreover, under such conditions, those norms not only guide my activity; they also serve as standards of assessment for my success or failure in trying to make a table. The basic constitutivist approach to *hypothetical* normativity is thus straightforward: I have reason to do what is constitutive of actions I already have independent reason to undertake.

More ambitious forms of constitutivism try to ground *categorical* normativity in the constitutive features of action. Perhaps the best-known example of such a view comes from Christine Korsgaard's (2009) *Self-Constitution*. Since I can't do Korsgaard's complex view full justice here, I only sketch the kernel of her argument to illustrate how such accounts work:

1. Action is inescapable.
2. The Categorical Imperative (CI) is the constitutive principle of action.
3. The CI has normative authority for all agents as such.

Although this tells us little about Korsgaard's view, it indicates how ambitious constitutivist arguments work. Namely, to borrow Ferrero's (2018) expression, they "ground the force of the *should* in the 'bind' of the *must*" (133). According to Korsgaard, we *must* act; the CI is constitutive of action; and so we *should* act (i.e., we have *reason* to act) in accordance with the CI. The demands of morality are thus categorical—every agent is bound by the CI simply in virtue of being an agent. The approach thus shuns the kind of subjectivism that anchors normativity in contingent psychological states, eschews the realism that commits us to agent-independent normative truths, and instead grounds claims to objective normativity in the constitutive features of our inescapable agency.

Since ambitious constitutivist arguments ground categorical normative claims on "the necessity of being *an agent*" (Korsgaard 2009: 26), agency's alleged inescapability is crucial for their success. But what does it mean to say that agency is inescapable? Korsgaard answers: "The necessity of choosing and acting is not causal, logical, or rational necessity. It is our *plight*" (ibid.: 2). But this response bewilders some critics. If neither causal, logical, nor rational, what sort of inescapability is it? It's clearly not ontological or metaphysical; after all, suicide can deliver us from our plight. In what sense, then, is agency inescapable?

I think Velleman (2009) and Ferrero (2009, 2018) offer the best answer: agency is *dialectically* inescapable. We cannot imagine a standpoint outside of agency from which to assess the standards that govern our deliberation and action. In other words, we must address every practical question—every question about what it's best to think or do or be, including whether it's best to go on thinking, doing, and being—from the standpoint of agency. To be sure, we can put an end to that standpoint in our own case, but we cannot think, act, or be anything outside of it. From here on, I speak of the inescapability of agency in this dialectical sense. It doesn't mean you're bound to be an agent; it means you're bound by the standpoint and standards of agency whenever you answer questions about what it's best to think or do or be.

2. HAUGELAND ON HYPOTHETICAL NORMATIVITY

Like Korsgaard, Haugeland (1998) builds his account of normativity around the notion of constitutive standards. (Although constitutive standards are only one kind of norm among many, they are the only kind that concerns me here, so from this point on I use "constitutive standard" and "norm" interchangeably.) Haugeland's initial characterization of constitutive standards leans heavily on the heuristic of games, such as chess. A chess piece, a knight, say, can only be what it is in the context of the game of chess. To understand a rook *as* a rook is precisely to see it in light of the constitutive standards that govern rook-related phenomena within the game. To *be* a rook is to be understood and used in accordance with the norms of chess. And this goes for all chess phenomena: the constitutive standards of chess "govern all phenomena which occur in the game and *determine what they are*" (Haugeland 1998: 329; my emphasis). Moreover, there are no chess pieces outside the constitutive standards of chess. Constitutive standards are constitutive, then, because they *let beings be*—they allow us to make sense of beings *as* the determinate kind of beings they are.

For Haugeland, all beings are constituted in this sense. Even the objects of natural science only show up as the objects they are in virtue of a scientific theory—a highly refined constellation of constitutive standards. This doesn't mean that scientific theories *create* the objects they describe; nor does it mean that natural objects can't serve as independent criteria that constrain, "push back" against, and falsify the scientific theories that constitute them; it just means that the constitutive standards of a theory make sense of the relevant natural objects as a particular kind of object. The theory "lets them be" what they are "by finding and showing that they make sense in some determinate way" (ibid.).

Such constitutive standards are rarely made explicit. Instead, Haugeland argues, they tend to operate implicitly in our skillful activity. Structured and guided by constitutive standards, our skills allow us (a) to competently interact with phenomena in accordance with constitutive standards and (b) to tell "whether the phenomena . . . are, in fact, in accord with" those standards (ibid.: 341). This implies an intrinsic correlation between our skills and the way phenomena show up for us: beings appear as the determinate kind of beings they are in virtue of the norm-governed skills we use to make sense of them. Our skills give us access to a spontaneously intelligible, constituted world.

Haugeland (2000) finds a similar account of the constitution of beings in *Being and Time*. At the center of that account lies Heidegger's notion of understanding. Understanding, for Heidegger, denotes our everyday practical know-how in terms of which we make sense of things. To understand is to be able to "manage something" or to be "competent to do something" (BT 143–183). And, Heidegger argues, we owe such understanding to our shared social practices. Practice here denotes a set of purposive activities organized around particular human interests and structured by an open-ended set of norms that measure success or failure in those activities. Growing up in a form of life, we learn to participate competently in such practices, and when socialized into a practice, we acquire what Heidegger calls a *Seinkönnen*[2]—the "ability-to-be" someone, or to do what "one does," in a practice. An ability-to-be entails the kind of skills identified by Haugeland and so allows us to manage and make sense of entities within a practice. For example, having been socialized into the practice of teaching, I can competently use whiteboards, markers, and erasers as teachers do, and they show up to me *as* teaching paraphernalia in light of the constitutive standards of teaching. Moreover, such objects could not show up *as* teaching paraphernalia to me if I were not to some extent familiar with the holistic context of meaning in which they serve their purpose. Thus, in the sense of constitution Haugeland clarifies in *Having Thought*, the constitutive standards that govern our abilities-to-be constitute the being of worldly entities. Like Haugeland, Heidegger insists, "'Constituting' does not mean producing in the sense of making and fabricating; it means letting the entity be seen in its objectivity" (HCT: 97).

But it's not just the being of entities that we understand in terms of constitutive standards; we also understand ourselves in their terms. For Heidegger, whenever I act, I always do so as a participant in some social practice, for-the-sake-of some ability-to-be, and in light of constitutive standards that measure my success or failure in taking up that ability-to-be. I'm a father, husband, teacher, and so on, and these abilities-to-be govern my actions and define who I am in the shared world. So I understand entities and myself in terms of my abilities-to-be, both of which are governed by the constitutive standards inherent in our social practices. Heidegger thus affirms the same correlation Haugeland identifies between our skills and constituted entities—there's an intrinsic interdependence between our abilities-to-be and the entities they disclose. When I engage in a practice, then, the constitutive standards that govern that practice serve as a measure (1) for my being, measuring how well I embody some ability-to-be, and (2) for the being of the entities and others within the practice, allowing me to make sense of them in a determinate way.

From here it's easy to cast Haugeland's Heidegger-inspired view as a constitutivist account of hypothetical normativity. As I explained earlier, constitutivism grounds hypothetical normativity in the constitutive features of actions we already have independent reason(s) to undertake. For Haugeland, that independent reason is what he calls "existential constitutive commitment" (1998: 341)—an insistence that my own being and the being of entities accord with the norms that govern some ability-to-be. In other words, *if* I'm committed to exercising some ability-to-be, then I have reason to act in light of the constitutive standards that govern that ability-to-be—those norms have normative force *for me*. Moreover, as we've already seen, those same norms will also serve as a measure for the appropriateness of the entities relevant to the ability-to-be, and they will furnish me with measures to assess my own success or failure in my attempt to exercise that ability-to-be. To stick with the teaching example, pedagogical norms have normative authority for me, and furnish me with reasons to think or act in light of them, *if* I'm committed to being-a-teacher. Moreover, so long as that commitment lasts, those norms serve as standards for assessing (1) my success or failure at being-a-teacher, (2) the appropriateness of my work context and paraphernalia, and (3) the performance of other people relevant to the context (such as students). Norms have hypothetical normative force for me, then, *if and to the extent that* I'm committed to exercising the ability-to-be they govern.

I want to consider two objections to this view before we move on to Crowell's work. First, critics might object that the view fails to identify any genuine normative standards. Some constitutivist views derive standards for action from the nature of action *as such*; and this allows them to argue that the norms they identify serve as genuine standards of success, because they serve as a measure for any and every action. But Haugeland's account relies on the norms of social practices, which are notoriously contested—my take on teaching differs from yours, yours differs from hers, and so on. Such disagreement seems to speak against the idea that the norms of social practices can serve as robust normative standards. Moreover, this worry resonates with another critique of social practices, namely, that performances within such practices lack sufficient similarity to warrant the claim that they are regulated by anything as rigid as rules. Finally, these criticisms also connect with recent arguments against the allegedly mindless character of skilled action. Skilled agents intelligently discriminate and adjust to subtle features of an action context, which seems incompatible with the notion that such action involves mindless rule-following. A mindless rule-follower, critics claim, could not respond sensitively to small shifts in circumstances.[3] To summarize the criticisms collected in this paragraph: within social practices we see (1) widespread disagreement about norms, (2) remarkable diversity across performances, and (3) context-sensitive skilled action; and 1–3 all seem to speak against the claim that the norms of social practices can actually serve as standards. Does this leave Haugeland's constitutivism without any genuine constitutive standards?

I don't think so. We can explain the disagreement about norms, performance diversity, and context-sensitivity of skilled action without denying the existence of social norms. Specifically, we can argue that there are indeed third-person norms, but that the individuals who take them up also act under first-person normative claims specific to their own agency and second-person normative claims placed on them by the particular people in their lives. In other words, as my coeditor puts it in her recent book, as agents, we always face normative claims that arise simultaneously from "three different domains of normativity within which human beings operate, namely, the claims posed by the self, other, and shared world" (McMullin 2018: 68). For example, I want to be a good father. In trying to do so, I draw on shared, third-person norms of fatherhood, but I take these norms up in light of my own personally inflected interests and in response to the specific second-person demands that my particular children place me under. Aiming to meet all these normative claims at once requires *phronesis*, the "concretely situation-specific discernment" (McDowell 2007: 340) that allows me to track the relevant claims from these three normative domains, while tailoring my action to my current circumstances. This, I contend, accounts for the disagreement about norms, performance diversity, and context-sensitivity of skilled action without denying the existence of shared norms endemic to social practices. There *are* shared norms, but we take them up in different ways to accommodate our first-person commitments, second-person obligations, and current circumstances.

Still: can this view furnish genuine standards of success? I think it can if we borrow and repurpose an insight from Paul Katsafanas's (2013) aim-based constitutivism; this is the idea that "*aims* generate standards of success" (39)—i.e., to aim at a goal is to generate a standard of success, namely, *achieving that goal*. The goals Katsafanas tends to focus on are specific outcomes (e.g., building a house, baking a potato, or banging a drum). Aim at any of these goals and you generate a standard of success—i.e., achieving your goal by executing the relevant action (or actions). Aim to φ and you thereby generate a standard of success (i.e., successfully φ-ing).

We can adapt this insight to Haugeland's constitutivism. To do so, we should accept Katsafanas's claim that we generate standards of success for action by aiming at discrete outcomes, but we should not focus on such cases. Given the existential orientation of Haugeland's view, we should instead focus on the fact that whenever we act, we not only aim at some discrete outcome, but we also aim *to be* a particular kind of agent by taking up some ability-to-be. Moreover, following McMullin (2018), we don't do this by aiming to merely instantiate generic third-person norms; rather, we aim to take up a norm-governed ability-to-be in light of our first-person interests, second-person obligations, and particular circumstances. Repurposing Katsafanas's insight, then, we can argue that such an aim generates a standard of success (i.e., successfully exercising the ability-to-be in a manner that is suitably sensitive to the context and that meets the normative claims posed by self, other, and shared world). To illustrate this with my favorite example: when I teach, I aim to meet certain shared standards of the practice, to live up to my own aspirations as a teacher, to respond to the claims my students make on me, and to be sensitive to the requirements of *this* particular classroom setting. And such aiming generates a standard of success for my efforts.[4] (For the rest of the chapter, whenever I refer to an agent "committing to the norms of some ability-to-be," I ask the reader to take it as shorthand for "committing to *her take on* the norms that govern some ability-to-be in light of her first-person commitments, second-person obligations, and particular circumstances.") As I see it, this should keep Haugeland's view safe from the criticism that it cannot furnish agents with genuine standards of success.

But we're not out of the woods yet. Critics might also complain that Haugeland's notion of existential commitment amounts to an absurd voluntarism.[5] In other words, the critic might object that Haugeland's view makes hypothetical normativity rest *entirely* on the agent's free commitment, which falsifies the phenomenology of normative claims. Consider an example to illustrate the worry. Imagine you're in a romantic relationship with hypothetical normative value. No harm there—not every desire carries categorical demands. The worry, however, is the idea that your reasons for being in that relationship derive their normative force *entirely from your commitment*. Imagine explaining that to your partner:

Her: "Why are you in this relationship?"
You: "It's a sheer act of will."

Against this, the critic might insist that normativity has a dual aspect. For claims to have normative authority for me, commitment's not enough—I must first be claimed by them. That's why a normal answer in the above scenario would mention the way your partner affects you. *We don't make things normative for us* through commitment; rather, *things make normative claims on us* and our commitment acknowledges and reinforces those claims.[6]

To answer this objection, I think we need to flesh out some underdeveloped aspects of Haugeland's view and introduce a minor terminological revision. To begin with the former, when Haugeland speaks of commitment, what he has in mind isn't an extreme voluntarism but rather something closer to what Mark Lance (2015) calls a "lived commitment." To have a lived commitment is to be disposed to think and act in accord with that commitment. Lance illustrates this idea with the example of Joyce and Helen, two sisters whose father needs care after a stroke. Convention obliges both sisters to care for him, but Joyce is selfish and feels no obligation to do so. She knows what convention requires but she "simply *does not care*. . . . [She] has no *lived commitment* to caring for her father" (Lance 2015: 282). Helen, on the other hand, does have such a commitment: "The need to care for her father is something lived and experienced, something that is a salient part of her at all times" (ibid.: 283). Her lived commitment is a constitutive feature of her mental life that orients her thought and action.

Lance's idea can help us better appreciate Haugeland's view if we think more expansively about lived commitments. Lance focuses on the big commitments that shape an agent's life; but Haugeland's view implies that lived commitments orient *all* intentional experience. Commitment, he tells us, is the "transcendental ground of objectivity, subjectivity, and normativity" (1998: 304). I *always* understand myself, entities, and others in a normative light because I am spontaneously and constantly oriented to the world in terms of an implicit lived commitment to some ability-to-be.

This is no absurd voluntarism. Lived commitments don't depend *entirely* on my endorsement. Recall Joyce and Helen: the difference between them isn't Helen's superior willpower. The difference, rather, is that Helen is *claimed by* a felt sense of obligation to care for her father; Joyce isn't. If Joyce were to care for him, *her* commitment would likely collapse under minimal pressure. But Helen feels *claimed by* the normative expectation and she's *committed* to meeting it. Seen in light of Lance's notion of lived commitment, then, Haugeland's account of existential commitment escapes the charge of absurd voluntarism.[7]

Still, to put the second objection to rest, I think a small terminological revision is in order. Namely, instead of commitment, Haugeland should speak of "care" as the source of hypothetical normativity. Care harbors all the connotations that Haugeland attributes to existential commitment. To care about my engagement in some ability-to-be is to be committed to think and act in light of the norms that I take to govern that ability-to-be. Moreover, the term "care" doesn't imply that such commitment is explicit, nor that one would be able to articulate those norms if called upon to do so. You can care about X without knowing it, or even while explicitly thinking you don't care about X. Finally, caring is never purely a product of self-assertion. You can't will yourself to care about something. Caring presupposes a claim that precedes (or is at least coeval with) your commitment.

To sum up, this section defends three claims: (1) Haugeland offers a constitutivist account of hypothetical normativity—*if* I care about and am committed to exercising some ability-to-be, then the norms that I take to govern that ability-to-be have normative force for me and serve as standards of assessment for my conduct; (2) my commitment to those standards is best understood as a largely implicit lived commitment; and (3) the term "care" better captures what Haugeland identifies as the source of hypothetical normative authority.

3. CROWELL ON THE CATEGORICAL DEMAND TO BE AUTHENTIC

Let's turn now to Crowell's ambitious constitutivism. As I read his work, Crowell contends that from the constitutive features of agency we can derive a *categorical* normative demand to be authentic. I reconstruct his argument for this claim in this section, and I challenge it in the next.

Before doing so, however, I want to point out that Crowell's goal—to show that we have powerful reasons to be authentic—should be a priority for any charitable interpreter of *Being and Time*. For Heidegger insists that anyone who fails to be authentic thereby fails to be a self. Each Dasein, he tells us, "has its being to be, and has it as its own"; it must face a fundamental decision about its being: "to be itself or not itself" by "taking hold or neglecting" (BT: 33). Authentic Dasein takes hold of its existence and thereby succeeds in being itself; and inauthentic Dasein neglects this task and thereby fails to be itself. This strong normative language about authenticity pervades the text. Thus, Heidegger clearly thinks we *should* be authentic. What's less clear is *why* he thinks that. What justifies his insistence? What reasons do we have to be authentic? Why is it better to be authentic than inauthentic? Few Heidegger scholars raise these questions, while his critics contend that such questions have no answers, because the rhetoric of authenticity is mere jargon, the pseudo-ethical ideal of Heidegger's vacuous heroic nihilism (again, see our introduction: 2–5). As usual, then, Crowell's up to something important here. Although I disagree somewhat with his answers, he asks the right questions—questions too often ignored by Heidegger's epigones, and just as often weaponized by his critics.

Now for Crowell's argument. As an ambitious constitutivist, he needs to take the inescapability of agency as his starting point in order to "ground the force of the *should* in the 'bind' of the *must*" (Ferrero 2018: 133). Although he never explicitly appeals to such inescapability, I interpret his claims that Dasein faces "unavoidable task(s)" and answers an "unavoidable call" (2013: 253) in these terms, because I think it strengthens his case. For argument's sake, then, let's assume he agrees that agency is dialectically inescapable.

The next premise in my reconstruction of Crowell's argument is the claim that human agency is characterized by ontological responsibility. Unlike the inescapability premise, this claim takes center-stage in much of Crowell's recent work (2008, 2013, 2015, 2017a, 2017b, 2019). Understanding the premise requires familiarity with Heidegger's distinction between the ontic and the ontological—the so-called ontological difference between entities and the *being* of entities. The basic idea is this: ontic matters pertain to contingent aspects of our being, like the fact that I'm a teacher; ontological determinants, on the other hand, are constitutive features of our being as such. When Crowell speaks of *ontological responsibility*, then, he means responsibility not as a "contingent [ontic] property of certain acts" but rather as "an ontological determinant of Dasein's being" as such (2008: 264). How can we be responsible as such?

Crowell's answer emerges from his interpretation of Division II of *Being and Time*. As we saw above, for Heidegger, care makes norm-governed action possible by orienting us to the world in terms of an implicit commitment to some ability-to-be. In Division I, Heidegger argues that, for the most part, care thus orients us toward everyday abilities-to-be. In Division II, however, he analyzes "the call of conscience," an experience that disrupts this everyday intelligibility and thereby furnishes certain insights into the structure of agency.

This experience comes about, Heidegger famously claims, due to the unusual mood of angst. Most moods open us to the world such that we're drawn to some action possibilities and turned off by others. Angst works differently. Instead of polarizing the world into appealing and unappealing possibilities, it attenuates the claims that all such possibilities make on me. In the grip of angst, then, I'm still aware of my everyday abilities-to-be as potential ways for me to be a self, but none of them claims me sufficiently to motivate action. This doesn't mean that I fail to care about anything at all. After all, we've followed Haugeland and Crowell in maintaining that caring is a condition for the possibility of intelligible experience, and "the call" is certainly an intelligible experience. Thus, it's an exaggeration to suggest, as some do, that the experience involves a quasi-annihilation of agency in the face of life's sheer meaninglessness; if it were *utterly* meaningless, we wouldn't be able to describe its phenomenology. It's not that nothing matters to me when I hear "the call," then; it's rather that instead of caring about some particular ability-to-be, I care about my existence as such. I see my worldly abilities-to-be as possible ways to be a self that at present fail to motivate me to act, and this experience discloses certain truths about the structure of agency. Although there are many such truths, I mention only four here:

C_1: Since all of my worldly abilities-to-be can simultaneously fail to motivate my commitment, none of them defines me as such; the only ability essential to my being is my capacity to care itself.

C_2: To be someone in the world at all, I cannot *not* care about and commit to some ability-to-be.

C_3: Since submitting myself to a norm presupposes that I grasp my being as normatively assessable, my capacity to care—as a capacity to be claimed by and committed to norm-governed abilities-to-be—is "intrinsically oriented towards measures of success or failure" (Crowell 2013: 79)—i.e., my being is characterized by "responsiveness to the normative *as* normative" (ibid.: 24).

C_4: Finally, without my caring, the norms that govern the worldly abilities-to-be that typically define me lose their normative force; thus, care is the source of hypothetical normativity.

We can build Crowell's case for ontological responsibility out of these four insights. Nothing essentially defines me other than my capacity to care (C_1), I must care about and commit to some ability-to-be to be anything at all (C_2), caring is intrinsically oriented toward measures of better and worse (C_3), and which ability-to-be I project myself into will determine which norms have normative force *for me* (C_4), thereby determining which factic givens of my situation count as *my* reasons. To make any ontic commitment whatsoever, then, I must transform *some* factic givens into *my* reasons; and that unavoidable fact is what Crowell calls ontological responsibility:

"Ontologically, . . . to be responsible would mean that I am essentially called to view the givens of my situation as assessable in light of better and worse, that I cannot *not* view them in that way" (ibid.: 222). All "ontic commitments," Crowell claims, "are grounded in the unavoidable (Heidegger says '*unüberhörbar*') call to 'be responsible' as such" (2017a: 87). That's the basic case for Crowell's second premise.

The final step in my reconstruction of Crowell's argument is to ground the demand to be authentic (or to be a self) on the fact of ontological responsibility. In a number of places, Crowell argues that when we act, we're always subject to the possibility of failure on two distinct levels. On an *ontic level*, when I exercise some ability-to-be, I can succeed or fail at living up to my take on its governing norms. And at the same time, on an *ontological level*, "I can succeed or fail at being a *self*" (2019: 341); thus, my being as such is "assessable against a normative standard," that is, "the standard of authenticity (*Eigenlichkeit*)" (2017a: 78). I am subject to this latter possibility of failure, Crowell argues, because I am ontologically responsible. How does he justify this entailment?

His argument goes something like this. Ontological responsibility means that no matter which ability-to-be I take up, I cannot *not* transform some factic givens into reasons. However, there are two different ways that I can relate to this fact. I can act transparently in light of the fact that my caring is the source of my reasons, or I can fail to do so. If I act transparently in light of that fact, then I'm authentic—I take ownership of the fact that my caring is the source of my reasons, integrating that fact into the way I take up any particular ability-to-be. I make factic givens "my reasons by taking responsibility for endorsing them" (2013: 300). Ontological responsibility, then, denotes *the fact* that I am responsible for my being, because my care and commitment transform factic givens into my reasons; and authenticity is a mode of being in which I *take responsibility* for that fact—i.e., I act "in light of . . . my responsibility for the normative force of those standards (reasons) in light of which I act" (ibid.).

How exactly do I do that? Crowell tells us: I do so by putting "myself forth not as justified by the given rules of the game but as exemplary of what it means to succeed in some way of being" (2015: 89). In other words, rather than locating the authority of my reasons in norms whose normative force is externally fixed and in no way depends on me, I transparently own the fact that my caring is the source of their normative force. On this view, then, being authentic amounts to acknowledging my own first-person authority by acting in full light of the fact that my reasons are *mine* because my caring about them makes them so. On the other hand, if I locate the authority of my reasons in externally fixed norms, as if their normative force in no way depends on me, I fail to transparently acknowledge my own first-person authority. I relate to the factic givens of my situation not as reasons in light of which I think and act but rather as external forces (e.g., causes) that determine what I'm bound to think and do. In doing so, I'm inauthentic, failing to live up to the normative standard built into agency: I fail to acknowledge my own first-person authority, and I fail to transparently acknowledge my reasons as *mine*. Moreover, according to Heidegger's existentialist use of the term, I thereby fail to be a self.

To translate this into constitutivist terms, Haugeland grounds *hypothetical* normativity on an agent's care for and commitment to some ability-to-be; and Crowell grounds a *categorical* normative demand to be authentic on the fact that responsibility is a constitutive feature of agency. In other words, Crowell identifies a *categorical* normative demand to transparently acknowledge and take ownership of the fact that my caring is the source of *hypothetical* normativity. And this demand must be categorical: Crowell, following Heidegger, doesn't argue that *if* I care about being a self, *then* I'm subject to the possibility of failing to be one. His claim, rather, is that *any* agent who fails to be authentic thereby fails to be a self. The call to be authentic is a normative demand, then, because we can fail to meet it; and it's categorical, because it doesn't depend on a contingent psychological motive—*any* agent who fails to be authentic thereby fails to be a self. Responsibility is a constitutive feature of agency. You can try to deny that fact with self-serving platitudes (e.g., "I'm just playing by the rules of the game."). But you can't stop making givens into reasons. The demand to *take* responsibility is unavoidable because responsibility is a constitutive feature of your inescapable agency.

To summarize Crowell's argument:

1. Agency is inescapable.
2. Ontological responsibility is a constitutive feature of agency (i.e., I cannot not transform factic givens into reasons by caring about some ability-to-be).
3. All agents face a categorical normative demand to be authentic—*the fact of ontological responsibility* faces me with a categorical normative demand to *take responsibility* for my reasons by transparently acknowledging my own first-person authority.

4. A CHALLENGE TO CROWELL'S CONSTITUTIVISM

I agree with Crowell's claims that care transforms factic givens into reasons, and that to be someone in the world at all we cannot *not* make givens into reasons. But I think it's a mistake to construe this latter necessity as a form of "responsibility." In this section, then, I criticize the notion of ontological responsibility. And since Crowell relies on that notion to motivate the claim that we ought to be authentic, my criticism also constitutes a challenge to his overall constitutivist strategy.

So, what's wrong with using the term "ontological responsibility" to characterize the fact that we must transform factic givens into reasons? I see at least two problems with it.

First, it fails to respect responsibility's normative character. Take any major conception of responsibility, and you will notice that it specifies normative satisfaction conditions for responsibility attributions. That is, all major conceptions of responsibility maintain that we are (or would be) responsible for actions that satisfy certain conditions, and we are not responsible for actions that fail to satisfy those conditions. Every viable account of responsibility has this feature, because responsibility is an intrinsically normative concept: it must specify a standard that *you can fail to meet*. What Crowell calls ontological responsibility lacks this feature: as an ontological determinant, constitutive of agency as such, it specifies something *you cannot fail to be*. Therefore, it cannot be a kind of responsibility. If we cannot fail to be R, then R does not specify a way to be responsible.

We can frame the second problem as a *reductio*. Assume responsibility is an ontological determinant of our being. On that assumption, we are responsible as such even when no reasonable person would consider us responsible for what we do. For example, imagine an impressionable person subjected to systematic brainwashing who acts on the orders of her manipulators. For the sake of argument, assume the manipulation runs so deep that no reasonable person would think her responsible for her action. (If it helps, go ahead and imagine an evil neuroscientist uses advanced technology to control her behavior.) If Crowell's right about ontological responsibility, then it seems that even this person, acting under the influence of extreme manipulation, would be *responsible for her being as such*, because, from the first-person point of view, her caring would still transform factic givens into reasons. She *is not* responsible, and yet she *is* responsible. Of course, we need not appeal to outlandish hypotheticals to make this point. In ordinary life, sorting out what we're responsible for, and what we can hold others accountable for, is hard work, because so many factors can compromise our capacity for responsible action. And yet, even when such factors undermine our capacity for responsibility, if we continue to have intelligible experiences, then we continue to care about our norm-governed abilities-to-be and so to transform factic givens into reasons. If we call that unavoidable fact "ontological responsibility," we imply that even in cases when we are not responsible for our actions, we are still responsible as such. To my ear, the word responsible loses its meaning here.

At this point, someone might object that Crowell's doctrine of ontological responsibility amounts to a reframing of Kant's "Incorporation Thesis" (IT), which licenses the claim that we're responsible as such.[8] I disagree. It's certainly true, as Golob makes clear in chapter 3, that Crowell reformulates

Kant's IT. But the IT fails to license the claim that we're responsible as such. The IT is the claim that psychological incentives don't simply cause us to act but rather determine our behavior *only* once we incorporate them into a maxim. For a Kantian like Korsgaard, it is the "space of reflective distance" that underwrites the IT, because that space allows us to ask "whether [or not] incentives give us reasons" to act (2009: 115). For a Heideggerian like Crowell, it is "the call of conscience" that discloses me as "a being for whom thrown grounds can never function simply as causes . . . [because] it is I who make them normative for me, reasons for what I do" (2013: 209; cited by Golob: 82). This link to Kant's IT, however, in no way warrants a commitment to the idea of ontological responsibility. The capacity to distance myself from psychological incentives and to take (or reject) them as reasons doesn't make me responsible for my being as such. The term "responsible" must refer to something we can fail to be; to claim otherwise is to strip the concept of its normative dimension and to fall prey to the *reductio* sketched above. If we cannot fail to be R, then R does not specify a viable conception of responsibility. Appealing to the IT changes nothing.[9]

In some places, Crowell (forthcoming; this volume) calls the fact that we must convert givens into reasons by other names (e.g., "answerability" and "freedom"). I have no problem with these alternatives, because I don't think they're vulnerable to the same criticisms. Without the term "ontological responsibility," however, it's hard to see how he can motivate the claim that there's a categorical normative demand to be authentic built into the very structure of human agency. The move from the claim that we are *in fact responsible* to the claim that we *ought to take responsibility* for ourselves seems reasonable. It's a tricky move, but it looks like one you might be able to justify. If we're not responsible as such, however, why *should* we act responsibly in light of the fact that our caring converts factic givens into reasons? Why not flee that fact inauthentically and shirk the burden of self-responsibility?

Crowell's interpretation of Heidegger shows us why we *can* authentically take responsibility for what we do, then, but I don't think it tells us why we *should*. Of course, Crowell's not alone in this—I'm unaware of any better attempt to justify the normative language that surrounds the concept of authenticity in *Being and Time*. I am aware, however, of critics who insist that Heidegger gives us *no substantive reasons* to be authentic.

5. GETTING IT RIGHT

In this section, I want to draw on the foregoing discussion to develop an alternative ambitious constitutivist strategy. Before I do so, however, I need to highlight another constitutive feature of agency. In §2, I took a cue from

McMullin (2018) and argued that agents always take up third-person norms in light of specific first-person commitments, second-person obligations, and circumstances. Thus, balancing the claims of these three normative domains while tailoring your action to your current circumstances is an unavoidable task for all agents. In other words, the task of negotiating these plural, oft-conflicting, and incommensurable normative claims is a constitutive feature of agency as such. Moreover, this feature of agency has synchronic and diachronic dimensions. Synchronically, I have to take up *this* particular ability-to-be governed by *these* third-person norms in light of *these* first-person commitments, second-person obligations, and circumstances; and I can be assessed in the here and now by how well I do so. But this balancing act also has a diachronic dimension: my life as a whole can be assessed over time according to how well I negotiate first-, second-, and third-person normative claims.

Now I can offer a formal representation of my own proposal for an ambitious constitutivist strategy:

1. Agency is inescapable (see §1).
2. To be someone at all, I have to care about and commit to some ability-to-be (C_2).
3. Committing to the norms of an ability-to-be presupposes that I grasp my being as intrinsically normative, that is, as oriented toward distinctions of better and worse (C_3).
4. I cannot *not* transform factic givens into reasons in light of my sense of what's best (see §4).
5. To take up any ability-to-be, I must strike a balance between first-, second-, and third-person normative claims in some particular circumstances (see preceding paragraph).
6. To be an agent over time, I must strike a balance between first-, second-, and third-person normative claims across a variety of circumstances (see preceding paragraph).
7. By (1)–(6), I must aim to get the balance identified in (5) and (6) right.
8. Aiming at ϕ generates a standard of success for ϕ-ing (see §2).
9. ∴ I *should* get the balance in (5) and (6) right, as measured by the standard in (8).

Key to this argument is the claim that we must act in light of our own sense of what's best. In a number of places, Crowell, following Heidegger, cashes the idea of an intrinsic orientation toward the normative in terms of Plato's idea of the agathon (or the Good). To have an existence intrinsically oriented toward the "normative, the agathon," he claims, is to always relate to your existence "in light of what is best" (2013: 211). This doesn't mean that we are good by nature, or that we always try to act in light of some objective notion of the good, or that we try to live up to what "people in general" consider good. It means that whenever I take up an ability-to-be, I must do so in light of *my own sense* of what's best. The idea is thus very close to Price's account of the "abstract agathon," which McManus discusses in chapter 5 of this volume (133–42). Crowell agrees that to act at all, an agent must try to "identify what, for him then and there, is *the thing to do*" (Price 2011: 68; cited by McManus: 32). The difference is that Crowell offers a transcendental justification for why doing so is unavoidable.

Agency is inescapable (1). To be anything at all, I must care about and commit to some *norm*-governed ability-to-be (2); thus, my being is *intrinsically normative*—I must in every case relate to my existence in terms of distinctions of better and worse (3). And that means that I must always convert factic givens into reasons in light of *my own sense of what's best* (4). I cannot not do so. Thus, trying to identify *the thing to do* is constitutive of agency as such.

Moreover, if I must always act in light of my own sense of what's best, and I cannot avoid striking a balance between first-, second-, and third-person normative claims in a specific set of circumstances—both at a time (5) and over time (6)—then I must strike that balance in light of my own sense of what's best. In other words, I must aim to get the balance identified in (5) and (6) *right*—for aiming to get that balance right just means trying to do what's best. There's no guarantee that I will get it right, but I must try. Thus, (7) follows from (1) to (6). Moreover, I have a standard of success in aiming to get the balance in (5) and (6) right, because aiming to ϕ generates a standard of success for ϕ-ing (8).

And my conclusion in (9)? Why *should* I get the balance identified in (5) and (6) right? Because caring gives me *reasons* to act (4), and to act at all, I must try to get that balance right (7). If I have *reasons* to act, and I must aim to get that balance right to act at all, then I have reasons—i.e., I *should*—get that balance right (9).

What would getting it right look like? Broadly speaking, it would involve "successfully responding to and balancing the legitimate claims arising from the three different domains of normativity within which human beings operate, namely, the claims posed by the self, other, and shared world" (McMullin 2018: 68). Simply in virtue of being agents we face a categorical demand to get that balance right. The demand is not based on a *contingent* psychological state, nor does it get its force from some agent-independent normative truth; it's a demand we face in virtue of being agents. In other words, my argument in this section could be construed as a constitutivist justification for the phenomenological virtue ethics McMullin offers in her *Existential Flourishing* (2018).

Although my argument here is far from conclusive, I think it warrants further thought. To think it through a bit more, I close this section by testing the proposal against two standard objections to constitutivism.

The first is the objection that constitutivism derives an "ought" from an "is." Crowell offers an innovative way around this objection. On his view, no derivation of the normative from the natural is necessary, because *our being is intrinsically normative*. This isn't just an assertion. As we saw, Crowell defends the claim with a transcendental phenomenological argument: to be anything at all, we have to submit to the norms of some ability-to-be; thus, our being as such is intrinsically oriented toward normative measures of better and worse. Put otherwise, to be anything at all is to be subject to the possibility of failing to be who you're trying to be. Deriving "oughtness" from "being" isn't necessary, then, because in our case there's no norm-neutral natural fact to cover in normative plating. Our being is normative from the ground up.

The second objection is the so-called bad action problem (Railton 1997; Clark 2001): constitutivists claim that action has the constitutive feature F; they then claim that F is a constitutive standard of action; this implies that bad (or defective) action is impossible, because any action that fails to meet the standard that F provides ipso facto lacks a constitutive feature of action, and so *cannot actually be an action*.

This objection makes no contact with my argument. I never claimed that getting the balance in (5) and (6) right was constitutive of agency as such. I claimed that we have to *aim at* getting it right to act at all. Thus, the bad action problem is not a problem for my view. I can aim to get it right while getting it horribly wrong. A bad action is still an action.

5.1 Reasons to Be Authentic

Before drawing things to a close, I want to return to the question of whether we have reasons to be authentic. In section 4, I criticized Crowell's constitutivist answer to this question, but I also said that his goal—to show that we have good reasons to be authentic—should be a priority for any charitable reading of *Being and Time*. Strong normative language pervades Heidegger's discussion of authenticity; no one has sufficiently justified that language; and that fact fuels deflationary critiques of authenticity as mere "decisionistic" blather. What reasons do we have to be authentic?

We can begin to answer this question by thinking about authenticity in relation to my constitutivist argument. That argument concludes with the claim that, at a time and over time, we should aim to balance first-, second-, and third-person normative claims in light of our sense of what's best. Now I want to argue that the demand to achieve that balance also gives us reasons to be authentic, because it would be very difficult to achieve that balance without being authentic (at least much of the time). I can't make a full case for this claim here, so I will only try to motivate it in a preliminary way.

Authenticity is a stance of transparent self-ownership in which I take responsibility for the fact that my caring and commitment make certain factic givens *my* reasons. As we saw above, taking this stance toward my existence entails that I refuse to act as if my action is simply "justified by the given rules of the game"; instead, I put myself forth "as exemplary of what it means to succeed in some way of being" (Crowell 2015: 89). In doing so, I acknowledge that my reasons for what I think and do are *up to me*, that my caring transforms factic givens into my reasons in light of my own sense of what's best. Part of what's at stake in authenticity, then, is the possibility of estrangement from the grounds of my beliefs and actions. For this reason, John Haugeland (2000) translated *Eigenthlichkeit*—the Heideggerian term typically translated as authenticity—as "ownedness." This not only makes etymological sense (*eigen* means "own"); it also makes philosophical sense, because, as an authentic agent, I take ownership of my reasons for what I think and do. I don't allow myself to be determined by whichever factic givens happen to claim me or seem expedient or socially convenient at the time, losing myself "in those '*opportunities*' which are closest" (BT: 347). Instead, if I'm authentic, I determine for myself which factic givens to take as reasons, again, in light of my own sense of what's best. This is how I understand Heidegger's claim that each Dasein faces a fundamental decision "to be itself or not itself" by "taking hold or neglecting" (BT: 33). When I'm authentic, I take hold of myself by refusing to just "follow the rules of the game" as if everything were fixed in advance for me, as if I had no say regarding which factic givens I take as reasons. As an authentic agent, *I* determine for myself what it's best to think, do, and be.

There's a lot we could say about how authenticity helps us respond well to first-, second-, and third-person claims, but I'll only scratch the surface here. Let's begin with first-person normative claims. These are claims that the self, so to speak, makes on itself—the desires, goals, and intimations of a calling to become "who one is." One of the difficulties in responding well to these claims is the self's partial opacity—it can be hard to know which factic claims, if taken up, would genuinely express one's deep sense of self, and which would express mere fleeting desires, conformist tendencies, self-destructive urges, and so on. Authenticity can help us win the self-knowledge we need to make this determination. After all, to be authentic is to determine for myself which factic givens I should take as reasons in light of my own sense of what's best. Relating to factic givens authentically, then, seems important—if not necessary—if we hope to separate the first-person wheat—the claims that resonate with my deep sense of self—from the chaff—the factic givens that draw me toward thoughts and actions that I would, all things considered, reject. Given the self's partial opacity, this kind of authentic self-scrutiny is no guarantee against mistakes in these matters; but it should at least make it less likely that you'll get carried away by first-person claims that don't reflect your own sense of what's best.

Turning to second-person claims, one major challenge in interpersonal relationships is giving each other enough space for autonomous self-expression within the relationship. Therapists sometimes call this "respecting boundaries." Authenticity can help with this too. First of all, to respect another person's boundaries, one needs a strong sense of one's own. Thus, the first-person knowledge discussed above (i.e., ensuring that one takes factic givens as reasons in light of one's own sense of what's best) is important for drawing boundaries within a relationship. For example, let's say I act inauthentically and take certain gender norms as fixed, feeling compelled to conform to them, even though they are out of joint with my own all-things-considered sense of what's best. At least implicitly, this will in turn put normative pressure on my partner to adhere to the complementary set of norms, potentially breeding resentments that poison the relationship, just because I've failed to get straight about which way of being-in-the-world actually tracks with my own sense of what's best. In contrast, by being authentic and nourishing my ability to think and act in light of my own sense of what's best and refusing to allow alien grounds to determine who I am, I simultaneously improve my capacity to recognize and respect that ability in others. In Heidegger's terms, I teach myself not to "*leap in*" for and "take away 'care' from the Other" (BT: 158), and instead I "*leap ahead*" in order to help "the Other to become transparent to himself *in* his care and to become *free for* it" (BT: 159). In at least two respects, then, authenticity can help us respond well to second-person claims: (1) it can help us avoid taking up alien factic grounds that indirectly put unwelcome normative pressure on other people, and (2) it can help us better respect other people's efforts to shape their lives in light of their own sense of what's best.

Finally, in the normative domain of third-person claims, I face the difficulties of determining which norms merit my commitment and what my take on those norms will be. It seems authenticity should help us negotiate these difficulties as well. For to determine which norms merit my commitment and what my take on those norms will be, I will once again have to ward off fleeting desires and conformist tendencies, and I will have to make both calls in light of my own sense of what's best. I might not have to do this in every single case—now and then I can just get on with things and go with the flow—but, to respond well to third-person claims, much of the time I will need to take an authentic stance toward my existence.

Arguably, then, without the kind of transparent, responsible stance toward our existence that Heidegger calls authenticity, we cannot reasonably expect to successfully balance the first-, second-, and third-person normative claims that life makes on us. This isn't exactly a constitutivist argument that we have reasons to be authentic. We don't have reasons to be authentic "merely in virtue of the fact that we are agents" (Katsafanas 2016: 367). However, we do have reasons to get our existence right merely in virtue of the fact that we are agents; it's hard to imagine getting that right without being authentic (at least much of the time). If we have reasons to get our existence right, then we also have reasons to be authentic.

6. CONCLUSION

In this chapter, I recast Haugeland and Crowell's work in terms of constitutivism; I argued that we find a constitutivist account of hypothetical normativity in Haugeland's work (§2); I identified an ambitious constitutivist strategy in Crowell's work (§3); I criticized a key premise in Crowell's argument (§4); and, finally, I tried to develop an alternative Heidegger-inspired constitutivist strategy to justify a categorical normative demand to get our existence right, a demand that I argued also gives us reasons to be authentic (§5). If my attempt has failed, I hope this chapter at least calls more attention to what Heideggerian phenomenology can offer contemporary conversations about normativity and reasons.

NOTES

1. I dedicate this chapter to my friend and mentor Steve Crowell. For helpful comments on an earlier draft, I'd like to thank Bill Blattner, David Cerbone, Steve Crowell, Maxime Doyon, Sacha Golob, Gabrielle Jackson, Leslie MacAvoy, Irene McMullin, Mark Okrent, Joseph Rouse, Joseph Schear, Matthew Shockey, David Suarez, and Kate Withy. I'd also like to thank the Independent Social Research Foundation for funding the research leave during which I worked on this project.
2. *Seinkönnen* has no perfect English translation. Past attempts include "possibility," "potentiality-for-being," "practical identity," "existential ability," and "ability-to-be." I opt for the latter here.
3. For a discussion of these issues, see Burch 2018.
4. Crowell (2017b) offers his own solution to this problem by appealing to the notion of an exemplar; McMullin (this volume) speaks of a "schema." Considerations like these lie beyond the scope of my current concerns, but I consider their views broadly compatible with mine.
5. See Golob (this volume) for a helpful discussion of what makes some forms of voluntarism absurd.
6. This objection dovetails nicely with the influential "Decisionism Critique" of Heidegger's practical philosophy. For an appraisal of that critique, see Burch (2010).

7. Crowell (2017a, forthcoming) has defended Haugeland's view against this criticism in several places, arguing that the phenomenology of commitment does not entail an absurd voluntarism.

8. Thanks to Sacha Golob for calling this potential objection to my attention at the 2019 meeting of the International Society for Phenomenological Studies.

9. Kant himself seemed to recognize this. Thus, in *Religion within the Limits of Reason Alone*, he argues that full responsibility for our agency requires that we are responsible not only for our individual immoral choices but also for the condition that makes us prefer self-love to respect for the moral law. He therefore identifies "radical evil" as a supposedly freely chosen "supreme maxim" to "neglect the incentives springing from the moral law in favor of others which are not moral" (1960: 25)—a maxim whereby we systematically subordinate the claims of the moral law to the incentives of self-love. Only through such a supreme maxim, he argues, could we be fully responsible for ourselves. How Kant thought we could be responsible for this inscrutable choice is unclear. On the one hand, he calls radical evil a "natural propensity" that is "*inextirpable* by human powers" (1960: 32; original emphasis); on the other, he insists that radical evil must be understood as a product of free choice. The idea, then, looks like a philosophically unsatisfactory secularization of "original sin," another failed attempt to make us responsible for our being as such. The point here, however, is that by Kant's own lights, the IT wasn't enough to make us responsible as such. For an illuminating look at Kant's doctrine of radical evil, see McMullin (2013).

REFERENCES

Burch, Matthew. 2010. "Death and Deliberation: Overcoming the Decisionism Critique of Heidegger's Practical Philosophy." *Inquiry* 53, no. 3: 211–34.

———. 2018. "Making Sense of Akrasia." *Phenomenology and the Cognitive Sciences* 17, no. 5: 939–71.

Burch, Matthew, and Katherine Furman. 2019. "Objectivity in Science and Law: A Shared Rescue Strategy." *International Journal of Law and Psychiatry* 64: 60–70.

Clark, Philip. 2001. "Velleman's Autonomism." *Ethics* 111: 580–93.

Crowell, Steven Galt. 2001. *Husserl, Heidegger, and the Space of Meaning: Paths Toward Transcendental Phenomenology.* Evanston, IL: Northwestern University Press.

———. 2008. "Measure-Taking: Meaning and Normativity in Heidegger's Philosophy." *Continental Philosophy Review* 41, no. 3: 261–76.

———. 2013. *Normativity and Phenomenology in Husserl and Heidegger.* Cambridge: Cambridge University Press.

———. 2015. "Second-Person Phenomenology." In *The Phenomenology of Sociality: Discovering the "We,"* edited by Thomas Szanto and Dermot Moran, 70–92. London: Routledge.

———. 2017a. "Competence over Being as Existing: The Indispensability of Haugeland's Heidegger." In *Giving a Damn: Essays in Dialogue with John Haugeland*, edited by Zed Adams and Jacob Browning, 73–102. Cambridge, MA: MIT Press.

———. 2017b. "Exemplary Necessity: Heidegger, Pragmatism and Reason." In *Pragmatic Perspectives in Phenomenology*, edited by Ondrej Svec and Jakub Capek, 242–56. London: Routledge.

———. 2019. "A Philosophy of Mind: Phenomenology, Normativity, and Meaning." In *Normativity, Meaning, and the Promise of Phenomenology*, edited by Matthew Burch, Jack Marsh, and Irene McMullin, 329–54. London: Routledge.

———. Forthcoming. "Commitment: What Is Self-Binding, and How Is it Possible?"

Ferrero, Luca. 2009. "Constitutivism and the Inescapability of Agency." In *Oxford Studies in Metaethics*, Vol. 4, edited by Russ Shafer-Landau, 303–33. Oxford: Oxford University Press.

———. 2018. "Inescapability Revisited." *Manuscrito* 41, no. 4: 113–58.

Haugeland, John. 1998. *Having Thought*. Cambridge, MA: Harvard University Press.

———. 2000. "Truth and Finitude: Heidegger's Transcendental Existentialism." In *Heidegger, Authenticity, and Modernity: Essays in Honor of Hubert L. Dreyfus*, Vol. 1, edited by Mark Wrathall and Jeff Malpas, 43–77. Cambridge, MA: MIT Press.

Kant, Immanuel. 1960. *Religion within the Limits of Reason Alone*. Translated by Theodore M. Greene and Hoyt H. Hudson. New York: Harper & Brothers.

Katsafanas, Paul. 2013. *Agency and the Foundations of Ethics: Nietzschean Constitutivism*. Oxford: Oxford University Press.

———. 2016. "Constitutivism about Practical Reasons." In *Oxford Handbook of Reasons and Normativity*, edited by Daniel Star, 367–94. Oxford: Oxford University Press.

Korsgaard, Christine M. 2009. *Self-Constitution: Agency, Identity, and Integrity*. Oxford: Oxford University Press.

Lance, Mark. 2015. "Life Is Not a Box-Score." In *Meaning Without Representation: Essays on Truth, Expression, Normativity, and Naturalism*, edited by Stephen Gross, Nicholas Tebben, and Michael Williams, 279–306. Oxford: Oxford University Press.

McDowell, John. 2007. "What Myth?" *Inquiry* 50, no. 4: 338–51.

McManus, Denis. Forthcoming. "On a Judgment of One's Own: Heideggerian Authenticity, Standpoints, and All Things Considered." *Mind*. https://doi.org/10.1093/mind/fzx045.

McMullin, Irene. 2013. "Kant on Radical Evil and the Origin of Moral Responsibility." *Kantian Review* 18, no. 1: 49–72.

———. 2018. *Existential Flourishing: A Phenomenology of the Virtues*. Cambridge: Cambridge University Press.

Price, A. W. 2011. *Virtue and Reason in Plato and Aristotle*. Oxford: Oxford University Press.

Railton, Peter. 1997. "On the Hypothetical and Non-Hypothetical in Reasoning about Belief and Action." In *Ethics and Practical Reason*, edited by Garrett Cullity and Berys Nigel Gaut, 53–79. Oxford: Oxford University Press.

Smith, Michael. 2015. "The Magic of Constitutivism." *American Philosophical Quarterly*, 52, no. 2: 187–200.

Tugendhat, Ernst. 1986. *Self-Consciousness and Self-Determination*. Translated by Paul Stern. Cambridge, MA: MIT Press.

Velleman, J. David. 2009. *How We Get Along*. New York: Cambridge University Press.

Part II

PRACTICAL DELIBERATION AND THE UNITY OF AGENCY

Chapter 5

Heidegger and Aristotle on Reason, Choice, and Self-Expression

On Decisionists, Nihilists, and Pluralists

Denis McManus

1. SELF-EXPRESSION AS THE TRANSCENDENCE OF REASON

Decisionist readings of Heidegger's discussion of authenticity set him in a familiar historical narrative, which runs from Kant through Nietzsche to Sartre. Radicalizing the insistence that heteronomy—our acting on principles that are not "our own"—is a life beneath "the dignity of a human being and of every rational nature" (Kant 2012: 52, 48), there can be for the authentic individual "no Good nor Evil unless he [brings] them into being" (Sartre 1986: 243): "each one of us should devise *his own* virtue, *his own* categorical imperative," an "invention" expressive of a "deep personal choice" (Nietzsche 1968: sec. 11).[1] Only through such a choice does one truly express *oneself* and become capable of truly acting on one's own behalf—rather than, say, acting out the collective wishes of one's community that one has uncritically accepted. As Michael Friedman puts it in his reading of Heidegger, rather than merely following dictates "taken up unquestioningly from tradition or society," when authentic, I recognize that

> [my] normal or everyday practical context is simply one possibility among others, *one which is thereby subject to [my] own free choice*. . . . [This] opens up the possibility of a very particular kind of liberation—the possibility of a truly "authentic" existence in which [my] own choices and decisions rest on no taken for granted background framework at all. (Friedman 2000: 51)

125

One way in which such a framework can be—heteronomously—taken for granted is by seeing it as expressive of supposedly objective values; a refusal to project such values on to what is, in fact, a value-free world—or so the story goes—then seems a requirement for that choice that is our free self-expression to exist: as Iris Murdoch puts it in her critical reflections on such decisionism, "[i]f the will is to be totally free the world it moves in must be devoid of normative characteristics" (1970: 42).

Decisionist readings of Heidegger such as Friedman's are not without foundation. Heidegger depicts the authentic as somehow distinctively choosing for themselves, while inauthenticity "relieves Dasein of th[at] task," of "all choosing and deciding" (HCT: 247). He tells us that "Dasein can *choose itself* and determine its existence primarily and chiefly from that choice, that is, it can exist authentically" (BP: 170, cf. HCT: 319):

> *Dasein* can comport itself in such a way that it chooses between itself and the world; it can make each decision on the basis of what it encounters in the world, or it can rely on itself. *Dasein's* possibility of choosing offers the possibility of fetching itself back from its having become lost in the world, that is, from its publicness. When *Dasein* has chosen itself, it has thereby chosen both itself and choice. (WDR: 168)

Rather than rely on supposedly objectively available values—"relying on the world"—or the established opinions of one's community—on a "public" through which Dasein would "let itself be determined in its being by others and thus exist *inauthentically*" (BP: 170)—authentic Dasein makes up its own mind, relying only on itself. Only "in terms of that potentiality-for-Being which it has chosen" does Dasein "let[] its ownmost Self *take action in itself*," its "ownmost Self tak[ing] action in itself of its own accord" (SZ: 268, 295).[2]

Moreover, Heidegger can seem to endorse the nihilist denial of objective, normative reasons upon which decisionism and its account of free self-expressive agency rest, most obviously in his remarks on anxiety. Heidegger tells us that "[a]nxiety reveals an insignificance of the world" (SZ: 343). "[W]hat is environmentally ready-to-hand," which Heidegger typically identifies with entities with which we can actively engage, "sinks away" and an "utter insignificance . . . makes itself known," the "insignificance of what is within-the-world" (SZ 187). Most commentators understandably take such remarks to describe "an experience of utter meaninglessness" (Dahlstrom 2013: 208), one in which "all meaning and mattering slip away" (Dreyfus and Rubin 1991: 332). If we take this experience to be a veridical experience of our world,[3] then we seem to witness a stripping of "normative characteristics" from that world, a denial of the normative reasons for action that they might seem to provide; and the insight that Heidegger seems to be trying to convey through such remarks he ties closely to the requirement that Dasein instead "rely on itself":

> In anxiety there lies the possibility of a disclosure which is quite distinctive; for anxiety individualises. This individualisation brings *Dasein* back from its falling, and makes manifest to it that authenticity and inauthenticity are possibilities of its Being. These basic possibilities of *Dasein* ... show themselves in anxiety as they are in themselves—undisguised by entities within-the-world, to which, proximally and for the most part, *Dasein* clings [*klammert*]. (SZ: 190–91)

"Anxiety," Heidegger tells us, "makes manifest in *Dasein* . . . its *Being-free for* the freedom of choosing itself and taking hold of itself" (SZ: 188).[4]

But as critics such as Murdoch have pointed out, decisionism is deeply problematic. If the decisions it envisages do not rest on reasons of some sort, then they seem to be arbitrary: "I may as well toss a coin" (Murdoch 1970: 91). And why think of these choices as somehow distinctively expressive of *me*? As Ernst Tugendhat puts it, "A choice ... that is not made in the light of reasons ... is a choice in which I leave how I choose to accident; and in this respect we have to say that it was not I who chose" (Tugendhat 1986: 216). The decisionist believes that only by transcending reason—denying its authority—can we save free, self-expressive agency. But this renders the "pure choices" that are left the "wild leap[ing]" of a "substanceless will" (Murdoch 1970: 8, 16, 27). In such moments, "are we really choosing at all," and "are we right indeed to identify *ourselves* with this giddy empty will?" (1970: 8, 36). It is unclear then why we should think of this supposedly "deep personal choice" as deep or personal.

In light of such criticisms, today most commentators on Heidegger's discussion of authenticity see their task as that of explaining why decisionist readings are mistaken. Indeed "decision" has become something of a dirty word in the literature, as has "choice." But if we are to understand Heidegger's stress on these notions not as expressive of decisionism and his discussion of anxiety not as expressive of a normative nihilism that might underpin such a decisionism, how ought we to understand these striking features of Heidegger's work?

What makes our interpretive task more difficult is the fact that notions such as "choice" are themselves philosophically perplexing. Richard Holton has recently observed that choice is an "under-explored phenomenon" (2006: 2). That might seem an odd claim given its central role in the free will literature. But choice is, one might say, puzzling in its own right, in particular with respect to how it stands to other mental states. For example, consider Holton's presentation of a trilemma. If choices merely express a "judgment of what is best" "determined by our prior beliefs and desires," then choice can seem simply redundant, "constrained by th[at] judgment" and "no more than an echo" of those beliefs and desires (Holton 2006: 6, 4). This is unappealing inasmuch as it seems to rob us of our sense that choice is special in having a close connection of some sort with *self*-expression. It can appear that the agent herself has been "left out of the picture," at best a "passive vessel" "pushed along by [her] beliefs and desires" and with no "*discretionary* contribution" to how she behaves: "there is no place for an independent contribution from an act of choice" (Holton 2009: 55, 57). But if instead choices are *not* determined by—do not simply echo—a judgment of what is best, we seem to have only two remaining options, neither of which appeals: either there is some issue here beyond such judgment—in which case, as Holton echoes Murdoch and Tugendhat, "how can choosing ever be more than arbitrary picking?"—or choice is simply that which makes it possible for us to "fail to make that echo"—in which case our capacity for choice has become "a *liability*," the capacity to "fail[] to do that which we judge best" (Holton 2006: 7, 6, cf. 2009: 58).[5] Efforts to arrive at a sympathetic reading of Heidegger depend then on our also making some progress at least with this philosophical issue.

2. RECONTEXTUALIZING HEIDEGGER: ON MISTAKING AN ARISTOTELIAN FOR A DECISIONIST NIHILIST

As indicated above, decisionist readings assign *Being and Time* a familiar place in a certain reading of the history of philosophy. But the subsequent publication of other works of his from the 1920s suggests a rather different story, identifying influences on Heidegger's thought that were largely invisible in the years in which decisionist readings became popular. A crucial influence is a figure, who, as Anthony Price has recently put it, also "aims to bring to light . . . the focal importance" not only of "*action* . . . as the mode by which we express our moral character" but also, "for each agent, of *acting oneself*" (Price 2011: 315).[6] That figure is Aristotle.[7]

Steven Galt Crowell has recently claimed that "it has become something of a commonplace to see *Being and Time* as an existential re-working of Aristotle's practical philosophy" (2015: 284) and what I offer here can indeed be described in those terms too.[8] But continuing to pursue such an approach promises to be productive, I believe, because continuing to read Aristotle is: as one might put the point, we are still finding out what Aristotle's practical philosophy is and, hence, what *Being and Time* as an existential reworking of it would be. A claim I have defended elsewhere,[9] and will develop further here, is that Aristotle's *phronimos* provides a model for Heidegger of authentic Dasein. Other commentators certainly have made the same claim; but the accounts of authenticity that we offer differ because we understand *phronêsis* differently.[10] Aristotle clearly influenced Heidegger profoundly. But what that tells us about the latter's thought depends on how we—and the latter—understand the former; and in what follows we will touch on a number of other controversies in the Aristotle literature.[11]

I argue below that, in his 1920s lectures on Aristotle, Heidegger sets out an account of something one could naturally call "authenticity," understood as a readiness to bring to bear one's own judgment on how to act best in situations in which one finds oneself. The first half of the chapter presents themes that emerge in those lectures. The theme of section 3 is that establishing a determinate sense of how to act depends on the identification of an all-encompassing good, although it ends by noting remarks of Heidegger's that seem to deny that there can be such a thing. Section 4 identifies two different ways in which one might understand such a good, drawing on a distinction identified in the Anglophone Aristotle literature; and section 5 then argues that Heidegger's apparently conflicting remarks address these different understandings of the good: "the good" that Heidegger denies he denies on the basis of an Aristotelian normative pluralism, and "the good" that he affirms is the abstract good, "what is best here and now," which—through its weighing of diverse concrete goods—*phronêsis* identifies. The significance of this seemingly thin good—I go on to argue—is that the authentic act in light of it and the inauthentic do not.

On the basis of this claim, the second half of the chapter provides an alternative interpretation of those features of Heidegger's discussion that inspire decisionist readings. Section 6 argues that acting in light of the above abstract good requires free, self-expressive choice—in Aristotle's vocabulary, "*proairesis*." But this choice does not require that room be made for it by a normative nihilism—by our transcending reason in order to be free, and ourselves. Instead it requires that we draw all our many reasons together in a judgment of what is best. The discussion of Heidegger's most evocative of normative nihilism—that of anxiety—is also better understood, section 7 argues, in light of sections 3–5's Aristotelian themes. No concrete, "inner-worldly" good that we encounter can determine "what is best here and now," because that depends on *all* of the concrete goods that we find around ourselves; only an agent who addresses that set as a whole—that weighs the totality of reasons that her situation presents—can determine what realizes here and now that abstract good. That judgment, as section 6 argues, comes in the form of a necessarily self-expressive choice; and thus the experience that Heidegger calls "being-anxious" that, first, reveals the "insignificance of what is within-the-world" by, second, "disclos[ing], primordially and directly, the world as world [*die Welt als Welt*]," also, third, "individualises"

Dasein (SZ: 187, 186, cf. SZ: 188). Heidegger's "failure" to identify "concrete (ontic) determinations, perhaps even norms, for being-here and being-with-others" that might characterize the life of the authentic is not then, as Daniel Dahlstrom has proposed, a failure to "adequately clarify" "the factical ideal of a death-anticipating resoluteness" (2015: 157). Nor does it show that, in light of a normative nihilism's "very particular kind of liberation," the authentic "invent" their own Good and Evil.[12] Rather, the authentic are distinctive in pursuing the abstract good, "what is best."

3. THE NEED FOR AN ENCOMPASSING GOOD

Phronêsis guides action in the light of an understanding not of particular goals—of "what sorts of things promote health or strength, for instance"— but of "living well in general," as Irwin translates a key passage (NE 6.5 1140a25–31, cf. 6.2 1139b1–4). As Heidegger puts it, the *phronimos* acts not "in relation to particular *Beiträglichkeiten* which promote Dasein in a particular regard"—particular ways in which one's acts might be conducive to the achievement of particular objectives or the satisfaction of obligations associated with particular roles one occupies—but instead with regard to how Dasein should act "as such and as a whole [*als solchen im Ganzen*]" (PS: 34).

Heidegger explains the need for such an all-encompassing goal in a striking discussion in his 1924 *Basic Concepts of Aristotelian Philosophy*.[13] Heidegger tells us that "the world in which human beings move themselves is encountered . . . in the character of the *sumpheron*"—the term that Heidegger translates as the *Beiträglich*, and his translators as "the conducive" (BCArP: 41)—the objects around us presenting themselves to us as soliciting acts that serve particular ends. But for us human beings, "a *manifoldness of concerns* is given" and, "with this manifoldness of concerns, there will also be a *manifoldness of tele* at which concern reaches its end," at which we aim (BCArP: 49).[14] For this manifold to be "not a mere aggregate" or "heap [*Menge*]" of *tele*—of goals—it must be the case, Heidegger tells us, that "among these concerns a certain *guiding* appears": "a *guiding connectedness* is presupposed by the manifold of concerns" such that "there is thus one whole manifoldness [*eine ganze Mannigfaltigkeit*] of concern," rather than a "mere heap" (BCArP: 49, 50, cf. 63). Here, Heidegger proposes, we see why "Aristotle says that there must be . . . a telos that is *di auto*"—"a *telos* with which we are concerned 'for its own sake'" and that "encompasses the others, encloses them in itself" (BCArP: 51, cf. NE 1.2 1094b6). Heidegger identifies this with the *agathon*, which is standardly translated in English as "the good." As "the being of human beings . . . is determined by a manifoldness of *praxeis*," they must "have a guiding connectedness among them, so that one finds an *akrotaton agathon*, 'highest good,' implicit in them, an *agathon* that is *di auto*" (BCArP: 59).

But why must there be such a thing? Why can't our *tele* merely be a "heap"? Heidegger's discussion suggests a reason. Without such an encompassing *agathon*, the significance of any member of our "*manifoldness of concerns*" is moot: "Action *x* may well be conducive to goal *y* . . . but so what?" one might ask, as achieving that *telos* might be incompatible with the achievement of others to which we are committed: the maintenance of one's health, for example, might clash with fulfilling one's obligations to others or nurturing one's talents. If one is to determine what one should do, these *tele* must then be brought together through an ordering or "guiding connectedness," one that would settle which *telos* ought to be pursued at the expense of the rest. The many solicitations of the *Beiträglichen* lack significance *in themselves*, one might say, because, without an encompassing *agathon*, their significance remains indeterminate. If Dasein "obtains no *peras*"—fails to throw a limit or boundary around its concerns to draw them together in "one whole manifoldness"—then its concern "becomes . . . empty and vain" (BCArP: 64, 51, quoting NE 1.2 1094a19–21). "The completion [*Vollzug*] of concern is only possible in that . . . the concern is not grasping at straws [*ins Leere greift*]"; only if "that concern has the character of the *peras* . . . is it possible for a concern in general to come into its being" (BCArP 51). Such an encompassing good is a horizon for the weighing of the multiple *tele* that we find given and an evaluative selecting from among the many *praxeis* that the entities we find around us—understood in light of those *tele*—solicit. In light of such an *agathon*, a determinate concern—a determinate sense of what should be done—can "come into being"; otherwise, one's concern remains "empty and vain," "*grasping at straws*."

Yet isn't it one of the most striking respects in which Heidegger and Aristotle *differ* that the latter believes that there is such a highest good—and goes to some lengths to explain what it is in, for example, his discussions of *eudaimonia*, "the mean," *theoria*, and a supposed defining *ergon* for human beings—whereas the former doesn't? Put another way, isn't it implausible that *phronêsis*—which guides our actions in light of "living well in general"—should play an important role in Heidegger's thought when he seems to disavow any attempt to provide us with a substantive, general account of— "some concrete (ontic) determinations, perhaps even norms, for"—"living well in general"?[15] There are points in the discussion presented above at which Heidegger seems to try to persuade us that Aristotle doesn't either; he claims that "Aristotle comes to the conclusion that there cannot be a good in itself," that "a 'good in general [*Guten überhaupt*]' makes no sense" (BCArP: 207, 55).[16] But isn't that just one more example to cite for those who think Heidegger an utterly unreliable reader of his forebears? I think not, and to see why, let us note a distinction that the Anglophone literature on Aristotle has marked. It has been articulated with reference to his notion of "*eudaimonia*" in particular, but I suggest it can help us understand Heidegger's reflections on the *agathon* too.[17]

4. TWO UNDERSTANDINGS OF THE GOOD—ABSTRACT AND CONCRETE

J. L. Austin proposed that "Aristotle means to ask firstly: what is the analysis or definition of *eudaimonia*? And secondly: what life . . . satisfies that definition or specification?" (1961: 16). This points us to two different ways in which one might take an interest in *eudaimonia*: it is one thing, as Austin puts it, to ask "what fills the bill" and another what the bill to be filled is (16). For example, while one might understand *eudaimonia* as the abstract goal of "living well" or "acting well," "[w]hat *counts as* [doing so] from context to context is concrete and variable," as Price puts it (2011: 4).

Despite the widely held sentiments with which the last paragraph of the last section began, opinions differ quite markedly on whether Aristotle believed it was possible to specify a *concrete* understanding of "living well" in general terms. One view—that renderings of *eudaimonia* as "happiness" or "human flourishing" might encourage—is that he believed in what Sarah Broadie has called a "grand end": "an explicit, comprehensive, substantial vision of th[e] good," a "blueprint of the good [that] guides its possessor in all his deliberations, and in terms [that] his rational choices can be explained and justified" (Broadie 1991: 198). Rejecting such a reading—as Broadie does and, the next section will suggest, Heidegger does—leaves open a range of possible views.[18] But let us consider first how the abstract objective of "living well" is specified.

An interesting property of this objective is that *all* who decide how to act share it. They may differ in what they think "living well" amounts to in concrete terms here and now. But they aim to act in a way that they deem to be their acting well, seeking what they seek "under the guise of the good," as the current rendering of the medieval slogan goes. As Price puts it, "Acting well . . . is the end inherent in all deliberate action. The kernel of this is simply that, in deliberating, an agent tries to identify what, for him then and there, is *the thing to do*" (Price 2011: 68). This endows this abstract objective with a further interesting property: it is not an objective that one might question or for which one might propose a better alternative. As Anselm Müller argues, "[i]t would not be up to me not to tend towards this aim . . . for *any* option I took would already be inspired by *it*" (1989: 236). Any alternative would only be pursued because I deemed it better, deeming it instead to be what it is to act well here and now, "*the thing to do*." Hence, one might say of the latter, "It is an aim I do not *set* myself. It is there as soon as I am there; it is as little of my choosing as my existence is; it is somehow set before me" (Müller 1989: 238). As Price puts it, the abstract objective of "living well" is then "*the* good of choice and action," although this is a "pure object of will" rather than a substantive, concrete end; it is a "bare abstraction," "the mere notion of *the thing to do*" (Price 2011: 39, 5, 68). Following Müller (1989: 236), Price suggests that "living well" serves as the goal for our actions as the truth serves as the goal for belief. But the question "Why do you believe that *p*, rather than that *q*?" is not happily answered by replying, "Because it is true that *p*, but not that *q*" (Price 2011: 23). In this sense, "living well" "isn't a reason for doing one thing rather than another" and so "doesn't properly belong *within* practical reasoning at all" (Price 2011: 40n8).[19]

This might tempt one to say that there is nothing here worth discussing in the "bare logic" of this "thinnest of abstractions" (Price 2011: 76, 221). But that would be mistaken. "[T]here *is* no choice unless *eudaimonia* is the goal," understood as the "bare target of acting well" (Price 2011: 211, 5). But what makes it a significant normative goal, nonetheless, is that I may fail to choose. Sometimes such a failure is forced upon us, such as when sudden stimuli call for immediate reactions: as Aristotle says, we do not describe "acts done on the spur of the moment . . . as chosen" (NE 3.2 1111b9–10). Hence, Price proposes that the good is *the* aim of action only where we have in mind "action in a restricted," "privileged" or "rich sense," specifically that in which "all action is chosen" (Price 2011: 39, 2, 80, cf. 40 and 46). In what follows, I will suggest that Heidegger's distinction of authenticity from inauthenticity identifies another way in which action may be impoverished, the result of another way in which we may fail to choose.

What I propose is that the *agathon* that Heidegger depicts as essential if our concern is not to be "empty and vain" is essentially Price's "bare abstraction," which I will suggest we understand at least in the context of Heidegger's thought, as "what matters most" or "is best here and now"; and the "good in general" that Heidegger denies is Broadie's "grand end," the dream of a substantive and general "blueprint" for what concretely satisfies that abstraction in any particular situation. Crucially, as we will see, some think Aristotle himself denied that there is such a thing, and called thereby for neither normative nihilism nor decisionist "pure choice," commitments that—as section 1 argued—we would do well to spare Heidegger too.

5. AN ABSTRACT *AGATHON* AFFIRMED AND A CONCRETE *AGATHON* DENIED

As I indicated at the end of section 3, in the context of the argument presented there, Heidegger's rejection of a "good in general" is puzzling, and he elaborates on this rejection in what can seem equally puzzling ways. He says of such a "good," "And if there were such a thing, it would not settle anything. Useless!" (BCArP: 253, cf. EE 1.8 1217b25). In contemplating some "good that hovers over being," "there would be nothing there for *praxis* to be concerned about," because "the view of *praxis* goes right to . . . the 'here and now' under such and such circumstances"; "*[a]gathon* is in itself always *peras* of a *praxis*, and this *praxis* is, however, here and now" (BCArP: 207, 208, 55, cf. also BCArP: 95 and PS: 96). What is puzzling about these claims is why they should be taken to show that "a 'good in general' makes no sense": a central hope in the history of moral philosophy has been to identify a good in general that would precisely—and usefully—settle what it would be good to do here and now by subsuming such particular situations under a broader claim about what it is good in general to do.

To understand Heidegger's remarks, we need to recognize, I believe, the influence of a broader Aristotelian claim about our normative predicament that I believe he inherits: as another important neo-Aristotelian puts this claim, "practical worthwhileness is multi-dimensional" (McDowell 1998: 41). Human lives are subject to multiple norms interacting in complex ways, with some trumping others in some situations and being trumped by others in others; as a result, as McDowell proposes, it is "hardly plausible that a conception of how a human being should live could be fully captured in terms of . . . universal prohibitions" (1998: 27n9), or indeed prescriptions. As Heidegger would seem to make the point, "*[f]or our being, . . . no unique and absolute norm can be given*" (BCArP: 126).[20] As we saw in section 3, for us human beings "a *manifoldness of concerns* is given," "a *manifoldness of tele*"; affirming this is precisely one way in which one might deny that there is a "good in general" in the form of a concrete "grand aim." This is not to deny that there is such a thing as "what is best" in any particular situation, but rather that there is much that can be said of a general nature and in concrete terms about such things. As Heidegger renders NE 2.2 1104a6–9, "[t]here is no *paraggelia* [set of instructions], something like a universal military field order, an *a priori* ethics, by which humanity becomes better *eo ipso*"; instead "[e]veryone must have, for himself, his eyes trained on that which is at the moment and which matters to him" (BCArP: 123). In the absence of such a "blueprint," the challenge we face is, I suggest, that of weighing multiple, competing normative demands in order to establish which matters most in each here and now in which we find ourselves.[21] Doing so is the work of *phronêsis*, which "disclos[es] the concrete individual possibilities of the being of Dasein"—the many *Beiträglichkeiten* that its situation presents and the many courses of action they would solicit—with a view to uncovering "what is best among th[ose] possible actions" (PS: 96, 95).

"What is best here and now" is the abstract *agathon* that Heidegger retains and that informs his understanding of authenticity, or so I propose: "The being-character of the *agathon*," Heidegger declares, "is oriented to the *kairos*, determined by its position" (BCArP: 208)—the here and now in which one finds oneself. This *telos* shares with Price's "pure object of will" that it is not one end of choice among others, such that it might be questioned or an alternative proposed. A question that section 3's discussion may have raised concerns the standard set there for concern "coming into being." That we must act on a consideration that *nothing* can trump—a *telos* that not only "encompasses the others . . . in itself" but "is *di auto*"—may have struck the reader as an odd and implausibly demanding thought. Certainly it is a struggle to identify any plausible, *concrete* candidate: to take two apposite proposals, neither happiness nor flourishing—if identified in concrete terms—will clearly do. But the abstract *agathon* that is "what is best here and now" meets that demand, because—to adapt a related thought of David Wiggins's— "nothing suitable by way of practical or ethical concern . . . would be left over (outside the ambit of [this *telos*])" (1987: 223) on the basis of which it might be challenged: there is nothing left over that might trump "what is best," so this *telos* is indeed "*the* good of choice and action."

6. *PHRONÊSIS* AND *PROAIRESIS*: CHOICE AND SELF-EXPRESSION REVISITED

The remainder of the chapter will argue that the aspects of Heidegger's texts that inspire decisionist nihilist readings make better sense if we read them in light of the above Aristotelian concerns and their distinction between the *agathon* as abstract and as concrete. Section 7 will make that case for Heidegger's reflections on anxiety, the present section for the role in authenticity that he ascribes to choice.

The reader will have noticed how the—or at least, a—notion of "choice" has quietly inserted itself into our discussion—of "*the* good of choice and action"—and *phronêsis* is "a task . . . that must be seized in a *proairesis*" (PS: 36), typically translated as "choice" or "decision."[22] Crucially, though, this is a non-decisionist conception of choice. While the decisionist calls for a choice that is the expression of "pure will"—one that transcends reasons— "[f]or Aristotle," Price proposes, "to choose an act is also to judge that *it is to be done*" because "choice is of something one discriminates as *best*" (Price 2011: 310, 121).[23] Aristotle offers a "dual characterisation of choice" (Price 2011: 197): "all choice is of something and for the sake of something" (EE 2.11 1227b36–37, cf. 2.10 1226a11–13 and Price 2011: 121, 215). As

Heidegger puts it, "*[p]roairesis* always aims at a *prakton agathon*" (BCArP 100). From this perspective, that decisionism runs into the profound problems that section 1 identified is no surprise: whatever act of will or inner exertion one performs with "no taken for granted background framework at all"—with no *prakton agathon* in view—it can be, at best, one might say, half a choice.[24]

But what does the making of such judgments have to do with authenticity? Indeed, typical translation or not, if *proairesis* is the making of such judgments, what does it have to do with *choice*? Doesn't this simply leave us on the first horn of Holton's trilemma, rendering choice a redundant "echo" of judgment?[25] Key to answering these questions, I believe, is recognition of an alternative conception of self-expression, one that understands it precisely as judging what is best and that Heidegger also finds in Aristotle.

In the BCArP lectures, we find an argument arising out of Heidegger's reading of Aristotle's *Rhetoric* (and R 2.1 1378a in particular) that identifies exercise of *phronêsis* precisely with arriving at a judgment that is truly one's own. Heidegger asks what it takes for "we as hearers [to] take [a] speaker to be *himself* bearing witness to the matter that he represents"—to judge "that the speaker speaks for the matter *with his person* [*mit seiner Person*]" (BCArP: 112). In settling this, Heidegger returns to now-familiar notions: "He can ... recommend something as *sumpheron* that he believes is *sumpheron*, and yet ... the hearer can notice in the course of discourse that the speaker does not bring himself to say what is best" (BCArP: 112). "In the counsel he delivers," the speaker "holds back what his *phronêsis* makes available to him"—"puts at his disposal [*die er aus seiner phronêsis heraus verfügt*]": "[h]e is satisfied with presenting ... a serious proposal, though not the best" (BCArP: 112)—the *sumpheron* but not the *agathon*. As a result, the hearer "withdraws his trust from the speaker," because the speaker "screens his own position" (BCArP: 112). But why say that? In what sense is a speaker who sincerely recommends something as conducive to some particular end—"something as *sumpheron* that he believes is *sumpheron*"—"screening his own position"?

We see a sense in which he does so when we note that we can respond to his recommendation with the question, "Yes, but what do *you* think ought to be done?" (To return to a notion from section 3, we can ask of his recommendation, "So what?") That which the speaker has said so far leaves indeterminate what one might then naturally call his "own view." The same follow-up question would not seem to make sense, however, were he to "bring himself to say what is best" and present it as such. Rather, there would be something akin to Moore's paradox in adding to such a statement "though that is not what *I* think ought to be done." When the speaker "recommends something as *sumpheron* that he believes is *sumpheron*," there is room, so to speak, for such a further clause distinguishing that which is recommended from what he might believe to be—and might yet present as—the *agathon*, as that further clause may express some further thought or valuation of the speaker's: as Heidegger puts it, the speaker then "does not say everything" and it is possible that he "knows still more" (BCArP: 112). But if instead the speaker "bring[s] himself to say what is best," then he "presents himself in what he says" (BCArP: 112): to articulate what one takes to be not merely *sumpheron* but the *agathon* is to express oneself. To fail to do so can take a superficial form and a deep form, where the latter connects at most indirectly with interpersonal trust or lack thereof. The superficial form is a lie: my hiding from others what I think is best. The deep form, I suggest, is inauthenticity, where that is hiding from myself—and hence also perhaps others, although only derivatively—by failing to *settle* what I myself think, failing to *decide* what is best.[26]

This outcome is not, I think, as counterintuitive as it might seem: if I am asked whether I have expressed my own view of what should be done, I am asked whether there are other thoughts or feelings I have about my situation that I have yet to bring to bear. I am being asked whether I have "presented myself in what I have said," or might instead have "not said everything" and "know still more": have I expressed *all* of myself, or merely a part?

Moreover, this tallies neatly, of course, with Heidegger's depiction of authentic existence as "being-a-whole," while inauthentic life is one of "dispersal": "the inauthentic being of Dasein" is "*als unganzes*"—as "*less* than a *whole*," or as Stambaugh puts it, "fragmentary" (SZ: 233, 235, 371). This fragmentation manifests itself in a distinctive myopia, of which our discussion above also makes sense. Rather than address the full range of demands that its situation places upon it—rather than "gaze directly and concernfully at life"—Dasein "take[s] easy refuge in . . . the supposedly indispensable resolution" of "some pressing mundane task [*welthafte Dringlichkeit*] or other" (PIA: 92). *Phronêsis*, Heidegger claims, is "involved in a constant struggle against a tendency to concealment residing at the heart of Dasein," a "tendency to be concerned" "with things of minor importance [*nebensächliche Dinge*]" (PS: 36–37). Similarly, Heidegger later depicts the inauthentic person as "understand[ing] himself in terms of those very closest events and be-fallings which he encounters . . . and which thrust themselves upon him"; he "abandon[s] [him]self to whatever the day may bring," to "what is proximally at [his] everyday disposal," "distracted by"—"*entangled* in," "lost in"—"the objects of [his] closest concern" (SZ: 410, 345, 195, 338; HCT: 281), rather than determining in light of the full range of possible actions actually available to him which would be best.[27] Inauthentic Dasein has "not authentically chosen"; instead it "allow[s] itself to be chosen by whatever it [has] immersed itself in" (CTR: 50, 45).

According to the above vision, the authentic person differs—chooses rather than being chosen—in making an overall judgment of the demands for action that her situation makes upon her: she takes a position on these multiple *tele* in a unifying judgment of what matters most, collapsing what is otherwise a "mere aggregate" in an "encompassing," "guiding connectedness." Until she does, she reacts as no more than a part—a fragment—of herself: herself as a professor, a mother, a daughter, a socialist, etc. Only in a phronetic judgment of what is best do we see "the bursting forth of the acting person as such" (PS: 103), a person truly "act[ing] from out of himself" (BCArP: 123).

To return then to our earlier worry, the choices distinctive of the authentic are indeed judgments but not *mere* judgments, in that they bear two features that section 1 identified as key to why choice seems to matter to us: these judgments distinctively embody free self-expression.[28] Rather than expressing some unique "own voice" that somehow stands apart from, or transcends, the reasons one has—making some "independent," "*discretionary* contribution" (Holton, quoted earlier)—one expresses oneself when one judges what is best, in that one brings all of one's beliefs and desires to bear on one's situation; none are silenced, one might say.[29] Such judgments can also be seen as self-determination, as expressive of freedom: I decide for myself, on the basis of my own judgment. I do so when I look to see what is best—to see clearly for myself the situation in which I find myself. This is, however, "a finite freedom," as Heidegger says in a striking passage late in *Being and Time*; when authentic,

> Dasein understands itself in its own *superior power* [*Übermacht*], the power of its finite freedom, so that in this freedom, which "is" only in its having chosen to make such a choice, it can take over the *powerlessness* [*Ohnmacht*] of being abandoned to itself and come to have a clear vision for the accidents [*Zufälle*] of the Situation that has been disclosed. (SZ: 384)

This is a freedom that requires not that I transcend or deny reason but rather an openness to my many reasons and them as a whole. I exercise my freedom by looking for myself; but this power is a finite freedom in that, in exercising it, I direct myself to the situation in which I find myself, to the judging of which I am "abandoned." If I choose for myself, I look for myself; but I do not choose what I then see before me: my freedom "'is' only in [my] having chosen to make such a choice."[30]

Finally, in this section, let us note one further feature of Heidegger's depiction of authenticity that has taken on a natural sense. I have offered elsewhere an account of how some of the key concepts that we find in Heidegger's discussion of authenticity can be understood as articulating the vision set out above.[31] One example is that authentic Dasein can be seen to distinctively exhibit "resolution"—*Entschlossenheit*—in being true to its own judgment, deploying its capacity to judge for itself. Commentators have proposed that a further note that Heidegger may want us to hear in selecting this particular term is one of openness—*Ent-schlossenheit* is an un-closedness[32]—and the above vision accounts for that too. The *phronimos*, Heidegger tells us, "act[s] in the full situation within which it acts," in light of "the situation in the largest sense" (PS: 101); and the resultant *proairesis* is an "[o]rientation towards the whole moment" (BCArP: 98). The authentic agent does not subsume her situation myopically under the requirements of some role or the pursuit of some *telos*, but instead is open to all the ways in which her situation solicits action from her through her multiple roles and *tele*.

But what our presentation of these ideas here adds is a way of accommodating a further clear resonance of *Entschlossenheit*: this openness comes in the form of a readiness for *Entschluss*—for decision or choice. Heidegger translates *proairesis* as *Entschlossensein*—which his translators have rendered as "being-resolved" (see, e.g., BCArP: 98)—and as *Sichentschliessen*—his translators offering for that "resolving-oneself" (see, e.g., BCArP: 99), although "deciding," "choosing," and "making up one's mind" are equally natural: thus, "that I am resolved that a matter be done thus and so is *proairesis*" (BCArP: 97). In seeking to escape the suspicion of decisionism, commentators have been reluctant to acknowledge this further clear connection—that *Entschlossenheit* is a life of *Entschluss*. But decisionism does not own that notion and our Aristotelian account rehabilitates it, making it no longer the dirty word that in reaction to decisionism it has become.[33]

7. DISCLOSING THE WORLD AS AN ENCOMPASSING WHOLE INDIVIDUALIZES DASEIN: ANXIETY REVISITED

Our discussion above has exposed a question that we face that the citing of what one might call "innerworldly" achievements cannot answer; and this provides us with a new way of looking at anxiety, the other theme in Heidegger's discussion of authenticity that principally inspires the suspicion of a decisionist normative nihilism.

The significance of any outcome one might achieve in pursuit of particular goals or performing particular roles is always subject to question in that one can question whether achieving it is what is best here and now; identifying that is a matter that cannot be resolved simply by considering individual "innerworldly" "advantages." But according to the outlook that section 3 presented, it is in terms of such advantages that the entities that we find around us show up as meaningful: they are "encountered . . . in the character of the *sumpheron*," as soliciting acts that serve particular *tele*. No such entity on its own presents us with a determinate reason to act then, in that identifying such a reason requires that we settle which of the multiple *tele*—for which the multiple acts solicited by the multiple entities that we encounter are *sumpheron*—ought to be pursued at the expense of the rest. One might say indeed—as Heidegger does—that the entities we discover within the world are "in themselves completely without significance [*an ihm selbst . . . völlig belanglos ist*]" (SZ: 187): they lack significance *in themselves* in that—even though "encountered . . . in the character of the *sumpheron*"—none considered on their own can settle what is best here and now.[34] To settle that, one must be open to *all*, and *as* a whole.

One need not be a value nihilist to think this: for example, as we saw above, Aristotle may have, and wasn't. Indeed, in one sense, the above claims need not at all entail that such entities—and such "innerworldly" ends, products and achievements—lack meaning or significance; and it is important—if we wish to avoid a life of "arbitrary picking"—that they don't. Rather, to repeat, they lack significance *in themselves*. The concrete goods for which they are *sumpheron* may be ends, but none is a "grand end" that might by itself determine "what is best." Any number of normatively significant facts could hold then—concerning what is *sumpheron* in light of role *x* or goal *y*—without their resolving the identity of the *agathon*: however well-founded those facts are, without considering them *all* and *as* a whole, that matter remains outstanding.

One might see it as a category mistake to think otherwise; but, when inauthentic, we succumb to this thought all the same. Recall once again Heidegger's account of the inauthentic individual "immersing" himself in "the objects of [his] closest concern," in "those very closest events and befallings which he encounters." Heidegger describes this condition as Dasein's "flee[ing] towards . . . entities within-the-world" (SZ: 189); as other passages quoted earlier put it, Dasein "become[s] lost *in* the world," "cling[ing]" to "entities *within*-the-world" (WDR: 168, SZ: 190–91, italics added). More specifically, when inauthentic, I take the way that the world presents itself to me through the task in which I "take refuge" to simply and exclusively *be* the world—*the* world, "the facts"; all "other possibilities" are "levell[ed] off," "crowded out," or "closed off," and what remains—the world understood through the particular concern that grips me—"becomes the 'real world'" (SZ: 195): "[b]lind for possibilities," inauthentic Dasein "retains and receives the 'actual' that is left over" (SZ: 391).[35]

"Anxiety brings Dasein back from its falling absorption in the 'world'" to the need to address the "*world as world*" (SZ: 189, 187).[36] This is a need that only those who acknowledge the need to judge their situation as a whole meet. This need—the outstanding issue of the *agathon*—presses itself upon us when we recognize that anything less than all the facts about what here and now is *sumpheron* does not, and could not, resolve it:

> The utter insignificance which makes itself known in [anxiety], does not signify that the world is absent, but tells us that entities within-the-world are of so little importance in themselves that on the basis of this *insignificance* of what is within-the-world, the world in its worldhood alone is left to obtrude. (SZ: 187)

Authentic Dasein does not, therefore, look *beyond* its "innerworldly" concerns—the many reasons that are there pressing upon it—or away from those concerns—and those reasons—to consider itself somehow in isolation: it is not a "flight from the world" (CTR: 47). Nor does the "obtruding" of "the world in its worldhood" somehow provide some further *concrete* concern or reason in light of which Dasein should act—to echo Price, "a reason for doing one thing rather than another." Rather, having this further, abstract all-encompassing "object" in view distinguishes those who choose from those who don't. The world as world is a "pure object of will" in that only when Dasein takes in, and decides in light of, its many concrete reasons as the totality that they are does it express its own will: it "rel[ies] on itself" rather than on "what it encounters in the world" (WDR: 168, quoted earlier).³⁷ As section 6 argued, when I subject myself to the discipline of deciding what is best, I make judgments to which I precisely do not have discretion to append "though that is not what I think ought to be done." It is no longer an option to distance myself from such judgments by saying that I have "not said everything" and "know still more"; instead I have "presented myself in what I have said"—*all* of myself, my *own* judgment. Similarly, the world as world is "*the* good of choice and action" in that Dasein's adopting any perspective narrower than that which takes in this all-encompassing *telos*—judging what is best in light of its reasons for action considered as a whole—leaves it falling short of *proairesis* and *praxis*, "tak[ing] action in itself of its own accord" (SZ: 295, quoted above).³⁸

"Anxiety individualizes" then; and it does so in a double sense. Only when I take in my world *as* a world do I look *for* myself at how things stand, and *at* myself as the whole that I am. To see my situation as a whole is also to see how I am as a whole. I see the normative demands I am meeting, those I am failing to meet and how I am faring not merely as a teacher, as a father, etc., but how I am faring as a whole, as I myself, one might naturally say.³⁹ In anxiety, "*the world has been disclosed as world, and [Dasein] has been disclosed as a potentiality-for-Being which is individualised*":

> Anxiety individualizes Dasein and thus discloses it as "*solus ipse*." But this existential "solipsism" is so far from the displacement of putting an isolated subject-Thing into the innocuous emptiness of a worldless occurring, that in an extreme sense what it does is precisely to bring Dasein face to face with its world as world, and thus bring it face to face with itself as Being-in-the-world. (SZ: 188)

When authentic then, Dasein looks for itself and thereby at itself.

We can look now at some of Müller's formulations quoted earlier in a new light. The abstract *agathon* "is an aim I do not *set* myself": "[i]t is there as soon as I am there" and is "as little of my choosing as my existence is." But this does not entail that I cannot fail to pursue this aim, just that doing so is at the same time turning attention away from myself. In being willing to determine what is best here and now—in being open to its world *as* a world, the *totality* of reasons that its situation gives it—the authentic agent has "chosen both itself and choice" (WDR: 168): it has turned its attention to itself as a whole in accepting the need to exercise its own capacity to choose. In refusing to orient myself by the *telos* that is "what is best"—letting that abstract *agathon* be "set before me"—I refuse to let myself be set before me, but instead only a fragment of myself, which leaves how I myself am as a whole indeterminate, without *peras*. The all-encompassing "world" is there as soon as I am there, in that acknowledgement of it requires that I express myself; and I am there as soon as it is there, in that only when I judge in light of it do I see for myself myself as a whole. Inauthenticity is then to reject oneself as both an object—the whole that one might see to be thus-and-so—and a subject—one's capacity to see that object for oneself.

8. THE TRANSCENDENCE OF REASON REVISITED

Clearly much more needs to be said.[40] But I will end by returning to the title of this volume, a motif using which we can draw together in conclusion some of the issues that we have discussed.

To some, the fact that there is no *paragellia* that guides phronetic judgment will entail that it "transcends reason" in precisely the same way "arbitrary picking" does. But this reaction would be untrue to the phenomenology of such judgment—to "the torment of thinking, feeling and understanding," as David Wiggins puts it (1987: 237), that it can involve—and rests, I have proposed elsewhere,[41] on a crude picture of rationality—one that identifies it with application of a *paragellia* and that Aristotle too clearly rejects. As one might make the point in his terms, *phronêsis* is not *episteme* but it is still a mode of *aletheuein*—of uncovering or disclosure.[42] The distinctive "object" that *phronêsis*—and, if my reading is right, authenticity—uncovers is one's situation *as a whole*.

But the motif of "transcending reason" can play a more positive role here too. Our discussion began with reflections on the apparent incompatibility of the authority of reason and an agent's free self-expression. Decisionism responds to this by denying the former, although the version of the latter that it thereby saves is no more than the "wild leaping" of a "giddy empty will."

The reading I have offered shares with decisionism the commitment that, if we are to freely express ourselves, we must transcend the particular, concrete reasons that the entities around us present. It is this common feature that renders both readings prima facie plausible interpretations of Heidegger's remarks on choice and anxiety. But these readings differ in how they understand this "transcendence." They differ over the ultimate character of our normative predicament that presses the need for such transcendence upon us—a normative pluralism contrasting with a normative nihilism—and over the choice it elicits from us—phronetic *proairesis* contrasting with "pure," "arbitrary picking." Crucially, my reading also makes available a different conception of free self-expression—expressing oneself as a whole rather than as a "fragment"—and that requires us to transcend our particular, concrete reasons in order that we might disclose what we have *most* reason to do. Rather than their being incompatible, it is by opening ourselves to that for which our reasons *as a whole* call that we both give reason its proper authority *and* freely express ourselves.[43]

NOTES

1. Whether the narrative in question provides the best way to understand Sartre and Nietzsche—which I doubt and very much doubt respectively—will not be my concern here.

2. Other pertinent remarks can be found at SZ: 42, 188, 268, 270, 287, 288, 384, 385, 394, and HCT: 318 and 319.

3. Not all commentators do, as McManus 2015a discusses. The first third of that paper sets out in detail interpretive challenges that Heidegger's discussion of anxiety poses. Of the considerations that I offer later in that paper in attempting to meet those challenges, those in its second third play a part below; but those in the final third of that paper now seem to me mistaken.

4. Another pertinent theme that I set aside for another day is responsibility: the authentic individual is depicted in the narrative with which we opened as distinctively taking responsibility for her life and Heidegger too describes authenticity as "assuming self-responsibility [*Selbstverantwortung*]" (CTR: 45).

5. I won't discuss here Holton's own proposed solution to these difficulties—that "very often" a choice "will not be random picking" because it "respond[s] to features that we have registered but of which we are unaware" (2006: 9).

6. As will be apparent below, I have benefited greatly from Price 2011.

7. References to works by Aristotle use the following acronyms: EE—*Eudemian Ethics*, MM—*Magna Moralia*, NE—*Nicomachean Ethics*, R—*Rhetoric*. I generally follow the translations of Aristotle published in Aristotle 1984, but I also draw on Irwin's version of NE.

8. I won't attempt to determine here how the reading of Heidegger's discussion that I offer stands to Crowell's own reading. We turn to some similar-sounding

formulations in articulating ideas that inform our reading. But I suspect that the tasks we assign to those ideas are rather different.

9. See McManus forthcoming-b. Despite its date of publication, McManus 2018 offers a significantly earlier understanding of mine of how an appropriation of *phronêsis* might inform Heidegger's understanding of authenticity. The considerations that the first half of that paper offers still strike me as pertinent, those of the second half less so.

10. For example, the understanding of *phronêsis* upon which I draw here is consistent with its exercise being at least in part a deliberative feat, whereas the understanding of it on which Hubert Dreyfus draws, in one of his later accounts of authenticity, presents its exercise as the subject "simply *seeing* the appropriate thing to do and responding without deliberation" (2005: 51). For discussion, see Finnigan 2015.

11. *Being and Time* is also, of course, not *merely* a reworking of Aristotle's practical philosophy, as other influences matter greatly: in particular, Heidegger's reading of St. Paul and St. Augustine shape powerfully his discussion of "being-towards-death," or so McManus 2015b argues. (See also n. 30 below.) But I confine my attention here to how the appropriation of Aristotelian themes may also have shaped Heidegger's discussion of authenticity.

12. Our discussion may also have a bearing on the justice of the claim—when viewed in light of the Aristotle lectures—that "Heidegger's gesture toward the *agathon* is little more than a placeholder" (Crowell 2013: 277–78). To do justice to Crowell and his fascinating discussion, he makes this claim principally in light of EG and MFL and their comments on Plato's *agathon*.

13. In several respects, this discussion is clearly a model for a key and very well-known discussion in chapter 3 of division one of *Being and Time*. But I confine my attention here to only certain features of it.

14. Cf. NE 1.1 1094a6ff, to which Heidegger is alluding; see BCArP: 50.

15. See n. 20 below.

16. Cf. BCArP: 27, 49, 55, and 252.

17. That that should be so is no coincidence as Heidegger clearly sees the roles that these two notions play in Aristotle as very closely intertwined. See, e.g., BCArP: 63, PS: 95, 118–19, and GA27: 172.

18. See n. 21 and, for a defense of a "grand aim" reading of Aristotle, Kraut 1993.

19. To touch on issues that Matthew Burch addresses elsewhere in this volume, as "*the* good of choice and action" the abstract *agathon* is a constitutive good for both, but not a *concrete* good, which—to use Eric Wiland's expression (2012: 141)—is the rabbit that some constitutivists seek to pull from their hats.

20. McManus forthcoming-b provides further support for this being Heidegger's own view on the basis of discussion of his concept of "guilt." For an understanding of themes from Heidegger's discussion of authenticity premised on a rather different brand of normative pluralism, see McMullin 2019.

21. One might believe impossible a *paraggelia* that will settle unequivocally what is best in each here and now while also believing that quite a lot can be said about what is good in general. Indeed this is arguably what Aristotle does in giving for the virtues "character sketches of their possessors" (McDowell 2009: 45). Moreover, the

absence of any corresponding considerations in Heidegger stems not, I think, from a conviction that none would be intelligible but from the broader interests that drive his philosophy, interests we must recognize if we are also to understand the role that authenticity plays within the broader project he sets for *Being and Time*. These matters lie beyond the scope of the present chapter but McManus 2013 and 2015c offer what I believe are some relevant thoughts.

22. See, for example, Aristotle 1984 and 1999 respectively, and Finnigan 2015: 679.

23. Price's reasons for saying "is also" rather than simply "is" are complex and I won't explore them further here, although n. 33 touches upon them.

24. Compare Heidegger's observation that "[w]e know possibilities of preference [*Vorzugsmöglichkeiten*] only in areas where there are decisions about value or lack of value, higher or lower value" (MFL: 116). See also PIA: 135, where Heidegger notes that when presented with something that is a "matter of choice," we ask, "What are the choices based on?"

25. There are remarks of Aristotle's that might fuel this worry: "When a thing appears best to us after having thought it over, there ensues an impulse to act, and it is when we act in this way that we are held to act on choice" (MM I.17 1189a26–27).

26. McManus forthcoming-a and -b articulate this view using the concept of "all-things-considered judgment," and that may bring to mind a view that Gary Watson has defended: as Chandra Sripada has recently expressed it, "[t]he deep self consists of the judgments issued by one's valuational system," where these are "judgments of [the] form: 'the thing for me to do in these circumstances, all things considered, is *a*'" (2016: 1207, cf. Watson 2004: 25). This similarity may then also suggest that the view that I defend will face the same objections that Watson's does: as Sripada puts one of these, such "calm, cool reasoning" is often precisely not revelatory of the self, and "raw passion" often precisely is (Sripada 2016: 1207–8). All I will say here is that how we view such matters will depend upon, among other things, how we understand the relation between reason and emotion. McManus forthcoming-a proposes that, in light of Heidegger's understanding of that relation, one's capacity to make an all-things-considered judgment depends upon an openness to all of the emotions that my situation elicits from me. (I would like to thank Matthew Burch for pressing me on this issue.)

27. Delimiting what such a full range is, is a complex issue. All I will say here is that Heidegger's reflections on "thrownness" and "guilt" suggest that he at least believes such a delimitation possible.

28. The claim is not that everything we label "a choice" is such a judgment. There clearly are other kinds of choice that meet other kinds of need, such as those needed "to break the impasse" in "so-called Buridan examples" (Holton 2009: 4) and those through which we select from the dessert menu. But since the function of the former is precisely "resolving indifference" (Holton 2009: 59) and the latter "really do just depend on how you feel," as Charles Taylor puts it (1991: 38), it is hard to see either as "deep personal choices," or as bearing the kind of significance that Heidegger seems to ascribe to the choosing distinctive of the authentic. (In these other cases, "[n]o one would dream of making discriminating judgements about these preferences, but that's because they are all without importance" [Taylor 1991: 38].) We

should also note, of course, that, although I talk here of "choice," the word on which we really need to reflect is "*Wahl*." These terms have largely similar uses with some not-uninteresting exceptions: "*Wählen*" has more deliberative connotations than "choose," is used in referring to elections, and would be exaggeratedly formal when choosing dessert (where "*aussuchen*" would be more natural).

29. To merely touch on a complex matter and invoke a difficult distinction, the thought is not that one has "external reasons" (see Williams 1979) that one does not recognize, but that one has "internal reasons" that, on particular occasions, one "dims down" (SZ 195).

30. There are clearly connections here with St. Augustine's conception of freedom, for which, "the more primordially the *propensio* [propensity] is for the *bonum*, the more authentic the freedom of acting" (IPR: 111, cf. MFL: 116).

31. On the basis of the above account, McManus forthcoming-b develops an account of "guilt" and "*das Man*," and McManus 2015b provides the basis for a reading of "Being-towards-death" consistent with this account.

32. "The Origin of the Work of Art" retrospectively supports this: "The resoluteness intended in *Being and Time* is . . . the opening up of human being, . . . to the openness of Being" (BW: 192).

33. An interesting objection I won't pursue here concerns the relationship between a judgment of what is best and the *intention* to perform the act so judged: isn't this something that choice brings and judgment alone does not? Assessing this matter is difficult because, as Price notes, there is no explicit discussion of intention in Aristotle (Price 2011: 309) and the conceptual framework within which he works aligns poorly with the background Humeanism that provides at least some of the motivation for the objection.

34. Cf. Price 2011: 76: "*[S]tanding one's ground in battle*, say, counts as brave and virtuous only if, in context, it looks to serve some good purpose. . . . [W]hether doing some act *counts* as acting well is not independent of its function in context."

35. In this way, although the inauthentic are "fragmented" in being "immersed" in some "closest concern," this very "immersion" obscures from them both itself and that "fragmentation." See also Sec. 8.

36. As an early remark puts it, "in anxiety," one's life—one's relation to one's world—is "[d]ealing with, but not falling into!" (PRL: 200n36).

37. This is also, I think, an angle from which one might consider Heidegger's depiction of "the call of conscience" as silent (see, e.g., SZ: 273).

38. Issues I won't explore here are the extent to which my reading identifies Heidegger's "world" with his "concrete situation," and the justifiability of any such identification. But such an identification would not be totally off-the-wall or without textual support: see, e.g., Carman 1994: 203 ("the world is not fundamentally a collection of objects or objectives states of affairs but a practical context or situation") and Heidegger's claim that, in a "totality of involvements [*Bewandtnisganzheit*]," "there lurks an ontological relationship to the world" (SZ: 85), "*Bewandtnis*" being the term that most clearly inherits in SZ the role that "*Beiträglichkeit*" plays in BCArP. See also BCArP 41, quoted above.

39. As Heidegger puts it in an early remark, when "a genuine appreciation of the *bonum* is enacted, . . . the self always sees itself before itself" (PRL 180).

40. To note just one obvious outstanding matter, Heidegger declares that the authentic "choose choice," but my focus has been the first-order choice that—in some sense or other—this second-order choice chooses. But how are we to understand the latter "strange beast," as Beatrice Han-Pile has recently called it (2013: 311)?

41. See McManus forthcoming-b. The account presented here may also seem to invite the contrasting charge that it over-intellectualizes authenticity, to one version of which n. 26 alluded. Another version asks whether making the judgments described must be identified with "a conscious, first-personal activity of decision-making" (Finnigan 2015: 692). All I will say here is that the resources available to Aristotle's commentators in responding to the same question—see, e.g., Broadie 1991: 79–80 and McDowell 2009: 36 and 49—are available to Heidegger's too, and that we should again be wary here of the influence of caricatures of what phronetic judgment must involve.

42. Cf. PS: 16 and 39.

43. An obvious line of further exploration would examine the ways in which Heidegger himself weaves the concept of "transcendence" together with "world" and "anxiety"—themes of Sec. 7—and "freedom" and "self"—themes of Sec. 6—in works such as WM, EG, FCM, and OET that he composed in the aftermath of SZ. For example, in EG, Heidegger declares that "[t]ranscendence means surpassing [*Überstieg*]," and "*[w]hat* is surpassed is precisely and solely *entities themselves*" (EG: 107, 108). "Whatever the entities that have on each particular occasion been surpassed in any Dasein, they are not simply a random aggregate"; "rather, entities, however they may be individually determined and structured, are surpassed . . . as a whole"; and "[w]e name *world* that *toward which* Dasein as such transcends" (EG: 109). But such "[s]urpassing in the direction of world is freedom itself"; and "[t]ranscendence constitutes selfhood" (EG: 126, 108). Conspicuously here too, Heidegger speculates, "may we interpret the *agathon* as the transcendence of Dasein?" (EG: 124).

For helpful comments on earlier versions of this chapter and on work upon which it draws, I would like to thank Bill Blattner, Taylor Carman, Filippo Casati, David Cerbone, Ursula Coope, Steven Galt Crowell, Daniel Dahlstrom, Guy Elgat, Francisco Gallegos, Sacha Golob, Martin Hägglund, Gabrielle Jackson, Stephan Käufer, Elselijn Kingma, Leslie MacAvoy, Wayne Martin, Samantha Matherne, Conor McHugh, Adrian Moore, Dermot Moran, Mark Okrent, Graham Priest, Aaron Ridley, Joseph Rouse, Joseph Schear, Matthew Shockey, David Suarez, Iain Thomson, Jonathan Way, Daniel Whiting, Edward Witherspoon, Kate Withy, Fiona Woollard, and the editors of this volume.

REFERENCES

Aristotle. 1984. *The Complete Works of Aristotle, the Revised Oxford Translation.* Edited by J. Barnes. Princeton, NJ: Princeton University Press.

———. 1999. *Nicomachean Ethics.* Translated by T. Irwin. Indianapolis: Hackett.

Austin, J. L. 1961. "*Agathon* and *Eudaimonia* in the *Ethics* of Aristotle," in his *Philosophical Papers.* Edited by J. O. Urmson and G. J. Warnock. Oxford: Oxford University Press.

Broadie, S. 1991. *Ethics with Aristotle*. Oxford: Oxford University Press.
Carman, T. 1994. "On Being Social: A Reply to Olafson." *Inquiry* 37: 203–23.
Crowell, S. G. 2013. *Normativity and Phenomenology in Husserl and Heidegger*. Cambridge: Cambridge University Press.
Dahlstrom, D. 2013. *The Heidegger Dictionary*. London: Bloomsbury Academic.
———. 2015. "Authenticity and the Absence of Death." In *Heidegger, Authenticity and the Self: Themes from Division Two of* Being and Time, edited by D. McManus. London: Routledge.
Dreyfus, H. L. 1991. *Being-in-the-World*. Cambridge, MA: MIT Press.
———. 2005. "Overcoming the Myth of the Mental: How Philosophers Can Profit from the Phenomenology of Everyday Expertise." *Proceedings and Addresses of the American Philosophical Association* 79: 47–65.
Dreyfus, H. L., and Rubin, J. 1991. "Kierkegaard, Division II, and Later Heidegger." Appendix to Dreyfus 1991.
Finnigan, B. 2015. "*Phronêsis* in Aristotle: Reconciling Deliberation with Spontaneity." *Philosophy and Phenomenological Research* 91: 674–97.
Friedman, M. 2000. *A Parting of the Ways: Carnap, Cassirer, and Heidegger*. Peru, IL: Open Court.
Han-Pile, B. 2013. "Freedom and the 'Choice to Choose Oneself' in *Being and Time*." In *The Cambridge Companion to* Being and Time, edited by M. A. Wrathall, 291–319. Cambridge: Cambridge University Press.
Holton, R. 2006. "The Act of Choice." *Philosopher's Imprint* 6: 1–15.
———. 2009. *Willing, Wanting, Waiting*. Oxford: Oxford University Press.
Kant, I. 2012. *Groundwork of the Metaphysics of Morals*. Translated and edited by M. Gregor and J. Timmermann. Cambridge: Cambridge University Press.
Kraut, R. 1993. "In Defence of the Grand End." *Ethics* 103: 361–74.
McDowell, J. 1998. *Mind, Value, and Reality*. Cambridge, MA: Harvard University Press.
———. 2009. *The Engaged Intellect*, Cambridge, MA: Harvard University Press.
McManus, D. 2013. "Ontological Pluralism and the *Being and Time* Project." *Journal of the History of Philosophy* 51: 651–74.
———. 2015a. "Anxiety, Choice and Responsibility in Heidegger's Account of Authenticity." In *Heidegger, Authenticity and the Self: Themes from Division Two of* Being and Time, edited by D. McManus. London: Routledge.
———. 2015b. "Being-towards-Death and Owning One's Judgment." *Philosophy and Phenomenological Research* 91: 245–72.
———. 2015c. "On Being as a Whole and Being-a-Whole." In *Division III of* Being and Time: *Heidegger's Unanswered Question of Being*, edited by L. Braver. Cambridge, MA: MIT Press.
———. 2018. "Vision, Norm and Openness: Some Themes in Heidegger, Murdoch and Aristotle." In *Aspect Perception after Wittgenstein: Seeing-As and Novelty*, edited by M. Beaney, B. Harrington, and D. Shaw. London: Routledge.
———. Forthcoming-a. "Affect and Authenticity: Three Heideggerian Models of Owned Emotion." In *Heidegger on Affect*, edited by C. Hadjioannou. London: Palgrave-Macmillan.

———. Forthcoming-b. "On a Judgment of One's Own: Heideggerian Authenticity, Standpoints, and All Things Considered." *Mind*. https://doi.org/10.1093/mind/fzx045.
McMullin, I. 2019. *Existential Flourishing*. Cambridge: Cambridge University Press.
Müller, A. F. 1989. "Absolute Requirement: A Central Topic in Wittgenstein's *Lecture on Ethics*." *Revue Internationale de Philosophie* 43: 217–48.
Murdoch, I. 1970. *The Sovereignty of Good*. New York: Routledge and Kegan Paul.
Nietzsche, F. 1968. *The Antichrist*. Translated by R. J. Hollingdale. In F. Nietzsche, *Twilight of the Idols and The Antichrist*. Harmondsworth: Penguin Books.
Price, A. 2011. *Virtue and Reason in Plato and Aristotle*. Oxford: Oxford University Press.
Sartre, J.-P. 1986. *The Age of Reason*. Translated by E. Sutton. Harmondsworth: Penguin.
Sripada, C. 2016. "Self-Expression: A Deep Self Theory of Moral Responsibility." *Philosophical Studies* 173: 1203–32.
Taylor, C. 1991. *The Ethics of Authenticity*. Cambridge, MA: Harvard University Press.
Tugendhat, E. 1986. *Self-Consciousness and Self-Determination*. Translated by P. Stern. Cambridge, MA: MIT Press.
Watson, G. 2004. *Agency and Answerability*. Oxford: Oxford University Press.
Wiggins, D. 1987. *Needs, Values, Truth*. Oxford: Oxford University Press.
Wiland, E. 2012. *Reasons*. London: Bloomsbury.
Williams, B. 1979. "Internal and External Reasons." Reprinted in his *Moral Luck*. Cambridge: Cambridge University Press, 1981.
Wittgenstein, L. 1979. *Wittgenstein's Lectures Cambridge 1932–35*. Edited by A. Ambrose. Oxford: Blackwell.

Chapter 6

Heidegger on Deliberation

Patrick Londen

There is a traditional view about human agency that sees an intimate connection between deliberation and action. Deliberation on this view is the activity of engaging in motivationally effective—or practical—reasoning. This model of action centers on the idea that intentional action flows from a judgment of what one has reason to do, and that this is the kind of judgment one forms at the end of a process of successful practical reasoning. This is a view arguably found in Aristotle, who claimed that the "starting-point" of action "is deliberate choice, and of deliberate choice, the starting-point is desire and reason," which "is why, without understanding and thought on the one hand and a state of character on the other, there is no deliberate choice."[1] On this view, distinctively human action originates in our rational capacities, which guide the actions of rational animals like us. Kant is well known for claiming that action issues from the standpoint of practical reasoning, for example, in his so-called Incorporation Thesis, which asserts that a motive leads to action only *"insofar as the human being has incorporated it into his maxim* (has made it into a universal rule for himself, according to which he wills to conduct himself)."[2] Only actions that issue from motives that are rationally chosen—that is, incorporated into a deliberative rule—can be properly attributable to the agent's will.

Although Heidegger makes important contributions to the phenomenology of agency, he seems to make little room for deliberation. Heidegger rejects traditional accounts of agency that attribute the intelligibility of our actions to the activity of the thinking subject. How we understand what to do, for the most part, is not the result of stepping back to reflect on the psychological states directed at potential actions or on the rational grounds of those actions. Most of what we do is not mediated by acts of reflection. Instead, our actions are drawn out of us by our pretheoretical and prereflective grasp of what the particular situation demands of us on any given occasion.

Readers who are otherwise sympathetic to this account of "everyday" prereflective activity may see Heidegger's near silence on the nature and role of deliberation as an important lacuna in his practical philosophy. Without an account of deliberation, Heidegger might be understood as offering an account of human agency in which action is automatic, instinctual, or otherwise unguided by capacities that are recognizably agential.

In response to this challenge, Steven Crowell has pointed out that Heidegger does discuss deliberation, albeit only briefly. Heidegger says that our everyday prereflective comportment toward entities is "subject to the guidance of a more or less express overview" of the practical situation, and Heidegger equates this "overviewing" with "deliberation" (SZ: 359). Crowell elucidates this conception of deliberation by showing how it usefully resembles Christine Korsgaard's account, which is itself a fusion of Aristotelian and Kantian models of practical reasoning (Crowell 2013). On Crowell's innovative reading, this traditional view of practical reasoning can fruitfully supplement Heidegger's account of everyday prereflective comportment: practical deliberation develops and makes explicit the way we guide our action prereflectively.

In this chapter, I will reconstruct Heidegger's conception of deliberation in a similar spirit. After reviewing existing interpretations of the account of deliberation in *Being and Time* that assimilate it to traditional conceptions, I argue that Heidegger's reading of Aristotle on deliberation actually leads him to a novel account that rejects basic tenets of the traditional conception. Deliberation is traditionally conceived as a process of reflective thought that enacts a rational procedure: when we deliberate we reflect on our reasons for acting. The goal of deliberation is to make an explicit judgment about which courses of action are the right courses of action to take—that is, the ones for which, at least from the agent's perspective, there is a justifying, normative reason. For Heidegger, by contrast, deliberation is a process of figuring out what to do that consists in seeing the world in a way that is conducive to one's projects. Deliberative guidance is thus modeled not on thinking about the world but on seeing it. I argue that this "aesthetic" account of deliberative guidance, as far removed from the tradition as it appears to be, actually agrees with it in seeing an intimate connection between deliberation and action.

EXISTING INTERPRETATIONS OF THE DELIBERATION PASSAGE

Let me begin with a brief sketch of Heidegger's account of everyday, prereflective agency, before turning to what he has to say about deliberation.

Heidegger's account starts with the idea that we are always practically engaged in a world that invites this engagement. For the most part, we engage with the world practically. He characterizes the attitude involved when we act in terms of a kind of sight he calls "*Umsicht*" or "circumspection" (SZ: 69). The German term plays on the prefix *um*, which means both "around" and "in order to," suggesting that the kind of sight in operation when we act is *situated*, in that it is immersed in the context of a world in which we are already practically engaged, as well as *purposive*, in that the sight is in the service of doing something. He contrasts this with another kind of sight, observation (*betrachten*; SZ: 69) or merely looking (*Nur-hinsehen*; SZ: 69). Observation exemplifies the intentional attitude involved in judgment. For Heidegger, judgment paradigmatically involves predicating something of an object. The attitude paradigmatic of action, however, is not one in which we ascribe a property to an object.[3]

Circumspection expresses our understanding of entities in action. On this view, entities always appear as part of an articulated, purposively organized context that Heidegger calls a "whole of affordance" (*Bewandtnisganzheit*). When I am actively engaged in the world, things show up as directly inviting action, as affordances for acting in specific ways: we don't notice the doorknob when we use it; we simply see it as a way of opening the door. In ordinary action, things show up as "equipment" (*Zeug*) in the sense that they show up directly as available for use (*zuhanden*, ready-to-hand). The way that equipment is meaningfully organized into a functional whole is in terms of the role that it plays in a practice—i.e., in a more or less functionally organized network of other equipment, familiar activities, and other participants. Practices, like teaching, baking, or dating, provide more or less standardized norms for distinguishing between appropriate and inappropriate behavior. In this sense, our familiarity with common practices guides how we use the equipment that makes sense within those practices. Our engagement in any given practice is guided by—"for the sake of"—forms of life that develop around these familiar practices. When I bake a cake for my niece, my use of bowls, whisks, and baking tins is guided by my sensitivity to how these items are typically used in baking practices, but also by my understanding of how a baker or an uncle lives—that is, my understanding of what it means for baking cakes for one's niece to matter and to show up as appropriate to do. Being an uncle is a form of life, what Heidegger calls a "possibility of being" or an "ability-to-be." The purposively organized structure of any activity always refers back to some form of life that gives that practical engagement its purposive orientation.

Circumspection involves interpreting entities *as* the entities they are. When we interpret available entities like bowls and whisks, we see them in terms of the dual aspects of their practical context—that is, in terms of their role in the practice of baking, and in terms of some possible way of being or ability-to-be. This situated and purposive kind of interpretive sight is how we express our understanding of entities when we see them with a view to interacting with them.

Heidegger sees a close connection between circumspective interpretation and deliberation. In the passage in which Heidegger discusses his conception of deliberation, he refers to it as a kind of sight that guides interpretation. Heidegger writes:

> Circumspection [. . .] is subject to the guidance of a more or less express overview [*ausdrückliche Übersicht*] of the equipmental totality of the current equipment-world and of the public environment which belongs to it. The overview is not just one in which things that are occurrent are scraped together. What is essential to it is that one should have a primary understanding of the whole of affordance within which factual concern always takes its start. Such an overview illumines one's concern, and receives its "light" from that ability-to-be on the part of human existence *for the sake of which* concern exists as care. In one's current using and manipulating, the "overviewing" circumspection of concern *brings* the available *closer* to human existence, and does so by interpreting what has been sighted. This specific way of bringing concern close by interpreting it circumspectively, we call *deliberation* [Überlegung]. (SZ: 359)

While Heidegger's description of deliberation as an overview of the "current equipment-world" does not sound like a process of rational reflection, he does seem to appeal to a familiar form of instrumental reasoning to fill out his picture: "The scheme peculiar to this is the 'if—then'; if this or that, for instance, is to be produced, put to use, or averted, then some ways and means, circumstances, or opportunities will be needed" (SZ: 359). This suggests that deliberation involves having an end in view and searching for the means that might bring it about.

Hubert Dreyfus reads the passage this way: Heidegger's discussion here is meant to situate the traditional conception of deliberation within his own account of prereflective agency. On Dreyfus's reading, everyday action is fluidly responsive to solicitations from the environment. We only deliberate when we experience a disturbance or obstacle to our ongoing, fluid comportment, forcing us to engage in "reflective planning." He explains, "In deliberation one stops and considers what is going on and plans what to do" (Dreyfus 1991: 72). Although for Dreyfus we never completely break from the ongoing background of engaged activity, deliberation marks a moment in which we step back from action to rely on mental states that represent the world, like beliefs and desires, in order to make plans that we can then try to bring about in action. On Dreyfus's reading, deliberation consists in a process of means-end thinking that involves representing a state of affairs and searching for the means to bring it about in the world.

Crowell argues against reading Heidegger's conception of deliberation as a narrowly instrumental form of reasoning. Instead, Crowell takes his cue from Korsgaard. For Korsgaard, deliberating about what to do involves evaluating possible actions on the basis of reflective judgments about some conception of one's practical identity—i.e., "a description under which you value yourself" (Korsgaard 1996: 101). Figuring out whether one should, for example, betray a friend's confidence for personal gain would involve evaluating that proposed action in light of one's being a friend to that person, or in light of some other conception of one's practical identity that might justify the action. On Crowell's reading of Heidegger, we do the same on the basis of our abilities-to-be.[4] The point of deliberation, on this reading, is not just to figure out necessary means to one's ends, but to endorse whole actions that are supported by one's practical identity. One's practical identity is not something to be brought about or produced, but functions instead as the source of the standard by which one can evaluate courses of action. On Heidegger's model of deliberation, Crowell concludes: "The reasons we draw upon in deliberation do not have the structure of instrumental reasons; instead, they provide normative justification for what I do—that is, they state not what must be done but what is *best* to do in these circumstances, given a particular practical identity" (Crowell 2013: 292).

On this view, the kind of guidance that deliberation provides is rational guidance through reflection. Deliberation guides action by seeking "normative justification" for possible courses of action by reflecting on one's reasons for acting. Furthermore, what this rational guidance amounts to, on Korsgaard's view, is *evaluative* in nature. What it means for a reason to provide "normative justification" is for a reason to identify a value that one might ascribe to certain courses of action or states of affairs. The way that practical identities generate reasons, on Korsgaard's view, is by "confer[ing] a kind of value on certain whole actions" (Korsgaard 2009: 21). In other words, there is a reason to cook for someone if you are that person's friend because valuing yourself as a friend also involves judging this action to be of value, to be good to do from the standpoint of being her friend.

Both readings assume that deliberation is a recognizable variant of a traditional conception of practical reasoning, and that deliberation occurs when the flow of prereflective action is obstructed and the agent needs to step back and think about what to do (Crowell 2013: 289). Crowell seeks evidence for his reading in the fact that both Korsgaard and Heidegger were inspired by Aristotle's thinking on deliberation. So to assess these proposals, we turn first to Heidegger's reading of the passages from Aristotle that Crowell cites as the inspiration for Heidegger's view.

HEIDEGGER ON ARISTOTLE ON DELIBERATION

Two years before publishing *Being and Time*, Heidegger begins a 1924–1925 lecture course on Plato's *Sophist* with a reading of Books VI and X of Aristotle's *Nichomachean Ethics*. In an effort to understand Aristotle's notion of practical wisdom or *phronêsis*, Heidegger looks to the structure of *bouleuesthai* or deliberating for a "structural analysis of action" (GA19: 146). Here is how deliberation works on this account:

> *Phronêsis* begins with a *prohairesis* [decision or choice]: for the sake of this, for the sake of an *agathon* (whichever one it may be), such and such is to be done. That is the first premise. And now the circumstances and the situation of the action are such and such. That is the second premise. The consequent is: hence I will act in such and such a way. The first premise concerns the grasping of the *hou heneka* [for the sake of], which is an *endechomenon* [possibility]. The second premise concerns the finding of the *eschaton*, the outermost point, at which the *logizesthai* comes to a halt. Now Aristotle says: *toutôn oun echein dei aisthêsin, autê d' esti nous* (1143b5). "What is needed now is *aisthêsis*, straightforward perception." In the deliberation over the situation in which I am to act, I finally touch upon the straightforward grasping of the determinate states of affairs on hand, the determinate circumstances, and the determinate time. All deliberating ends in an *aisthêsis*. This straightforward perceiving within *phronêsis* is *nous*. (GA19: 159)

Given that Heidegger lays out deliberation as a kind of syllogism, with "premises" and a "consequent," it seems that he takes deliberation to be a process of rational thought. And the fact that deliberation is oriented by an "*agathon*," usually translated as "good," suggests that deliberation guides action by pointing out what is good to do. A closer look, however, shows that Heidegger is intent on opening up a conception of deliberation in his reading of Aristotle that is an alternative to the traditional one. Specifically, Heidegger rejects attributing to Aristotle a model of instrumental reasoning, and his reading resists a view of deliberation as Korsgaardian reflective evaluation.

According to Heidegger's reading, deliberation is a *logizesthai*, which he construes as a process not of ratiocination but of "circumspective talking through" (*umsichtiges Durchsprechen*) what is involved in taking action, in a way that gives expression to entities in the world (GA19: 159). Although the term *logos* is sometimes translated as "reason," Heidegger wants his audience in these lectures to rid themselves of some of the assumptions of medieval and modern philosophy that might cloud their reading of Aristotle. Despite what Heidegger calls "a veritable history of nonsense," he contends that "*logos* means discussion, not reason" (GA19: 151). *Logos* is a form of speech, "the asserting of something about something," where "[t]o assert means to articulate what is spoken about" (GA19: 144–45). Here *logos* is the expression of our understanding of entities as they are "articulated" in themselves, in the sense of having proper parts. In another lecture course given the same year, Heidegger notes that for Aristotle, in practical deliberation "the world explicitly keeps to its primary character of *as* such and such, *as* conducive to, . . . and precisely because *legein* in its primary manner and mode addresses the world *as* something. [. . .] In speaking about something, I make it present, I bring it into the there, *as* this or that, in the character of *as*" (GA18: 60). When we deliberate, on this model, we talk about the circumstances of action in a way that gives expression to the elements of the practical context, such that those elements stand out as conducive to action.

Heidegger argues that the term "'premise,' *protasis*, is here understood in a broad sense as that which is posited in advance, that which stands before the consequent" (GA19: 159). Examples of "premises" include the "esteemed opinions" (*endoxa*) that rhetoricians rely on to persuade their audience (ibid.). These *endoxa* should not be thought of as a set of beliefs or propositions from which to infer a conclusion. They should be read as a foreshadowing of Heidegger's notion of *das Man*, the prevailing norms of conventional behavior that constitute the background of our familiarity with common practices. That which comes before action—the "premises" in this broad, original sense—is a kind of context or background.

The view seems to be one in which figuring out what to do involves talking about the circumstances of action, drawing on one's familiarity with the way things work in familiar shared practices. At times, Heidegger suggests that this is a kind of talking to oneself about what to do, a "circumspective self-counsel" (*umsichtige Mit-sich-zu-Rate-Gehen*) (GA19: 143); at other points, he suggests that we deliberate by talking things through with others (GA18: 60–61). Heidegger strongly suggests that, on his reading, deliberation involves "actual discussion" (*wirkliche Durchsprechen*). For example, if I am trying to decide what to do for my niece's birthday, I may find it helpful to talk it through: I say (in my head to myself or aloud to someone else), "My niece's birthday is coming up. Her parents are organizing a party, but neither of them cooks. You can't have a kid's birthday without a cake. I'll check with her parents about bringing over a cake for the party." Articulating the practical circumstances involves highlighting certain features as salient, given my grasp of the relevant practices, such that baking a cake shows up as the thing to do. Of course, this picture of deliberation is not incompatible with a kind of practical reasoning, nor with specific acts of reflection. Nonetheless, for Heidegger's Aristotle, discussion is well-suited to guide action not because in discussion we engage in reflective thought (although we might). Discussion does not guide action by tracking the rational relationships between the contents of the propositions expressed in speech. Rather, the importance of talking through what to do lies in the fact that when the circumstances are discussed, we can see things more clearly, since things are best understood when they are expressed in speech. When certain conventions (such as that expressed in, "You can't have a kid's birthday without a cake") are made salient by being expressed, it allows the agent to see the situation a bit more clearly, and this helps guide action. (In his own philosophical view, Heidegger claims that elements of the practical context are not best expressed in speech, but rather in interpretation; we'll investigate that view in the next section.)

Perhaps the goal of discussing the circumstances of action is to find the best course of action by *assessing* the alternatives. After all, on this account deliberation proceeds from a grasping of the "for the sake of an *agathon.*" Does deliberation identify what to do by issuing a judgment of what courses of action are good? Some of Heidegger's remarks on the *agathon* suggest otherwise: "The *agathon* is nothing else than an ontological character of beings: it applies to those beings which are determined by a *telos* [end]. To the extent that a being reaches its *telos* and is complete, it is as it is meant to be, *eu* [well, good]. [. . .] If we take the *agathon* as value, then this is all nonsense" (GA19: 123). The primary sense of *agathon* for Heidegger is an ontological feature of entities that are defined in terms of ends. In the passage cited earlier, Heidegger equates the *agathon* with the grasping of the for-the-sake-of, which in turn he identifies with a "possibility." We can make sense of these connections if we recall Aristotle's distinction between two senses of the "for-the-sake-of": the doctor practices medicine for the sake of the patient—the beneficiary of the action—and for the sake of health—the general aim of the action.[5] Only health is a possibility in the relevant sense, but how is health a "possibility of Dasein's being" as Heidegger identifies the for-the-sake-of? In a discussion of Aristotle's *hou heneka*, Gabriel Richardson Lear explains, "One way a thing can act for the sake of an end [. . .] is to become it. In other words, when a living thing realizes its own form, it acts for the sake of an [. . .] end" (Richardson Lear 2004: 77). When an acorn grows into an oak tree, it does so for the sake of its form, in the sense that the form of the tree makes sense of why it matures the way it does. The general aims that guide human interaction with entities aren't predetermined by the nature of human existence "as if it were a table, house or tree" (SZ: 42). Instead, human agents are who they are in virtue of how they lead their lives. The general end for the sake of which we act is a form of life, an ability-to-be.

Of course, the concept of an end introduces a notion of normativity that could serve as the basis of an evaluation. But Heidegger's point here is that the kind of normativity involved does not require ascribing value to anything. As Heidegger will later argue, evaluative judgments are ascriptions of "value predicates" to objects (SZ: 99). The issue is not that Heidegger thinks that deliberation and the actions that result from it are insensitive to normative discrimination. The problem is that the form of intentionality that evaluative judgments embody is not germane to the way we guide action (at least not paradigmatically).

If what guides deliberation, on Heidegger's reading of Aristotle, is not an ascription of value, what is the standard of "correctness" (*orthotês*) in deliberating? Heidegger says that success in deliberation concerns not the choice of the starting point of this process, but rather only that process itself. It thus concerns the "middle term" of the "syllogism," that is, the way of carrying out the "*agathon*" or "possibility" that provides the starting point of the deliberation. Heidegger adopts an example from *Nicomachean Ethics* III, 5, in which the doctor or the orator have clear projects to carry out, and in their deliberating, "they look around, in each case within the concrete situation of their acting [. . .] until their deliberation touches the first *aition* [cause] when they can intervene, that which, in the uncovering of the whole state of affairs, is the outermost of the deliberation" (GA19: 162). This "outermost of the deliberation," Heidegger specifies, is the starting point for *poiesis*, the "making" that Heidegger will later interpret in terms of his account of the available. When a doctor carries out the project of healing, she may talk over the patient's case, surveying the range of equipment at her disposal. The standard of success in deliberating is "correctness with regard to what matters for the carrying out of the *prohaireton agathon*, which is more precisely determined as [. . .] what it needs, how it is used, and when" (GA19: 155). The doctor needs to have a sense of the range of equipment that is relevant for the task at hand, so that she can use it in the right way and at the right time. The process of deliberation can fail if the "middle term" in the syllogism of deliberation is *pseudês*, distortive, in such a way "that it distorts [or hides; *verstellt*] the circumstances, the means, and the ways, that is does not provide me with them as they should be in relation to the *prohaireton* [what is decided—i.e., the *agathon*]" (GA19: 155). That is, when one's grasp of the relevant practices distorts what is called for—what one needs in order to carry out one's project—then deliberation has missed the mark.[6]

While success in deliberation on this view consists in seeing what needs to be done in carrying out a project, Crowell is right to emphasize that this should not be understood as a form of instrumental reasoning in a narrow sense. A form of life, or ability-to-be, is not something that one seeks to produce or bring about. But to the extent that engaging in practices serves to carry out a form of life, and moreover that we can fail to find a way to carry it out, recommends understanding the relation between practice and form of life in particular normative terms.

We can think of the relation as consisting of a *constitutive* means rather than a narrowly instrumental means, provided we understand this relation in the right way. Calling my friend on her birthday is a way of being a friend to her. This doesn't mean that calling her is an instrumental means to attaining the end of being a friend. Being her friend lies in part *in* the act of calling her; or better, calling her is how I manifest being her friend. The phone call doesn't bring about the friendship, but part of being her friend is to do things like this. A form of life is an end, but not in the sense that I seek to bring it about; the end is formal in the sense that I can carry it out or embody it in particular acts. The relation of constitutive means to formal end is normative in the sense that there is a way of succeeding to carry out the end and a way to fail. I can fail to be a friend just as much as I can manifest being one. This is the sense in which deliberation can "distort" "the circumstances, the means, and the ways": we can find ways of acting that can fail to manifest the form of life to which those ways of acting are constitutive means. When, for example, out of kindness I lie to my friend to protect her feelings, I can in effect fail to manifest friendship as a form of life, if I don't ultimately recognize in this act what it means to be a friend. I can be misguided in regarding dishonesty as a way of manifesting the friendship. The fact of introducing a normative relation that can be described as one of means to end does not imply that the relation must obtain among propositions, or that one must make judgments about the relation to be influenced by it as a standard of success. Success in carrying out a form of life lies in the degree to which the practice hides or reveals the form of life that engaging in it is supposed to manifest. Responsiveness to this standard, Heidegger's reading suggests, lies in a kind of sight rather than a discursive act.

On Heidegger's reading of Aristotle, deliberating involves giving expression (in speech) to the different aspects of the situation of action, to clarify what is at stake and what is needed, until the point at which the *phronimos* can leave this discussion behind and see directly what is to be done. Heidegger suggests that the result of deliberation is not a judgment, not a discursive act. The endpoint of deliberation is an exercise of *nous*. Heidegger translates *nous* as "perception" rather than "intellect" (as another standard translation, "intuition," also suggests). This perception, *noein*, "is a matter of a simple presentifying [*Vergegenwärtigen*] of something, so that it speaks purely out of itself and no longer requires discourse or a demonstration on our part. Here it can still be said: *phainetai*, the things show themselves in this way. The only possibility here is to look on and, in looking, to grasp" (GA19: 161). Talking through the circumstances and situation of action gives expression to what is at stake in the act, what kinds of things are needed to act, how those things are to be used, all so that one can find a way of acting that manifests the form of life that's guiding the deliberation; once this endpoint is reached, what is to be done is seen directly and invites action without the mediation of judgment. As Heidegger notes, the result of deliberation is "circumspection"; when deliberation goes well, "the objects grasped in it have the character of the *sympheron* [useful]" (GA19: 163).

Regardless of whether this view can be accurately attributed to Aristotle, Heidegger's unorthodox reading of him resists easy assimilation to either the narrowly instrumental reasoning model or the Korsgaardian reflective evaluation model. Heidegger's reading of Aristotle gives important insights into his own account, but those views are importantly different. In the next section, we turn to Heidegger's account of deliberation in *Being and Time* to see what he takes from Aristotle, and what makes his own account different.

DELIBERATION IN *BEING AND TIME*

It is worth remembering that these lectures on Aristotle come several years before the publication of *Being and Time*, during a period in which Heidegger is still developing a systematic view. So we should not be surprised to find some discrepancy between his reading of Aristotle on deliberation and his own account. In *Being and Time*, Heidegger points out that the Greeks (especially Plato and Aristotle) thought that speech is the best expression of our understanding of things in the world: they took explicit assertion in language to be the best expression of our understanding of entities as they are. According to Heidegger, what the Greeks were after with the term *logos* was "discourse" (*Rede*), the way things lend themselves to be expressed as the things they are, which is not, for Heidegger, wholly or primarily a linguistic phenomenon.[7] He notes, "because the *logos* came into [the Greeks'] philosophical ken primarily as assertion, *this* was the kind of *logos* which they took as their clue for working out the basic structures of the forms of discourse and its components" (SZ: 165).[8]

According to the Heidegger of *Being and Time*, the best expression of our understanding of entities is not explicit assertion in language, but what he calls "interpretation" (*Auslegung*). Interpretation is not primarily a linguistic phenomenon, but rather encompasses a much broader variety of ways in which we express what entities are. When we act, we interpret entities by treating them as the kind of entities they are: when I pick up a fork to start eating, I take the utensil *as* a fork, as serving a particular role in a whole network of equipment. This form of intentionality gives expression to the fork as the thing it is within and in terms of the context that gives this entity its significance as the thing it is. In this sense, practical interpretation gives expression to the entities we interact with as the entities they are. Interpretation can also take the form of an explicit assertion about an object, as in "This is a fork," or "This fork is useful." But Heidegger thinks that what is expressed in explicit speech is not exactly our understanding of entities as we understand them when we interact with them. Heidegger claims that assertions are a derivative mode of expression of our understanding of equipment. We can't explore this claim here, but Heidegger's point is that when we express these entities in an explicit assertion, in a declarative sentence, what we express is detached from the practical context that constitutes these entities as equipment.

For Heidegger, Aristotle was interested in how entities can be expressed as they are, but because he focused exclusively on expression in speech, he missed the more basic form of expression that Heidegger identifies as interpretation. While the point of deliberation, for Heidegger's Aristotle, is to talk through the situation of action to find expression of what is to be done, for the Heidegger of *Being and Time*, asserting what is to be done does not yet put one in a position to *see directly* what is to be done and so to act. Thus, as Heidegger develops his own views of expression, he would have to adjust his reading of Aristotle's model of deliberation to fit his account of interpretation.

This is why the passage on deliberation in *Being and Time* focuses on the role of deliberation in practical interpretation. Recall that deliberation is a kind of "overview" that guides circumspection in that it "*brings* the available *closer* to human existence," and he says that it accomplishes this "by interpreting [the available] circumspectively" (SZ: 359). Heidegger is here targeting a different phenomenon than is traditionally identified with the term "deliberation." Instead of a process of reflective thinking, Heidegger suggests that deliberation is a process that can operate within prereflective, practical interpretation. We can call Heidegger's conception (as he does in passing) "circumspective deliberation" (SZ: 359). Consider the following example. When I am on the bus, I generally observe the conventions of public transit, minding my own business, avoiding eye contact, and generally keeping to myself. Imagine, however, that I notice the person sitting next to me is crying, and I am moved to make a gesture like offering her a pack of tissues. Here there is a shift in perspective, from one in which it makes sense to ignore my neighbor as much as possible, to one in which acknowledging her may be appropriate. My initial practical orientation is given by the forms of life associated with the practice of riding the bus: people typically ignore each other as best they can when in transit. But my crying neighbor upsets any straightforward enacting of the typical way of being on public transit: I feel something that prevents me from just ignoring this person. I am, on this occasion, invited to enact a different form of life, a spirit of fellowship, associated with different practices, like that of showing sympathy. It may take a moment to readjust to this change of aspect in the practical situation: I no longer simply enact the way of being that is typical of riding the bus but must read the whole scene anew, taking stock of my neighbor and the situation more generally. That shift in perspective enables a shift in what shows up as conducive to action. While initially my belongings are to be kept close, once my perspective shifts, it makes sense to dig out a pack of tissues from my bag and offer them to my neighbor. I can determine what to do, and change course in my way of acting, without having to engage in reflective thinking about what to do. On this view, we deliberate when we stop to "read the scene," and look for new openings for action given a new guiding form of life.

Heidegger suggests that deliberation is an activity that can be "performed" or "carried out" (*vollziehen*) (SZ: 359), but he also suggests that it plays a structural role in circumspective interpretation. At times he seems to indicate that the act of deliberating seems to enable circumspective interpretation in the first place: "The affordance-character of the available does not first get discovered by deliberation, but only gets brought close by it, so that it [i.e., deliberation] lets that *in which* something *has* an involvement [or affordance], be seen circumspectively *as* this very thing" (SZ: 360). While entities are "discovered" by understanding, they aren't interpreted until they are "brought close" by deliberation. Heidegger seems to be saying that deliberation lets what is understood be interpreted. This suggests that deliberation is a necessary condition for the interpretation of available entities. This is surprising because Heidegger also claims that interpretation is pervasive; it is involved in all cases of interacting with the available: "All prepredicative straightforward seeing of the available is in itself already understanding-interpreting" (SZ: 149).[9] If every meaningful engagement with available entities is marked by an interpretation of them *as* the things they are, and if deliberation is required for interpretation, then deliberation must be involved in every action of this sort. If deliberation is a deliberate (if not necessarily reflective) act of considering what to do, one might think this means that all practical interpretation, and thus all intelligible action, is necessarily preceded by this kind of deliberate act of taking stock of things. There would thus be no room for the way of acting when one is caught up in the flow of ongoing activity, the kind of activity that Heidegger thinks characterizes much of our everyday engagement in the world.

To see how deliberation can play a structural role in mediating between understanding and interpretation, even in cases of "flow-like" ongoing activity, let's first recall how understanding and interpretation are related in Heidegger's thinking. Heidegger identifies *understanding* with our general capacity to engage with entities in the contexts in which they make sense as the entities they are. As we have seen, available entities are ontologically constituted by the twin contexts of practices—networks of referral networks among equipment—and projects—possible forms of life or abilities-to-be that organize equipment according to how the agent understands herself in acting. Heidegger says that understanding has the character of projecting onto possibilities; this means having a grasp of the contexts that constitute them as the entities they are.[10]

Interpretation, Heidegger says, is "the development [*Ausbildung*] of the understanding" (SZ: 148). In interpretation, the available entities that are constituted by their practical context are given expression as such: "that which is *expressly* [ausdrücklich] understood—has the structure of *something as something*" (SZ: 149). When Heidegger argues that interpretation is *ausdrücklich*, he is not claiming that interpretation is primarily background understanding made explicit in concepts, in propositional form, or a deliberate act.[11] Rather, interpretation is understanding made salient, as expressed in some act or other—sometimes in an act of judgment, but also in fluid action.

In order to interpret an available entity as an invitation to act, I need to understand the entity. I need to have a grasp of the contexts that determine how it is to be used, as well as the conditions under which it proves useful. But a grasp of these contexts alone is insufficient for me to see it as an invitation. To grasp these contexts is to open up a range of possible ways of interpreting the entity. For example, laptops can play roles in various practices and can serve various projects. Since understanding entities means seeing them within the possible contexts in which they can be intelligible as the entities they are, understanding an available entity means asking the question of *how to take* such an entity, of what the entity is. To ask such a question is already to sketch out a range of possible answers. So if understanding poses the question of what there is to engage with, interpretation offers an answer: "the circumspective question as to what this particular thing that is available may be, receives the circumspectively interpretive answer that it is for such and such a purpose [*es ist zum* . . .]. [. . .] The 'as' makes up the structure of the expressness of something that is understood. It constitutes the interpretation" (SZ: 149). Answering the leading question of what is available means narrowing the possibility space in which the relevant entities are to be understood. Living out a particular form of life is a way of narrowing this possibility space. If I orient myself toward study as a form of life, this restricts the range of ways that I can take entities. An entity like a laptop is lifted into prominence by the stance I take up when I am oriented toward the project of study. This is so because laptops play particular roles in the practice of taking notes and writing papers, which serves study as a form of life. An entity like the laptop only invites action when it is seen from the perspective of a particular form of life.

The passage on deliberation suggests that what marks the transition from an understanding to an interpretation of an available entity is the act of "bringing the available closer to human existence," and that this act is accomplished in deliberation. The available is "closer" to human existence when it has been interpreted as manifesting the form of life that is the agent's project in acting. In order to effect the transition from an understanding to an interpretation of an entity, then, one needs to see that entity in terms of the form of life that provides one's practical orientation in acting. The moment of seeing in terms of this context is a moment of seeing the entity as part of a whole; this means having a view of this whole itself. When we engage in circumspective deliberation, we step back to get an "overview" of the situation as a whole. What distinguishes an overview is that what is seen is the whole. On the basis of the overview or view of the whole, certain referral and affordance relationships stand out. When an entity is seen as playing a role in a practice that carries out or manifests some form of life, the entity must be seen within the proper relation of practice and form of life. This is not to say that, to interpret an entity as it is, one must see three discrete items (the entity, its practice, and the form of life it serves) and then put them together. Rather, the model is closer to the Gestalt theory of perception, in which individual elements are only seen as shaped by the overall pattern in which they fit. Seeing an element requires seeing the whole to which it belongs. The "overview" that Heidegger associates with deliberation is the moment of seeing the whole, which is a necessary condition of interpreting an entity in light of that whole.

When Heidegger seems to suggest that the transition from understanding to interpretation is made possible in deliberation, he does not mean that we need to deliberate (even in Heidegger's sense of circumspective deliberation) every time we interpret something as inviting action. His point is that the act of deliberating exemplifies a structure that shapes every instance of circumspective interpretation. When we deliberate, on his model, we look for a way to engage with entities in some practice, which allows us to carry out a form of life. Any instance of interpreting available entities as an invitation to act presupposes this structure: the entity plays a role in a practice that serves to carry out a particular form of life.

Because practical interpretation bears the structure of deliberation, it is subject to the same normative constraints. We saw earlier in Heidegger's reading of Aristotle that deliberating about what to do is subject to a particular standard of success. The relevant normative relation can be described as that between means and end. More specifically and accurately, we can call this a relation of constitutive means to formal end: the practice is a "constitutive" means because the end is not something external to engaging in the practice, but is *in* that engagement; and the end is "formal" in the sense that the end is a form of life, a way to be. In claiming that practical interpretation bears the same structure as that embodied in an act of deliberation, Heidegger is also claiming that built into every practical hermeneutic whole is a standard of success in interpretation. Practical interpretation is successful to the extent that equipment, the paraphernalia of a given practice, is interpreted so as to provide a way of manifesting a particular form of life. When we are solicited to act by the environment, we are subject to this standard of agential guidance. This doesn't mean we need to deliberately guide action in order to act; often, action is experienced as being drawn out of us. But the way we interpret that solicitation to action is always in terms of a practice and a form of life that are related in the way that we relate them when we stop to consider what to do.

For the most part, on Heidegger's view, we respond fluidly to what the situation demands of us. This form of comportment is not merely instinctive or "automatic" behavior; rather, it bears the complex structure of a particular expression of our understanding. Occasionally, we need to express this structure more overtly. Sometimes we need to consider our options in acting more deliberately, by surveying the situation of action in light of some more or less specific project. This kind of careful consideration, which Heidegger identifies as "deliberation," does not necessarily involve trying to bring about a determinate state of affairs. Nor does it require asking oneself for reasons for action. But the consideration of features of the practical situation can help clarify what stands out as an opportunity to act. At other times, clarifying what calls for action requires isolating determinate features of the context of action and reflecting on them and their relation to other features in a determinate judgment, which may include evaluating alternatives as good or bad. In any of these cases, when deliberation goes well, the agent is able to express her understanding in action by interpreting things in a way that allows her to manifest a particular way of being in the world.

ÜBERLEGUNG AND DELIBERATION

Dreyfus and Crowell interpret what Heidegger says about deliberation on the basis of traditional views of that term. On these readings, what Heidegger calls "deliberation" refers to acts of reflective thinking. Since Dreyfus recognizes that, for Heidegger, action is paradigmatically prereflective, action that issues from reflective deliberation is a derivative mode of human agency: reflective thinking distorts the form of intelligibility that is most characteristic of human agency. By contrast, Crowell argues that this account of deliberation develops and makes explicit the way we guide our action prereflectively. On the view sketched in this chapter, what Heidegger calls "deliberation" is not reflective thinking. He adopts a radically new model of deliberation that fits in line with his views of prereflective (circumspective) action. So while deliberation makes explicit the way we guide action prereflectively, this doesn't imply that everyday circumspective action bears the intelligible structure of reflective thought.

The reading sketched in this chapter raises some pressing questions: If Heidegger does not want to talk about reflective thinking, why does he use the term *Überlegung*, and even granted that he does, why translate this term as "deliberation"? How does this model relate to more traditional (or perhaps even conventional) views of deliberation?

On the view sketched above, Heidegger draws from his reading of Aristotle on *phronêsis* and deliberation to give an alternative account of how agents guide action with understanding. On that reading, Heidegger appears to equate "the structure of *bouleuesthai* [deliberating]" with a "[s]tructural analysis of action" or "[t]he constitutive moments of action" (GA19: 146). The point of that analysis for Heidegger was not to claim that only actions that issue from deliberation are full-fledged actions. Rather, deliberation plays a normative role in an account of action: deliberation makes explicit the intelligible structure of action, because in deliberation we allow our understanding to guide action explicitly, and action that is *properly* guided is action that is guided by understanding. The philosophical tradition has often construed *proper* agential guidance in terms of rationality. Let me sketch out two ways in which rational deliberation has been given this kind of priority in accounts of human agency, and then how circumspective deliberation plays similar roles on Heidegger's account.

First, deliberation marks the occasion by which the agent actively guides her action with understanding, so action should originate in capacities that are exercised in that guidance. Since we think of human action paradigmatically as *meaningful*, in the sense that it is responsive to and expressive of our understanding, the capacities that are operative in action should be those that are exercised in deliberation. The process of deliberating relates the agent to her action in the right way, such that the action is explained by the proper functioning of agential capacities rather than in some other mechanism (like reflex or instinct). On a model of rational deliberation, the relevant deliberative process involves rational capacities, so consummate action issues from a process that is responsive to reasons for acting. Rationality thus plays an *explanatory* role in accounts of action that prioritize rational deliberation.

Second, deliberation makes explicit how action is normative for the agent. Deliberation solves a problem for a common way of thinking about action. Intentional actions are sometimes motivated by what the agent wants or desires. But the agent's desires do not always conform to what the agent regards as appropriate or right to do. This suggests that having a desire to φ doesn't by itself mean that the agent regards φing as the appropriate or right action to take. Part of the concept of agential guidance is that the actions performed by the agent actually seem appropriate or right on the agent's own lights. This is the idea that the agent's actions are in an important sense an expression of what matters to her. The point of deliberating is to arrive at an action that is appropriate or right on the agent's own lights. On the traditional rational model, the action that is regarded as the right one is the action that is supported by reasons. So to say that an action motivated by a desire expresses what matters to the agent is to say that the action issues from (or could have issued from) a conclusion of practical reasoning that takes that desire as an input or premise.[12] The action "speaks for the agent"—has subjective normative authority for the agent—when the action bears the structure of practical reasoning.

Deliberation on Heidegger's model clarifies how action is normative for the agent, even in everyday prereflective action. Interacting with equipment prereflectively involves acting in ways that the agent regards as appropriate, and not just in the sense that the agent acts in accordance with the norms of a given practice. As we have seen, circumspective interpretation requires being sensitive to the appropriate use of equipment in a given practice. It also requires being purposively oriented in action by a guiding form of life. What makes actions normative for the agent on this view is the *connection* between the practice and the form of life: equipment invites action when it provides a way of manifesting a form of life. The action "speaks for" the agent when the action successfully manifests the way of life that guided the agent in acting. The subjective normative authority of intentional action, on this view, is thus grounded in the standard of success that the concept of deliberative guidance brings with it.

This helps account for the fact that, on Heidegger's view, too, actions should originate in the same capacities that are exercised in acts of deliberation. Heidegger thinks that our practical engagement is always subject to the guidance of deliberation. As we have seen, this doesn't mean that all actions must issue from prior deliberation; rather, whenever we act, we are being guided by an attitude that bears the structure of deliberation. Every act of practical interpretation is guided by a view of the whole practical context, and this context is determined by the proper relation of familiar practices with ongoing forms of life. When we deliberate, we relate forms of life to particular practices, to find a way to manifest these ways of living within the practices. Thus the capacities enacted in deliberation play an important explanatory role in Heidegger's account of action, since these capacities are responsible for all motivationally effective practical interpretation.[13]

NOTES

1. See *Nicomachean Ethics* VI.2, 1139a (Aristotle 2014: 99).
2. See *Religion Within the Boundaries of Mere Reason* (Kant 1998: 49).

3. For critical discussion of this point, see Schear 2007.

4. "Korsgaard's concept of practical identity tracks Heidegger's for-the-sake-of" (Crowell 2013: 291).

5. See *De Anima*, 415b2–3 (Aristotle 1991: 26) and *Metaphysics*, 1072b1–3 (Aristotle 2016: 205).

6. The fact that deliberation aims at manifesting a form of life suggests that deliberation takes its guiding "for-the-sake-of" as fixed. In fact, this is exactly what Heidegger suggests in his reading of Aristotle: "A doctor does not deliberate about whether he is going to heal; on the contrary, that belongs to the meaning of his existence itself, because as a doctor he has already resolved in favor of healing" (GA19: 162). Burch (2010) distinguishes "ordinary deliberation," in which one takes the for-the-sake-of as fixed, from "deep deliberation," in which one deliberates about one's commitment to a particular for-the-sake-of. For the purposes of this chapter, Heidegger's account of deliberation is restricted to ordinary deliberation. Thanks to Matt Burch for pointing this out.

7. For a discussion of the claim that *Rede* is not primarily linguistic, see Carman 2003, especially chapter 5.

8. See also SZ: 154.

9. See Wrathall 2013 for an explication of the pervasiveness of interpretation, and an account of the relationship between understanding and interpretation.

10. "In the projecting of the understanding, entities are disclosed in their possibility. The character of the possibility corresponds, on each occasion, with the kind of being of the entity which is understood. Entities within-the-world generally are projected upon that world—that is, upon a whole of significance, to whose referral-relations concern, as being-in-the-world, has been tied up in advance" SZ: 151.

11. See Wrathall 2013: 196.

12. A historical version of this thought can be found in Kant's "Incorporation Thesis." For a different, contemporary version, see, e.g., "How Is Weakness of the Will Possible?" and "Intending" (Davidson 1980).

13. I would like to thank the editors of this volume for helpful comments, as well as Pierre Keller, Jozef Müller, Andy Reath, and Mark Wrathall for feedback on earlier versions of this chapter.

BIBLIOGRAPHY

Aristotle. 1991. *Complete Works*. Translated by Jonathan Barnes. Princeton, NJ: Princeton University Press.

———. 2014. *Nicomachean Ethics*. Translated by C. D. C. Reeve. Indianapolis: Hackett.

———. 2016. *Metaphysics*. Translated by C. D. C. Reeve. Indianapolis: Hackett.

Burch, Matthew. 2010. "Death and Deliberation: Overcoming the Decisionism Critique of Heidegger's Practical Philosophy." *Inquiry* 53, no. 3: 211–34.

Carman, Taylor. 2003. *Heidegger's Analytic: Interpretation, Discourse, and Authenticity in* Being and Time. Cambridge: Cambridge University Press.

Crowell, Steven. 2013. *Normativity and Phenomenology in Husserl and Heidegger*. New York: Cambridge University Press.
Davidson, Donald. 1980. *Essays on Actions and Events*. Oxford: Clarendon Press.
Dreyfus, Hubert. 1991. *Being-in-the-World: A Commentary on Heidegger's Being and Time*. Cambridge, MA: MIT Press.
Kant, Immanuel. 1998. *Religion Within the Boundaries of Mere Reason and Other Writings*. Translated by Allen Wood and George Di Giovanni. Cambridge: Cambridge University Press.
Korsgaard, Christine. 1996. *The Sources of Normativity*. New York: Cambridge University Press.
———. 2009. *Self-Constitution*. Oxford: Oxford University Press.
Richardson Lear, Gabriel. 2004. *Happy Lives and the Highest Good: An Essay on Aristotle's Nicomachean Ethics*. Princeton, NJ: Princeton University Press.
Schear, Joseph. 2007. "Judgment and Ontology in Heidegger's Phenomenology." *New Yearbook for Phenomenology and Phenomenological Philosophy* 7: 127–58.
Wrathall, Mark. 2013. "Heidegger on Human Understanding." In *The Cambridge Companion to Heidegger's Being and Time*, edited by Mark Wrathall. New York: Cambridge University Press.

Chapter 7

Grice and Heidegger on the Logic of Conversation

Chad Engelland

In his autobiography, Benjamin Franklin lists "silence" as the second of the thirteen virtues that he wishes to make his own. He expresses this virtue with the following precept: "Speak not but what may benefit others or yourself; avoid trifling conversation" (Franklin 1906: 86). He explains that he has a penchant for "prattling, punning, and joking," and he accordingly wishes to listen more and to speak less (Franklin 1906: 88). In an earlier chapter, he mentions the reason he rarely wished to listen to the only Presbyterian preacher in Philadelphia: because his sermons were concerned with confessional rather than ethical matters, Franklin found them "very dry, uninteresting, and unedifying" (Franklin 1906: 84). In this way, Franklin counsels us to speak to benefit others and thereby avoid the censure of being uninteresting. His musings raise the question concerning the logic of conversation. This logic is implicit in the ordinary ways in which we evaluate conversational moves, whether those of our own or of others.

When we judge that a move in a conversation is interesting, we do not attend to the words but the articulation of the world that is so offered; to say that something said is interesting is to say that the person who says it is perceptive and it is therefore worthwhile to see the world from the proffered vantage point. To say that something is uninteresting is to say that in this case one does not gain much from viewing the world from that person's point of view—that in this case the person is not particularly perceptive or insightful. Conversation aims at having the world articulated, highlighted, and intensified through the interchange of points of view.

The question of what we should say if and when we speak is a topic of considerable interest today. Paul Grice (1991) introduced the theme into contemporary analytic philosophy by clarifying the communicative motives implicit in speech acts. According to his "Cooperative Principle," a conversation ought to unfold according to the implicit expectations of the interlocutors, although he calls attention to the puzzling phenomenon in which a conversation can profitably shift expectations. Grice's Cooperative Principle has also spawned contemporary speech pragmatics. Sperber and Wilson think conversation, like all communication, is governed by the principle of relevance: I think what I have to say is beneficial enough to be worth your effort of listening, and I listen to you on the assumption that what you have to say will be beneficial enough to me to be worth my effort of listening (Sperber and Wilson 1995: 156–57). The Gricean-pragmatist approach raises foundational questions concerning what counts as beneficial and so relevant, which trade on questions concerning the nature of the two interlocutors. Also pressing is the question concerning what conditions might obtain that would justify subverting the expected horizon of a given discourse.

The puzzling but central character of cooperation and relevance for conversation happens upon terrain earlier explored by phenomenological authors, especially Martin Heidegger. According to phenomenology, conversation is not in fact a species of joint action whose horizon is determined by prior purposes; conversation is instead a joint activity whose end is to share the truth of the world more explicitly (Engelland 2014; McMullin 2013: 174–76; Carman 2003: 238–41; Taylor 1985: 259). There is therefore the obligation to disrupt the presumed horizon of a given conversation if it be possible and advisable to occasion a deeper understanding of the truth of things. Even before deciding to cooperate for the purposes of a given conversation, we are geared toward one another in care.

In this chapter, I would like to focus on the logic of conversation and the question of what justifies one interlocutor to challenge the conversational expectations of the other. I first turn to Grice, who approaches conversation as one instance of joint action that, like all such action, is governed by the Cooperative Principle. He thinks the expectations of the interlocutors must align, although he acknowledges that expectations can and do shift in the course of a conversation through a process he finds strange. I then attend to Martin Heidegger's analysis of discourse as governed by the normativity of care for self and for another. It is the structure of care that warrants disrupting the presumed cooperative horizon of a conversation in order to occasion some new insight. Finally, I expand Heidegger's ontological conception of care to make sense of the exigencies of conversation. In my view, conversation requires taking cognizance of (1) the human good, (2) the specifics of the conversational context, and (3) one's responsibilities for the other. This threefold understanding can provide directives for subverting the interlocutor's expectation for the purposes of a given conversation. Care moves us to bear witness to the human good, in this situation, with others for whom I am responsible given my practical identities.

1. GRICE ON COOPERATION AND CONVERSATION

Question: "How was the flight?" Reply: "Let's just say I'll never fly again." Here the statement, "I'll never fly again," does not literally answer the question. It is also false in its literal meaning; the speaker has no intention of avoiding air transportation in the future. But it answers the question by way of implicature: the flight must have been really bad to motivate a (feigned) resolution never to fly again. In order to explain how such implicatures work, Grice needs to explain their context, everyday conversation. To do so, he identifies the basic principle present in conversation, the Cooperative Principle, which he formulates as follows: "Make your conversational contribution such as is required, at the stage at which it occurs, by the accepted purpose or direction of the talk exchange in which you are engaged" (Grice 1991: 26). He then draws from Kant's categories to articulate four groups of supporting maxims.

Under the category Quantity, he specifies that a conversation contribution should provide neither too much nor too little information. One can here think of a conversation gone awry because one of the participants is making personal disclosures out of keeping with the context. Under the category Quality, he provides more important guidance. First there is what he calls a "supermaxim" that governs conversation: "Try to make your contribution one that is true" (Grice 1991: 27). Second, he adds two specific maxims: do not utter falsehoods and do not speak without sufficient grounds for thinking what you say is true. Truthfulness or veracity anchors most types of conversation, although one could imagine an acceptable language game that involves telling tall tales; Grice's point, I take it, is that the purpose of the speaker should match the purpose of the hearer; if the hearer expects truth, which the hearer usually does, that's what the speaker should provide. Under the category of Relation, Grice adduces a single maxim, "Be relevant." A conversation can get sidetracked, stalled, or come to grief due to inappropriate conversational contributions. While the first three categories relate to what is said, the fourth category, Manner, concerns the how of what is said. The supermaxim he adduces is "Be perspicuous," under which he specifies various goals such as clarity, distinctness, brevity, and orderliness. One cannot help but think of student papers, the worst of which are not conversational contributions because they are obscure, ambiguous, and jumbled. With these four categories, Grice provides some content to his Cooperative Principle governing conversation, the observance of which makes conversation possible.

Grice gives his analysis of the Cooperative Principle as background to making sense of implicature, in which we mean and can be taken to mean more than what we say. In this connection, it is noteworthy that the word "interesting" can carry an implicature. We may be asked for our opinion of something we found deeply unsatisfactory but, because it would be indelicate of us to say so, we reply, "It was interesting." We may share with our friends an article advocating a controversial point and say we found it "interesting," which expresses a noncommittal attitude that is projected to avoid coming across as overbearing. It may seem that we offer a measured positive evaluation when in fact we do no such thing. Now, our interlocutor will be able to detect such implicatures provided they know us well enough. That we should use the vague term "interesting" could appear to undermine the Cooperative Principle; in the category Quantity, it provides too little information; in the category of Manner, it is ambiguous; in the category of Quality, its ambiguity erodes confidence in truthfulness; and in the category of Relation, such a conversational contribution can appear flippant and irrelevant. However, this pressure on the Cooperative Principle alerts the thoughtful hearer that the speaker is meaning more than what is said. The specific context of the conversation and the background beliefs mutually known to hearer and speaker can serve thereby to make the conversational contribution known as a contribution that supplies the right amount of information, is perfectly clear in its expression, is truthful, and is relevant. To make sense of this implicature, it might be useful to add another maxim under the category of Manner: "Don't needlessly offend." This would accommodate various submaxims, such as "If you can't say something nice about it, say it was interesting" or "Offer challenging views as suggestive rather than assertive." For his part, Grice gives the example of "Be polite," noting that there are aesthetic, social, and moral maxims outside of the conversational ones he has identified that may lead to implicatures (Grice 1991: 28). My own sense is that the maxim "Don't needlessly offend" is a requirement of conversation rather than an extraneous social maxim; if, as Grice suggests, conversation has as its aim mutual illumination of the truth, it requires a mutually supportive context that excludes unnecessary conflict.

Grice's appeal to the logic of conversation also provides some direction for understanding what is happening when we use the word "interesting" in a straightforward way without any implicature. Something that is interesting is not something particularly associated with Quantity, Quality, or Manner—the amount of information, its reliability, or its mode of expression—although these are not unrelated to something's being taken to be interesting. Too much or too little information might deaden or fail to enkindle interest in a thing, and fiction can sometimes outperform fact in terms of interest. Something that is interesting, however, does especially concern the category of Relation and its supermaxim of relevance, which specifies that contributions must be appropriate. Grice, for his part, seems to think this category the most interesting to think about; its simplicity masks a host of complex issues:

> Though the maxim itself is terse, its formulation conceals a number of problems that exercise me a good deal: questions about what different kinds and focuses of relevance there may be, how these shift in the course of a talk exchange, how to allow for the fact that subjects of conversation are legitimately changed, and so on. I find the treatment of such questions exceedingly difficult, and I hope to revert to them in later work. (Grice 1991: 27)

What makes something interesting and so relevant? How can relevance constrain the horizon of a conversation and rupture the horizon of a conversation? How can conversation as cooperative behavior presupposing a shared goal come to adopt a new goal in its unfolding? What's at the bottom of relevance that makes it shared and dynamic?

John Searle follows Grice in zeroing in on the question of relevance for making sense of the logic of conversation. He notes that "a topic must be, as such, an object of interest to the speaker and hearer" (Searle 2002: 187). The invocation of interest in turn involves the purpose of the interlocutors, a purpose that is not determined by conversation in general and that, in fact, may shift in the course of a conversation. Precisely because conversation remains open to different purposes, Searle cannot render its logic with the same sort of precision he rendered speech acts (Searle 2002: 193). Nonetheless, he does proceed to characterize conversation as a kind of joint action that calls upon a preintentional background, and it is just this involvement with a preintentional background that determines the relevance at work in a conversation (Searle 2002: 198–99). What I find valuable about his engagement with Grice is the recognition that the principle of relevance entails something prior to a specific conversation for its comprehension. Referring to this as the background rightly suggests an a priori dimension, although Searle's account of the background is notoriously ambiguous (Dreyfus 1991: 103–5, Ratcliffe 2004). What is this background, and how does it explain shifts in relevance?

2. HEIDEGGER ON CARE AND RETICENCE

From Grice, we have a rich account of conversation as a joint action that operates in light of a joint commitment to being helpful, truthful, relevant, and clear. This account of conversation gives us resources to understand possible implicatures concerning the word "interesting." As Grice and Searle note, it also raises important questions about the nature and scope of relevance. But it leaves the ordinary plain sense of interesting underdeveloped, and it leaves the background of relevance underdetermined. To shed light on this sense of interesting and its context, it is helpful to turn to Heidegger, who distinguishes between being interested in something and finding it interesting:

[1] Inter-est [*Inter-esse*] means to be between and among things, to stand in the midst of a thing and to remain near it. [2] But today's interest accepts as valid only what is interesting [*Interessante*]. And interesting is the sort of thing that can freely be regarded as indifferent the next moment, and be displaced by something else, which then concerns us just as little as what went before. Today, one often takes the view that one especially honors something by finding it interesting. The truth is that such a judgment has already relegated the interesting thing to the ranks of what is indifferent [*das Gleichgültige*] and soon boring. (WCT/WHD: 5/6–7)[1]

The etymological sense of interest expresses something of Heidegger's research into the condition for the possibility of intentionality. It fulfills Heidegger's formulation of care from *Being and Time*: "the being of Dasein means ahead-of-itself-being-already-in-(the-world) as being-near [*Sein-bei*] (entities encountered within-the-world)" (BT/SZ: 237/192). This formula compactly expresses the interplay of affectivity and spontaneity enabled by timeliness in which the manifestation of things is possible. The human is not only thrown open in terms of disposed understanding, but in virtue of this being thrown open the human can encounter things in his or her otherness (Engelland 2017: 32–38). And, so encountered, things can show themselves from themselves via a phased structure: human beings begin by directing-themselves-toward a topic of investigation; then they grow into a dwelling-with that item; on that basis, they can apprehend or interpret the item; finally, they can preserve that apprehension as a modification of their original directing-themselves-toward the thing (HCT/GA20: 163/219–20). The authentic sense of interest, its placing us near a thing, enables us to know the thing in question.

Heidegger also mounts a criticism of contemporary talk, namely that it has reduced interest to what is interesting. What's interesting functions like the index finger—it singles out but only momentarily; in the next moment it will point out something else. When it comes to what is interesting, Heidegger thinks we are all-too-easily determined by what everyone (*das Man*) thinks, which constitutes the Public (*die Offentlichkeit*). By reading the newspaper, watching television, or reading blog posts we are habituated to a certain interpretation of what counts as pleasurable, entertaining, fearful, and shocking: "we do not say what we see, but rather the reverse, we see what *everyone says* [man . . . sprichte] about the matter" (HCT/GA20: 56/75). The Public treats everything as equally important. By consequence, it never attains the things that really matter (BT/SZ: 165/127). To reach the thing pointed out, to reach the thing that is interesting, requires an authentic devotion, a break from the logic of distraction warding off boredom. It requires entering into wonder in order to bring something near and exhibit it as such. The word "interesting" is thus ambiguous and slippery. While we appeal to it thinking we have fulfilled the authentic sense of being in the midst of something, we all-too-easily express a superficial attitude of fundamental indifference to the topic in question.

How does Heidegger's meditation on interest and care illuminate the logic of conversation? He roots conversation in the joint openness afforded by care: "Words emerge from that *essential agreement* of human beings with one another, in accordance with which they *are open in their being with one another for the beings around them*, which they can then individually agree about—and this also means fail to agree about" (FCM/GA29/30: 309/447). Heidegger spends much of his thought unpacking what constitutes this essential agreement, an agreement that, among other things, makes conversation possible. "In discourse being-with becomes 'explicitly' *shared*; that is to say, it *is* already, but it is unshared as something that has not been grasped and appropriated" (BT/SZ: 205/162). Like Grice, Heidegger sees conversation as a specific possibility of a more general ability. Beyond Grice, he situates the possibility of joint action within the transcendental structure of human existence and its shared truth (Crowell 2013, Golob 2014, Engelland 2015, Engelland 2017). Heidegger thereby grounds the Cooperative Principle in care-for or solicitude (*Fürsorge*). Talking to others about things is a matter of letting them see what is pointed out (BT/SZ: 197/155).

Heidegger observes that solicitude admits of negative and positive modes as well as inauthentic and authentic ones. Quite often, we are indifferent to those we encounter, an indifference that is deficient in solicitude. But we can show our care for others positively in two ways: either by leaping in for them and completing the task in their stead, which creates a relation of dependence, or by leaping ahead of them and enabling them to complete the task for themselves, a move that frees them to come into their own. Heidegger applies these possibilities of solicitude to joint action in a way that is applicable to a conversation. Participants may mistrust each other and thereby exercise solicitude in a negative mode, but it is also possible for them to exercise an authentic positive mode that frees each to deal with the thing in question together:

> When they devote themselves to the same thing [*Sache*] in common, their doing so is determined by the manner in which their Dasein, each in its own way, has been affected. They thus become *authentically* bound together, and this makes possible the right kind of objectivity [*die rechte Sachlichkeit*], which frees the other in his freedom for himself. (BT/SZ: 159/122)

Heidegger, then, would see Grice's Cooperative Principle as governing a certain positive and indeed authentic possibility of solicitude for others. He does not refrain from using the language of maxim to discuss such existential possibilities: "Insofar as it determines the execution of a possibility of the very existence of Dasein, a principle is also called a *maxim*" (HCT/GA20:

85/104).[2] In this way, to do justice to the logic of conversation, we might follow Heidegger and expand the category of Relation to accommodate various modes of community. It would then carry certain maxims such as "Care for others," "Help by enabling (rather than substituting for) their freedom," and the like.

Among the possibilities of discourse, Heidegger identifies "discretion" or "reticence" (*Verschwiegenheit*) as an authentic one. Rather than fall prey to idle talk, which talks carelessly about something and flits from topic to topic, reticence is prone to silence. In the space of that silence it can really listen to another and it can take time to ponder before speaking (BT/SZ: 208/165, 218/174). In this way, reticence makes room for the silent summons of conscience, which brings the self thoughtfully back to itself and its openness to the world (BT/SZ: 318/273). Reticence makes us answerable to others through fostering a readiness to give reasons for our decisions (Crowell 2013: 225–27). What Heidegger gives us to understand is that all too easily we will keep to what is merely interesting and thereby remain immune to the truth of things. Silence, opened up by reticence, holds such talk at bay. In doing so, it allows us to hear the other who speaks to us, to become thoughtful about what is, and to be attentive to the quiet call of conscience that provokes us to care. In this way, Heidegger's analyses give us reason to expand Grice's table of maxims still further:

Quantity: Remember that silence can be richly communicative (BT/SZ: 208/164–65).
Quality: Avoid idle talk by first making the topic one's own (BT/SZ: 270/169). Making the topic one's own wards off hearsay, gossip, and superficiality.
Relation: Avoid empty curiosity that seeks new experiences for the sake of novelty instead of for the sake of achieving understanding (BT/SZ: 216/172).
Manner: Endeavor to be reticent rather than fall prey to idle talk (BT/SZ: 342/296).

Grice wonders how the presumed aims of a conversation can be upended in the course of a conversation. Heidegger thinks that reticence enables such a transformation. In the "Letter on 'Humanism,'" he illustrates this power by recalling the charming story Aristotle relates about Heraclitus (Aristotle 1941: 645a17–22). Moved by curiosity, a group of strangers seeks out the great thinker, Heraclitus, only to be shocked that instead of finding him in meditation or disputation they find him silently warming himself by the kitchen stove. Heidegger comments, "The vision of a shivering thinker offers little of interest [*Interessanten*]. At this disappointing spectacle even the curious lose their desire to come any closer" (PM/GA9: 270/186). The seekers do not really seek; they remain at the level of admiration. Heidegger again comments, "The group hopes that in their visit to the thinker they will find things that will provide material for entertaining conversation [*Gerede*]—at least for a while" (PM/GA9: 270/185). Aristotle tells us that Heraclitus invites them through the door with the words, "Come in and don't be afraid, for here too the gods are present." Heraclitus is inviting them to shift from marveling to wonder, from a search for the unusual to a recognition of the usualness of the usual. He could have chased them off, of course, or let them wander away into the darkness, but he saw the opportunity, in the conversation, of challenging them to expand their horizon of inquiry. His conversational contribution, the fruit of reticence, expresses his having become the conscience of the strangers in such a way that he frees them from superficiality so that they might come into their own. As Heidegger writes in *Being and Time*:

> Dasein's resoluteness towards itself is what first makes it possible to let the others who are with it "be" in their ownmost potentiality-for-being, and to co-disclose this potentiality in the solicitude which leaps forth and liberates. When Dasein is resolute, it can become the "conscience" of others. Only by authentically being-their-selves in resoluteness can people authentically be with one another—not by ambiguous and jealous stipulations and talkative fraternizing in the "everyone" and in what "everyone" wants to undertake. (BT/SZ: 344–45/298)

What Heraclitus says to the strangers is relevant to their good but not relevant to their preconceptions for what a conversation with the famous thinker would amount to. Heraclitus leaps ahead to set them free to care more deeply. In this case, the thinker disrupts Grice's Cooperative Principle by challenging the strangers' expectation regarding the conversation, but the thinker does so in light of a deeper commitment to the demands of solicitude for others, a demand that involves helping others be perceptive about what is most important.

Heidegger takes us further than Grice into the logic of conversation by detailing the solicitude and authenticity that can justify changes of relevance. Reticence challenges the presumed horizon of idle talk in order to make effective the words that really matter. If we are to revise Grice's Cooperative Principle in light of Heidegger's care, we might add a new maxim from Heraclitus: "Expect the unexpected" (Heraclitus 1979: 129). That is, an agreed aim of conversation is to be surprised, even concerning the presumed horizon of that conversation.

3. FILLING IN THE CONTEXT OF CARE

Steven Crowell helpfully characterizes the content of conversation as follows: "What it means to be a good father, friend, or carpenter—and so also what it means to be a good person, morally good—is always the substance of 'the conversation that we ourselves are'" (Crowell 2013: 303). Conversation takes its bearings from the concrete context and content of care: that's what we spend our time talking about and that's what's involved in navigating shifts in relevance. Does Heidegger have the resources for making sense of the vicissitudes of conversation in terms of its concrete context and content?

Suppose a student calls upon a professor during office hours. What determines what the professor *should* and *should not* say? The student wants to figure out how to get an A in the class so she can get into medical school; the professor wants to alert her to the issue of truth and wisdom. Yes, by all means, the professor should exercise care, but in what way? Here one is mindful of Sartre's critique of Kantian ethics as being too formal (Sartre 1993: 47). Yes, do not use another as a means to an end, but how might one decide what to do here and now? The alternative, pace Sartre, is not some sort of decisionism. Rather it is a matter of a prudential mindfulness of the specific contours of the situation, contours sketched but not fully outlined by Heidegger: "when the call of conscience summons us to our potentiality-for-being, it does not hold before us some empty ideal of existence, but *calls us forth into the situation*" (BT/SZ: 347/300). I would like to follow Heidegger and work out care in terms of its threefold context: the good to be expressed, the possibility for conversation here and now, and the inherited identities for speakers available for repetition and correction (BT/SZ: 437/385). In this way, I recall and exceed Heidegger's temporal analysis as filling in the context of conversation in order to render intelligible disruptions in conversational expectations concerning content.

A. Futural: Wonder and the Human Good

While appropriating the theme of care from the Augustinian tradition via Scheler, Heidegger jettisons what he regards as a neo-Platonic overlay in both Scheler and Augustine (PRL/GA60: 199/265). The *ordo amoris* or order of love specifies not descriptively how one loves but prescriptively how one ought to love if one is to love well. Heidegger wishes to reduce the tiered sense of goods to the basic opposition of authenticity and inauthenticity. In terms of enacting fundamental ontology, the opposition is perhaps sufficient; but in terms of making sense of the human good, it is not. What disappears in this way is the good's complexity, which involves not only perspicacious self-awareness but also various grades of apprehended goods. Scheler observes that there are idolatrous, inverted, and inadequate loves (Scheler 1973: 124). A student might want lots of money as if that were the highest good; he might want grades instead of learning; he might have an insufficient appreciation for the goods of the intellect. Or again a father might wish to be eminently successful in his career even if that means being woefully deficient in his fatherhood. Part of what we should talk about, as Crowell observes, is the question concerning what we should care about. For such a conversation to be worthwhile, the interlocutors must assume there is a difference between how one in fact loves and how one does well to love. That difference provides an important justification for exceeding the presumed horizon of relevance in a given conversation.

In challenging that horizon, an interlocutor does not seek to impose an external constraint but to elicit inward recognition of what, in truth, care should be about. The normativity can be found within each of us, but the truth of the goods must come to light for them to be appreciated rightly. Instead of the careless indifference of boredom's *interesting*, which levels all differences, one appeals to the careful difference of wonder's authentic *interest*, which prioritizes more important topics. Curiosity and boredom rest content in superficial sameness; wonder and awe open up the stratification of goods. In truth, the student not only cares about money and the father not only about his career; there is a still deeper, if uncultivated, interest that must be awakened via wonder. Care naturally cares, but the truth of the grades of goods must be made plain so that we might care about the right things.

A sense of the various ingredients in the complete human good provides essential direction for determining conversation's content. The professor invites the student to find the contemplative character of human life—a responsibility for the truth of things operative in every mode of human life thoughtfully lived out—but part of this thoughtfulness involves recognizing the importance of money for rightly caring for oneself and one's loved ones. Similarly, a friend might suggest to the professor that success in his career, which is a laudable goal, is secondary to success in raising his children. Both are goods but they are not equally important, and confusion on this point will prove blameworthy. Heidegger is right, of course, that there is no table of goods that can simply be intuited, but the stratification of goods can arise in experience due to differences in fulfillment (Engelland 2004). Precisely because of our finitude we can only pursue one good at a time and can therefore not pursue all goods at once. Finitude requires prioritization, requires serially choosing from among competing goods in order thereby over time to bring about the variegated human good. Just what constitutes the human good is, as Crowell suggests above, central to the human conversation, and it is more complicated than Heidegger realizes (Engelland 2017: 228–34).

B. Moment of Vision: What Is Appropriate in This Situation

Insight into the human good is not sufficient to warrant subverting the presumed aim of any and every conversation. Consider a Saturday morning conversation over the breakfast table. "What are we going to do today?"

"Pursue the good and avoid the bad." Or, even if that conversational move is welcome it is only as a humorous statement of the obvious that will then call for a reissue of the question: "Are you heading to the store? Is there another birthday party this weekend?" Conversation involves not only a sense of the human good but also a sense for the moment, what is possible and relevant in this context, which trumps absolute considerations of the good. The reason for this is that we do need to attend to lesser goods in order to share life with others and only specific goods can be achieved via action.

The understanding of the human good is being offered to others as their own. Hence they must be induced to see it. Introducing it outside the appropriate moment will only serve to harden them to its allure, for a shift in relevance requires a previously established rapport, trust, and openness. Consider sitting on an airplane: one's in-flight neighbor might be buried in a book or engrossed in a movie in such a way that he or she would tolerate a request to move so that one can go to the bathroom but would not regard that exchange as an opening for questions concerning the nature of the travel, the content of the book or movie, or one's life ambitions. Rapport relaxes and makes others available to conversational turns and surprises: it makes solicitude something that is felt. On the basis of the established rapport of solicitude, and given the specifics of the situation including the perceived mood of the moment, a shift in relevance becomes possible.

In this way, one must attend to what can and cannot be accomplished given the specific historical horizons of the conversation that are in play in the present moment (BT/SZ: 345–48/298–300). As Heidegger points out, authentic resolve sizes up the situation in its peculiar juxtaposition of elements and realizes just what it is for. The question of what possibility this specific moment with its peculiar complex of factors might afford proves essential.

C. Having-Been: One's Responsibility Given One's Inherited Role Relative to This Person

What care calls for depends on the roles at play for the people in the situation. Yes, one has an obligation to everyone one meets, everyone who thanks to proximity is a neighbor, but more robust obligations come in being a spouse, a parent, a child, a friend, a teacher, a judge, a doctor, a mechanic, etc. Crowell appeals to Christine Korsgaard's "practical identity" as determining reasons for acting as we do, as filling in the content of care (Crowell 2013: 290–91; Korsgaard 1996: 100–102). A professor has reasons to mentor her students, doctors have reasons to care for their patients, a mother has reasons to parent her children, a friend has reasons to care for a friend, and so on.[3] To value these identities is to have obligations to do certain actions. To be able to defend one's conversational choices, to answer the question, "Why did you say that?" (a question rarely verbalized but frequently expressed in a dumbfounded countenance), requires not only appealing to care but also what care requires for a father or mother, friend or neighbor, in just this situation. The roles specify arcs of solicitude that shape our understanding of our responsibility for disrupting suppositions about conversational purpose.

Practical identities help fill in Heidegger's invocation of the repetition of possibilities into which we are thrown (BT/SZ: 437/385). We inherit an understanding of what these roles specify and in repeating these identities we simultaneously make them available to others. A professor, for example, not only aspires to be a good professor; in doing so she aspires to be memorable and formative so that any students who later assume the role will do so at least in part in light of the understanding of the role as shaped by their teacher's exercise of her practical identity. Similarly, what it means to be a parent is at least in part informed by our experience of parenthood and by the sorts of expectations our culture has regarding these roles. We say the sorts of things that a father or mother should say rather than the sorts of things that a friend, teacher, or doctor should say. Never do we strive to do simply what has been done; rather we strive to do what should be done, taking inspiration from what has been done but never aping it except thoughtlessly. Thus these practical identities are always made our own as we separate what is exemplary from what is not. We strive to emulate the intervention of an inspiring teacher or parent rather than the talk of an incompetent teacher or parent.

Consider Heraclitus's visitors trekking to see the philosopher or the student frequenting a professor's office hours: here the philosopher or professor has a rich practical identity that specifies obligations toward the visitors or students. In particular, just to be a philosopher (or to a lesser extent, a philosophy professor) means to be obliged to risk unwelcome disruptions of the expectations of one's conversational interlocutors for the sake of their good, to bear witness to a higher good than the one presumed as the topic of the conversation. That indeed is a great part of what it means to be a philosopher, to resolve to be a gadfly, a conscience in the first place for oneself but also for others. After all, if the philosopher does not bear witness to the priority of wisdom, who on earth will? Heidegger recalls Aristotle's recollection of Heraclitus, but we might also attend to an even more famous episode of philosophical exchange. Socrates, on his deathbed, makes his last conversational contribution as follows: "Don't be careless" (Madison 2002). By bidding his disciples to take care, he recalls his central teaching as summarized in the *Apology*: "are you not ashamed of your eagerness to possess as much wealth, reputation and honors as possible, while you do not care for nor give thought to wisdom or truth, or the best possible state of your soul?" (Plato 1997: 29d–e). Socrates's obligation as a gadfly is to enjoin his fellow citizens to care for wisdom, truth, and virtue rather than money or honor. The substance of what the philosopher should say is to take care; to bear the practical identity of a philosopher is to have reason to look to disrupt conversational expectations by enjoining interlocutors to attend to the truth of things. In doing so, philosophers might not make the most convivial of interlocutors. In the context of a conversation with a philosopher, one should expect to be challenged; one should expect shifts in relevance. Of course, there are other practical identities—doctor, carpenter, neighbor, citizen, and so on—that might oblige us to handle relevance with a lighter touch. The art of conversation involves harmonizing and prioritizing one's practical identities in order to achieve insight into the requisite good of this particular conversation.

CONCLUSION

Benjamin Franklin counsels us that conversation ought to be beneficial and that we should accordingly avoid prattling on and speaking trifles. Pragmatics valuably recognizes that a given speech act calls upon an interpersonal context for its proper interpretation. The principle of relevance from pragmatics holds that I think the benefit of what I have to tell you will outweigh the trouble of your having to listen to what I say. This approach wrongly suggests a framework in which we are silent unless compelled to speak. Human beings, however, naturally talk just as naturally as they share the world with one another. Heidegger writes, "We are continually speaking in one way or another. We speak because speaking is natural to us. It does not first arise out of some special volition" (PLT/US: 189/11). The relation to the interlocutor is not established by a particular exchange; rather the exchange comes later, after a relationship has already been established by proximity. A conversation, moreover, need not inform in order to still achieve some good. To speak to someone means that that person is worth speaking to; the act as such embodies care and fortifies the interpersonal relationship even if the content is uninformative. Precisely because talking is the default, silence can be communicative; it alerts the puzzled interlocutors to the weight of speech by inviting them to pause and consider what really is worth saying, what really will benefit oneself and others. It thereby disrupts the hold that ordinary ruts of conversation has on us and enables us to plow new furrows.

When should we challenge the expected horizons of a conversation? The Grice-Searle worry about shifts in relevance receives clarification from Heidegger's appeal to care and solicitude as the background of conversation. Authenticity enables us to achieve insight into the good for ourselves and for others, although the content of this good is more complex than Heidegger realizes. Some practical identities involve becoming a conscience for others. A mother, father, or friend has an obligation to elevate conversation to focus on higher human goods. A philosopher or other leader has the obligation to counsel others to take care. Other practical identities direct us to be less robust in our challenge to conversational expectations. The human good, the specific dynamics of this situation, and the obligations and possibilities specified by one's own role help fill in the specific content of care. Relevance takes its bearings from a solicitude constrained but also liberated by the context—constrained insofar as it makes certain conversational contributions out of bounds; liberated insofar as it makes certain conversational contributions needful and appropriate—that is, it frees us to be meaningful. What should we say when we speak carefully? That depends on our sense of the good, of this moment, and of the manner of our responsibility for the other. In this way, Heidegger's reticence, like Franklin's silence, frees us up to converse about things of genuine interest rather than things that are merely interesting. In doing so, it gives life to our conversations with each another.

NOTES

1. For quotations of Heidegger, the first page number refers to the English and the second to the German edition: E/G. I have frequently modified the translations in view of uniformity and clarity.
2. Heidegger has in mind the phenomenological "return to the things themselves" as the cardinal maxim.
3. Such roles hearken back to Plato's rejoinder to Thrasymachus's voluntarism: to be a ruler is to have a practical identity determined by the good of the ruled. Korsgaard specifically mentions the disintegration of the tyrant's identity in *Republic* IX (Korsgaard 1996: 102).

WORKS CITED

Aristotle. 1941. *Parts of Animals*. In *The Basic Works of Aristotle*, edited by Richard McKeon. New York: Random House.
Carman, Taylor. 2003. *Heidegger's Analytic: Interpretation, Discourse, and Authenticity in* Being and Time. Cambridge: Cambridge University Press.
Crowell, Steven. 2013. *Normativity and Phenomenology in Husserl and Heidegger*. Cambridge: Cambridge University Press.
Dreyfus, Hubert. 1991. *Being-in-the-World: A Commentary on Heidegger's* Being and Time, *Division I*. Cambridge, MA: MIT Press.
Engelland, Chad. 2004. "Augustinian Elements in Heidegger's Philosophical Anthropology: A Study of the Early Lecture Course on Augustine." *Proceedings of the American Catholic Philosophical Association* 78: 263–75.
———. 2014. *Ostension: Word Learning and Embodied Mind*. Cambridge, MA: MIT Press.

———. 2015. "Heidegger and the Human Difference." *Journal of the American Philosophical Association* 1: 175–93.
———. 2017. *Heidegger's Shadow: Kant, Husserl, and the Transcendental Turn.* New York: Routledge.
Franklin, Benjamin. 1906. *The Autobiography of Benjamin Franklin.* New York: Houghton Mifflin and Co.
Golob, Sacha. 2014. *Heidegger on Concepts, Freedom, and Normativity.* Cambridge: Cambridge University Press.
Grice, H. Paul. 1991. "Logic and Conversation." In *Studies in the Ways of Words.* Cambridge, MA: Harvard University Press.
Heraclitus. 1979. *The Art and Thought of Heraclitus: An Edition of the Fragments with Translation and Commentary.* Edited and translated by Charles Kahn. Cambridge: Cambridge University Press.
Korsgaard, Christine. 1996. *Sources of Normativity.* Cambridge: Cambridge University Press.
Madison, Laurel. 2002. "Have We Been Careless with Socrates' Last Words? A Rereading of the Phaedo." *Journal of the History of Philosophy* 40, no. 4: 421–36.
McMullin, Irene. 2013. *Time and the Shared World: Heidegger on Social Relations.* Evanston, IL: Northwestern University Press.
Plato. 1997. *Plato: Complete Works.* Edited by John M. Cooper. Indianapolis: Hackett Publishing Co.
Ratcliffe, Matthew. 2004. "Realism, Biologism, and 'the Background.'" *Philosophical Explorations* 7, no. 2: 149–66.
Sartre, Jean-Paul. 1993. *Existentialism and Human Emotions.* Translated by Bernard Frechtman and Hazel E. Barnes. New York: Carol Publishing.
Scheler, Max. 1973. *Selected Philosophical Essays.* Translated by David R. Lachterman. Evanston, IL: Northwestern University Press.
Searle, John. 2002. "Conversation." In *Consciousness and Language.* New York: Cambridge University Press.
Sperber, Dan, and Deirdre Wilson. 1995. *Relevance: Communication and Cognition*, 2nd ed. Malden, MA: Blackwell.
Taylor, Charles. 1985. *Human Agency and Language: Philosophical Papers*, vol. 1. Cambridge: Cambridge University Press.

Chapter 8

Rational Ideals and the Unity of Practical Agency

Kant's Postulates of Practical Reason and Their Heideggerian Reconceptualization

Irene McMullin

The aim of this chapter is to uncover a structural similarity in Kant's and Heidegger's conception of how practical reason copes with the unification work with which it is tasked—unification work seemingly at odds with the dissolution, temporal dispersal, and agential division that characterizes the worldly self. In both thinkers, I suggest, this unification work involves commitment to a practical belief in the realizability of self-unity. The question of why we pursue this unity—or indeed whether we ought to—will be bracketed in the interest of thinking through the phenomenology of agency operative in its pursuit.

According to a Heidegger-inspired model of practical rationality, human beings are care-driven agents who act in light of the norms governing the various practical roles and abilities by which they specify who they are trying to be. Such norm-governed practical action is a fluid non-deliberative mode of responsivity to the context and the possibilities of better and worse ways of being that it affords. This fluid agency of everyday coping with the world—whereby things show up as appropriate or inappropriate and are immediately responded to as such—is itself grounded in the agent's commitment to the projects and roles in terms of which those affordances are meaningful: "things can show up as serviceable or suitable . . . only because I am trying to be something, only because some 'possibility for being' (*Seinkönnen*; ability-to-be) is at issue for me" (Crowell 2017: 247).[1] Even the most "mindless" manifestation of such practical action always involves an implicit sense of being at stake in those abilities to be and a commitment that underwrites their bindingness.

For the most part these identity possibilities are delineated for us by public rules and conventions. We simply do what one does, immersed in *das Man*. But the specification that conventional norms provides can never be entirely definitive of what ought to be done in any given situation since they must be sufficiently general to cover an enormous range of persons and circumstances. The fact that my identity is at issue in these practical possibilities—coupled with their indeterminacy—means that I experience myself as tasked with interpretation and application work that reflects my individual sense of who I am trying to be and hence what it is best to do.

Steven Crowell has argued that this process of creative interpretation can be understood according to the Kantian idea of "exemplary necessity," which involves holding oneself up as a kind of model for others—an exemplar of how best to interpret the norms constitutive of the practical identity in question: one "stands as an exemplar (*Vorbild*)"—testifying to what all agents *ought* to recognize as being at stake in that particular possibility (Crowell 2017: 249). In these cases, the agent embodies a judgment that makes a claim to be recognized as what is best—but which cannot be *justified* as such (Crowell 2017: 249) since the limits of the relevant standards of legitimacy have been shown up as insufficient or at issue through that very creative interpretation work. On the Heideggerian picture, this is characterized in terms of the concept of transcendence—a normatively oriented striving that nevertheless lacks the definitive normative criteria in terms of which judgments typically have legitimacy.

This lack of definitive normative guidance raises worries about decisionism—namely, that the model of life that one holds up as best is simply an arbitrary preference. But as Crowell argues, our sense of what is best in these situations is ultimately constrained only by a commitment to universal answerability: that we offer to others our reasons for believing that this is best and hope that they too can understand the claim to validity that the meaning possibility we're staking out makes.

I will return to the question of intersubjective answerability below. But first I would like to think a bit further about the phenomenology of agency that is operative when one "stands as an exemplar." On one reading, doing so is no more than publicly displaying to others a possibility that one has already realized in one's own life. But it seems that "standing as an exemplar" can also be a relationship that one has to *oneself*, and in particular, to one's potential self. What is the relationship one has to the potential or exemplary version of oneself? How can we identify with the version of ourselves toward which we are striving? Can this be understood as an activity of practical reason?[2]

David Velleman speaks of this issue in "Motivation by Ideal," arguing that when we identify with the self we are trying to become it is like "a game of make-believe, in which we pretend to be that with which we identify" (2002:

91).[3] This kind of make-believe requires an agent to get "carried away" with the new identity possibility and put "his real identity and his real relations to other participants temporarily out of mind. In order to enact his fictional identity and his fictional relations to others, he must devote his mind to the fiction" (Velleman 2002: 97). A problem with this, Velleman notes, is that this kind of "putting out of mind" of the real or actual identity configuration in favor of a possible or yearned for one can lead an agent to violate his already-existing commitments and interests.[4] Nevertheless, Velleman suggests that "the temporary irrationality of getting carried away can sometimes be exploited for more permanent gains in rationality. For an agent can get carried away with the better of his motives as well as the worse" (2002: 99). For example, quitting smoking demands thinking of oneself as no longer *being* a smoker and eventually the reality conforms to the ideal.[5]

In the case of smoking, what the new identity possibility demands is fairly straightforward. One can look to others to see what "nonsmoker" looks like in broad outline such that the interpretation work necessary to apply it to one's own life—to imagine oneself into that possibility and inaugurate it through specific actions—is fairly minimal. This kind of self-transformation work involves both other people serving as role models and a sort of bootstrapping maneuver in which a potentiality of the self is first demonstrated as a possibility through an expressive first instantiation of the new identity—an inaugural enactment that can then itself serve as an exemplar for the agent to follow.[6] That kind of exemplary action makes real for the first time a possibility previously only imagined or yearned for, and in so doing one "stands as an exemplar" *for oneself*. In other words, having experienced what it is like to resist smoking in a context where one typically smoked, one is then able to recognize an instantiation of the nonsmoking version of the self *as oneself*. Having encountered an instance of the ideal version of the self *as* a realizable possibility, further work toward its realization can build on that initial exemplary instantiation. Hence we can understand progression toward a potential self as a kind of step-change, each step arising out of concrete choices that manifest the style of being that one is attempting to bring about in one's life. As a result, the irrationality of the "make-believe" in these types of cases seems quite minimal. Of course, this process can proceed in both good and bad directions: having experienced the delights of smoking at a party, one can more easily imagine oneself enjoying a smoke with an afternoon coffee, say.

Velleman has argued that imaginative projection into a potential self is itself an irrational behavior that is only made legitimate by the rationality of the payoff.[7] The "irrationality" of conceiving of oneself otherwise can be mobilized in the service of both rational and irrational ends. But what about these ends themselves? We regularly face choices not simply about how to best instantiate a given practical identity, but also about whether to do so, given the shape of our lives as a whole—both how it is and how it ought to be. How do we enact the self that we envision ourselves capable of becoming in such cases—namely, not simply as a nonsmoker, but as a self more broadly understood, in which a plurality of practical identity possibilities forms a unified whole encompassing a more general sense of who one is striving to be? In such cases a coherent and self-expressive configuration of a plurality of specific practical identities is itself what we're striving to realize. Clearly we look to role models in such cases to give us a sense of "the kind of person" we wish to be, but the creative specification work necessary to apply their model to our own lives is such that they can only offer so much guidance. Hence it seems that we must stand as exemplars for ourselves not simply in terms of the localized specification work necessary to instantiate a particular practical identity, but also in terms of an ideal vision of the shape of our lives as a whole—a vision of how to organize the plurality of claims by which we are bound.

We have seen that Velleman has suggested that the process of ideal-inspired self-becoming is a kind of "fantasy" or "make-believe"—an irrationality only made good by the realization of a rational end product (for example, the status of being a healthy nonsmoker). But most of our practical identities are not characterized by the realization of some end point but rather require the ongoing work of trying to be that thing—teacher, parent, friend. This ongoing process of open-ended self-becoming is only more obviously the case when the end in question is an integrated state of selfhood more globally understood. This temporal open-endedness and dispersion only further complicates a possibility of self-unity that is already compromised by entrenched structural tendencies toward worldly falling (Heidegger) and toward conflict between duty and desire (Kant). All of this seems to rule out a clearly realized end state that could be used as a norm for guiding or assessing one's self-unification and self-specification work. Hence the various forms of agential division and dispersal by which we are characterized would seem to militate against achieving any kind of global agential unity. And yet it seems we must give an account of how the various components of one's identity can be integrated in a nonarbitrary way. How do we arrange their relative priority in our lives?

KANT'S POSTULATES OF PURE PRACTICAL REASON

In many ways, this is a problem for which Kant's postulates of pure practical reason are the solution. Namely, they specify the way that reason posits a unity that is not accessible in the domain of worldly appearances but that enables its coherence. Kant distinguishes between *Vernunft* (reason) and

Verstand (intellect or understanding)[8]—the latter focused on knowledge of the given empirical world of appearances, the former concerning itself not with objects but with their conditions of possibility. As Arendt puts it, "The intellect (*Verstand*) desires to grasp what is given to the senses, but reason (*Vernunft*) wishes to understand its *meaning*" (1981: 57). Hence while the former is concerned with facts about the real—with the requisite criteria for certainty and evidence by which they can be determined as such—reason is not.

A condition for the possibility of unified empirical knowledge, for example, is commitment to the idea of the world as a unity of all appearances—a unity that cannot itself be intuited. Although the constitutive role of the categories assures the basic coherence of our experiences of the physical world, we are also tasked with the practical work of making sense of how variation and multiplicity in that coherent experience can be understood to fit together. Reason enables us to grasp the transcendent whole—the world—in terms of which the empirical parts can be seen to be meaningful in relation to each other. This work of meaning-making in light of a background sense of the whole occurs in an everyday way in the basic forms of coping by which we attempt to organize our disparate experiences. But we also see the unifying function of this "idea of reason" at work in the sciences, for example, when we try to find in our empirical experiences the kind of systematic unity we specify in scientific laws. Hence "world" is an idea of reason that strays beyond the realm of experience but nevertheless has a kind of reality insofar as it serves a regulative role in the organization of our varied experience. It contains "a certain completeness that no possible empirical knowledge can attain," but rather represents "a systematic unity" that reason "tries to make our empirically possible unity approach, without it ever being fully attained" (EG: 117). "World" serves as a unifying condition for discrete empirical experiences that are themselves understood as aspiring to that systematic wholeness.[9]

But as Heidegger points out in "On the Essence of Ground," "world" as Kant understands it bears within it a necessary reference to *finite* experience—it is the name for the total possible unity of *human* experience in its relationship to beings: "bringing world before itself is the originary projection of the possibilities of Dasein, insofar as, in the midst of beings, it is to be able to comport itself toward such beings" (EG: 123). Hence Heidegger argues that Kant is ultimately speaking of "world" not simply as the arena of scientific laws and the natural entities of which human beings are one species, but also of "world" as the total arena of human freedom and striving (EG: 119–20). Understood properly, Heidegger argues, "world" is a regulative idea of reason by which to make sense of the unity of human beings in their relationship to beings as a whole—a system of significance and coherence that is a condition for the possibility of any particular practical activity of truth-finding or meaning-making. In keeping with his other works, Heidegger argues in "On the Essence of Ground" that the wholeness in light of which we organize our experience is not simply the unity of present-at-hand objects, then, but rather the unity of the entire context of significance within which all of Dasein's intentional activity occurs.

Kant's practical philosophy makes use of several different tools for understanding the sense-making activity of creatures who are governed not simply by the drive for theoretical knowing but also by individual practical striving. Kant argues that the coherence of such striving rests on a practical belief in what he calls "the highest good": roughly speaking, a *moral* world. This has two elements:

> First of all, it includes virtue, as the "supreme" good, that is, as that which is unconditionally good. In order to be the "complete" good, however, Kant adds, the highest good must also include happiness. The two elements are to be connected in such a way that the first is the cause of the second. (KpV 5:110) (Kleingeld 2016: 38)

In other words, reason posits a world in which there is a realized unity between subjective desires and objective reason; a world in which happiness—the satisfaction of our wishes[10]—is caused by virtue. "In sum, the highest good, when conceived as a moral world, is the world that moral agents would bring into existence if their agency faced no obstacles, that is, if all moral agents were fully virtuous and their actions would achieve their moral ends" (Kleingeld 2016: 41). The problem, however, is that this appears to be impossible for non-holy finite wills. The impossibility is twofold. On the one hand, the happiness that the highest good promises presupposes a moral author of the world who is capable of ensuring that good people prosper and bad people don't. In other words, it presupposes that the *worldly* conditions necessary for allocating happiness in proportion to duty are realized. On the other hand, the highest good demands that one's wishes and one's duties are not in conflict (i.e., that one becomes a holy will). In other words, it presupposes that *agential* obstacles to the highest good can be overcome such that the unity of desire and duty can be realized within a single agent.

While theoretical reason looks to observe the unity that it takes to exist in the world (e.g., by formulating scientific laws expressive of that unity), practical reason looks to *create* the unity that it takes as potentially existing in the world. But it needs assurances of the realizability of this unity if this end is to be motivationally efficacious. Hence Kant argues that committing to the highest good as a practical possibility (i.e., such that it actually governs our actions) requires commitment to two further practical postulates: the existence of a god who could guarantee this harmony of desire and reason by making happiness proportional to virtue, and an immortal soul by which we can earn it.[11] Kant defines the postulates as beliefs that "reason finds itself constrained to assume; otherwise it would have to regard the moral laws as empty figments of the brain" (Kant 1929: 639; KrV A811/B839). The postulates are essentially subjectively necessary hypotheses about reality. Without the practical postulates, the claims of morality would be "objects of approval and admiration, but not springs of purpose and action" (Kant 1929: 640; KrV A813/B81).

Although these two postulates are typically understood in terms of our ability to realize the *worldly* conditions of a happiness allocated in proportion to virtue (i.e., we must believe in God to believe that good people will be rewarded with happiness) here I wish to think through the role that these beliefs play in testifying to the realizability of the agential conditions of the highest good—namely, the agent's self-conception *as* a potential unity of desire and duty. What role does belief in "God" and "immortality" play in conceptualizing oneself as a potentially holy will (i.e., the self understood as a constituent element of the highest good)? We have seen that for both Kant and Heidegger it is the "world," properly understood, that serves as the whole in terms of which finite experience can be coherently organized. But this wholeness, as we will see, also requires a particular grasp of *oneself* as a whole in terms of which specific experiences can be coherently organized. In what follows I will both unpack these claims in a Kantian register and examine the extent to which we can understand there to be Heideggerian analogues to the postulates that enable this self-grasping. In other words, I will examine the postulates of God's existence and the immortality of the soul through a phenomenological lens.

IMMORTALITY AND GOD'S EXISTENCE

According to Kant, it is necessary to adopt the view that there is a possible reality in which one's given, affective self—one's "wishes and wills" (moral or otherwise)—could be brought into perfect unity with one's rational agency—one's duty. Practical reason demands that we believe in the existence of God and the immortality of the soul as necessary conditions of belief in the realizability of this highest good. Since it appears impossible to realize this end—given that we are finite creatures in the grip of incentives or wishes at odds with morality—it seems practically impossible to set and pursue it.[12] The postulates can help us resolve this practical conflict since, "if the soul is immortal, and God exists, the morally required ends may after all be realizable . . . [and so] the agent's action in pursuit of those ends may be seen as consistent, not irrational" (Zuckert 2018: 201). Or, in Kant's words:

> The ideas of *God* and *immortality* . . . [are] the conditions of applying the morally determined will to its object given to it a priori (the highest good). Consequently, their possibility in this practical relation can and must be *assumed*, although we cannot theoretically cognize and have insight into them. (Kant 2015: 4; KpV 5:4)

A good deal of Kant scholarship is dismissive of these two postulates insofar as they appear to be contaminated by thinly disguised metaphysical speculation of the kind that Kant's critical project had purportedly ruled out.[13] They appear so insofar as they purport to be theoretical propositions about an ideal or transcendent state that go beyond the limits of the intellect—thereby ruling out the epistemic warrant by which such propositions are typically legitimated. Of course, Kant insists that they are *beliefs*, not *knowledge*: they lack this epistemic justification but are nevertheless firmly held convictions about the nature of reality.[14] Kant's views on how the legitimate positing of propositions without epistemic warrant is possible changes over the years,[15] but for our purposes, the claim that the postulates are things in which we must *believe* for practical purposes ("their possibility in this practical relation can and must be assumed") amounts to the claim that conviction and commitment (subjective necessity) is legitimate—indeed, required—in the case of the practical postulates (i.e., it is justified that we hold them to have objective reality), despite the absence of the epistemic warrant that typically provides legitimacy to such convictions.

Hence Kant appears to hold that our relationship to postulates like God's existence and our own immortality must be one of *belief*.[16] As Rachel Zuckert argues, however, that belief in God and immortality may also threaten to undermine moral agency by giving rise to fanaticism or fatalism (2018: 208). Hence if these postulates are indeed to be understood as *propositions* about objective reality, they will have to be recognized as antinomial. In light of this she proposes an alternative interpretation of the postulates as regulative ideas guiding action that are not endorsed or even postulated as objectively true propositions. In other words, the postulates are not to be approached with the cognitive attitude of belief in their objective reality, but rather with a more fundamentally practical orientation—which she specifies in terms of hope: "The attitude of hope is, then, both weaker than belief—it does not assert that the world is so but only that it may be—but also more strongly practical, for it holds the future open before the agent" (Zuckert 2018: 214).[17] Difficulties arise with this reading, however, insofar as Kant seems to explicitly deny that mere *hope* is sufficient: "the theological postulates are intended by Kant to *ground* hope, not merely to express it" (Gardner 2011: 193). Hence it is essential that the postulates are present to reason as objects with sufficient content that they make a kind of claim to reality on us and in so doing serve their motivational and organizing role.[18] Zuckert recognizes this, arguing that they are best understood on the model of regulative ideas: "For practical reason as for theoretical reason, the ideas of God and soul are thus (properly) treated not as presenting actual entities, subject matters of cognitive claims, even belief. Rather, they are regulative ideas, which hold open, direct, and promote striving" (2018: 216). Hence if we take the postulates of God's existence and our own immortality to be regulative ideas akin to the idea of "world" discussed above, we might read them as practically efficacious orientations toward a systematic unity that transcends but helps to organize experience—an orientation, qua practical, that presents this unity to the agent as *realizable* through her own agency, not merely as observable in the world.

How, specifically, do the postulates of immortality and God function to enable pursuit of the unity of the self, despite the inherent conflict between affect and reason? They do so by allowing us to conceptualize that inherent conflict as able to be overcome. Think first of what Kant says about the postulate of immortality. For creatures like us, a perfectly good will—whereby what we want is exactly what reason demands—could only be attained through endless progress (Kant 2015: 99; KpV 5:122). And since endless progress is only possible on the presupposition of the same being continuing endlessly, we must presuppose the immortality of that being. In other words, it is necessary to commit to an understanding of oneself as *immortal* because only on its basis could we be motivated to pursue a reality in which desire and duty form a unity whereby both are satisfied. But as Allen Wood points out, Kant can hardly mean that a condition in which the complete correspondence of incentive and duty is actually attained at a particular point *within* or at the *end* of this endless progress, since that would mean that at some point we somehow completely eradicate our sensuous nature and become holy wills—in other words, cease to be human. In order to deal with this problem, Kant suggests that God is able to see in the endless progress from less holy to more holy a kind of *principle* of holiness. God supposedly takes this to be good enough for allocating a perfect happiness commensurate with that moral goodness (i.e., for establishing the highest good).[19] Hence the two postulates go together: the idea of the infinity of the immortal soul makes reasonable the endless striving of selfhood in its projection into a seemingly unrealizable possibility, while God's capacity to discern some principle governing that open-ended striving gives us a way to think of ourselves as nevertheless available to the kind of definition necessary to conceptualize this possibility *as* realizable.

Because the Kantian model takes the complete harmony of reason and affect to be *impossible* for non-holy agents such as ourselves, its postulated realization—belief in which is necessary for us to be motivated to pursue this "highest good" at all—is conceptualized as a state of infinite becoming beyond the sensible realm, accompanied by belief in an extraworldly perspective by which this infinite development could nevertheless be defined as realized. Hence both postulates are necessary for grasping the self as a unitary whole that is nevertheless characterized by endless becoming toward a condition that is stipulated at the outset as impossible for us to achieve. They are necessary unifying self-conceptions that exceed the bounds of experience but are posited—at reason's behest—as realizable in order to render practical agency intelligible to itself.

But if we reject Kant's account of the self—according to which reason and affect, duty and desire are irrevocably at odds—is there any sense in which the coherence of practical agency still requires anything like these postulates? In what follows, I will argue that despite significant differences, the Heideggerian view also involves something analogous to these postulates of practical reason: modes of self-grasping that testify to the realizability of self-unity and transcend the bounds of worldly experience.

HEIDEGGERIAN "POSTULATES"

When read through a phenomenological lens, the Kantian idea of viewing oneself as immortal—and the role that this plays in organizing one's practical agency—is a conception of oneself as engaged in an endless task of self-becoming, challenged in its aim by forms of experienced disunity that appear irrevocable. And the Kantian idea of viewing oneself as standing in relation to a judging God is—in a phenomenological register—a conception of oneself as assessable in an exemplary moment that stands out from that endless striving as an event in which disunity is overcome.

Like Kant, Heidegger takes our worldly way of being to be characterized by certain fundamental forms of division and disunity. Also like Kant, Heidegger thinks we must grasp this disunity as something that can be overcome—a vision of realizability that informs the work of self-unification with which we are tasked. Unlike Kant, however, Heidegger's view makes room for exemplary instances of this realized unity that thereby attest to its possibility. Heidegger himself only explicitly provides an account of one of these forms of attested-to unity, but it is one that relies on phenomenological analogues of Kant's postulates discussed above—namely, Heidegger's account of anxiety/death/conscience demonstrates the possibility of an exemplary instance of unity despite the temporal and fallen dispersal that characterizes worldly Dasein's mode of being. After discussing the comparison between Kant's postulates and Heidegger's account of anxiety/death/conscience in greater detail, I will turn, in the final sections of the chapter, to a discussion of a second form of practical unity—and the one with which the chapter began: namely, a unified personal identity achieved in the face of the plurality of practical identities by which we are gripped. Making use of Kantian resources, I will suggest that this too demands something like a postulate of practical reason: in this case, in the form of a creative schema of personal unity.

The Dispersed Self

The problem of grasping oneself as a whole—despite being dispersed across time and fallen, anonymous modes of self-understanding—is a problem that Heidegger attempts to solve using the notions of existential death, anxiety, and conscience.[20] In *Being and Time* these ideas are used as tools for grasping Dasein as a whole despite the fact that such wholeness is at odds with our way of being as temporally dispersed and engaged in publicly specified projects of trying to be that are characterized by openness to possibility and falling. Experiences of death/anxiety/conscience enable exemplary instances of the kind of lived integrity or authenticity that Heidegger specifies as the norm governing a unified mode of being: authenticity is the stance of self-ownership that makes *you*—and not the anonymous "they" of *das Man*—answerable for the specific choices that you make. This is accomplished in an exemplary moment—the *Augenblick*—wherein past, present, and future are unified in a single point of self-understanding, thereby achieving a kind of unity and coherence despite the open-ended incompleteness that characterizes the temporally dispersed kinds of things that we are. In the moment of the *Augenblick*, when we "choose to choose," we stand as an exemplar for ourselves as the unified self now recognized as realizable.[21] Such exemplary experiences are then taken to serve as a model for organizing further specific manifestations of practical agency.[22]

The similarities to Kant's practical postulates discussed above should be obvious: here we see Heidegger wrestling with the fact that both an endless open-ended projecting into the future, along with a tendency to have one's identity dispersed in the multiple anonymous acts that make up one's days—can nevertheless be grasped *as* a whole if one conceptualizes this endless becoming in time as manifesting a principled unity that can be recognized as such in a single moment. Kant's God is one way to conceptualize our endless becoming as a kind of whole by way of the particular style or principle of striving that it displays; in the same way, Heidegger's call of conscience is a way to conceptualize one's dispersal *as* a unity to be achieved through a principled stance of self-ownership.

Both approaches characterize the aimed-at unity as in some sense both transcending the bounds of worldly experience and as realizable. In Kant's case, the "immortal soul" is a placeholder for that which individuates us but without defining us in terms of a particular configuration of given worldly facts. And this is a promising way to understand what Heidegger's ideas of anxiety and death are also doing: namely, providing us with a way to think about a possible unity of selfhood that is not defined by any given configuration of worldly facts. Anxiety "takes away from Dasein the possibility of understanding itself, as it falls, in terms of the "world" and the way things have been publicly interpreted" (BT: 232/SZ: 187). Anxious Dasein displays a self-understanding in which particular worldly facts about who it is are no longer experienced as definitive; it grasps itself, instead, *as* an open-ended capacity for ongoing self-determination. Hence like Kant's notion of the immortal soul, we see Heidegger positing the possibility of a unity of the self that transcends worldly modes of manifestation.

The Kantian postulate of God's existence, on the other hand, involves adopting a conception of oneself as assessible in terms of success or failure based on the extent to which the discrete worldly elements of one's life display a general tendency toward the good—a tendency that is itself not reducible to or experienceable from within those specific worldly experiences and as such transcends the limits of experience. Like the Kantian God, Heidegger's notion of "conscience" serves a comparable purpose insofar as it is an experience of being judged from a perspective external to Dasein's worldly being, an extraworldly self-orientation in which the worldly dispersal of the self is grasped as able to be overcome. "In its 'who,' the caller is definable in a 'worldly' way by nothing at all. The caller is Dasein in its uncanniness: primordial, thrown being in-the-world as the 'not-at-home'—the bare 'that-it-is' in the 'nothing' of the world" (BT: 321/SZ: 276–77). Although Kant attributes this perspective of assessment to God and Heidegger attributes it to the potential authentic self, both characterize it as second-personal and extraworldly in structure.[23] It is not the everyday "me myself" to whom I experience myself as answerable in this experience, but an external perspective whose judgment imposes on me a sense of the realizability of a potential self-unity that is not possible to generate otherwise.

Despite these structural similarities, there are clearly important differences between the two accounts. Kant's view depends on a robustly moral characterization of the principle in terms of which the self is unified—namely, conformity to duty—whereas Heidegger's view (appears to be) amoral insofar as it simply requires a practical self-relation of responsibility and temporal unity.[24] It also appears to be the case that, for Heidegger, it is possible to experience exemplary *instances* of the ideal unity by which our everyday experiences might be organized—although they too are in a sense "extraworldly" experiences—whereas Kant's commitment to the impossibility of agential coherence for human beings means that his view suggests a more "as if" structure: that is, we must act *as if* the realizability of the highest good is possible, including the achievement of the status of holy will—but we can't directly *experience* its realizability. It is, rather, a matter of faith or hope—with the attendant problem of how to understand the relationship between theoretical and practical reason to which this gives rise. Or so it seems. Here a return to Velleman's article might prove helpful, since he argues that to obey the categorical imperative *just is* to realize an ideal image of the will (2002: 103). Hence we might think it possible, even on the Kantian picture, for an agent to achieve a kind of momentary exemplary instance of perfected will status, which then testifies to the nature and realizability of that ideal condition for which one strives in one's life as a whole.[25] Although this would not provide evidence of the guaranteed realizability of the highest good as such—which demands belief in the objective worldly conditions necessary for making happiness proportional to virtue—it might serve as testimony to the subjective realizability of the unity of agential desire and duty.

Despite these differences—or seeming differences—we can note how both accounts require commitment to a world-transcending idea of normatively governed self-unity in order for agents to cope with the everyday disunity that they experience themselves as bound to strive against.[26]

The Fragmented Self

Here I wish to consider whether there is another sense in which our mode of being is characterized by a lack of unity that we strive to overcome by way of a model of realized unity. We have seen that, for Heidegger, anxiety, death, and conscience give us a sense of ourselves as unified in the moment of responsible self-ownership despite our dispersal into anonymous worldly possibilities and our condition of temporal ecstasis. But as we saw at the outset of this chapter, we are also characterized by another kind of disunity: the fact that we are claimed by a plurality of (potential) practical identities and we must develop a means of coping with their conflicting demands. Responsible temporal unity gives us no tools for doing so. In this sense it seems that we need a different kind of practical postulate, a need that is satisfied neither by belief in God and immortality nor their Heideggerian analogues in authenticity and authentic temporality. Recall that when it comes to the actual choices that we are to responsibly and authentically make, Heidegger simply exhorts us to look to our unique situation—a fact that has led many to accuse Heidegger of decisionistic nihilism.[27] Within any given situation each agent is claimed by a plurality of (possible) normative demands depending upon the practical identities to which she commits and how she arranges their relative priority in her life. Hence if we are to achieve the coherence in our lives as a whole that is necessary for nonarbitrary relationships between plural practical identities, we require other practical "postulates"—other ways to grasp ourselves as realizable unities despite the worldly evidence testifying to our essential fragmentation. In other words, to avoid understanding ourselves simply as externally related agglomerations of acts and identities, we must be able to adopt a stance on ourselves as a coherent personal unity.

Of course, one might object that it is not, in fact, necessary to believe that it's possible that all of one's normative parts fit together in such a coherent personal identity. But without a regulative idea of such normative coherence—a principled way to relate our different practical identities to each other—we are in danger of having our condition of normative pluralism collapse into a state of fragmentation whereby commitment to one practical identity or value can stand in no meaningful relationship to another. Unless an agent has some means by which to try to organize her life into a practical unity, the choices she makes between the different practical identities to which she is (or might be) committed will be arbitrary. Since we must act—and doing so always prioritizes or inflects the different practical identities to which we are committed—we need some nonarbitrary way to manage their relative priority. The practical positing of a realizable ideal of coherence isn't a neurotic perfectionism, then, but the material application of the responsibility-taking that is specified in the idea of authenticity: I find myself answerable for the cares by which I am gripped—with the consequence being that I must organize the relative weight and meaning of those cares in my "situation" (i.e., in my life as a whole).[28] This is not to deny the possibility of experiencing ruptures or radical conversions in identity; we might, for example, denounce a practical identity that had previously played a central role in our lives. But when this occurs we find ourselves compelled to readjust the relative priority of the other roles we are committed to playing—to create a new balance among them, else we will have no means for principled decision-making when they come into conflict.

Since, when it comes to practical identities, the shape of any such organization must be idiosyncratic to each one of us, the content by which it provides such regulative guidance cannot arise solely from some shared (meta) practical identity.[29] The posited whole—if it is to function as an *individual* regulative ideal—requires more material content than temporal unity or authentic self-ownership or shared (public) norms can provide. Rather, we each require our own model or schema for how to integrate the unique set of practical identities to which we are committed in our lives as a whole. How are we to understand this?

Role models will, as we have seen, play an important role here—one wishes to lead a life like the admired other, thereby providing clues as to how to organize specific acts and identities into a coherent whole expressive of its many parts. But the idiosyncratic nature of being in the grip of commitments A, B, and C—and not X, Y, and Z—means that each of us will require a more individual model of possible unity than another person could provide.

In thinking through the experience of the potential unity of the self, it seems phenomenologically inaccurate to suggest that agents have anything like an explicit vision of unity that could simply be applied in particular situations. Instead, I would suggest that each person has an inchoate sense of what does or does not "fit" with the self she is striving to be; a general sense of the rough arrangement of the parts of her life in terms of which specific choices ought to be made. This sense of fit—an inchoate sense of who one is trying to be (or not be)—underwrites both our norm-responsivity within particular practical identities and our choice of which ones to take up at all.

MODELING PERSONAL UNITY

In the final sections of the chapter, I wish to explore the idea that a fruitful way to think about these models of personal unity is in terms of Kant's idea of the schematism, and in particular, the creative activity involved in schematizing.[30] The idea is that the agent creates something like a schema of her own personal unification, which can then serve a regulative role in the arrangement of particular worldly acts or events. For Kant, the schemata bring heterogeneous elements into relation by way of a mediating representation that is itself homogenous with both elements (Kant 1929: 180–81; KrV A138/B177). Hence to schematize is to create a relationship between two different things by way of a third middle term that shares features with both (Kant 1929: 180; KrV A137–38/B176–77). As Matherne puts it, a schema is like a pattern—or "sketch," "gestalt," or "outline" by which an intuition is synthesized such that it represents a concept, and by which a concept is manifest in a "unified sensible way" (2014: 188). Hence we might think of the schema as a general pattern or style of meaning-making that unifies seemingly incompatible elements. The activity by which a schema is produced is characterized by Kant as a kind of artistic creation or *Kunst*, which involves flexible, responsive, and projective modes of making sense of the manifold of experience by way of "indirect" or "symbolic" presentations (Matherne 2014: 192; 196). Heidegger characterizes "world-forming" in "On the Essence of Ground" as displaying a comparable structure, whereby Dasein gives itself a view of the whole by way of a paradigmatic form [*Vor-bild*] (EG: 122).[31]

Such creative schematizing work occurs on the level of *self*-grasping, I want to suggest, when a person understands a concrete instance of her own agency or state of being *as* an exemplary or paradigmatic form of the wholeness toward which she is oriented. It occurs when she understands a particular act as symbolically representing a normative pattern or style by which the whole of her personal identity can be understood. Hence we might return here to the idea of serving as an exemplar for *oneself* by way of individual experiential states or actions that are taken by the agent to instantiate a more globally expressive potential way of being. We schematize these concrete particular experiences when we understand them to represent a particular gestalt or style of possible personal unity.[32] The suggestion here, then, is that the work of unifying one's various practical identities and normative commitments relies on the possibility of conceptualizing specific moments of agency as symbolic manifestations of a particular style of normative ordering in one's life as a whole.

We might think here of how Heidegger speaks of artworks as "setting up a world" in "Origin of the Work of Art." Namely, artworks are characterized there as exemplary manifestations of a particular possibility of normative ordering: they "put up for decision what is holy and what is unholy, what great and what small, what brave and what cowardly, what lofty and what flighty, what master and what slave" (BW: 169). The suggestion, then, is that personal unity requires such a stance toward the *self*; it demands the creative work of seeing specific states or actions as paradigmatic forms that "set up a self."[33] This kind of creative self-schematizing work can correspondingly be thought in terms of Kant's idea of aesthetic genius, whereby the agent gives herself the rule or norm by which she will be governed (Kant 2002: 186; KU 5: 307), guided, as she does, by "no other standard than the feeling of unity in the presentation" (Kant 2002: 195; KU 5: 319).

In the case of the unification of personal identity, however, this "feeling of unity" cannot arise solely on formal grounds of mere coherence if it is to serve its normative organizing role: the relevant norm of self-unity must be a state of coherence that reflects one's sense of what genuinely matters. One might take some guidance from Nietzsche in *Schopenhauer as Educator* in this regard:

> What have you truly loved up to now, what has drawn your soul aloft, what has mastered it and at the same time blessed it? Set up these revered objects before you and perhaps their nature and their sequence will give you a law, the fundamental law of your own true self. Compare these objects one with another, see how one completes, expands, surpasses, transfigures another, how they constituted a stepladder upon which you have clambered up to yourself as you are now; for your true nature lies, not concealed deep within you, but immeasurably high above you, or at least above that which you usually take yourself to be. (1997: 129)

Positing oneself as a whole governed by such "fundamental laws of your own true self" can provide a regulatory role, helping the agent understand how the various disparate elements of her life can be marshalled to the task of becoming who she is trying to be. Nietzsche speaks of these "fundamental laws" as being revealed via one's love for some things and not others. These deep life-organizing cares are not specifying merely formal relationships of temporal unity or responsibility-taking, then, but bear more individualized and substantive content, positing a way in which the specific constituent elements of each person's "situation" might be organized to form a coherent and self-expressive whole.

INTERSUBJECTIVITY

The imaginative schematizing work that we each do in giving content to the ideal of wholeness by which we can organize the plurality of our practical identities is specific to each agent's life—each of us "sets up" a different self. But this self-creation is not only the work of an isolated genius; it is undertaken in conversation with others. Although this idea of aesthetic self-creation does—and should—have an element of radical individuality, this self-unification work also contains an intersubjective element insofar as these creative schemata are not inflexible forms but adaptive and projective patterns of response to the changing (intersubjectively structured) situation. The result is that there might be more than one way that the regulative idea of personal unity can be made concrete to agents. In closing, I would like to suggest that there are (at least) two ways in which the fact of intersubjectivity might shape the self-unification work of practical reason in this regard:

1. In our unique personal relationships, others can see particular acts we undertake as exemplary manifestations of personal unity and reflect back to us a different pattern or model of identity than the one with which we might be operating. By observing us from without, the others who stand in close relationships to us can sometimes show us alternative fruitful ways to grasp ourselves as a whole.
2. Similarly, social/political metaphors of unity might also shape our personal models of that unity. We might think of this in terms of Heidegger's history of being, which argues that different epochs operate with different background ontologies regarding the nature of self and world. As we saw with Kant, for example, we might conceive of ourselves as immortal souls in relationship with a God who discerns in our disparate acts a direction of travel. Hence the ideal of the unified self has, for Kant, a religious tenor that may shape the model of personal unity at work in one's efforts to organize multiple normative commitments.

The suggestion, in other words, is that others can provide content for different imaginative concretizations of the unified self, complicating the exemplar of selfhood with which the individual attempts to unify her practical experience. It is in light of this that we might understand Kant's increasingly intersubjective emphasis—for example, in his characterization of reason in political terms.[34] It is in the same way that we can understand Crowell's claim from the outset that, on the Heideggerian picture, we are governed by answerability to others in our attempts to specify a vision of the good life. Although Crowell tends to model this answerability on reason-giving—giving an account of oneself—I have suggested that this answerability might also involve sharing with others the imaginative metaphors or archetypes by which we attempt to grasp the possibility of our own self-unity. If this is so, then a key element of this kind of answerability to and with others is a commitment to holding open a space of creative expression in which unforeseen meaning possibilities can emerge through tensions that arise between our different metaphors of wholeness—our different models of how to be a unified self. Hence we should reject any conception of practical reason as simple ratiocination. Rather, we have seen that practical reason involves imaginative modeling—in dialogue with others—of the self-unity that we never fully encounter in the world but which nevertheless orients our worldly striving.[35]

NOTES

1. See also McMullin 2019, especially chapter 6; Wrathall 2015; Crowell 2014.

2. This is an idea discussed extensively in Nietzsche's writing, especially in "Schopenhauer as Educator" (1997). See also Zagzebski 2017: 136 and Golob forthcoming.

3. Velleman's discussion takes place in the context of an attempt to think about how different motives can mix. "One way requires the agent to think of himself as acting on both motives at once and hence to be guided, not only by their combined forces, but also by his conception of how those forces combine. In this case, the agent is consciously engaged in a mixed activity. . . . Another way for motives to combine is for the agent to conceive of himself as acting on only one of them, while the other tacitly modifies this activity. . . . What makes for the difference between these two ways of mixing motives is the motivational role of the agent's self-conception, which is not epiphenomenal on his behavior, not just an idle commentary. In one case, the agent deliberately acts on both motives, by enacting a story of both; in the other case, the agent enacts the story of one motive, while this enactment is subject to unheralded modification by the other" (2002: 96–97).

4. For Velleman, this points to a fundamental division in our motivational structure: "between the motives that are being enacted and the motives that can at most modify that enactment" (2002: 99). This "division in an agent's motives can lead to action that is irrational in relation to the totality of his desires and interests, as when it lets him get carried away in a debate, to his subsequent regret" (2002: 99).

5. Velleman defines such an ideal as "the image of another person, or a currently untrue image of oneself, that one can get carried away with enacting" (2002: 100).

6. I explore this idea in McMullin 2019, especially chapter 5: "Called to Be Oneself." Velleman offers a similar approach: "Suppose that one idealizes a person for his generosity and wants to resemble him in this respect. Insofar as this desire directly moves one to do generous things, those acts will not in fact be motivated by generosity, after all, and so one's attempted imitation of the ideal will be an obvious failure. Indeed, one would be unlikely to acquire or to learn generosity through acts motivated in this way. The desire to mold oneself in the image of a generous person will meet with better success if it moves one first to imagine being a generous person and then to enact this self-image, making believe that one is generous and using as props whatever motives one has that can be cast in the role of generosity" (2002: 100).

7. "The activity of pretending to be a non-smoker was irrational in the sense that it made the smoker insensitive to some of the reasons that actually applied to him, and consequently led him to do something that wasn't supported by the balance of actual reasons" (Velleman 2002: 102).

8. Although often translated as "understanding," in *The Life of the Mind* Arendt insists that it be translated as "intellect." See Bernstein 2000: 283.

9. As Heidegger points out, the rational idea of "world" transcends experience not in the sense that Kant's transcendental *ideal* does—which is the absolutely unconditioned—but rather as a transcending that nevertheless remains tied to finitude (i.e., to possible appearance): "But transcendence in the Kantian [49] sense of surpassing experience is ambivalent. On the one hand, it can mean: *within* experience, exceeding that which is given *within it* as such, namely, the manifold of appearances. This is the case for the representation 'world.' But transcendence also means: stepping *out* of experience as finite knowledge altogether and representing the possible whole of all things as the 'object' of an *intuitus originarius*. In such transcendence there arises the transcendental ideal, compared to which world constitutes a *restriction* and becomes a term for finite, *human* knowledge in its totality. The concept of world stands, as it were, *between* the 'possibility of experience' and the 'transcendental ideal,' and thus in its core means the totality of the finitude that is *human* in essence" (EG: 119).

10. "*Happiness* is the state of a rational being in the world in the whole of whose existence *everything goes according to his wish and will*, and rests, therefore, on the harmony of nature with his whole end as well as with the essential determining ground of his will" (Kant 2015: 100; KpV 5:124).

11. Freedom is also a practical postulate but one that has a special status for Kant insofar as it involves immediate cognition of the supersensible: "Nothing analogous is available for the propositions that God exists or that my soul is immortal: there can be no practical reflexive pressure to assent to the theological postulates in the way that there is for the postulate of freedom, since the question of whether God exists is not one that, in the very entertaining of it, allows and directs me to answer it through the determination of my will. So although practical reason can require theoretical reason to accept the theological postulates, as it does the freedom postulate, practical reason cannot *assist* theoretical reason in doing so in the way that it can with regard to the freedom postulate" (Gardner 2011: 199). We will largely bracket discussion of the postulate of freedom here. See also Pasternack 2011.

12. For the purposes of this chapter I will largely bracket the question of *why* we must pursue it, focusing only on *how* it is possible for practical reason to do so, assuming it must.

13. See, for example, Beck 1960: 268; Allison 1990: 172; Surprenant 2008.

14. For discussion of whether the postulates are objectively binding or just subjectively held, see Kuehn 1985 and Wood 1970.

15. Pasternack 2011 discusses this historical development at length.

16. See Pasternack 2011: 302–3. Pasternack goes on to show that only freedom genuinely counts as a proper belief for the mature Kant, while the practical postulates of God and immortality should be understood as *derivative* beliefs insofar as they provide epistemic warrant for belief in the Highest Good. The Highest Good is in turn not a direct but a derivative belief, on Pasternack's account, for two reasons: "First, it is not introduced as an explanatory condition but as a product of moral reflection about what ought to be. Second, it is not (to borrow the grammatical distinction) a declarative but an imperative. Our assent is to what *ought* to be. Whereas we assent to the Practical Postulates not as prescriptions but as facts: 'there is a God' and 'there is an afterlife,' not 'there *ought* to be a God,' 'there *ought* to be an afterlife.' Thus the conviction of our assent in the case of the Highest Good carries the additional sense of a commitment to do" (310).

17. Difficulties arise here, however, as Kant denies "that the mere *hope* of achieving the highest good is sufficient for moral purposes: the theological postulates are intended by Kant to *ground* hope, not merely to express it" (Gardner 2011: 193).

18. See Pasternack 2011 on how the postulates of God and immortality appear to play an explanatory or justificatory role in the possibility of commitment to the highest good, thereby undermining their status as "direct" beliefs as opposed to derivative ones (312). Gardner 2011 includes a lengthy discussion on the thorny relationship between theoretical and practical reason that this must involve.

19. Kant 2015: 99; KpV 5:123.

20. "The question hovering over us of an authentic wholeness of Dasein and its existential constitution can be placed on a viable, phenomenal basis only if that question can hold fast to a possible authenticity of its being attested by Dasein itself" (BT: 311/SZ: 267). This is particularly difficult because, as he puts it in *Fundamental Concepts of Metaphysics*, Dasein is "essentially *'absent.'* Absent in a fundamental sense—never simply at hand, but absent in his essence, in his *essentially being away*, removed into *essential having been* and *future. . . . Transposed* into the possible, he must constantly *be mistaken* concerning what is actual" (FCM 366).

21. For discussion of how "choosing to choose" is best understood as an exemplary instantiation of Dasein's potential authenticity, see McMullin 2013a, chapter 7. See also Kukla 2002, Crowell 2014.

22. How exactly this authentic moment is meant to inform consequent action is a matter of some debate. Some suggest, for example, that authentic Dasein "narrativizes" its situation to make sense of it via the resulting "life-gestalt" (Fisher 2010: 262–63). For a Heideggerian critique of narrative theory in this regard, see Altshuler 2015 and Crowell 2004. McManus 2018 suggests an alternative model: the "all-things-considered judgment model," which rejects narrative closure and understands authenticity as openness to the specificity and plurality of all of the multiple,

competing normative demands one faces at a time: "when we act we must take a position on these many obligations, collapsing this multiplicity in a unified judgment of what matters most. My failing to do so would leave me, in a recognizable sense, 'fragmented': I fail to—so to speak—pull myself together" (16). Although I am in agreement with much of what McManus says here, I object to his view on two grounds: (a) that this kind of situation-specific concrete unification work is the best way to understand what Heidegger means by *authenticity*—which I take to be describing a more formal stance of responsibility-taking, with further concrete specification and unification work falling outside the remit of that concept, and (b) that the work of unifying the self as a whole is best understood in terms of making *judgments*. See also McManus 2015, Varga 2011, Haugeland 2013.

23. See McMullin 2013a for further discussion of the second-personal and extraworldly nature of the call of conscience.

24. See McMullin 2013a for a problematization of this common interpretation of Heidegger's view.

25. One might also consider here the kind of conversion experience that Kant discusses in the *Religion* as "putting on the new man" (Kant 1996: 92; 6:47). See also McMullin 2013b for discussion.

26. The reason we are (or feel ourselves to be) so bound is an important and clearly related question that must be bracketed here. I would argue that in both cases the answer is that we are bound to sense-making; that it is constitutive of agency as such. For discussion of the relationship between Heidegger and contemporary Kantian approaches to this issue, see Burch, this volume.

27. See the introduction to this volume. The formality of Kant's moral constraints similarly leads—most famously in Hegel—to accusations that there is insufficient material content in Kant's account for making concrete decisions in specific lives about what kind of person to become. See Wood 1999 and Stern 2015.

28. Although we do not have space to discuss the "why" of unity-seeking in any detail, we might note that "On the Essence of Ground" notes that the different kinds of grounding "each in their own way *spring forth from a care for steadfastness and subsistence*" (EG: 132).

29. Although I do not discuss Korsgaard in this chapter, this can be read as a rejection of any suggestion that "humanity"—understood as a kind of master practical identity—could solve this problem (see Korsgaard 1996, 2009). On that view, meeting certain universal formal constraints is constitutive of unified agency. With this I am in agreement. But the empty formalism objection returns here: the idiosyncratic personal identity of the individual agent means that the universality of such formal constraints rules them out as being able to provide the required content for making decisions about the specific shape of one's particular life. See Crowell 2007 for a critique of Korsgaard's view. I also reject the view that this can be understood as a kind of Sartrean "ground project." Sartre's suggestion that all of our commitments can be subsumed to a single foundational practical identity—like "writer"—is at odds with the normative pluralism to which I am committed. See McMullin 2018.

30. This discussion is indebted to Matherne 2014.

31. Recent work on practical reason has invoked the idea of a schema as a way to think about the action-guiding power of certain kinds of practical templates or

"constellation[s] of interconnected practices and symbols" that are neither "particular evaluative attitudes nor features of practical reason *as such*" (Walden 2018: 127; 126). Although these tend to be thought of in social terms (e.g., the shared schema of "honor culture")—not as individual templates—we can see a similar function to what I am invoking here: they "interpret and organize information and coordinate action, thought, and affect," especially insofar as they structure our "choice architecture" or "possibility space for agency" by enabling or shutting down possibilities via templates of acceptability (Haslanger 2016: 126; 128).

32. See McMullin 2018, chapters 7 and 9, for further discussion of how an experience of the exemplarity of certain moments of choice functions in the virtues of patience and courage.

33. Although "world" and "self" are not separable for Heidegger, the point of this discussion has been to highlight the practical structures operative in the individual's work of self-unification, and as such the distinction is helpful.

34. For a helpful discussion of how Kant's practical postulates can be read in historical and political terms, see Dews 2013.

35. For helpful comments and questions on this chapter I would like to thank Bill Blattner, Matt Burch, David Cerbone, Steven Crowell, Peter Dews, Maxim Doyon, Sacha Golob, Gabrielle Jackson, Leslie MacAvoy, Denis McManus, Mark Okrent, Joseph Rouse, Joseph Schear, Matthew Shockey, David Suarez, and Kate Withy.

REFERENCES

Allison, Henry. 1990. *Kant's Theory of Freedom*. Cambridge: Cambridge University Press.
Altshuler, Roman. 2015. "Teleology, Narrative, and Death." In *Narrative, Identity and the Kierkegaardian Self*, edited by J. Lippitt and P. Stokes, 29–45. Edinburgh: Edinburgh University Press.
Arendt, Hannah. 1981. *The Life of the Mind*. New York: Harcourt Publishers Ltd.
Beck, Lewis White. 1960. *Commentary on the Critique of Practical Reason*. Chicago: University of Chicago Press.
Bernstein, Richard J. 2000. "Arendt on Thinking." In *The Cambridge Companion to Hannah Arendt*, edited by Dana Villa, 277–92. Cambridge: Cambridge University Press.
Brandom, Robert B. 2009. "Norms, Selves, and Concepts." In *Reason in Philosophy: Animating Ideas*, 27–51. Cambridge, MA: Harvard University Press.
Buchdahl, Gerd. 1992. *Kant and the Dynamics of Reason*. Cambridge: Blackwell.
Crowell, Steven. 2017. "Exemplary Necessity: Heidegger, Pragmatism, and Reason." In *Pragmatic Perspectives in Phenomenology*, edited by O. Svec and J. Capek, 242–56. London: Routledge.
———. 2016. "What Is It to Think?" In *Phenomenology of Thinking: Philosophical Investigations into the Character of Cognitive Experiences*, edited by Thiemo Breyer and Christopher Gutland, 183–206. London: Routledge.
———. 2014. *Normativity and Phenomenology in Husserl and Heidegger*. Cambridge: Cambridge University Press.

———. 2007. "*Sorge* or *Selbstbewußtsein*? Heidegger and Korsgaard on the Sources of Normativity." *European Journal of Philosophy* 15, no. 3: 315–33.
———. 2004. "Authentic Historicality." In *Space, Time and Culture*, edited by D. Carr and C. F. Cheung, 57–71. Dordrecht: Kluwer.
Dews, Peter. 2013. "Kant: The Perversion of Freedom." In *The Idea of Evil*, 17–45. London: Blackwell.
Fisher, Tony. 2010. "Heidegger and the Narrativity Debate." *Continental Philosophical Review* 43: 241–65.
Gardner, Sebastian. 2011. "Kant's Practical Postulates and the Limits of the Critical System." *Bulletin of the Hegel Society of Great Britain* 63: 187–215.
Gibbons, Sarah L. 1994. *Kant's Theory of Imagination: Bridging Gaps in Judgement and Experience*. Oxford: Clarendon.
Golob, Sacha. Forthcoming. "Exemplars, Institutions, and Self-Knowledge in *Schopenhauer as Educator*." *Journal of Nietzsche Studies*.
Haslanger, Sally. 2016. "What Is a (Social) Structural Explanation?" *Philosophical Studies* 173, no. 1: 113–30.
Haugeland, John. 2013. *Dasein Disclosed*. Edited by J. Rouse. Cambridge, MA: Harvard University Press.
Kant, Immanuel. 2015. *Critique of Practical Reason*. 2nd ed. Translated by Mary Gregor. Cambridge: Cambridge University Press.
———. 2002. *Critique of the Power of Judgment*. Translated by Paul Guyer and Erich Matthews. Cambridge: Cambridge University Press.
———. 1996. "Religion Within the Boundaries of Mere Reason." In *Religion and Rational Theology*, edited by A. W. Wood, 41–215. Cambridge: Cambridge University Press.
———. 1929. *Critique of Pure Reason*. Translated by Norman Kemp Smith. London: Macmillan.
Kleingeld, Pauline. 2016. "Kant on 'Good,' the Good, and the Duty to Promote the Highest Good." In *The Highest Good in Kant's Philosophy*, edited by Thomas Höwing, 33–49. Berlin: De Gruyter.
Korsgaard, Christine. 2009. *Self-Constitution: Agency, Identity, and Integrity*. Cambridge: Cambridge University Press.
———. 1996. *Sources of Normativity*. Cambridge: Cambridge University Press.
Kuehn, Manfred. 1985. "Kant's Transcendental Deduction of God's Existence as a Postulate of Pure Practical Reason." *Kant-Studien* 76, no. 2: 152–69.
Kukla, Rebecca. 2002. "The Ontology and Temporality of Conscience." *Continental Philosophy Review* 35, no. 1: 1–34.
Matherne, Samantha. 2014. "Kant and the Art of Schematism." *Kantian Review* 19, no. 2: 181–205.
McManus, Denis. 2018. "On a Judgment of One's Own: Heideggerian Authenticity, Standpoints, and All Things Considered." *Mind*. doi:10.1093/mind/fzx045.
———. 2015. "Being-towards-Death and Owning One's Judgment." *Philosophy and Phenomenological Research* 91: 245–72.
McMullin, Irene. 2019. *Existential Flourishing: A Phenomenology of the Virtues*. Cambridge: Cambridge University Press.

———. 2013a. *Time and the Shared World: Heidegger on Social Relations.* Evanston, IL: Northwestern University Press.

———. 2013b. "Kant on Radical Evil and the Origin of Moral Responsibility." *Kantian Review* 18, no. 1: 49–72.

Nietzsche, Friedrich. 1997. "Schopenhauer as Educator." In *Untimely Meditations*, edited by D. Breazeale; translated by R. J. Hollingdale, 125–94. Cambridge: Cambridge University Press.

O'Neill, Onora. 1992. "Vindicating Reason." In *The Cambridge Companion to Kant*, edited by Paul Guyer, 280–308. New York: Cambridge University Press.

Pasternack, Lawrence. 2011. "The Development and Scope of Kantian Belief: The Highest Good, The Practical Postulates, and The Fact of Reason." *Kant-Studien* 102: 290–315.

Stern, Robert. 2015. "On Hegel's Critique of Kant's Ethics: Beyond the 'Empty Formalism' Objection." In *Kantian Ethics: Value, Agency, and Obligation*, edited by Robert Stern, 139–56. Oxford: Oxford University Press.

Surprenant, Chris W. 2008. "Kant's Postulate of the Immortality of the Soul." *International Philosophical Quarterly* 48: 85–98.

Varga, Somogy. 2011. "Existential Choices: To What Degree Is Who We Are a Matter of Choice?" *Continental Philosophy Review* 44: 65–79.

Velleman, J. David. 2002. "Motivation by Ideal." *Philosophical Explorations: An International Journal for the Philosophy of Mind and Action* 5, no. 2: 90–104.

Walden, Kenneth. 2018. "Practical Reason Not As Such." *Journal of Ethics and Social Philosophy* 13, no. 2: 125–53.

Wood, Allen W. 1970. *Kant's Moral Religion.* Ithaca, NY: Cornell University Press.

———. 1999. *Kant's Ethical Thought.* Cambridge: Cambridge University Press.

Wrathall, Mark. 2015. "Autonomy, Authenticity, and the Self." In *Heidegger, Authenticity, and the Self: Themes from Division Two of Being and Time*, edited by Denis McManus, 193–214. New York: Routledge.

Zagzebski, Linda. 2017. *Exemplarist Moral Theory.* Oxford: Oxford University Press.

Zuckert, Rachel. 2018. "Hidden Antinomies of Practical Reason, and Kant's Religion of Hope." *Kant Yearbook* 10, no. 1: 199–217.

Part III

METHOD

Chapter 9

What Did Edmund Husserl's Phenomenology Want to Accomplish?

And What Now?

Burt C. Hopkins

In the following discussion I advance six interrelated arguments. One, that Eugen Fink's now classic essay published in 1934, "What Does Edmund Husserl's Phenomenology Want [to Accomplish]?" (Fink 1972 [1934]), answers its title's question by situating Heidegger's existential-ontological project of *Grundlegung* (laying the ground) within Husserl's project of radical self-reflection, toward the end of securing a transcendentally pure foundation of the system of sciences. Two, that contemporary philosophers working in the phenomenological tradition have rejected Husserl's transcendental criterion of purity and therewith phenomenology's fundamentally foundational aspiration. Three, that Steven Crowell, alone among contemporary phenomenologists, has embraced phenomenology's foundational aspiration by shifting the formulation of the ground in question to that of the existential-ontological condition of possibility for the normativity of all meaning, together with its rational self-justification. Four, that Crowell's endeavor to extract from Heidegger's analytic of Dasein's existence a fundamentally ahistorical first-personal authority as the phenomenological source of normativity follows Heidegger's formalization of Dasein's being Guilty, in order to secure the existential-ontological ground of Dasein's radical self-responsibility. Five, the formal ontological status of the being of the object yielded by formalization renders paradoxical Heidegger's employment of it for the purpose of disclosing the existential-ontological character of Dasein's being. And, finally, six, that the historicity inseparable from formalization's primal establishment in early modernity presents a challenge to Crowell's claim that Dasein's first-personal authority's foundation in the formalization of its being Guilty outstrips its history.

1. FINK'S CHALLENGE TO HEIDEGGER'S CRITIQUE OF HUSSERL

In "What Does Edmund Husserl's Phenomenology Want [to Accomplish]?" Fink's bold answer to the question raised by his title is that it wants to accomplish nothing less than the laying of the ground (*Grundlegung*) for *the* system of knowledge. Notwithstanding both the Heideggerian and Hegelian idioms in which Fink frames this answer, which includes respectively the former's notion of ground-laying and the latter's of *Geist*'s returning to itself from out of its worldly self-alienation, the argument behind Fink's articulation of the object of Husserl's phenomenological desire is firmly Husserlian. It is rooted in Husserl's articulation of phenomenology's method and results, right up until the time Fink's essay was published; that is, right before Husserl's last texts' phenomenological articulation of the crisis of European sciences and the phenomenologically novel historical reflection that he proposed in response to that crisis.

Conspicuously missing from Fink's discussion of Husserl's phenomenological philosophy, however, is the name Martin Heidegger. Whatever the political significance of this omission,[1] its philosophical significance can be grasped by reading between the lines of Fink's text. The main lines of Heidegger's critique of Husserl, which were well known to Fink, are effectively challenged in Fink's account of what Husserl's phenomenology wants to accomplish. In that account's articulation of the phenomenological method's laying of a ground, the prehension of the system of knowledge inseparable from that method, and the accomplishment of a radically new concept of philosophy that is its result, Heidegger's critique is quietly addressed. Indeed, it cannot be an accident that Fink formulates Husserl's phenomenology according to the guiding idea of "laying-a-ground," which is the very idea that Heidegger appeals to in order to characterize Dasein's existential mode of being as a thrown ground in *Being and Time* (BT: 284/330). Thus, Fink situates Heidegger's own fundamental ontology within the context of the transcendental attitude driving Husserl's method and the overcoming of the ontic self-understanding of the subjectivity of the subject. This is to say Fink's text presents as misunderstandings both Heidegger's critique of Husserl's reflective methodology and his critique of the putative ontic understanding of Being driving Husserl's theory of intentionality. And in the process, he also suggests that Heidegger's formulation of the "understanding of Being" (Fink 1972: 24) stands on the transcendental ground secured by Husserl's phenomenological reduction.

Fink characterizes Husserl's phenomenological method in terms of "the method of the most radical self-reflection" [*die Methode der radikalisiertesten Selbstbesinnung*] (ibid.: 17), which he distinguishes from the "'inner perception'" (ibid.: 14) characteristic of reflection as the common subjective psychological capacity to turn inward. Fink makes it clear that the subjective character of the self-reflection that grounds phenomenology *includes* rather than turns away from the things themselves, as its "material" [*sachlich*] concern with them is "exclusively based in self-reflection" (ibid.: 13). Fink's thematic distinction between inward-turning psychological reflection and phenomenology's method of radical self-reflection undercuts Heidegger's well-known critique that owing to its reflective character, Husserl's reduction turns away from the world, and with that, Dasein's fundamental mode of existence as being-in-the-world. It does so by exposing the conflation of the inward-turning reflection characteristic of inner perception with Husserl's method of radical self-reflection behind Heidegger's critique. The "self" at issue in the latter—transcendental—reflection is therefore not the psychological subject but the transcendental subjectivity that is the constitutive source of the things themselves in a manner that cuts across the traditional opposition between "inner" and "outer" perception. Moreover, for Fink, Heidegger's concern with not just Being but the *meaning* of Being presupposes the Husserlian reflection properly understood. That is, it presupposes a transcendental reflection that is not understood as the natural capacity of the human to turn inward but as the radical possibility of the transcendental philosopher to thematize the meaning of Being, and to do so by inquiring into the conditions of intelligibility that are inseparable from the worldly givenness of entities, including the human self as an entity.

Having responded to the main lines of Heidegger's existential-ontological critique of Husserl's phenomenology, Fink concludes his account of Husserl's phenomenology by articulating "the concept of system governing" it (ibid.: 25). The system in question is that of "the exclusive and persistent self-reflection," which means "the *constitutive interpretation of the world* made possible by the phenomenological reduction" (ibid.). As the "exhaustion of the *problem-area* which has been encompassed in advance" (ibid.) by radical and pure self-reflection, it is "no architectonically closed, esthetically satisfying phantasy, but a *philosophy of toil*" (ibid.). As such, "it has its analytical work in front of itself, an endlessly open horizon of concrete researches" (ibid.). Despite the system—"[i]n the work carried out by Husserl"—being "once and for all *secured*," it nevertheless "demands the work of many, many lives" (ibid.) to be realized. However, given the cardinal differences between the natural attitude's limited sight governing the mundane world and the spiritually awakened, which is to say, phenomenologically "pure" sight guiding the transcendental attitude, between the mundane subject and transcendental subjectivity, Fink is supremely confident of the following: that those "attempts of radical self-reflections [that] do not philosophize exclusively and purely in relentless consequence from out of self-reflection, but always carry into it a knowledge stemming from the natural (mundane-ontological) self-understanding" (ibid.: 17), will have nothing to contribute to what Husserl's phenomenology wants to accomplish. This is the case, above all, because "in phenomenology, the concept of 'ground,' in return to which the philosophical grasping of the world realizes itself, has lost its usual 'objective' sense precisely through the persistent adherence to self-meditation, carried out with a certain radicalism of 'purity,' as the exclusive thematic source of philosophy" (ibid.).

2. THE POST-HUSSERL REJECTION OF HIS "PURITY" CRITERION FOR GENUINE METHODOLOGICAL ACCESS TO THE PHENOMENOLOGICAL DOMAIN

That was, of course, then. Despite Fink's confidence in 1934 that Husserl's method of radical self-reflection had secured the ground for a new concept of philosophy, and that the reduction and system implicit in it had definitively demarcated both a problem domain and a philosophical criterion for deciding what work qualifies to contribute to concrete research in that domain, that's not the way it turned out. Reception of the criterion of "purity" governing both the radical self-reflection and the results of the phenomenological reduction proved to be more problematic than Fink realized when he wrote his article. Husserl's phenomenological desire to calibrate that criterion in terms of the epoché of the legitimacy of the objective units of meaning that originate in the natural attitude for the purpose of the constitutive analysis of the origin of that very meaning was either deemed impossible to accomplish in practice or itself philosophically undesirable.

On the one hand, two aspects of Heidegger's phenomenology, neither of which can be found addressed between the lines written by Fink, have been embraced by many who worked or are still working in the phenomenological tradition as definitively critiquing Husserl's criterion for purity. One aspect is found in Heidegger's so-called tool analysis in *Being and Time*. Many have found in that analysis a convincing account of the priority of practical involvement in the world over reflectively oriented "theory" and cognitive interests generally for the constitution of practical meaning—and perhaps *all* meaning. The other aspect is found in Heidegger's employment of his account of the historicity of the meaning of Being to critique what he argues is the historically dated derivative meaning of Being that guides the determination of objectivity in Husserl's phenomenology. Many, especially those influenced by the French tradition, have embraced a version of this critique developed by Jacques Derrida under the heading "metaphysics of presence." On the other hand, the dominant philosophical tradition in the world today, to the extent that it takes note of Husserl's phenomenology at all, sees it—unfavorably—through the lens of an internalist account of the philosophy of the mind. Despite their diversity, however, both critiques have the same target: the phenomenological criterion of purity, with its putative exclusion—respectively—of alterity and externality.

In light of this situation, it's legitimate to ask, what now? What does Husserlian phenomenology want to accomplish today? Which is to say, what do those still working in the tradition of Husserl's phenomenology want to accomplish? Especially now that the project of publishing his collected works is winding down, one reasonable answer would be the scholarly explication and reassessment of Husserl's thought on the basis of the completed publication of his *Nachlass*. There are many scholars worldwide who are engaged in this project. Related to this, another reasonable answer would be to argue for the contemporary relevance of Husserl's "classical" phenomenology for engaging the dominant contemporary, especially analytic, philosophical problematics. Many scholars worldwide committed to such a project are engaging contemporary issues in the philosophy of mind, values, emotions, ethics, aesthetics, mathematics, logic, etc.

3. CROWELL'S TRANSCENDENTAL PROJECT OF AN EXISTENTIAL-ONTOLOGICAL FOUNDATION OF THE CONSTITUTION OF NORMATIVITY

Notwithstanding the undeniable value of such undertakings, it's clear that underlying both these performative answers to the question what now does Husserlian phenomenology want to accomplish, is—however implicit—the abandonment of that phenomenology's philosophically foundational aspiration. And therefore, one could argue—and I certainly would—that to abandon phenomenology's foundational aspiration is to abandon phenomenology. However, there is one contemporary thinker working in the Husserlian tradition, Steven Crowell, who has not only not given up on the foundational quest of Husserl's classical phenomenology, but who has engaged contemporary analytic philosophy with a powerful argument for the relevance of Heidegger's existential-ontological transformation of the transcendental project behind Husserl's phenomenology for the contemporary analytic discourse on normativity. Thus Crowell argues that the relevance in question is foundational, in the precise sense that only transcendental phenomenology in a—what for many is a paradoxical—Heideggerian register is capable of providing a philosophical account of the *sine qua non* for their *being* something like a norm—namely, the first-personal awareness of *the* existential necessity of projecting one's own being normatively. Inseparable, then, from the problem of *normativity* for Crowell, that is, from the philosophical interrogation of the conditions of possibility responsible for there being something like a norm per se, is the constitution not just of an agent, but of *the* normative agent. Thus, the heart of Crowell's argument is that no formal or conceptual account of normativity can provide, on principle, an account of the being of something like a norm, because whatever else a norm is, the *normative* per se shows up first and foremost as an existential-ontological claim that cannot be avoided. It cannot be avoided, since any attempt to do so necessarily already presupposes the agent's normative constitution—that is, as Crowell puts it, its "being beholden to norms in the first place" (2013: 122).

On Crowell's view, then, transcendental phenomenology's task is to unpack this presupposition and to demonstrate that any *philosophical* account of the rationality of normativity must make it. However, the transcendental phenomenology he elicits for this task is that which emerges when the *phenomenological* shortcomings of both Husserl's and Heidegger's phenomenologies are addressed in the service of providing a foundational account of the transcendentally phenomenological origin of normativity. Crowell traces that origin to the constitution of the imperative to provide both oneself and others with justificatory accounts of one's existential-ontological self-determination, that he argues fundamentally characterizes Dasein's response to the call of conscience. To get to that origin, Crowell makes the case that the fundamental concern of both Husserl's and Heidegger's phenomenologies is the constitution of meaning and that inseparable from the meaning in question is its normative structure. By "normative" Crowell understands two interrelated things. One, the implicit or explicit connection between meaning's constitution and something like rules that guide its constitution. Two, the likewise implicit or explicit recognition that that constitution is measured in terms of its capacity to satisfy conditions that are somehow predelineated or otherwise adumbrated in and by those rules. Given the phenomenological register of Crowell's argument, his claims about the rule-like structures in question, as well as the conditions for their satisfaction, are—fundamentally—respectively neither formal nor logical. And, indeed, they need not even be explicitly known or for that matter intrinsically knowable. Crowell's claim, rather, is that inseparable from the phenomenon of meaning, that is, the way it shows up in the world, is both the possibility of it not meaning what it presents itself to mean (its failure) *and* its successful appearance lending itself to being measured—in terms of better and worse—in relation to the standard of something like an optimum (in Husserl's case) or the Platonic idea of the Good (in Heidegger's case).

Crucial to Crowell's argument, of course, is that normativity is—in some sense—recognized or otherwise exhibitable in both Husserl's and Heidegger's phenomenological accounts of meaning as a *sine qua non* for its constitution. Crowell's general strategy, then, is first to make perspicuous the phenomenological connection between meaning and normativity and then to assess the phenomenological adequacy of each phenomenologist's account of meaning in light of its normative connection. Moreover, given both Heidegger's debt to and criticism of the method and content of Husserl's phenomenology, Crowell's execution of this general strategy necessarily involves the presentation of that debt and an assessment of the criticism within the framework of his general assessment of their respective accounts of meaning's normative constitution.

Crowell locates the normative dimension of meaning in Husserl in his account of intentionality. Specifically, Crowell locates it in the empty intention constitutive of the intentional act that refers to the acts of fulfillment that intuitively give the emptily intended object *as* something. The normative dynamic exhibited here, according to Crowell, involves, on the one hand, the law-like regularity of the manifold lived-experiences that Husserl maintains composes the "consciousness of" constitutive of the empty intention. On the other hand, it involves the measure of the optimum that Husserl holds characterizes the intentional object's range of intuitive givenness (Crowell 2013: 137). Following the foundational role of perception in Husserl, Crowell advances his exhibition of the normative in Husserl's phenomenology by focusing on the intentionality proper to the perception of transcendent objects. Husserl's perspectival characterization of the consciousness moment proper to the manifold of lived-experiences in which the transcendent object of perception appears is clearly normative on Crowell's view, insofar as it articulates an invariant rule inseparable from the meaning constitutive of transcendent perceptual objects: their perspectival givenness to the perceptual consciousness that intentionally refers to them (ibid.: 18). Likewise, normative for Crowell is the invariant by which Husserl characterizes the objective meaning proper to the transcendent object's givenness, namely, its intrinsic inadequacy, in the sense that the unity of the object as a whole can be given neither in one particular perspective nor to an infinite totality of such perspectives. That is, Husserl's account of the essential incompleteness of the transcendent perceptual object's givenness is exhibited by Crowell as functioning in a normative fashion, precisely insofar as it is inseparable from the phenomenal meaning "transcendent perceptual object" that it is lawfully governed by its intrinsically incomplete givenness in perception (ibid.: 137).

Having exhibited the appeal to normative structure in Husserl's account of perceptual meaning, Crowell next assesses Husserl's account of the conditions of possibility for that structure, that is, of its normativity. On Crowell's view, Husserl's account is deficient. On the one hand, Husserl's appeal to the sense-giving (*Sinngebung*) function of the empty intention to animate nonintentional sensation contents (*hyle*) is problematical. It is so because the descriptive account of sense-giving's capacity to constitute both the objective unity of the object and the reference to that unity, turns out to presuppose rather than account for both the normativity of the unity in question and that of the reference (ibid.: 138–39). It does so insofar as the schema of intentional form and material content assumes not only the pre-givenness of both the reference to objective unity and that unity itself, but also the conditions of possibility constitutive of their normativity. On the other hand, Crowell maintains that Husserl's own criticism of his form and content schema, as well as his recognition of the role that consciousness's embodiment plays in the constitution of the meaning of the transcendent perceptual object, signals the founder of phenomenology's own recognition that the "static" descriptive accounts of both the empty intention's reference and the objective referent's unity do not address the following: (1) the normative conditions of possibility for that reference (i.e., the constitution of the rules that govern it); and (2) those of the referent (i.e., of the criteria for both the referent's constitution as the successful realization of the unity that is predelineated by the reference and the standard of the measure to which the calibration of the degree of this realization's success is determined).

Husserl's attempt to extend the referential scope of the empty intention beyond the significative reference intrinsic to linguistic meaning, and thus beyond the formality proper to its conceptual reference that is presupposed in the form-content schema, focuses on the perceptual function of sensations to adumbrate through perspectival profiles the unity of the perceptual object. It does so in the effort to account for the perceptual reference and referent presupposed by the conceptual (signitive) structure of intentionality. In the function of these sensations to adumbrate perspectivally the prepredicative (prelinguistic) appearance of the perceptual object's unity, Husserl seeks to locate a reference to the non-appearing aspects of the object. Crowell shows, however, that Husserl himself arrives at the realization that these adumbrating sensations do not manifest a descriptive basis for attributing to them an intentionally empty reference to the non-appearing aspects of the perceptual object that are continually fulfilled in the object's perspectival appearance. Specifically, Husserl realizes that there's nothing in the motivational relations between sensations and the associations of similarity, contiguity, and contrast that they give rise to, that is able to account for the intentional phenomena of either the reference characteristic of the empty intention or the objectivity of the profiled aspect of the referent that fulfills this intention (ibid.: 133).

Husserl's further attempt to uncover the conditions of possibility proper to the rules and criteria for the reference and referent in question, by tracing their genesis in passive syntheses, according to Crowell does not succeed in overcoming what he maintains is the formal presupposition guiding Husserl's analysis of intentionality. Husserl's genetic descriptions of the constitution accomplished by passive syntheses appeal to eidetically structured laws of association, to the end of uncovering the passively constituted "unities" of the prepredicative (prelinguistic) proto-reference and proto-object that he claims are originally generative of both the reference and referent constitutive of intentionality. Husserl, of course, thinks that the eidetic lawfulness of passive synthesis is sufficient to overcome the constitutive limits of the empirical formulation of association, which formulates the functioning of associative laws in terms of causality. When understood instead in terms of the description of eidetically lawful associations of phenomena, Husserl is confident that the descriptive account of the associative genesis of the preconceptual "unities" of sense contents and prethematic references to these contents is able to provide an account of the foundation of the intentional phenomena in question. However, Crowell argues that these descriptive appeals to the passive synthesis of manifolds of sensation refer to the very same relations of similarity, contiguity, and contrast, which Husserl had already rejected in his attempt to account for the reference and referent on the basis of the motivation of the sensations associated with the adumbrations of the perceptual object (ibid.: 139).

Husserl's appeal to the embodiment of consciousness to account for the constitution of perceptual normativity likewise falls short of accomplishing that feat according to Crowell. Husserl's exhibition of consciousness's embodiment on the basis of systems of kinaesthetic capability, which are expressed by conscious awareness of "I can" and which Husserl maintains function to motivate the adumbrations of the perceptual object's profiled appearance, fail to account for what Crowell argues is the key to embodiment, namely, the facticity of the body. The latter cannot be reduced on his view, as Husserl does, to a foundation in consciousness, "understood as a monadological 'absolute' flow" (ibid.: 141), in which presenting acts of sensation are motivated by kinaesthetic systems. These latter, in turn, being supposed by Husserl to constitute a second system of "'orthoaesthetic perceptions'" that manifest normal appearances of things and their properties. Normal meaning here, "'the "optimal givenness" in which the thing comes to the fore along with the properties that "befit it itself"'" (ibid.). The body and its role in perceptual normativity cannot be so reduced for Crowell, since despite Husserl's recognition of what Crowell calls "perceptual practice,"

> he held that the relevant normativity arose from the co-ordination of kinaesthetic with presentative sensations. Practices and abilities like walking around a candle or playing tennis or typing, however, are bodily skills that cannot be reduced to covariance relations between systems of appearances in consciousness. The body cannot itself be constituted as a function of temporal associations, nor can the norm of proper functioning relevant to bodily skills be understood as arising

from a system of kinaesthetic sensations. For a skill (sensorimotor knowledge) gains its normative sensitivity from its being "out for" something, its trying to accomplish a task, and trying is not any kind of sensation. The task in question need not be conceptually mediated—my concept of walking is not involved in my exercise of that skill—but any such task must be responsive to the distinction between success and failure. Thus while sensorimotor knowledge does involve the body's sense or feeling of itself as being appropriately situated within its project, the normative concept of the "appropriate" does not arise from the feeling but from the body's own way of being. (ibid.: 143)

Crowell's analysis of the normative limits of Husserl's transcendental phenomenology can be seen to have two interrelated foci, one methodological and the other structural. It is important to stress that for Crowell both limits are immanent to Husserl's transcendental project, in the precise sense that the limits in question do not challenge the philosophical cogency of its guiding principle, that descriptive evidence of the experience of meaning provides the sole basis for the justification of meaning's intelligibility. Rather, what Crowell calls into question is the scope and limits of the evidence Husserl provides to account for the conditions of possibility proper to the normativity that is inseparable from that intelligibility. The structural limit in question concerns Husserl's descriptive account of consciousness as the foundation of intentionality. As we've seen, Crowell shows that neither Husserl's appeals to eidetically governed laws of association nor the kinaesthetic constitution of the embodied "I can" are capable of providing the evidential warrant capable of justifying both the normative claim behind the intentionality of meaning and the related criteria for the success or failure of the intentional response to that claim. We've also seen that Crowell argues this because the moment of intentionality that is constitutive of the normativity in question is fundamentally *practical*. It is so in the precise sense that the condition of possibility for the normativity in question is characterized in terms of "being out for something," "trying to accomplish a task," whose conditions of possibility include both bodily facticity and engagement with worldly entities.

This structural limit, in turn, points for Crowell to the methodological limit of Husserl's transcendental phenomenology, namely, to the scope of the legitimate employment of the epoché. Crowell's disclosure of the role practical intentionality plays in the constitution of normativity provides grounds immanent to Husserl's project for endorsing Heidegger's claim that the performance of the epoché expresses a possibility of the being of the subject, and it is therefore a possibility inseparable from its subjectivity. One consequence of this is the intrinsic limit to the scope of the beings whose being is such as to lend themselves to bracketing by the epoché in the service of accounting for the constitution of meaning, and that's the being of the subject.[2] Crowell therefore insists that what is at issue in Heidegger's existential analytic of

Dasein—not just philosophically but for Heidegger himself—is a transcendental phenomenological account of the *being* of the subjectivity of the subject. Moreover, Crowell argues that that being is most properly characterized in its being in terms of its *first-personal* self-awareness as a being whose being is fundamentally at issue. And, finally, Crowell endeavors to show that this first-personal awareness constitutes the transcendental phenomenological foundation not only of normativity, but of the rationality proper to the self-responsibility that itself grounds all normativity.

But to show this, Crowell must first address the "gap" he finds in Heidegger's existential analytic of Dasein. He locates this gap in Heidegger's account of Dasein's inauthentic mode of its everyday being in the world, or better, in his account of that mode of being's self as the "one-self" (*Mann selbst*). According to Crowell, Heidegger's account of the one-self is articulated as an identity that is entirely determined by the conformity to the norms of "the one" (*das Man*), norms that are co-extensive with the typicality of the practical tasks and social roles everyday Dasein must assume in order to strive to realize the myriad of projects it must undertake for the sake of caring for its being. Dasein's normative engagement with the referential totality of tools necessary to fulfil these tasks is what determines the significance of any given tool *as* that which is appropriate for the task at hand, as well as what determines the awareness of the self of the one who exercises the existential capacity (*Seinskönnen*) to perform such tasks by conforming to the norms associated with them. Inauthentic Dasein's conformity to norms, then, determines not only the meaning of the entities it encounters as ready to hand in the world, but also its awareness of the meaning of itself as an entity, insofar as that meaning is determined by what is "'reflected back to [myself] from things'" (ibid.: 175) (e.g., as the chopper of *wood*, seller of *insurance*, *mother*, etc.). The typicality of the meaning that is reflected back in this manner rules out for Heidegger the individuality of the one-self that is determined thereby. And it also rules out for Crowell an account of the first-person awareness that nevertheless must be a condition of inauthentic Dasein's non-individuated relation to itself as "one-self." Such *first-person* awareness is ruled out in Heidegger's account according to Crowell, because all of what can be reflected back to Dasein's self by the totality of the tasks it assumes under the guidance of the norms proper to *das Man* is the anonymity of itself as "'another' or as 'anyone.'" Thus, inauthentic Dasein's self-relation in Heidegger's account is completely mediated by "third-person terms."

That Heidegger's account of the "one-self" nevertheless "owes us" (ibid.: 176), as Crowell puts it, a phenomenological account of something more than a third-person identity and presumably awareness of that identity, despite the fact that one can find in Heidegger's account "no difference between the way things come by their as-structure and the way I come by mine" (ibid.: 175), can be traced to the differences Heidegger's analyses recognize between Dasein's concern for things, solicitude of others, and care for self. Because of the instrumentality of Dasein's self-awareness as "the one," that awareness cannot account for the implicit awareness of these differences that are operative in Heidegger's analyses. This is the case because Dasein's goal-oriented tasks, structured by "an in-order-to" in the totality of its involvements, must originate in "'a towards-which in which there is *no further involvement*'" (ibid.). They must so originate, because the definite significance of these tasks is not intrinsic to them as tasks but rather has its source in that which "'has assigned *itself* to an "in-order-to"'" (ibid.), and has done so "in light of the for the sake of which *I*" (ibid.) am doing or using something. The crucial question, then, for Crowell, concerns the identify of this I, an identity that in Heidegger's account of the "one-self" is assigned instrumentally. Because of this instrumental assignment, Crowell argues that it leaves the totality of involvements "underdetermined and the intentionality of experience" (ibid.: 176) determinative of "one-self" unexplained. Heidegger's identification of the very being of Dasein "'as the sole authentic "for-the-sake-of which,"'" and thus "as a 'towards which' in which there is no further involvement," provides no account of what it is in "the kind of self-awareness belonging to the one-self [that] allows us to see why it has no further involvement, why it is not just another instrumentality" (ibid.). Without such an account, Crowell argues that Heidegger's account of intentionality contains a "gap" and thus remains incomplete, and it does so above all because its third-person account of the one-self provides no evidential basis for Heidegger's claim that the tasks and roles "can *matter*" for it, because in its being that being is necessarily an issue for itself.

4. CROWELL'S EXTRACTION OF FIRST-PERSONAL AWARENESS FROM HEIDEGGER'S EXISTENTIAL ANALYTIC AS THE FOUNDATION OF BOTH DASEIN'S ONE-SELF AND AUTHENTIC SELF

Missing, then, in Heidegger's account of the "one-self" for Crowell is "an account of the subjectivity that belongs to, but remains invisible in, the one-self" (ibid.). Crowell finds, or better, extracts such an account from Heidegger's existential analytic of the ostensibly negative phenomenon of angst. The subjectivity at issue for Crowell is the first-personal mode of awareness that he maintains alone has the evidential authority capable of exhibiting—in its full existential dimensionality—the innermost being that is in back of Dasein's self. Crowell accomplishes the extraction of the first-personal mode of awareness from Heidegger's existential analytic by first carefully delineating what he is not claiming can be extracted from it. To wit, on the one hand, a first-personal reference to an I that in turn formally refers to an ego, transcendental or otherwise, both distinct from and the ground of the first-personal I in question. On the other hand, first-personal access to lived-experiences that are foundational for intentionality. Thus, the first-personal authority in Heidegger that is Crowell's quarry is to be radically distinguished from its Husserlian guise (ibid.: 178). While one might wonder if not this what then could characterize first-personal authority, following Zahavi, Crowell (ibid.: 177), articulates three criteria as its *sine qua non*: infallible reference of the I to the entity it purports to refer to; the immediate, noncriterial, and noninferential identification of the self-referent in question; and, the absence of any type of third-person reference.

But Crowell follows neither Zahavi nor anyone else in connecting this last criterion to the radical unintelligibility of the first-personal awareness that he will extract from Heidegger's existential analytic. Thus, in marked contrast to contemporary discourse about first-personal authority that connects it with some kind of privileged intuition, epistemic or otherwise, following Dreyfus, Crowell argues (ibid.: 179) that Heidegger's existential analytic locates intelligibility in the third-personal norms that determine both the "as structure" of the entities encountered by everyday inauthentic Dasein as well as the one-self that is the agent of those encounters. Because of this, the first-personal awareness Crowell extracts from Heidegger's analytic of angst will be, strictly speaking, unintelligible. That is, it will be unintelligible when the measures of intelligibility are precisely the third-personal norms that are behind the gap Crowell finds in Heidegger's existential analytic's account of the one-self. But notwithstanding that, and in radical departure from Dreyfus and his students, Crowell will argue that in an existentially peculiar way the first-personal authority disclosed in the breakdown of the one-self initiated by angst has the ineluctable status of being the *ground* of all intelligibility, and indeed, of rationality itself.

Crowell's argument takes as its point of departure Heidegger's claim that "'what Dasein, *from its own standpoint*, demands as the only ontico-ontological way of access to itself'" (BT 182/226; cited in Crowell 2013: 180) is the "breakdown of the one-self," which Crowell maintains therefore has "special methodological significance" for Heidegger. Crowell argues that this "is equivalent to providing phenomenological access to subjectivity as the condition of possibility of authentic selfhood" (Crowell 2013: 180). As the latter's condition of possibility, Crowell maintains that the subjectivity in question, in its guise as "the place of the first-person in *Being and Time*," is neither the one-self nor the authentic self, "but the hidden condition of both" (ibid.: 183). The role the latter will assume in Crowell's account of the "*constitution* of the space of reasons" (ibid.: 189) in Heidegger's existential analytic, is what is behind Crowell's claim that "Heidegger's great achievement in *Being and Time* is to have demonstrated that care is prior to reason—that *homo cura* is more fundamental than *animal rationale*" (ibid.: 183–84). Situated within the context of the philosophy of mind, Crowell holds that the priority of care over reason in the being of *homo* "means that intentionality is not to be 'constructed' according to non-phenomenological 'logical' conditions but disclosed phenomenologically as a consequence of the care structure" (ibid.: 184). And for phenomenology, this priority means that, suitably modified, following the one-self's breakdown, Dasein's first-personal authority is not only not "anti-transcendental philosophical" (ibid.: 188), but that the Self that emerges is robustly foundational, insofar as it is driven, as Heidegger puts it, by the transcendental necessity of having "'to lay the ground for itself' [*Grund seiner selbst zu legen*]" (BT 284/330; cited in Crowell 2013: 188).

Crowell's bold claims here have their basis in a meticulous analysis of Heidegger's account of the breakdown of the one-self initiated by angst. That account takes its lead from the tripartite structure of care disclosed by the existential analytic: mood (*Befindlichkeit*), understanding (*Verstehen*), and discourse (*Rede*). Despite Heidegger's own apparent self-understanding of the existential-ontological "equiprimordiality" of these structures, Crowell's analysis shows that mood, in the guise of anxiety (angst), has priority in that it is what initiates the breakdown of the one-self. Following this breakdown, discourse—in the guise of conscience (*Gewissen*)—functions to reveal Dasein's Self in terms of first-personal authority. Understanding, meanwhile, the middle term as it were, discloses Dasein's self-understanding of its finitude in the one-self's breakdown.

According to Heidegger, anxiety gives the world "in such a way that it no longer matters" (Crowell 2013: 180), such that the entities within it withdraw and it becomes uncanny (*unheimlich*). Coincident with this, the one-self's involvements with others recede, "'until I grasp myself as the *solus ipse*'" (ibid.). The cumulative result of this, according to Crowell, is that "I discover my subjectivity, a dimension of my being that is irreducible to any "'totality of involvements.'"" Moreover, in the absence in anxiety of the capacity of its identity to be reflected back to itself from out of those involvements, Dasein can no longer be aware of itself "*as* anything" (ibid.: 182). Despite, however, this irreducibility to "any definite description," Dasein is able to identify itself. First in its broken-down self-understanding as a way to be which is not an ability to be (*Seinskönnen*) but rather the "'possibility of the impossibility of being there'" (ibid.: 180), that is, as death understood as Dasein's "ownmost" possibility. Second, in conscience's "kind of first-person self-reference" (ibid.: 182) as "Guilty." Indeed, conscience "'gives us to understand' something: the self-understanding that Heidegger terms 'death' gets articulated as '*Guilty*'" (ibid.: 221), such that "guilt 'turns up as a[3] predicate for the "I am."'"

According to Crowell, Heidegger's claim that the articulation of Dasein's self-understanding *as* guilty is not inconsistent with Heidegger's previous claim that following the breakdown of its one-self Dasein can no longer be made intelligible "as something." This is the case because for Heidegger, following the breakdown of the one-self initiated by anxiety, Dasein's Guilt, like its death, no longer refers to any of its possibilities measurable in the third-person terms that determine its everyday, inauthentic being in the world. That is, it no longer refers to a *determinate* capacity (*Seinskönnen*) of Dasein's being but to that being's existential-ontological condition of possibility. The key to Crowell's extracting of the latter from Heidegger's existential analytic, in terms of the disclosure of the Self behind Dasein's one-self as a first-personal mode of awareness that embodies ontico-ontological authority, is found in his analysis of the transformation of discourse initiated by the breakdown of the one-self. Crowell elicits from Heidegger's account of conscience two crucial moments: one, the addressee of its characteristic broken-down discourse and two, what is said in the address. The first of these discloses Dasein's factical, individuated being, manifest in the phenomenon of first-person awareness. The second discloses the authority of that first-person awareness, in the guise of its being the condition of the possibility of the *ought* that is constitutive of not this or that norm but of normativity per se.

The addressee in the breakdown of the one-self initiated by anxiety is Dasein's uncanny self-understanding following that breakdown, in which the ownmost possibility of its impossibility—death—is disclosed precisely in terms of a capacity intrinsic to its being that is incapable of being rendered intelligible in third-personal terms. Specifically, the breakdown of all ties to the world and others originally initiated and then accomplished by anxiety makes manifest Dasein's status—not just as a being among other beings—but as an individual being who is at once thrust into a situation in which what supports that being is the totality of conventional tasks it must assume to care for itself, and its own powerlessness to bring it about that the realization of any one—or however large a set—of those tasks will be sufficient to function as an enduring foundation of its being. Or in Heidegger's terminology, the addressee of conscience is Dasein's self-understanding as a thrown-projection who, as such, "'has to lay the ground for itself,'" because "as 'existing' it 'must take over being-a-ground'" (ibid.: 188).

What is said by conscience—its "call"—to its addressee is "the accusation 'Guilty'" (ibid.: 185). Subsequent to the breakdown of its one-self, the guilt in question is not such as would render Dasein's being intelligible by determining it "as" guilty of this or that infraction of the law or broken agreement. Because the author of the call of conscience is none other than

Dasein itself, Crowell points out that Dasein's "'being-guilty' is not contingent upon some worldly relation; rather it is *the*[4] 'predicate for the "I am"'" (ibid.: 186). Dasein is guilty therefore means something more like Dasein is "responsible" for laying not this or that ground but for laying the ground as such for itself. The linchpin of the move in Heidegger's analysis, from guilt as a worldly relation to guilt as the existential-ontological condition of possibility, is his *"formalization"* (ibid.: 186) of guilt. That is, the formalization of "the everyday notion of guilt in such a way that 'those ordinary phenomena of "guilt" which are related to our concernful being with others will *drop out*—phenomena related to everyday "reckoning" as well as to "any ought or law"'" (ibid.: 185). According to Crowell, despite seeming "[a]rtificial, this formalization simply reflects the character of the call as that mode of discourse which articulates the *un*intelligibility of Dasein when, as angst/death, its ordinary ties to the world break down" (ibid.: 186). Being guilty in this formalized sense, then, as the (or a) predicate for the "I am" of the Self behind the broken-down one-self, is for Crowell what "articulates the fundamental condition of subjectivity as such, the radically indexical first-person" (ibid.).

From the call of conscience Crowell then extracts three things: (1) the enabling of "the various (practical and theoretical) modes of knowing in the broadest sense, that from which *episteme*, *phronesis*, etc. primarily unfold"; (2) the tie of "the notion of conscience to that of reason"; and (3) the first-person authority of Dasein signifying "a being who no longer merely conforms to norms but who can act in light of them" (ibid.: 187).

Regarding conscience's enabling of modes of knowing in general, Crowell holds that the *"Ge"* of *Gewissen* is cognate with the *"Ge"* in the notion of *"Gestell"* (ibid.: 187). Thus conscience, like *Gestell*, signifies a primordially unfolding gathering, wherein what is gathered is no mere collection but rather "that which delimits the 'essence' or being of what is gathered" (ibid.: 185). Significant in this regard for Crowell is that Heidegger attributes to *nous* (in his lectures on the *Sophist*), as "one sense of 'reason,'" "just this role" of enabling "modes of knowing in the broadest sense" (ibid.). Tied to this is something that is heard in the call of conscience, even though it is silent when measured by the acoustics of the one-self's conventional worldly engagement. What is silently heard, in the sense of its *Vernehmlichkeit*, "is a hearing whose acoustic dimension is subordinated to a responsiveness to meaning" (ibid.). Indeed, given that *vernehmen* "is the root of the German word for reason (*Vernunft*)," Crowell thinks "[t]his might suggest that conscience (*Gewissen*) is the gathering-enabling of knowing and deliberating precisely as the hearing-perceiving (*vernehmen*) of a call, or meaningful claim, the response to which (*ver-antworten*) is a unique 'possibility' for being: *Vernunft*" (ibid.). Finally, for Crowell, given the lack of worldly relations highlighted by the formalization of Dasein's being-guilty, the call of conscience is "an understanding of one's being prior to any sense of owing or indebtedness—any sense of having, through one's actions in the world, incurred debts or obligations" (ibid.: 186). This is the case because Dasein's being-guilty "articulates the self-understanding (self-awareness) of that being who is the ground of obligations," and thus, of the obligations inseparable from worldly norms (e.g., that of appropriate exchange). Thus "*being*-indebted cannot merely be a state but it is something that I, from a first-person point of view, must be 'able-to-be'; and this means that I must be able to acknowledge the norm as normative—that is, as a claim addresses to me—and not merely as a pattern descriptive of 'one's' normal behavior" (ibid.). The capacity to act "in the light of norms" (ibid.: 187) means, then, "to measure myself *against* a standard of success or failure, to grasp *myself* in terms of the very idea of better or worse" (ibid.). The standard in question here, what Heidegger following Plato "occasionally names 'the Good,'" is characterized by Crowell as "the sort of first-person authority that derives from first-person self-awareness as conscience" (ibid.). As such, first-person authority is responsibility, which "transforms a creature who is 'grounded' by social norms into a ground of obligation—one who 'grounds' norms by giving grounds, that is reasons" (ibid.).

Suitably revised in accord with Crowell's masterful account of the first-personal phenomenological constitution of normativity, the updated version of the question raised in Fink's classical article can thus be reformulated as follows: what now does classical phenomenology want to accomplish? And likewise, its answer: the laying of the existential-ontological ground of the first-personal essence of subjectivity, toward the end of providing *the* transcendental foundation of normativity, in the all-encompassing sense of that ground's articulation in terms of an appropriation of Plato's idea of the Good. Despite its family resemblance to the foundational function of the transcendental in both Kant's and Husserl's thought, however, the transcendental foundation in Crowell's phenomenology is radically different from both. Moreover, the transcendental "space of meaning" at issue for Crowell in the constitution of meaning does not share with Kant and Husserl a preoccupation with the transcendental foundation of the exact meanings at issue in the formal sciences. Of course, this should hardly be surprising, given both Crowell's critical appropriation of Heidegger's existential-ontological concerns while nevertheless stressing their proper transcendental provenance and his filling in of the gap in Heidegger's existential analytics' account by disclosing the one-self's *necessary* first-personal *awareness* of its third-person identity. That said, despite the arguably tangential concern to Heidegger's existential analytic of the thematic problem of exact meaning in phenomenology, I want to pursue a line of thought that begins by identifying the unthematic presence in Heidegger's analysis of angst of—arguably—the crucial abstractive process in the constitution of the meaning that makes possible modern symbolic mathematics. Subsequent to this, I shall interrogate the function of this abstractive process in the existential analytic, with a focus on the question of whether it is consistent with the immanent intention of that analytic. Finally, I will raise but not answer the question of the impact of all of this on Crowell's account of what classical phenomenology now wants.

5. HEIDEGGER'S PUZZLING APPEAL TO FORMALIZATION IN THE EXISTENTIAL-ANALYTIC OF CONSCIENCE

As we've seen, Heidegger's existential analytic characterizes the breakdown of Dasein's one-self as the *sine qua non* for it to encounter the ground of both its inauthentic and authentic Self, in the guise of its existential-ontological necessity of having to lay the ground for itself. The breakdown of the one-self required for the access to this necessity is initiated by angst, which effects it by negating the existential-ontological dimension of Dasein's being that is the source of its self-care; that is, by negating Dasein's being-in-the-world as something that *matters* for it. Heidegger characterizes the being-in-the-world in question in terms of the *totality* of Dasein's involvements with tools and others. Because a necessary condition for these involvements is the world with which they are engaged being given in a way that matters to Dasein, the existential ontological structure of the totality in question has what at the very least must be called an "affective" dimension. Indeed, this affective dimension proves crucial in Heidegger's analysis, since it is precisely its disruption—and not any mechanical or performative disruption of Dasein's tasks or social conformity—that is crucial for initiating the breakdown of the one-self. As we've seen, for Heidegger—as Crowell's analysis makes patent—the complete breakdown of the one-self initiated by angst, which is the condition for the necessity of Dasein both having to lay its ground and take over *being* a ground, is *not* brought about by angst but by Dasein's everyday notion of guilt being "sufficiently formalized so that those ordinary phenomena of 'guilt' which are related to our concernful being with others will *drop out*" (BT: 283/328). The formalization in question is characterized by Heidegger as being in the service of realizing the goal of conceiving "the idea of 'guilty' in terms of Dasein's kind of being" (ibid.).

Heidegger's appeal to formalization in this context is very puzzling, to say the least, given the contrast between his intended purpose to conceive of Dasein's guilt in accord with Dasein's existential-ontological kind of being, with the theoretical character formalization enjoys both in the history of philosophy and in Heidegger's own account of it. In its starkest terms, the contrast is that between Dasein's existential-ontological mode of being and that of the mode of being proper to "the object as such [*Gegenstand überhaupt*]" (GA60: 61/42), that is, "a something as object [*enies Etwas als Gegenstand*]" (GA60: 61/42). Heidegger's most extensive discussion of formalization presents it in terms of Husserl's distinction between generalization and formalization, which Heidegger holds that although known to mathematics from at least the time of Leibniz, is only logically explicated for the first time by Husserl (Husserl 1976: 26–27). Formalization's origin is characterized by Heidegger, again following Husserl, in terms of a turning away from "the particular 'what' of the object to be determined" in order to determine it "as that which is grasped; as that to which the cognizing relation refers" (GA60: 61/42). As such, the "something as object" for Heidegger is the "'to which'" of the "theoretical attitudinal relation" and not the "what content" in general of something that is materially determined. According to Heidegger, "this attitudinal relation contains a manifold [*mannigfaltigkeit*] of senses that can be explicated," such that the "manifold" proper to the attitudinal relation "is formed out into a formal object-category to which a 'region' corresponds" (GA60: 62/42). Heidegger's discussion of formalizing guilt, of course, is not necessarily bound in *Being and Time* to his account of formalization in a lecture course on religion given some seven or so years before that book was written. However, elsewhere in *Being and Time* precisely this understanding of formalization, as both theoretical and abstractive of the object's what content, is operative.[5] This lends credence to the ontological puzzle, as it were, of how the formalization—in this, theoretical sense—of ordinary guilt, which subsequent to being formalized would presumably yield formalized guilt as a materially empty something as object, is consonant with Dasein's existential-ontological kind of being.

Setting aside for a moment what is behind the puzzle I'm calling attention to—that of the radically different kinds of being at issue in Dasein's existential-ontological mode of being and that of the something as an object—I want to address the question whether there might be some methodological exigency behind Heidegger's appeal to formalization in connection with the call of conscience. That is, I want to ask whether there's a methodological problem to which the formalization of ordinary guilt is the answer—besides that of securing the idea of being guilty according to Dasein's way of being. Working backward, as it were, from what it is that formalizing everyday inauthentic guilt brings about, namely, the dropping out of the ordinary phenomena of guilt "related to our concernful being with others," the following methodological exigency can be identified. For the complete breakdown of the one-self necessary in order for Dasein's way of being—in terms of its having to lay its own ground and take over *being* a ground—the *totality* of its involvements with the world must no longer be given in a way that matters to Dasein. Heidegger's appeal to "totality" here articulates the element of the completeness of the one-self's breakdown necessary to disclose Dasein's being thrown and the existential-ontological necessity that follows from that. Anxiety, which initiates this breakdown, is clearly an *affective* phenomenon, and as such it is ill-suited to effect the completeness of the one-self's breakdown requisite for disclosing Dasein's own way of being. This is the case, I submit, because the affective phenomenon is *intensive*, and the proper measure of such a phenomenon is the sliding scale of the *more and less*. And this is why, then, something more than anxiety is required to bring about the *complete* breakdown of the one-self, because the requisite for the completeness at issue here concerns a phenomenon—*totality*—that cannot be arrived at in terms of the more and less. Put differently, were it the case that coincident with Dasein's encounter with the phenomenon of anxiety the totality of its worldly involvements would "drop out," there would be no need to "formalize" the ordinary phenomena of "guilt" to the same end, since anxiety would have already done the trick.

6. THE AMBIGUITY OF GUILT AS "THE" OR "A" PREDICATE OF DASEIN'S AUTHENTIC BEING: THE QUESTION WHETHER THE AUTHENTIC BEING OF DASEIN HAS ROOM FOR HISTORY

Granting for the sake of argument that this account of the methodological exigency behind Heidegger's appeal to formalization in his existential-analytical account of the full realization of the call of conscience, the question of its legitimacy—given the immanent aims of the analytic—immediately arises. Before taking up this question, however, I want to consider Crowell's account of the formalization of guilt in the context of what I've laid out here. Perhaps significantly, Crowell himself noticed something of its seemingly "[a]rtificial" (2013: 186) character. But that said, he was content to remark that "this formalization simply reflects the character of the call as that mode of discourse which articulates the *un*intelligibility of Dasein when, as *Angst*/death, its ordinary ties to the world break down" (ibid.). On Crowell's view, then, formalization doesn't really do any work for Heidegger, beyond reflecting the breakdown of the world mattering for Dasein, which apparently has *already* been accomplished. Heidegger's appeal to formalization in the instance of the call of conscience, then, functions uniquely in *Being and Time* for Crowell, in that it has neither the theoretical nor formal ontological meaning that it has elsewhere in the text. Crowell also sees Heidegger's appeal to the formalizing of ordinary guilt as "an example of what Heidegger calls 'formal indication,' a method that he employs ubiquitously, but mostly tacitly, in *Being and Time*" (ibid.). Crowell's view that formalization instantiates formal indication is inconsistent with Heidegger's account of formal indication in *Introduction to the Phenomenology of Religious Life*. There Heidegger clearly distinguishes the two, as he maintains that the meaning of "formal" in "talk of formal indication" (GA60: 59/41) is something that "has nothing to do" with the "the sense of universality" that "is common to formalization and generalization." Thus, he writes: "the meaning of 'formal' in the 'formal indication' is more original." Within the formalized, the differences between "something is an object" and "experience as such" go together with the "sense of 'universal,'" whereas "the formal indication has nothing to do with this" (ibid.). Formal indication is nevertheless called formal because "the formal is something relational," albeit the "relational" in formal indication concerns neither the "direct" (PRL: 63/44) ordering in generalization nor the "indirect" (GA60: 61/42) ordering of formalization.[6]

But rather than pursue these issues any further here, I want to close these reflections by calling attention to two phenomenological issues lacking in both Fink's and Crowell's answers to the question of what it is that phenomenology wants to accomplish and to end them with the suggestion that they are not unrelated to the problem, if I may call it that, of the role Heidegger assigns to formalization in his account of Dasein's authentic response to the call of conscience. The first is that of the constitution of mathematical meaning, both of the ideality of the formal structure of Euclidean mathematics and the formalized structure of symbolic mathematics. The second is the historicity inseparable from both ideal and formalized mathematical meaning. The absence of the problem of the transcendental constitution of the exact meanings that compose the foundation of the exact sciences is conspicuous in both Fink's and Crowell's account of what transcendental phenomenology wants to accomplish, since the intention behind Husserl's phenomenology is uncontroversially distorted by the elision of the phenomenon of formalized meaning, especially in the guise of formal ontology. The absence, however, of the issue or problem of the historicity of ideal and formalized mathematical meaning—at the time Fink wrote his article—did not distort Husserl's intention then, since at that time Husserl was only just making the connection between epistemology and history, although it would now. These two problems can be seen to come together when the inconsistent attribution of "guilt"—as either "the" or "a"—predicate of Dasein's own-most being in Crowell's text is considered.[7] Behind this textual equivocation, I submit, is the issue of whether Dasein's authentic being outstrips, in the own-most core of its mineness, history. If being guilty is *the* predicate of that being, in the sense of its completeness and totality, then there would be no "room" in that being for history, as Crowell maintains.[8] If, however, being guilty is *a* predicate Dasein's authentic being, then there would be room for history as another predicate, beginning, perhaps, with the implications of the historicity of the formalized meaning behind the process of formalization that Heidegger saw fit to subject ordinary guilt to in order to "conceive the idea of 'guilty' in terms of Dasein's kind of being" (BT: 283/328).

CODA

The implications I have in mind regarding this latter scenario can be sketched very briefly. Phenomenological accounts of the process of formalization that seek to account for its origins in either intentional modifications of perception, where Husserl sought them, or in the "theoretical attitudinal relation's" turning away from the what content of generalized cognition in order to thematize the "toward which" intrinsic to that relation, where Heidegger sought them, are doomed to failure. This is the case because sedimented in both of these accounts is the historicity of the transformation of the premodern mathematical method of analysis and synthesis that was behind premodern algebra's transformation into modern symbolic mathematics.[9] The origins of the latter may be traced to the analytic method of François Viète and the analytic geometries of Descartes and Pierre de Fermat. Intrinsic to their "primal establishment" of modern symbolic mathematics is the formalization of the ideal objects of traditional mathematics. In its exact original sense, formalization is the methodological replacement of the traditional objects of mathematics—determinate numbers and determinate geometrical shapes—by sense perceptible symbols whose mathematical "being" is not determined by the traditional ontological category of quantity but by the computational rules that function to govern the indeterminate—which is to say, general—solution of mathematical problems. The indeterminate and in precisely this sense ontologically formalized object that corresponds to the symbolically general method of solving mathematical problems constitutive of modern mathematics was termed by Husserl the "*Etwas überhaupt.*" And Heidegger, of course, followed Husserl's terminology for both the object of the new modern science and for the science charged with the task of investigating it: "formal ontology."

That said, it seems to me the phenomenon proper to the historicity behind the paradox of Heidegger's existential analytics' employment of the process of formalization to secure—phenomenologically—the foundation of Dasein's existential ontological self-responsibility warrants closer scrutiny.

NOTES

1. In April of the year Fink's article was published, Heidegger stepped down after eleven months as the rector of Freiburg University during the initial period of its Nazification.

2. In connection with this, Crowell notes that Husserl's late recognition of the "paradox of subjectivity," that it is, seemingly at once, constituting and therefore to that extent beyond the world of constituted beings, but also a constituted being and therefore in that sense a worldly being, presented serious challenges for Husserl's account of the transcendental constitution of embodiment, sociality, and history (Crowell 2013: 53ff).

3. See the next note.

4. Earlier, Crowell was quoted to the effect that "being guilty" was "a predicate for the 'I am.'" Whether this is a question of Crowell changing his mind (he wrote the definite article's stronger claim earlier than the indefinite article's weaker claim) or if other factors explain the inconsistency, the issue raised by the difference is substantial. The occasion will arise to come back to it when Crowell's foundational project is considered as the answer to the question what, now, does phenomenology want to accomplish.

5. Heidegger, BT, 78, 108 (formalizing being a sign), 159, 202 (formalizing binding and separating), 209, 252 (formalizing being-in-the-world), 433, 484 (formalizing the sequence of "nows").

6. On my view, the possibility that Heidegger's appeal to "idea of 'Guilty'" being "sufficiently *formalized*" is an appeal, as it were, to the idea of Guilty functioning or otherwise having the sense of a "formal indication," has to be rejected on strictly philological grounds as well. This is the case, because however the respective meanings of "formalization" and "formal indication" are interpreted philosophically, the following is clear: the word "formalization" refers to a process in Heidegger's texts, while the words "formal indication" refers to a relation. Thus, if in our passage the "formal" in the word "formalized" is interpreted to mean "formal" in the sense of "formal indication," it would necessarily follow that "sufficiently *formalized*" means "sufficiently formally indicated"—and not the *relation* that composes the *Sache* of "formal indication."

7. See note 4 above.

8. "The first-person cannot be absorbed into its history" (Crowell 2013: 182).

9. For Husserl's shortcoming in this regard, see Hopkins 2011a, chs. 34–35. For Heidegger's, see Hopkins 2011b. For an account of the primal institution of symbolic mathematics and the origination of formalization behind it, see Klein 1969.

BIBLIOGRAPHY

Crowell, Steven. 2013. *Normativity in Husserl and Heidegger*. Cambridge: Cambridge University Press.

Fink, Eugen. 1934. "Was Will Die Phänomenologie Edmund Husserls?" *Die Tatwelt* X: 15–32. Reprint:1966. *Studien zur Phänomenologie 1930-1939*, edited by Herman Leo van Breda, Jacques Taminiaux, and Rudolf Boehm, 157–78. The Hague: Martinus Nijhoff. English: "What Does the Phenomenology of Edmund Husserl Want to Accomplish?" Translated by Arthur Grugan. *Research in Phenomenology* 2 (1972): 5–27.

Hopkins, Burt C. 2011a. *The Origin of the Logic of Symbolic Mathematics: Edmund Husserl and Jacob Klein*. Bloomington: Indiana University Press.

———. 2011b. "Deformalization and Phenomenon in Husserl and Heidegger." In *Heidegger, Translation, and the Task of Thinking: Essays in Honor of Parvis Emad*, edited by Frank Schalow, 49–69. Berlin: Springer.

Husserl, Edmund. 1976. *Ideen zu einer reinen Phänomenologie und phänomenologischen Philosophie, I, Buch: Allgemeine Einführung in die reine Phänomenologie*, hrsg. Karl Schuhmann. Hua III, Den Haag.

Klein, Jacob. 1969. *Greek Mathematical Thought and the Origin of Algebra*. Translated by Eva Brann. Cambridge, MA: MIT Press.

Chapter 10

"Die angebliche Frage nach dem 'Sein des Seienden'"

An Unknown Husserlian Response to Heidegger's "Question of Being"

Jered Janes and Sebastian Luft

In this chapter, we aim to do four things. First, we attempt to rectify a historical detail that sheds new light on Husserl's relation to Heidegger. This detail concerns a Husserlian response to Heidegger that was published in *Husserliana* XXXIV in 2002, but that has not been sufficiently noticed to date and has also not been understood as what it presumably was: Husserl's attempt at writing an "article against Heidegger." Second, we reconstruct the train of thought in this text. Third, we unpack how the text can be understood as a direct response to Heidegger's work. Finally, we discuss how Heidegger—who was almost certainly unaware of the text—might have responded to it.

1. A CORRECTION OF THE HISTORICAL RECORD: HUSSERL'S PLAN FOR WRITING AN ARTICLE "AGAINST HEIDEGGER" (1930–1931)

In the spring of 1931, Husserl receives an invitation from the Kant Societies in Berlin, Halle, and Frankfurt to speak on "phenomenology and anthropology" (cf. Schuhmann 1977: 379). In preparation for these lectures, as he explains to his former student Roman Ingarden in a letter from April 19, 1931, "I have to read closely my antipodes Scheler and Heidegger" (ibid.).[1] It is clear from various sources, however, that Husserl began his close study of Heidegger already in the summer of 1927, continued it in the winter of 1927–1928 and the summer and fall of 1929, only to return to it here in the spring of 1931, at which time he reread Heidegger's *Sein und Zeit* and read his *Kant und das Problem der Metaphysik* of 1929 (alongside Max Scheler's *Die Stellung des Menschen im Kosmos* and *Umsturz der Werte*) (see Sheehan 1997 and Schuhmann 1977: 349).[2] Several months prior to this latter sustained engagement, Husserl summarizes his view of Heidegger's work in the famous letter to Alexander Pfänder from January 6, 1931, as follows:

> Immediately after the printing of my last book [*Formal and Transcendental Logic* appeared in July of 1929], in order to come to a sober and ultimate estimation on Heidegger's philosophy, I turned, for two months, to the study of *Being and Time* as well as the newer writings. I came to the crushing result that I have nothing to do philosophically with this Heideggerian profundity, with this genial unscientificity, that Heidegger's open and veiled critique rests on a grave misunderstanding, that he is in the throes of constructing a system of philosophy of the sort to which I have devoted my life's work of making something like it forever impossible. All others have seen this for a long time, only I did not. I have not beaten around the bush with Heidegger concerning this result. (BW II: 184)[3]

Husserl spends the spring months following his letter to Pfänder and prior to his Kant Societies lecture preparing for the latter, and he delivers the lecture in Frankfurt on June 1, in Berlin on June 10 (to an audience of some 1,600 listeners), and in Halle on June 16. The lecture, which he titles "Phenomenology and Anthropology," does not mention the name of Heidegger (and Scheler only in passing, cf. Hua. XXVII: 180),[4] although it is clear that the enemy of his transcendental phenomenology is the new (existential) anthropology promoted by these newer thinkers.[5] The lecture is entirely positive, even celebratory, taking its point of departure from Descartes and showing how Descartes's philosophical intentions become true with Husserl's transcendental phenomenology (cf. Hua. XXVII: 164 f.).

These facts contradict Heidegger's claim in his 1966 interview with *Der Spiegel* that "Husserl at the beginning of the 1930s gave a public condemnation [*Abrechnung*] of Scheler and myself, whose explicitness left nothing to the imagination. Husserl spoke before students in the Berlin Sports Palace" (quoted in Schuhmann 1978: 603).[6] This claim is wrong on two points. First, Husserl gave the talk in the Auditorium Maximum of Berlin University. Arthur Liebert—professor in Berlin at the time and later publisher of the *Krisis* in exile in Belgrade—writes in the newspaper *Berliner Tagblatt* on June 11, 1931, that "if one were to count the scores of guests who had to be turned away, because the Auditorium Maximum could not seat them, one might have been able in fact to fill the Sports Palace" (quoted in Schuhmann 1978: 604 f.). Perhaps Heidegger was confused by the formulation Liebert used to convey the size of the crowd in Berlin, or perhaps he deliberately misrepresented the facts. Second, the claim that this lecture was "a public condemnation . . . whose explicitness left nothing to the imagination" is clearly wrong, and it is in no way supported by the text itself or by the newspaper articles Schuhmann quotes and that Heidegger presumably read at the time.[7]

Instead, the major part of the lecture is Husserl's celebration of the project of a transcendental phenomenology. As a whole, the lecture provides an outline of the contours of this project and its method of investigation through the "method of correlational investigation, the method of questioning back from the intentional objectivity, concretely expository" (Hua. XXVII: 177). Thus, the talk is really only about the *first* term mentioned in the title. In a brief conclusion, Husserl turns to the second term and asks "whether an anthropology in any sense of the task whatsoever is possible as a philosophical one" (ibid.: 179), which he answers with a resounding "no": "I cannot but declare . . . all philosophies, also those which call themselves phenomenological, as aberrations that in principle can never reach the actual philosophical dimension" (ibid.: 179). This "declaration," however, is not supported with further arguments. Thus, rather than dealing with anthropology critically, he simply declares it as unphilosophical *ab ovo*, as a form of "positive science," in which the cognizing agent "remains trapped in finitudes" (ibid.: 181). In short, in this text, Husserl misses the opportunity to deal directly with, and attempt to refute, his anthropological antipodes.

After giving the lecture in Frankfurt, Berlin, and Halle, Husserl returns to Freiburg on June 21 and reports to Alexandre Koyré on June 22 that he is exhausted but also excited about having returned from his "first and presumably only lecture tour through Germany" (quoted in Schuhmann 1977: 382). In another letter to Helmut Kuhn from July 2 of that year he writes that he has plans to publish the "anthropology-lecture in a separate volume (enlarged and as time allows)."[8] Half a year later, on January 7, 1932, Husserl writes to his student Boyce Gibson: "I hope to let Yearbook XII appear in the summer, perhaps, as an addition, with my lecture (to the Berlin Kant society of June 1931)" (BW 6: 142). As with so many of Husserl's projects, however, this one, too, never saw the light of day during Husserl's lifetime. In this case the discontinuation of the Yearbook after issue XI might have been an additional factor. But is this "Phenomenology and Anthropology" lecture—which was ultimately first published in English translation in 1941[9]—Husserl's only *Auseinandersetzung* with his anthropologistic antipode Heidegger, or is there perhaps another text that has been overlooked so far?

Indeed, already earlier, on March 23, 1930, Ingarden reports that Husserl is planning on writing "an article against Heidegger" (BW III: 265). This means that already before the invitation to Berlin Husserl must have been contemplating something of this nature: an article that would take on newer tendencies in phenomenology that he considers pernicious. It is clear, however, that regardless of how Husserl had initially planned it, "Phenomenology and Anthropology" turned out differently. As shown, the promise the title makes, to contrast phenomenology with anthropology, is not kept. It is known that, by the polemical term "anthropologism," Husserl means a philosophy that claims that "in the human being *alone*, indeed in an eidetic account [*Wesenslehre*] of its *concrete-worldly* Dasein, is supposed to lie the true foundation of philosophy" (quoted in Schuhmann 1978: 606; italics added).[10] The implicit argument of "Phenomenology and Anthropology" seems to be that transcendental phenomenology undermines any anthropology's claim to being fundamental. But Husserl does not deal head-on with Heidegger in this lecture. And any plan that he might have had for an extended version of the lecture was, once again, aborted in favor of Husserl turning to his two larger projects, which took precedence over this shorter project. These projects are his reworking of the *Méditations Cartesiennes*, which had appeared in 1931 in French translation but which (as he believed) needed extensive work to be published for a German audience, and the work on his systematic project, both in collaboration with his assistant Eugen Fink.

But if "Phenomenology and Anthropology" is thus not the planned "article against Heidegger," then what happened with that planned article? While it is clear that Husserl never published such a text, there are reasons to believe that he at least began it.[11] In fact, if our speculation is correct, then the article, or an outline thereof, exists and has been available to the public since 2002 in *Husserliana* XXXIV, although its connection to Husserl's plan to write an article against Heidegger has not yet been noted. In the critical edition of Husserl's unpublished manuscripts on the phenomenological reduction in Hua. XXXIV, the editor selected a manuscript as text #17, which is dated "May 1931" (Husserliana XXXIV: 264–78).[12] It is located in a smaller convolute of texts that Husserl wrote in the lead-up to his trip to the Kant Societies. The text is a fragment, but there are several reasons that lead us to believe that it is the outline of the article that Husserl intended to write "against Heidegger":

1. To begin with, text #17's dating of May 1931 may be incorrect. While the text was placed in a sub-convolute with Husserl's dating of "May 1931," that convolute was itself placed within a larger convolute with the note "St. Märgen 1931." In 1931, Husserl stayed at St. Märgen from July 1 to August 5 (cf. Hua. XXXIV: 584). Thus, while it is possible that Husserl wrote text #17 in May 1931, it is also possible (and also more plausible) that he wrote it sometime in July or August of 1931, after his Kant Societies trip.
2. The text is organized systematically in four sections, leading up to the phenomenological reduction, prefaced with a summary. Such a summary of handwritten texts from his manuscripts is not atypical for Husserl. But most such texts, which preface "real" manuscripts (and are, for that reason, oftentimes printed in italics), are mere summaries that Husserl wrote

afterward, to summarize for himself the most important results or points. In this case, the four points are more of the character of an outline, which Husserl follows but ultimately breaks off. Nonetheless, the four points present a structured outline and Husserl has followed that outline at least until the beginning of the last section, where the text breaks off with three periods, indicating "etcetera."
3. The idea that Husserl first wrote an outline which he would later fill in can be further supported by the several gaps in the text itself, indicated by " . . . " (266) and the staccato-style of the enumeration of words without a sentence structure (278), which would indicate that in the composition of this piece, Husserl was jumping ahead (in the case of 266) from a point he knew he would have to fill in later and, in the case of the end, he could confine himself to a few words to serve as a reminder for later fleshing out: "Basic distinction: to live in the enactment and to have ontological themes, ontological questions and answers, and to practice reflection that encompasses the former universally. Phenomenological Epoché—reduction" (278).
4. The text addresses directly what Husserl criticizes most about his contemporaries, of which Pfänder, Heidegger, and Scheler would have been recent reminders: that they all did not grasp the meaning of the phenomenological reduction. But in the present text, Husserl deals most explicitly with Heidegger. In fact, the text is structured such that it starts off from Heidegger's "alleged question as to the 'being of the entities'" (264) and has as its *terminus ad quem* the phenomenological reduction. As will be shown, Husserl's overarching argument in this short text is that thinking through the consequences of Heidegger's signature question leads directly to the reduction; that the reduction would be the end point of the very question of Being. What better and more convincing argument could one make against one's "antipode"? The very phrasing from text #17 "reflections starting out from the alleged question as to the 'being of the entities'" makes it abundantly clear that Heidegger is the target of this text.[13]
5. Moreover, of all the texts in Husserliana XXXIV, text #17 is the most widely and carefully edited by Husserl. It is known that Husserl reworked his manuscripts as he went through them, but seldom with an eye toward final editing. In this text, he appears to have done just that or something like that. Judging from his reworkings (which are contained in the *apparatus criticus*, Hua. XXXIV: 586–92), Husserl must have spent a great deal of time with this text before, for unknown reasons, aborting work on it. As one can see, his corrections are detailed to the point of tiny linguistic corrections and are clearly intended to bring this text into a publishable shape.

6. Finally, it is not a typical "research manuscript" intended for private use, but is in the shape of a text composed for publication, despite its fragmentary character. For instance, the article has considerable rhetorical flourish, which would be out of place in a private research manuscript. Consider, for instance, the following phrasing, which is clearly meant to be the rhetorically elegant conclusion of a *reductio ad absurdum* argument: "But do we not have to reach for our head and cry out: into what nonsense have we fallen!" (273). Husserl rarely writes in such an engaged manner in his private manuscripts. The quoted sentence is clearly addressed to a putative reader.

Taken together, these points support the following conclusion. The fact that the "Phenomenology and Anthropology" lecture does not deliver on the promise of its title, and the fact that text #17 deals directly with Heidegger both suggest that text #17 *is in fact* the fragment of the "article against Heidegger" that Husserl intended to write. If this is correct, then Husserl began this article but did not finish it and did not publish it. Since there is no direct factual support for this claim, it must remain speculation to an extent; however, the evidence presented here should lend plausibility to it.

But regardless of whether text #17 is in fact *the* promised "article against Heidegger," it is certainly philosophically important because Husserl articulates in it a different and perhaps more direct response to Heidegger's work than he does in other well-known and published texts. For this reason, if for no other, text #17 deserves closer study. In order to provide such a study, in the next section we give an account of the train of thought in this text, and in the third section we summarize the core argument of the text and discuss how it can be understood as a direct response to Heidegger's work.

2. THE TRAIN OF THOUGHT IN TEXT #17

The text starts out from the question that stands at the outset of Heidegger's *Being and Time*, the question as to the being of entities. Husserl clearly intends to reconstruct the salience of this question, "starting from the question, what it can mean" (264), that is, trying to think through it by phrasing and framing the question *in his own terms*, how the question would *properly* have to be asked, in Husserl's view. Husserl eventually reaches two results: first, he is not so much against asking the question as denying it its status as primary or essential; second, he argues that the truly radical asking of this question results in the necessity to perform the phenomenological reduction.

Heidegger starts out his analysis of the question of being by insisting that what is desired—essentially since Plato—is an ontology that has the status of a basic science underpinning our grounding of all other sciences or all other (regional) ontologies. However, this base-science can only be executed by starting out from an understanding of being, more precisely from a being that *has* this understanding, and this being is nothing other than human Dasein.[14] As Heidegger concludes in the introduction to *Being and Time*:

> Thus Dasein's understanding of Being pertains with equal primordiality both to an understanding of something like a "world," and to the understanding of the Being of those entities which become accessible within the world.... Therefore *fundamental ontology*, from which alone all other ontologies can take their rise, must be sought in the *existential analytic of Dasein*. (BT: 33–34)

This understanding of ontology, Cassirer points out in a review of Heidegger's *Kantbuch*, goes against all traditional views (including the neo-Kantians). Citing approvingly the neo-Kantian Alois Riehl, Cassirer writes: "Riehl assumes that the task of a philosophy, which makes the claim to be a rigorous science, can consist in nothing else than a doctrine of principles" (Cassirer 1931: 2). And such a scientific philosophy can only come forth as "*science of cognition*" (ibid.). Cognition does refer back to a subject, but only insofar as it *cognizes*, nothing else (as, for instance, being finite and having understanding). We shall keep these determinations of ontology in mind as we now turn to Husserl.

Thus, the text starts out by asking "does the Heideggerian 'working out' ['*Ausarbeitung*'][15] of the question as to the 'being of entities' ['*Sein des Seienden*'] have a good meaning and which meaning can the question, first begun by Aristotle, as to being qua being have?" (264 f.). The way Husserl approaches this question is in four steps, starting out with two short paragraphs[16] on (1) formal and (2) material ontology, then (3) turning to human intentionality within the "natural doctrine"—that is, remaining "first in the naïve-natural attitude" (264)—"of intentionality according to the basic distinctions. Everything that is valid for me as human being as being, being-thus, in all ontic modalities ... is valid for me in my own life of validity" (ibid.). The fourth step (4) is the radicalization of the third, broaching the "radical problem: I and world" (ibid.). The third section is the longest and best developed in this text; it serves as the hinge to turn to consciousness from ontological questions. Its style is also the most in the form of a "rehearsal" of familiar lines of thought.

It is evident from this order that Husserl's initial understanding of the question regarding being has to start out from *formal* ontology, which frames being as "substrate of possible true judgments" (ibid.), followed by the *material* ontological question "which includes the material content of ontic validity, the substrates of judgments. Form in the second sense: The form of the world as essential structure of all that is worldly 'real' and of the totality world. [. . . Material ontology deals with] the real categories, regions; total region world" (ibid.). The way Husserl approaches the question regarding being, thus, is familiar from his ontological approach known from *Ideas II*, which distinguishes formal from material ontology, with the latter in the plural, that is, as the disciplines dealing with the ontological regions within the world (regional ontologies) and ultimately the all-region "world." In his constitutive analyses in *Ideas II*, the regional ontologies are "guiding clues" to correlative modes of consciousness constituting them for a world-experiencing subject. "Consciousness" enters only when being is understood as *constituted*. Such an understanding, however, only becomes possible after the break with the natural attitude, by construing consciousness as transcendental. With the theme "consciousness," Husserl is not positing a new realm of being beyond what could be experienced in principle, but clarifying the a priori conditions of experience of being *in* the natural attitude.

"Formal ontology" Husserl understands in the Aristotelian sense of a discipline about "being qua being" as a matter of predication, "in order to predicate determinations of it" (265) "in pure, unconditioned generality" (ibid.). By being one understands "following the tradition" (ibid.) "*worldly entities, and in a free as-such-generality*" or simply "something as such" (ibid.). Formal ontology, thus, is about judging and predicating being "as actuality or possibility" (ibid.), that is, in general modalities that hold valid for all (possible) entities. If we encounter a worldly entity, we know, thus, "a priori that it is interpretable in its essential determinations proper to it" (ibid.).

Formal ontology, then, is a matter of making "categorial determinations" about entities. "All concepts which arise here are categories and possible determinants for something or entities as such and in generality. . . . These are the formalia of logic" (266). Formal ontology is thus about attributing to being determinants "spoken in the most empty, most extreme formal generality as substrate of possible determinations, possible individualities of groups, individual possibilities" (ibid.). This formal ontology, "which includes the entire mathematics, is intimately related to the formal science of predicative 'meanings,' of *apophantic logic*" (ibid.). Thus far, this is the formal ontology already known from Husserl's earlier work, a discipline correlated to formal logic as its correlative discipline and thus part of the most general *mathesis universalis*.

Next we arrive at material ontology, which is the "*a priori of these worldly substances*, thus their determinability through worldly 'specialized' categorial deductions (*material ontology*)" (ibid.), thus an ontology of the material "world" with its ultimate substrates, "and every such totality [called substrate] is substance in the pregnant sense" (267). Material ontology thus, "vis-à-vis the general questions regarding being as such in the sense of the 'real' ... raises the questions regarding the totality world according to its universal structures, its construction from realities, its categories of reality, that is, the essential types of worldly realities as such, which belong to the world and every possible world ... and whose concepts (*predicabilia*) are precisely categories of determinations of judgment related to the world as such and in essential generality" (ibid.). Material ontology thus talks about being as *worldly* being, as part of the all-region "world" and its sub-regions. Thus, the region "animal" is material in that it is a region belonging to this specific nature on this specific planet. The "general" category "animal" is thus, to use Husserl's terminology, a "bound" generality, as bound to its specific region (living creatures). It is a priori insofar as it is necessarily bound to a specific world, receiving its guiding clues from the world as it is encountered in experience.

To repeat, these two sections rehearse familiar themes from Husserl's views on ontology.

Now Husserl concludes these two sections on ontology with the important remark: "Thus, all of these questions [regarding formal and material ontology] are questions in natural-worldly attitude, and the only possible questions, as to the *being* of the entities, as to that, thus, which can be predicated in truth of entities as such, be they logically formal or worldly material" (ibid.). Ontology, thus, is a matter of "worldly" science; "in the natural attitude" is shorthand for "without a consideration of its relation to experiencing subjectivity." The being of the world, Husserl is fond of saying, "does not care" about subjects experiencing it. Hence, any ontology about worldly being *must not* take into consideration the subjective viewpoint of the world. It is about worldly being, period, regardless of its being-experienced. The fact that we know of worldly being only because we experience it is, *in the natural attitude*, trivial, and to "be subjective" would be an impediment to getting at objectivity. To properly understand worldly beings in their objective being-such, scientific methods and tools and devices are needed. So for instance, there are sounds that humans cannot hear (as in dog whistles). It is a scientific measuring of the sound waves alone that can inform us that they exist; otherwise, if we do not hear them, we might come to think (erroneously) that they don't exist. Anybody who denies that they exist because she does not hear them simply has a faulty ontology of sound waves. This is why any "worldly" ontology cannot and in fact must not relate itself back to a being that has an understanding of being. As Husserl insists many times, phenomenology neither takes away nor adds anything to worldly sciences that attempt to grasp the world objectively, in truth.

But what about an ontology of consciousness as another entity in the world? This question is tackled in the third section on "human intentionality," that is, as part of an account within the natural attitude of "things in the world." Among entities in the world are other human beings with their psyches as well as their bodies. When studying the former, psychic life, one discovers as a decisive feature of this life its relatedness to something: intentionality. In studying this feature of consciousness as a thing in the world, one inadvertently makes a distinction between the experience-of-something and this something that is experienced, thus between the "inner" life of the subject and the "outer" world. "Inner" and "outer" are categories of the world, and not a distinction into "non-worldly" being here and "worldly" being on the other hand. The latter *would be* a distinction that, as we will see, indeed breaks with the natural attitude if properly understood. The way Husserl depicts this discipline of the "inner" world of the subject when studied by intentional psychology is that the distinction between "inner" and "outer" are worldly distinctions, similar to an account of a box as seen from the outside or the inside. What follows is a genetic reconstruction of what results when one takes this approach to the question of the psyche—namely the paradoxical stance of solipsism.

Naturally, now, this regional ontology of consciousness will have its main distinctions, which Husserl briefly rehearses in the following. So, for instance, Husserl discusses the modalities of *Vermeinen*, as pure intending, believing, having as certain, doubt, negation, etc., furthermore, the distinction between intending in positionality or neutrality (quasi-positionality), the distinction between derived perceptions and a fundamental, primordial perception with its primordial form of intentionality [*Urintentionalität*] and its correlate, the world as "streaming total perception in harmonious synthesis of identity" (271). This discussion leads up to the dramatic finale of this short text, when Husserl raises the question of how it is possible that the subject knows that its subjective appearance is identical to the entity "out there," and this (quasi-)problem is heightened when the question comes to *other minds* as experienced in other respective lived bodies. Thus the question arises, "how can [the subject] know that such unities of appearances of possible or actual *peculiarities which appear as inner-psychic* can indeed refer to that which is real external to it? And how can another know who is in the same situation in relation to any other human ego and its external world, by thinking he can say something about it, believing that he and every other 'represent' the same objective world?" (272 f.). At this point Husserl counters with a *reductio* argument, exclaiming: "But must we not grasp our head and cry out: into which nonsense have we gotten!" (273). The problem only arises because one has made a faulty inner-outer distinction before; this was the very way Husserl reconstructed the genesis of the problem. The discussion in this section, thus, can be read as a *genetic reconstruction of the paradoxical stance of solipsism*. It amounts to a misunderstood "reduction to soul self-encapsulated for itself" (275). It is not necessary that every regional ontology of consciousness result in this paradox, but in such a radicalization of the inner-outer distinction, *this* is the necessary point of arrival.

And indeed, the last section begins with a newly reached critical standpoint, from which Husserl can say, "Thus it was complete nonsense to find a riddle in how a psychic subject in its immanence can know that the intentional formations of validity ... are indeed actualities and possibilities of the world, of the 'world itself,' as it is objectively, in itself. I have no other world than that which is 'constituted' in my immanence" (ibid.). Indeed, what I need to distinguish (in effect after having left the natural attitude) is *"my representation of the world*, my subjective manner of experiencing the world ... from the world itself, from the things themselves that exist, whether or not they are ever experienced as this or that by me or by anyone else" (ibid.). Thus, the reduction must not reduce to the famous "needle point" of an ego within the world, but instead to that subject that has a representation of the world writ large, the transcendental sphere of experience in which the world itself is constituted from the perspective of the natural attitude. The transcendental subject is, instead, the "ultimate bearer of all validity" (277), since all being is relative to and manifests itself for it. But seeing this distinction requires the performance of the phenomenological reduction.

What we learn to discern, from seeing through the "nonsensical riddle of the world" (ibid.), is the "true riddle of the world, which arises with radical self-reflection that I [not the worldly, but transcendental ego] am the ultimate, absolute bearer of validity of all and every entity for me" (ibid.). This distinction is something that has to be "put into play in an investigation taking its course in radical and concrete evidence" rather than "remaining stuck in formal arguing" (ibid.)—in other words, through the execution of phenomenological description. The text ends with a summary of the "basic distinction" that Husserl has attempted to hammer home here: "living in the execution [of the natural attitude] and having ontological themes, questions and answers [on the one hand, and on the other] practicing the universal reflection covering all this. Phenomenological epoché—reduction" (ibid.).

With this sketch of the text's train of thought before us, in the next section we summarize the core argument of the text and unpack how it constitutes a direct response to Heidegger's work. But in order to do these two things, it is first necessary to provide some additional context regarding the philosophical relationship between Husserl and Heidegger.

3. HUSSERL'S ARGUMENT IN TEXT #17

As can be gathered from Thomas Sheehan, several of Heidegger's core criticisms of Husserl go back to at least his first lecture course after the First

World War, a course—"The Idea of Philosophy and the Problem of World-View"—that began in January 1919 (Sheehan 1997: 14).[17] These criticisms are substantially developed over subsequent years, and Heidegger articulated them clearly in his 1925 summer lecture course—later published as *History of the Concept of Time: Prolegomena*—before they explicitly and implicitly appear in publication in 1927's *Being and Time*. In fact, around Christmas of 1926, Heidegger reports to Karl Jaspers that "[i]f the treatise [*Being and Time*] has been written 'against' anyone, then it has been written against Husserl" (Sheehan 1997: 22).

With help from Steven Crowell, a brief account of Heidegger's critique of Husserl can be gleaned from *History of the Concept of Time* and *Being and Time*. Heidegger disagrees with Husserl, as Crowell has shown, on the "matter" and, relatedly, the "method" of philosophy. Whereas Husserl understood philosophy to be fundamentally a transcendental "science of consciousness," Heidegger understood it to be fundamentally an "inquiry into being" (Crowell 2013: 64). On Heidegger's view in *Being and Time*, as indicated above, the inquiry into the being of entities or being *as* being—that is, general ontology—grounds all regional ontologies. But, as also noted, this inquiry can be carried out only by first confronting the being that already has an understanding of being, that is, Dasein. This means that, on Heidegger's view, general ontology presupposes a fundamental ontology of Dasein that consists in the "existential analytic of Dasein" (BT: 13; see also Crowell 2013: 66). Heidegger thus holds here that philosophy is fundamentally not only an inquiry into being, but one that must begin with an inquiry into the ontology of Dasein.

Furthermore, the latter inquiry reveals *Dasein* to be being-in-the-world (BT: 78ff.). And as Crowell has argued, Heidegger's view is that it is the "structures of being-in-the-world [that] make consciousness in Husserl's sense—the intentionality of acts of perception, judgment, imagination, etc.—possible" (Crowell 2013: 66). More specifically, it is Dasein's understanding of being that enables beings to "show up *as* what they *are*" (ibid.). For this reason, on Heidegger's view, consciousness in Husserl's sense presupposes Dasein, and any investigation of consciousness in this sense therefore presupposes an inquiry into the ontology of Dasein. In claiming that philosophy is fundamentally an inquiry into being that must begin with an inquiry into the ontology of Dasein, Heidegger is thus also claiming that this inquiry is more fundamental than, and presupposed by, Husserl's transcendental science of consciousness.

Now, as Husserl conceives of it, this science essentially involves the phenomenological reduction to phenomena that are immanent to transcendental consciousness, a reduction that requires bracketing the existence not only of these phenomena but also of the transcendental subject that is correlated with them. On Heidegger's view, this means that Husserl's science cannot provide "a positive account of being" in general and, because the "*'essence' of Dasein lies in its existence*," that it cannot provide a proper account of Dasein in particular (Crowell 2013: 47; BT: 67; HCT: 109–10). Thus, from Heidegger's perspective, not only does Husserl's transcendental science of consciousness fail to clarify the conditions of its own possibility, but in doing so it also fails to provide a positive account of being and a proper account of Dasein.

For his part, Husserl had been told often that "Heidegger's phenomenology is something totally different" from his (Husserl 1997: 481), but he appears not to have begun to realize the extent of their differences until he started reading the published version of *Being and Time* in the summer of 1927. This realization continued and deepened when he unsuccessfully attempted to collaborate with Heidegger on the *Encyclopedia Britannica* article in the fall of 1927, when he finished reading the published version of *Being and Time* in the winter of 1927–1928, and when he undertook a second reading of *Being and Time* alongside a reading of other more recent Heidegger texts in the summer and fall of 1929 (see Sheehan 1997: 22–29). In the midst of the latter effort, Husserl attended Heidegger's inaugural lecture, "What is Metaphysics?" in Freiburg in July 1929, an experience that, as Sheehan notes, undoubtedly served to further clarify the substantial differences between him and his now successor (Sheehan 1997: 29). By December 1929, Husserl was confident enough in his grasp of Heidegger's work to conclude—in a letter to Ingarden that anticipated what he wrote in the aforementioned 1931 letter to Pfänder—"that I can *not* admit his work within the framework of my phenomenology and unfortunately that I also must reject it entirely as regards its method, and in the essentials as regards its content" (Sheehan 1997: 29). And before referring to Heidegger (along with Scheler) as his "antipodes" in April 1931 and delivering the "Phenomenology and Anthropology" lecture that June, by March 1930 Husserl had further realized, as noted, the need for his own "article against Heidegger."

Thus, whereas Heidegger realized his philosophical opposition to Husserl early on and wrote 1927's *Being and Time* in some sense "against Husserl," Husserl realized his philosophical opposition to Heidegger much later and accordingly realized much later the need for his own article "against Heidegger." Now, regardless of whether text #17 is this latter article, it is certainly, as noted, a text in which Husserl articulates a different and perhaps more direct response to Heidegger's work than he does in other well-known and published texts. More specifically, it is a text in which he attempts to come to terms directly with Heidegger's *Seinsfrage*. In order to clarify what his position on the *Seinsfrage* is here and thus how text #17 constitutes a direct response to Heidegger's work, it is necessary to succinctly state—on the basis of the sketch provided in the second section above—Husserl's core argument in the text as follows.

Heidegger's work takes its start from the question of the being of entities. Any attempt to ask about the being of entities is an attempt to ask either formally or materially about the being of the world as either the totality of all entities or as the entity or entities of a specific region. In other words, it is an attempt to ask about ontology from the perspective of the natural attitude, a perspective from which all ontology is worldly ontology. But investigating worldly ontology from the perspective of this attitude requires investigating the being of the world independently of any subject who experiences the world. (Otherwise, what results is not an ontology but a form of transcendental realism, for which access to the world is considered crucial to an account of the being of the world.) For this reason, an inquiry into the being of entities cannot properly begin with an inquiry into a subject, even into a subject that has an understanding of being; this would be an arbitrary starting point for an ontology. In other words, general ontology—that is, the ontology of being as being—cannot begin with what Heidegger called fundamental ontology—that is, the ontology of Dasein.

If it did, this worldly ontology would begin with an analysis of the subject or consciousness as an object in the world. This analysis or regional ontology would reveal that consciousness has the defining characteristics of intentionality, that is, that the subject is capable of experiencing objects. And in investigating this characteristic, a distinction would naturally be drawn between the experience of objects, which is construed as part of the subject's inner life regarded as part of the world, and the objects that are experienced, which are construed as part of the external world. But this distinction inevitably raises the question of how we can know that the subject's experiences actually refer to what is external to the subject. In other words, it raises the problem of solipsism.[18] This problem can be overcome by leaving this worldly ontology and the natural attitude and focusing attention instead on consciousness or the subject regarded, not as a being in the world, but as the transcendental subject to whom all being is relative because it is the "ultimate bearer of all validity" (277). Once this transition from the natural attitude to the phenomenological attitude is made, and once the transcendental subject is recognized as the ultimate bearer of all validity and therefore as that to which all being, insofar as it can be meaningful, is relative, the above-noted problem dissolves because it becomes clear that this subject has "no other world than that which is 'constituted' in [its] immanence" (275). Furthermore, once this transition has occurred, we are no longer providing an ontology of the worldly subject or of the world; instead, we are providing a transcendental science of consciousness as the necessary condition of the meaningful appearance of the world and of all beings in it, including the human subject with the property of being "intentional."

There is little doubt that Husserl here intends to show that Heidegger's own *Seinsfrage* leads from the natural attitude and the human person to the phenomenological attitude and the transcendental subject. In other words, it is clear that the argument sketched in this text is an attempt to show that the *Seinsfrage* itself motivates the phenomenological reduction to pure consciousness. It is, in short, a way to the reduction via Heidegger's *Seinsfrage*.[19] It is crucial to emphasize that Husserl's direct engagement with Heidegger's signature question here does not have the character of a direct argument against Heidegger. Instead, Husserl here attempts to work through the question for himself and to articulate why he thinks it should be addressed through his transcendental phenomenology. Thus, while the text does not constitute a direct argument against Heidegger's work, it does constitute a direct response to it that is tantamount to an *implicit* argument against it. It is possible to note the following two ways in which the text can be understood as such an implicit argument.

First, as noted, because it involves bracketing the existence of the phenomena to be investigated, the phenomenological reduction, on Heidegger's view, precludes providing a positive account of being in general and a proper account of Dasein in particular. And because Husserl's transcendental science essentially involves this reduction, on Heidegger's view this science is incapable of providing these accounts. If Husserl's sketched argument is good, then this aspect of Heidegger's critique is off the mark. This is because, as the argument has it, the reduction reveals the necessity of an investigation into the sphere of transcendental consciousness and the transcendental subject, an investigation that itself reveals this subject to be the "ultimate bearer of all validity" and therefore that to which all being, insofar as it can be meaningful, is relative. As a result of this, any attempt to provide a fundamental clarification of being *as* being or the being of Dasein must begin with this transcendental subject that constitutes all being insofar as it is meaningful. Thus, far from precluding an account of being in general and a proper account of Dasein in particular, the phenomenological reduction is the proper first step to providing them. Crucially, in Husserl's implicit argument, this first step is motivated by Heidegger's *Seinsfrage*. This rhetorical move by Husserl is likely an attempt to show not only that his transcendental science can address Heidegger's fundamental questions, but also that Heidegger would recognize this fact himself if he were only to properly understand the reduction.[20]

Second, as also noted, because Heidegger held that Dasein as being-in-the-world is the necessary condition of consciousness as intentionality, and because consciousness in this sense is the focus of Husserl's transcendental science, Heidegger held that his inquiry into being is more fundamental than, and presupposed by, Husserl's science. If Husserl's sketched argument is good, then Heidegger's view here is also off the mark. This is because, as the "ultimate bearer of all validity" to whom all being, insofar as it can be meaningful, is relative, the transcendental subject is actually the necessary condition of Dasein as being-in-the-world. In other words, this is because the latter is a constitution or mundanization of the transcendental subject. As a result, Husserl's transcendental science, as the investigation of the transcendental subject and its constitution of the world—including the constitution of Dasein as being-in-the-world—is more fundamental than and presupposed by Heidegger's inquiry into being. For these reasons, if the implicit argument is good, then philosophy is not fundamentally an inquiry into being in Heidegger's sense; it is fundamentally a transcendental science of consciousness.

4. A HEIDEGGERIAN RESPONSE TO HUSSERL'S ARGUMENT

Of course, none of this is to say that Husserl's implicit argument in text #17 is in fact good. It is merely to say that, if it is good, then it amounts to an implicit argument against Heidegger's work in those two ways. It is crucial to remember that the text is a fragment or outlined rough draft that Husserl did not complete and did not publish. It is possible that he set it aside intending to return to it; but it is also possible that he found it to be fundamentally flawed and intentionally abandoned it. Bearing in mind the text's incompleteness and the uncertainty surrounding Husserl's assessment of it, it is nevertheless fruitful to consider—once again, relying on Crowell—the following two ways that the Heidegger of *Being and Time* could have responded to it.

First, Husserl utilizes a clearly un-Heideggerian conception of ontology when thinking through the *Seinsfrage*. According to Husserl's conception, because being insofar as it is meaningful is relative to the transcendental subject, being—again, insofar as it is meaningful—is *constituted* objectivity. This means that ontology is the study of beings as objects (Crowell 2001: 249). Furthermore, as indicated above, this is more specifically an a priori study of objects regarded either formally or materially. Whereas formal ontology describes the essence of any possible object *as* an object, material or regional ontologies further describe the essence of possible objects insofar as they are objects *of this or that particular region* (for example, of nature) (see Crowell 2013: 65; Husserl 2014: 20–24). As Crowell points out, Husserl's distinction between material and formal ontologies appears to be paralleled by Heidegger's distinction between regional ontologies and fundamental ontology (see BT: 31 f.). But this appearance is deceiving, for crucially, Heidegger distinguishes between beings as objects and being as such; and, also crucially, whereas Husserl's material and formal ontologies address beings as objects, they neglect being as such. As Crowell puts it, "Beyond the formal category 'something in general' there is, for Husserl, nothing to say about being as such, but for Heidegger it is precisely phenomenology's task to overcome such 'forgetfulness' and ask about the sense of being presupposed in formal and regional ontologies alike" (Crowell 2013: 65). Thus, Husserl's ontology neglects precisely the component of Heidegger's ontology that motivates his very project, and Husserl is, from Heidegger's perspective, but a more recent example of a philosopher who is forgetful of being.

The discrepancy between their conceptions of ontology is important because it means that, in utilizing his own conception, Husserl not only thinks through the *Seinsfrage* in a framework that is different from Heidegger's; he thinks through it in one that Heidegger would not accept. More specifically, in text #17, because Husserl holds that any question about being is a question about objects, he notes—as is evident toward the beginning of the implicit argument—that ontology is essentially a worldly science directed at objects as a whole or at the objects of a particular region. Of course, from Heidegger's perspective, this is simply not accurate. Heidegger recognizes that an ontology of worldly objects in this sense is possible, but he is not primarily interested in this; he is primarily interested in a more fundamental ontology that precedes that kind and any other kind of ontology, a fundamental ontology that must begin with an analysis of Dasein. To be sure, Heidegger understands Dasein as being-in-the-world, and for this reason his fundamental ontology is in a sense an ontology of the world. But as Crowell has argued, Dasein is in-the-world in a sense essentially different from the way merely worldly objects in Husserl's sense are in the world (Crowell 2002: 136 f.; Crowell 2001: 177 f.); and as a result, Heidegger's fundamental ontology is not a worldly ontology in the sense discussed in text #17. Given that in thinking through the *Seinsfrage* Husserl utilizes a conception of ontology crucially different from Heidegger's, and given that this different framework fundamentally shapes the conclusions that Husserl comes to in thinking through it, Heidegger could easily reject the conclusions by understandably rejecting this different ontological framework. In short, Heidegger could respond to the implicit argument in text #17 by pointing out that Husserl is simply "talking past" him.

Second, as noted, one of the upshots of Husserl's implicit argument is that, far from precluding an account of being in general and a proper account of Dasein in particular, the phenomenological reduction to the transcendental subject is the proper first step to providing them because, as the ultimate bearer of all validity, the transcendental subject is that to which all being, insofar as it is meaningful, is relative. Repeating his criticism from *History of the Concept of Time* and other writings, Heidegger can point out here that

Husserl is yet again failing to properly consider the question of the *being* of the transcendental subject (see HCT: 108 f.). It may be the case that any ontology of beings as objects must begin with the transcendental subject that constitutes these objects, but what about the ontology of the transcendental subject that constitutes? As Heidegger points out, for Husserl, this question is nonsensical (Crowell 2001: 180; HCT: 113 f.). This appears to be the case for Husserl because he thinks that to ask about the being of the transcendental subject is to ask about a being that constitutes but is not constituted; and because constitution is the process whereby being becomes meaningful or sensical, to ask about an un-constituted being is to ask about something that may be logically possible but is materially non-sensical (Crowell 2001: 191 and Husserl 2014: 87 f.).

But Heidegger could respond that, far from showing that the question is nonsensical, Husserl has merely established that it is nonsensical when addressed using the resources of his transcendental science of consciousness. As a result, to answer this question may not require a move from the sensical to the non-sensical but rather one from Husserl's science to Heidegger's inquiry into being, an inquiry that begins, again, with a fundamental ontology of Dasein. In other words, Husserl's implicit claim that his science of consciousness is more fundamental than Heidegger's ontology, and his implicit claim that the transcendental subject is more fundamental than Dasein, are not—on Heidegger's view—the result of a thorough review of the evidence but rather of Husserl's failure in text #17 (and throughout his thinking) to account for the being of the transcendental subject, an accounting that would require not only an alteration of Husserl's conception of ontology but also a modification of his phenomenological method (see Crowell 2001: 180 f.). In short, Heidegger could point out that, even when directly addressing the *Seinsfrage* in text #17, Husserl's implicit argument there remains "forgetful of being" and thereby fails to properly establish its conclusions.[21]

CONCLUSION

Even though in text #17 Husserl directly confronts Heidegger's *Seinsfrage*, his utilization there of a different conception of ontology and, relatedly, his failure there to confront the question of the ontological status of the transcendental subject, leave him open to familiar and substantial Heideggerian objections. Addressing the question of whether Husserl's mature transcendental science of consciousness contains the resources to successfully respond to these objections is beyond the scope of this chapter.[22] But it is important to note that if Husserl can successfully respond to them, he does not appear to do so in text #17.

What we have in this text is simply a previously unremarked-upon attempt by Husserl to come to terms with the heart of Heidegger's ontological project in a way that shows the superiority of his own transcendental phenomenological project. Again, it is crucial to bear in mind that Husserl never finished and published this piece, and therefore that he himself might have had serious misgivings about its persuasiveness. But regardless of Husserl's assessment, in this text he constructs a hitherto unknown implicit argument against Heidegger by addressing the latter's own *Seinsfrage*. For this reason, the text deserves to be acknowledged in the scholarship on the relationship between these two seminal thinkers, a relationship that has largely defined the history of phenomenology. As the foregoing discussion of this overlooked text has shown, delving into this vexed relationship is not merely a historical but also a philosophical task, one that stands to yield even further interesting research.

NOTES

1. All translations into English, unless otherwise noted, are from the authors.

2. Cf. also the unpublished letter to Alexandre Koyré (10/21/1929): "I am here [in Tremezzo] with my wife for three weeks. . . . But really, I continue to work. . . . Ms. Peiffer [co-translator of CM] informed me unfortunately that she would not finish the translation until the new year. Accordingly I will include parts of the German edition for the sake of my French friends. For the German readers I intend, à la Descartes, to add *Objectiones* and *Responsiones*, not sure how, but in any case I will have to tackle Dilthey—Misch and Heidegger's method, likewise Scheler's misunderstandings." Thanks to Thomas Vongehr for making this passage available. Cf. also the letter to Ingarden of December 2, 1929: "The 'study of Heidegger'? I came to the result that I *cannot* fit the book into the framework of my phenomenology, unfortunately that I also am forced to reject it entirely in terms of method and essentially also in substance" (BW III: 254). Husserl's study of Heidegger's work is tracked in greater detail in Sheehan 1997.

3. The letter has gained notoriety as it is Husserl's "shocked" response (cf. BW II: 180) to Pfänder's angry letter to Husserl, in which he wants a clarification of Husserl's behavior. According to Pfänder, Husserl told "everyone who wanted to hear it and who didn't" that he would recommend Pfänder as his successor in Freiburg, although ultimately he recommended Heidegger without even a mention of himself, Pfänder. Husserl's chagrined reply is his longest comment about Heidegger, according to which Husserl was at first elated about having such a powerful thinker among his students who would carry on his legacy, and how disappointed he felt after learning about Heidegger's true philosophy and character. Although meant to assuage Pfänder, Husserl's letter is quite insulting, as he also tells him that he would not have been able to recommend him anyway, since he did not grasp the meaning of the transcendental reduction. Pfänder is incensed upon receiving the reply and suggests in his reply of April 7 that they meet in person to talk about this. Husserl's final answer

is even more insulting, as he replies, just two days later, that he does not wish to see him unless they agree to talk about "nice themes that unite us" (ibid.: 186).

4. Volumes in the *Husserliana* are quoted as "Hua." + volume number.

5. The historical surroundings of this event are detailed in Schuhmann 1978; the talk is now published in Hua. XXVII.

6. The *Spiegel* interview was not published until after Heidegger's death, in the issue of May 31, 1976 (cf. Schuhmann 1978: 591).

7. Schuhmann calls the claim "unduly exaggerated" (Schuhmann 1978: 606).

8. Unpublished letter stored in the Husserl Archives in Leuven.

9. This first translation was done by Richard G. Schmitt, and it was published in the second volume of *Philosophy and Phenomenological Research*. A second translation, by Thomas Sheehan and Richard E. Palmer, was based on the critically edited *Husserliana* XXVII text, and it was published in Husserl 1997.

10. We disagree with Schuhmann, however, when he claims that in Husserl's eyes anthropologism "is a contemporary form of objectivism" (ibid.: 605 f.). The force of Husserl's argument is not that anthropologism is a veiled form of objectivism, which would be rather absurd (an account of the subject is to be objective?); rather, his critique is that a theory of the human subject cannot be the foundation of philosophy in general. If anything, the foundation for philosophy would have to lie in a *transcendental account* of the a priori correlation between subject *and world*. It is a different question whether Husserl thought that there could be a positive sense of a *phenomenological anthropology* as a doctrine of the human being *within* the framework of transcendental phenomenology. Husserl seems to have thought of such a project affirmatively and, moreover, that this was what he had sanctioned Heidegger to do (in the way in which he had sanctioned Oskar Becker to work out a phenomenology of mathematical existence—both Becker's *Mathematische Existenz* and *Sein und Zeit* were published in the same Yearbook). That such a doctrine would be construed as *fundamental* turns anthropology into anthropologism.

11. This idea resurfaces for one last time in 1936, as quoted in the editor's introduction to Hua. XXIX, p. xliv.

12. All simple quotations in the following are from text #17 in Hua. XXXIV.

13. To further support this point, in a text from the same convolute (Beilage XV), Husserl notes explicitly that "this is against Heidegger" (259). Being placed in the same vicinity, this text stems from the same body of work as Text #17.

14. We leave Dasein untranslated here and will not discuss Heidegger's possible motivation for calling the human being literally "being there" instead of "Mensch" (human being) or other possible candidates from the tradition.

15. This is the term Heidegger uses in para. 4 of *Being and Time*: Heidegger's rhetoric suggests that the question is not obvious but has to be worked out for the first time. Macquarrie and Robinson translate "*Ausarbeitung*" as "restating."

16. Keep in mind that this was the sketch for an article. The different parts would have been, presumably, of equal length.

17. It is important to note two things. First, the often-repeated claim that Heidegger was at this or at any other time Husserl's assistant is wrong. Husserl made Heidegger—a student of Rickert's whom Husserl took over from the departed Neo-Kantian—an assistant to the department (cf. Schuhmann 1978: 593). At that time

Heidegger was a fully educated academic (with habilitation). Schuhmann approvingly cites Spiegelberg (ibid.: 592) that "Heidegger was therefore never Husserl's pupil in the sense of the term which would justify the expectation of a special personal loyalty to Husserl." Second, Heidegger's misgivings about Husserl's work began even earlier than January 1919. In January 1916, Heidegger wrote to a friend that Husserl was "lacking the necessary breadth of vision" (Ott 1993: 90; quoted in Carman 2006: 97).

18. Husserl was frequently accused of being a solipsist. Here, he is showing how the problem of solipsism can arise and why it is absurd.

19. One may call this the "Heideggerian way," not to be mistaken with the "ontological way" in the *Crisis*.

20. As noted above, Husserl repeatedly claimed that Heidegger (and others) did not understand the phenomenological reduction. See, for example, Cairns 1976: 43.

21. For more on the issue of the ontological status of the transcendental subject in the Husserl-Heidegger relationship, see especially Crowell 2001.

22. For more on this question and how Husserl's late conception of the transcendental person relates to it, see Luft 2005.

BIBLIOGRAPHY

Cairns, Dorion. 1976. *Conversations with Husserl and Fink*. The Hague: Nijhoff.
Carman, Taylor. 2006. "The Principle of Phenomenology." In *The Cambridge Companion to Heidegger*, 2nd ed. Edited by Charles Guignon, 97–119. Cambridge: Cambridge University Press.
Cassirer, Ernst. 1931. "Kant und das Problem der Metaphysik. Bemerkungen zu Heideggers Kant-Interpretation." *Kant-Studien* 36, no. 1: 1–26.
Crowell, Steven. 2001. *Husserl, Heidegger, and the Space of Meaning: Paths toward Transcendental Phenomenology*. Evanston, IL: Northwestern University Press.
———. 2002. "Does the Husserl/Heidegger Feud Rest on a Mistake? An Essay on Psychological and Transcendental Phenomenology." *Husserl Studies* 18: 123–40.
———. 2013. *Normativity and Phenomenology in Husserl and Heidegger*. Cambridge: Cambridge University Press.
Husserl, Edmund. 1988. *Aufsätze und Vorträge (1922–1937)*. (Husserliana XXVII). Edited by Thomas Nenon and Hans Reiner Sepp. The Hague, Netherlands: Kluwer.
———. 1994. *Briefwechsel*. In collaboration with Elisabeth Schuhmann, edited by Karl Schuhmann. Dordrecht: Kluwer (quoted as BW + volume number).
———. 1997. *Psychological and Transcendental Phenomenology and the Confrontation with Heidegger (1927–1931)*. Translated by Thomas Sheehan and Richard E. Palmer. Dordrecht: Kluwer Academic.
———. 2002. *Zur phänomenologischen Reduktion. Texte aus dem Nachlass (1926–1935)*. Edited by S. Luft. (*Husserliana* XXXIV). Dordrecht: Kluwer.
———. 2014. *Ideas for a Pure Phenomenology and Phenomenological Philosophy: First Book*. Translated by Daniel O. Dahlstrom. Indianapolis: Hackett.
Luft, Sebastian. 2002. *"Phänomenologie der Phänomenologie." Zur Systematik und Methodologie der Phänomenologie in der Auseinandersetzung zwischen Husserl und Fink*. Dordrecht/Boston/London: Springer.

———. 2005. "Husserl's Concept of the 'Transcendental Person': Another Look at the Husserl-Heidegger Relationship." *International Journal of Philosophical Studies* 13, no. 2: 141–77.

Ott, Hugo. 1993. *Martin Heidegger: A Political Life*. Translated by Allan Blunden. London: HarperCollins.

Schuhmann, Karl. 1977. *Husserl-Chronik. Denk- und Lebensweg Edmund Husserls.* Dordrecht: Kluwer.

———. 1978. "Zu Heideggers Spiegel-Gespräch über Husserl." *Zeitschrift für philosophische Forschung* 32, no. 4: 591–612.

Sheehan, Thomas. 1997. "Husserl and Heidegger: The Making and Unmaking of a Relationship." In *Psychological and Transcendental Phenomenology and the Confrontation with Heidegger (1927–1931)*. Translated by Thomas Sheehan and Richard E. Palmer, 1–32. Dordrecht: Kluwer.

Chapter 11

Phenomenology Rediviva

Thomas Sheehan

Steven Crowell's *Normativity and Phenomenology in Husserl and Heidegger* (Cambridge, 2013) is something of a manifesto: a wake-up call and much-needed therapy for phenomenology in general and for Heidegger studies in particular, especially in North America. His earlier coedited collection *Transcendental Heidegger* (Stanford, 2007) already laid the groundwork for a revolution in Heidegger research, one that just might save that field from the self-congratulatory irrelevance toward which much of it seems to be stumbling. This latest book continues Crowell's efforts to draw lines between Husserl and Heidegger, those apparent antipodes, as it probes questions bearing on normativity and the like.

In what follows I focus only on certain Heideggerian aspects of the book, and I do so in the form of a propaedeutic to Crowell's original rewriting of phenomenology as it might be (but mostly is not) practiced by Heideggerians. This is a necessary propaedeutic, I argue, because as Crowell now moves into important issues of normativity, responsibility, ethics, and agency, this book *presupposes* crucial elements of his rewriting of phenomenology, elements that many Heideggerians either overlook or deny or in any case have yet to take on board.

I will thematize only two of those issues, but the two that constitute ground zero of Crowell's robust reinstatement of phenomenological *method* in Heidegger research: the phenomenological reduction and the transcendental reduction. For now I will continue to use the usual term "reduction," but later in this text—following Heidegger himself, and in order to name his unique formulation of the matter—I will substitute the term "*induction*" (*Hinführung*, as in the Greek ἐπαγωγή) for "*reduction*" (*Zurückführung*, as in the Greek ἐπαναγωγή).

1. SUNT LACRIMAE RERUM

Unfortunately, a good deal of contemporary Heidegger scholarship seems to have left phenomenology behind as it cuts its way through the dark thickets of his later texts. Or else it reduces that phenomenology to the quaint simplicity of "letting a thing show itself as it is in itself"—something that is impossible for two reasons. First of all, as regards the "in itself" piece: at least since Plotinus and Augustine, the in-itself-ness of an entity has been understood as the thing's noumenal status before an intellectually intuiting νοῦς,[1] something that Kant placed decisively beyond the scope of human cognition. Secondly, *Sein und Zeit* (SZ) demonstrates that within phenomenology the so-called *inseitas* or in-itself-ness of a thing is that thing's current *promeitas*—relatedness to a human being—within a specific world of interests and concerns. In SZ Heidegger was clear on this:

> The *usefulness* of a thing is the ontological-categorial determination of that thing *as it is "in itself."*
>
> In our *concernful use* of a readily available thing we encounter that thing's specific and self-evident "in-itself-ness."[2]

In other words, in Heidegger's phenomenology the so-called in-itself-ness of a thing is not its οὐσία or substance or "being"—that is, its stand-alone, unchanging essential structure—but rather its current (*jeweilig*) and very changeable significance to the person or persons experientially engaged with that thing within a specific context of concerns and interests. Heidegger investigates entities not in terms of their status as out-there-now-real (Aristotle's ἔξω ὂν καὶ χωριστόν and ἔξω [τῆς διανοίας]),[3] but only in terms of their *Anwesenheit/Bedeutsamkeit*, their current meaningfulness *to* someone within specific contexts of human purpose, desire, need, and so on. The key for entering all phenomenology, Heidegger's included, is the principle of correlation, and it applies equally to his investigations of propositional knowing-that and practical knowing-how. For Heidegger as much as for Husserl, phenomenology is correlation research.[4]

That notwithstanding, some scholars, most notably Professor Richard Capobianco of Stonehill College, Massachusetts, claim that Heidegger refused the phenomenological reduction and focused not on the correlation between things and the acts and structures that constitute them as meaningful, but rather on the independent "being" of things in what amounts to a quasi-realist ontology. (Capobianco goes so far as to suggest Heidegger sought "not to 'overcome' metaphysics as such, but rather to *refashion* it" as some kind of "'process' metaphysics.")[5]

Throughout the history of Western philosophy, being (εἶναι, οὐσία, εἶδος, ἐνέργεια, *esse*, *Sein*, and so on) has always been the proper object of metaphysics. And in fact, Heidegger himself confused matters (and misled three generations of scholars) by adopting the shopworn term *"Sein"* to name the proper object of his own *meta*-metaphysical thinking. He admitted his mistake in the early 1950s when Professor Tomio Tezuka of the Imperial University of Tokyo confronted him with "the confusion created by your [Heidegger's] ambiguous use of the word *Sein*." Heidegger responded, *"Sie haben Recht"*—"You're right." But having made that admission, he tried, without much success, to salvage and justify the use of *Sein* in his own work.

> *Heidegger*: My own thinking has a clear sense of the distinction between *Sein* as the *Sein des Seienden* and *Sein* as *Sein* with regard to its own proper sense, which is openness (the clearing).
> *Tezuka*: Then why didn't you immediately and decisively hand back the word *"Sein"* exclusively to the language of metaphysics? Why didn't you immediately give your own name to what you were seeking as the "meaning of *Sein*" on your path through the essence of time?
> *Heidegger*: How can I give a name to what I'm still searching for? Finding that would depend on assigning to it the word that would name it.
> *Tezuka*: Then we have to endure the confusion that has arisen. (GA12: 104.16–105.3)

And that unnecessary confusion has thrown off the scholarship for more than eight decades. Fortunately, however, Heidegger relented in his later years:

> I no longer like to use the word *Sein*. (GA15: 20.8–9)

> *Sein* remains only the provisional term. (GA7: 234.13)

and even more emphatically:

> *Sein* is no longer the proper object of thought. ("das Sein, das im Geschick beruht, nicht mehr das eigens zu Denkende ist": GA14: 50.2–3)

> There is no longer room even for the word *Sein*. ("ist sogar für den Namen Sein kein Raum mehr": GA15: 365.17–18)

William J. Richardson noted a half-century ago that the word *Sein*

> has almost completely disappeared from [the later Heidegger's] vocabulary. . . . Even in SZ, presumably, Heidegger sensed the inadequacy of the term but could find no other way to designate the process under discussion."[6]

But alas, instead of abandoning that misleading term and (like Heidegger himself) designating his topic as "the appropriated clearing" (*die ereignete Lichtung*, GA71: 211.9), Heideggerians like Capobianco beat on, boats against the current, borne back ceaselessly into the metaphysics that Heidegger abandoned, as they struggle to salvage the word *Sein*/being, either by an idiosyncratic spelling ("beyng" in imitation of Heidegger's *Seyn*) or by writing it under erasure (b̶e̶i̶n̶g̶) or by offering lame distinctions (e.g., being-itself vs. being-*qua*-beingness) that only perpetuate the confusion.

Retaining the word "being" under very strong erasure might just possibly work, but only if Heideggerians first managed to get clear on two facts:

1. that Heidegger radically reinterpreted the word *Sein* in a phenomenological mode as the *Anwesen* or meaningful presence of a thing to and for human beings; and
2. that the phrase *das Sein selbst*, "being itself," is not a phenomenon at all but only a provisional heuristic term that stands in for the sought-for "X" of Heidegger's work.

The phrase "being itself" means little more than "*das Erfragte*, i.e., the thing we're after," which turns out to be *not* being (*Sein*)—and not even being-as-*Anwesen*—but rather that which makes possible such meaningful presence. And Heidegger is clear: what enables or "gives" all forms of the meaningful presence of this or that is ex-sistence (*Dasein*) as the appropriated clearing.

> Welt "gibt" Sein; das Dasein ist das je vereinzelte "es," das gibt; das ermöglicht und ist das "es gibt" (GA73, 1: 642.28–29).
>
> World is what "gives" being. Ex-sistence is the ever individual "it" that gives, that makes possible and is the "it gives."

Getting clear on the *first* fact—*Sein* reinterpreted as *Anwesen*—would require that Heideggerians abandon what Husserl called "philosophical naïveté" and finally embrace the phenomenological reduction. Getting clear on the *second* fact would entail rewriting reams of Heidegger scholarship.

2. INSTAURATIO PHAENOMENOLOGICA

Crowell insists that Heidegger's philosophy begins with a phenomenological reduction. Over the entrance to Plato's Academy was allegedly written: "No one ignorant of geometry may enter." Crowell suggests in effect that over the entrance to Heidegger's Academy should be inscribed: "No phenomenological reduction? Don't even *try* to get in."[7] But a significant number of Heideggerians would object that whereas such a reduction might be necessary in *Husserl's* phenomenology, it certainly is not necessary in Heidegger's, and that for three reasons.

***First objection*:** For Heidegger human ex-sistence is being-in-the-world, living inescapably in this very messy everyday world of people and things.

Unlike Husserl, therefore, SZ allegedly repudiates the phenomenological reduction and remains resolutely and directly embedded in that world of the everyday.

Second objection: Given the first objection, it follows that there can be no epoché of the natural attitude in Heidegger, no bracketing of the workaday worlds of the carpenter, the farmer, the hacker, or, for that matter, the philosopher. In line with this objection, instead of performing such an epoché SZ allegedly spends its time ferreting out the implicit ontology at work *within* the natural attitude: concern with tools and solicitude for people, along with the everyday structures of fallenness, care, temporality, and the like.

Third objection: After his *Kehre* or "turn" in the 1930s, Heidegger allegedly left phenomenology behind for what he called *Seinsdenken*, the thinking of being. In fact it was Heidegger himself who gave William J. Richardson the subtitle of his famous book: "*Durch* Phänomenologie in das Denken des Seins" (Heidegger's emphasis), that is, *through* (and *beyond*) phenomenology and into the thinking of being. Some take that phrase as virtually summarizing the later Heidegger's progress, namely, as a *turn away from* the correlational phenomenology of SZ and a *turn to* the unmediated understanding of being, as such being, in its fundamental independence of ex-sistence, reveals and conceals itself, indeed as it has currently abandoned beings in today's τέχνη-besotted world, but will once again, someday after the dark night of *Gestell*, show itself as it really is.

However: wrong on all three counts.

Regarding the first objection ("no phenomenological reduction"). Crowell cites chapter and verse on how Heidegger insisted on a phenomenological reduction, most pointedly on Thursday, May 4, 1927, in his course Die Grundprobleme der Phänomenologie (GA24: 29.12–15). Of course Heidegger did not mean a Husserlian reduction to "the transcendental life of consciousness, . . . in which objects are constituted as correlates of consciousness." Rather, for Heidegger the phenomenological reduction means

> leading one's phenomenological gaze back from the apprehension of a thing, . . . back to the understanding of the *Sein* of the thing, that is, taking the thing in terms of the way it is disclosed [*auf die Weise seiner Unverborgenheit*].[8]

We note that the word *Sein* in this passage refers to the mode of *Unverborgenheit*, that is, the meaningful disclosure of something to someone within a phenomenological correlation and in an already operative field of intelligibility. Heidegger's phenomenological revolution rewrites the *Sein* of a thing in such a way that it now means the way that thing is disclosively related to someone (*mich-bezogen*, GA58: 105.12–13), the way it happens to be meaningful in the present circumstances. In the natural attitude our intentional awareness focuses on *objects*, whether persons or things, and we overlook two things:

- how those objects appear to and are understood by a person; and
- the prior constituting (*ausmachen, festmachen*, GA9: 244.26–28) of the modes of the thing's appearance and understanding.

In contrast to the naïveté of the natural attitude, in a phenomenological reduction we draw our intentional gaze away from the object as "independently and objectively out there" (whether it be *vorhanden, zuhanden,* or *persönlich*), and lead our gaze back (*re-ducere, zurück-führen*) to the way the object is currently disclosed/understood. Once we have done that, we can begin analyzing *how* and *why* the thing is disclosed in the way it is within a phenomenological correlation. For example: When I'm out camping, why do I currently understand this rock as an ersatz mallet for pounding in tent pegs rather than as a specimen of granite from the Achaean Eon? That may have to do with the specific world of concern (camping in the woods vs. academic petrology) in which I now find myself.

Once Husserl had put "phenomenological eyes in my head," as he said in 1923 (GA63: 5.22–23), Heidegger fought against the naïve objectifying realism of the Aristotelian-Thomistic metaphysics he had been steeped in, which held that "the real" is *id quod habet esse* or *id cui existentia non repugnat* (i.e., that which exists independent of any subjective constitution by human beings). In that traditional view the realness of a thing is its *existentia* or *Vorhandensein*, its mere existing (1) outside of nothing and (2) in the real world. The phenomenological attitude breaks with that naïveté and draws us back reflectively and thematically to where we always already stand without noticing it: within fields of intelligibility. There we relate to things not merely as objects positioned spatio-temporally in the universe, independent of us. Instead, we relate to things in terms of their significance, their meaningful presence to us as personally, socially, linguistically, and bodily *engaged* with them.

From the start of his career Heidegger affirmed, "I live in a first-hand world of meaning; everything around me makes sense, always and everywhere" (GA56/57: 73.1–8: "In einer Umwelt lebend, bedeutet es mir überall und immer"). Heidegger's philosophy, like all phenomenology worthy of the name, is *correlation* research in which "the one who is philosophizing belongs together with the things being treated" (GA9: 42.27–27: "zu den Sachen ... der Philosophierende selbst ... mitgehört"). But part from philosophy, even in our everyday lives, once we wake up to this most obvious fact, "the real" is not simply what's-out-there-now; it is *the meaningful*—not necessarily the "true," but always the meaningful. *Huis clos:* there is no *horstexte*, no exit from meaning. For us who are condemned to λόγος, outside of meaning there is only death.

Regarding the second objection ("no epoché"). The second objection notwithstanding, Heidegger in fact *does* carry out an epoché and puts the brakes on (ἐπέχει) our natural tendency to overlook the constitution of meaning. Usually we look *through* (i.e., neglect) the meaning-giving world we currently inhabit; we focus directly on *things* without noticing what constitutes them *as meaningful*. It is against such neglect and overlooking that the phenomenological epoché militates. As Aron Gurwitsch famously declared, after the phenomenological reduction the only philosophical issues one may properly pursue are the hermeneutical questions of sense, meaning, and signification.[9]

This certainly holds for Heidegger, for whom the so-called being of things is now no longer their εἶναι or οὐσία or *esse* or *Sein*, as in the metaphysical tradition, but their phenomenological παρ-εἶναι, παρ-ουσία, or *An-wesen*, where the prefixes παρά and *An-* point to what the medieval philosophers called the *praesentia intelligibilis* of a thing.[10] In this regard Heidegger was simply channeling Aristotle, who states at *Metaphysics* II 1 993b30–31 (and spells out in IX 10) that a thing's degree of being (εἶναι) is the same as its degree of knowability: ὥσθ' ἕκαστον ὡς ἔχει τοῦ εἶναι, οὕτω καὶ τῆς ἀληθείας. This text in the *Metaphysics* was the source of the scholastic axiom *ens et verum convertuntur*: the realness of a thing is measured by its ability to be intelligibly accessed, as in Thomas Aquinas:

> Eadem est dispositio rerum in esse sicut in veritate (*Summa theologiae* I–II, 3, 7c)
>
> Unumquodque, quantum habet de esse, tantum habet de cognoscibilitate (*Summa contra gentes*, I, 71, 16)

This is an axiom that Heidegger himself accepts: "Die Wahrheit und das Seiende in seiner Seiendheit sind dasselbe" (GA45: 122.4–5)

This is the fundamental, show-stopping fact that is completely missed by the naïve-realist interpretations of Heidegger that Professor Capobianco proposes. In Heidegger "being" is always written under phenomenological erasure. This means that his provisional topic (as contrasted with his *Grundfrage*) was not *Sein* but *Sinn*, not the independent and unchanging "being" of things but their ever-changing significance in relation to one's specific interests and concerns. Heidegger repeatedly and unambiguously equated his own understanding of "being" with phenomenological *Sinn*, that is, with the intelligibility and meaningfulness of things.

- Phenomenology is about "the intelligibility" [*Sinn*] of things (SZ: 35.25).
- Phenomenological ontology is "the explicit inquiry into the intelligibility [*Sinn*] of things" ("das explizite Fragen nach dem Sinn des Seienden," SZ: 12:14–15).
- The *Seinsfrage* is "the inquiry into the intelligibility of things, i.e., the inquiry into being" ("die Frage nach dem Sinn des Seienden, nach dem Sein," GA19: 205.13–14).

Of course, neither Husserl nor Heidegger doubt that things remain "out there," independent of our minds, after the reduction. Heidegger is emphatic: "Questions like 'Does the world exist independent of my thinking?' are meaningless" (GA58: 105.15–16; cf. GA26: 194.30–31)—because after the reduction, what we had originally perceived as out-there-in-nature is not lost but instead is now seen within a phenomenological correlation as the *perceived of a perceiving*. (Heidegger in 1927: "The thing [now] belongs to the perceiving as its perceived.")[11] Yes, after the reduction things are still "out there," but as such they are not the focus of phenomenology. The subject matter of a phenomenological inquiry is things only in terms of our meaningful engagement with them, and to do phenomenology is to study one's *relation* to the objects of intentionality.

Regarding the third objection ("*after the turn*"). This objection notwithstanding, Heidegger in his later years insisted that his work was phenomenological from beginning to end. In 1962 he said that even his writings about *Ereignis* (obscure as they might seem to some), were *echt* phenomenology (GA14: 54.2–3). And in his last published tribute to Edmund Husserl (1969) he said the same about his "history of being": it, too, is unmitigated phenomenology (GA14: 147.15–16). And by "phenomenology" he did not mean the feckless gesture of "letting things show themselves as they are in themselves." He meant the phenomenological reduction and all that it entails.

3. ἐπαγωγή: *INDUCTIO PHAENOMENOLOGICA*

At this point we have to clarify and define what a "phenomenological reduction" means in Heidegger, and here we return to what I mentioned at the beginning of this text. The directional adverb *zurück* in the term *Zurückführung* corresponds to the "re-" in "phenomenological *re*duction," where "re-duction" means "leading the gaze *back*." However, the word "back" can be misleading. Heidegger and Husserl hold very different views of both (1) the phenomenological correlation and (2) *that-back-to-which* one leads the phenomenological gaze. We may illustrate that difference in figure 11.1.

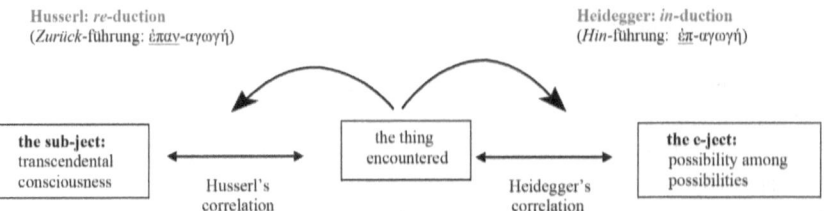

Figure 11.1

As we have said, all phenomenology, including Heidegger's, is correlation-research, and as such it is about meaning, and specifically about the meaningful presence of what one encounters (GA64: 23–25). But both (1) the structure of the correlation and (2) that which constitutes the meaning of things within the correlation turns out to be radically different in Husserl and Heidegger. For Husserl the correlation is between the meaning-constituting *sub-ject* (both psychological and ultimately transcendental) and the meaningfully constituted object. Hence, Husser's phenomenological *re*-duction shifts the gaze "in reverse," in the direction of the constituting sub-ject. In Greek that shift would be called an ἐπαν-αγωγή, a leading *backward*.

For Heidegger, on the other hand, the existential essence of human being is not sub-jectivity but e-jectivity, projected-ahead-ness into meaning. Exsistence is structurally a *geworfener Entwurf*, thrown *forward* as meaningful possibility into specific meaningful possibilities; and thus the phenomenological correlation lies between whatever we encounter and the meaningful possibilities we are living into. And that existential aheadness is precisely what accounts for the constitution of meaning. (GA14: 131.16–17: "Die transzendentale Konstitution is eine zentrale Möglichkeit der Existenz des faktischen Selbst").[12] For Heidegger, getting to the existential correlation is a matter of shifting our phenomenological gaze *forward* (ἐπί) toward the possibilities that we are living *into*, which give meaning to what we encounter. Thus, he radically recasts the *re*-duction as an *in*-duction—*Hinführung*—in Greek an ἐπ-αγωγή (GA62: 131.17–132.7; 191–92; GA22: 250.29; GA9: 244.12–35).

We could call Heidegger's refocusing of the gaze a phenomenological *re*-duction, as he himself did (GA24: 29.15, as above) but only if we remember that leading the gaze "back" means leading it back to *where we already are* without always noticing it, namely, a priori ahead as possibility among possibilities. To bring out that point, in what follows I will use the term Heidegger finally favored: in-duction rather than re-duction.

4. καταγωγή: *SUBDUCTIO PHAENOMENOLOGICA*

Once Heidegger had laid that foundation—phenomenological in-duction as the entrée to all his work—his thinking could go in one of two directions, either (1) to the *subsequent* question of how one's experience of meaningfulness can turn out to be true or false; or (2) to the *prior* question of how things become meaningful in the first place. He did deal with the question of apophantic correctness (e.g., in SZ § 44 and elsewhere), but he mostly followed the latter path back to the prior question regarding how things become meaningful at all.

Regarding the first option, the question of true/false: Heidegger distinguished three "levels" of what the Greeks called ἀλήθεια and what we may translate as "disclosedness," running from the most derivative to the most primary:

- ἀλήθεια-3: the truth of statements, in the sense of correct correspondence, *adaequatio intellectus et rei*
- ἀλήθεια-2: the immediate prior condition of such truth, namely, that the subject matter be already *disclosed as meaningful*, whether correctly meaningful or not
- ἀλήθεια-1: the "clearing," the prerequisite for—and that which makes possible—both of the above

Granted that discursive meaningfulness rather than intellectual intuition is the only form of meaningfulness we have, Heidegger was less interested in ἀλήθεια-3—or even ἀλήθεια-2 (i.e., meaningfulness). Instead, he was more focused on ἀλήθεια-1, that which must necessarily be already operative if the other two forms of ἀλήθεια are to hold at all. This issue rode under the rubric of *die Lichtung* or *das Offene*, the clearing or the "open."

Intimately bound up with this "open" is the question of the a priori *opening up* of the open—*das Lichten der Lichtung* (GA49: 41.25–28; GA4: 56.27; GA12: 127.14–15; GA66: 84.33–34)—or better, the a priori *opened*-ness of the clearing, a state of affairs that Heidegger referred to as *das Er-eignis*, *the* "ap-propri-atedness" of ex-sistence, i.e., the fact that that ex-sistence is always already brought into its *proprium*, its ownmost way of being—indeed "thrown" into it. *Ereignis* is not an "event" in any normal sense of that term; it is not a "happening" that has not yet occurred at t^1 but then takes place at t^2 and may stop at t^3. Indeed, as Heidegger constantly declared, *Ereignis* is not an event at all, not even the so-called event of appropriation (see GA11: 45.19–20; GA12: 247.10; GA14: 25.33–26.2; GA70: 17.19; GA98: 161.8; GA98: 341.25).

Rather, it is the ever-operative *factum*, the fundamental existential fact that ex-sistence, by its very nature, has always already been brought-*ad-proprium*, ap-propri-ated to its proper state as the open clearing that makes discursive meaningfulness possible and necessary. Insofar as this already-opened-ness of the clearing is a priori—that is, ex-sistential-structural—it is not *effected* by anyone's personal-existentiel will-act; rather, it can only be *taken over* in a subsequent ex-sistentiel-personal act of resolve (SZ: 325.37; GA65: 322.6–9). As ex-sistential, *Ereignis*—one's having been appropriated to be the clearing—comes with the territory of being *Da-sein*, having ex-sistence as one's structure. The focal topic of all Heidegger's work—what the heuristic term "being itself" provisionally stands in for—is ex-sistence as appropriated to sustaining the clearing: *die ereignete Lichtung*.

Two questions arise at this point:

1. How does the appropriateness of ex-sistence (and thus ἀλήθεια-1) make discursive meaningfulness (ἀλήθεια-2) possible and necessary?
2. What kind of "reduction" would be the proper procedure for discovering the appropriateness of ex-sistence?

First: How does the appropriateness of ex-sistence make discursive meaningfulness possible and necessary?

In the *philosophia perennis*, being (εἶναι, *esse*) shows up for us not in an intellectual intuition but only in a synthesis.[13] Analogously in Heidegger's phenomenology we experience the meaningfulness of something only in discursive acts of λέγειν, taking-something-as, whether propositionally or practically. That is what Aristotle meant by τὶ κατὰ τινὸς λέγειν/σημαίνειν: saying/signifying something (τί) about something (κατὰ τινός), as when we assert this predicate about that subject.[14] All sense-making is discursive, where *dis-currere* means "to run back and forth"—in this case between things and their possible meanings. For example, "I take Socrates *as* a Theban" (which is not correct but nonetheless is still meaningful) or "I take this rock *as for* hammering in tent pegs" (whether the rock works successfully to that end or not). Such synthetic activities are properly classified as "intentional," and to be able to perform them, I must "reach across the gap" between a thing and its possible meanings or possible uses. As Heidegger puts it, in all discursive activity I must "traverse an open space."[15]

But what makes intentional acts of traversing-of-the-open both possible and necessary? In answering that question, Heidegger follows the medieval axiom *operari sequitur esse*: a thing's activities follow from its nature; or to reverse the direction: natures determine operations.[16] As Heidegger puts it: "Each thing only performs/carries out what it is" ("Jegliches . . . je nur das leistet, was es ist": GA4: 65.26–28). He applies that axiom to his existential analysis of human being. By way of a phenomenological description of various operations—for example, hammering nails (SZ) or uttering declarative sentences (GA21: 135–62)—Heidegger first uncovers patterns that always recur in those activities; he then resolves those recurrent patterns into the essential structures they share in common. Those, formally speaking, are (1) structures in the absence of which the operations in question cease to be those very operations; and (2) structures the denial of which instantiates the very structures that are denied (*retorsio argumenti*).[17]

Whether in practical activities or declarative sentences, Heidegger discovers that the recurrent, essential pattern is aheadness-and-return, "Sich-vorweg-sein als Zurückkommen" (GA21: 147.23–26). In practical activities (whether ποίησις or πρᾶξις) we first "look ahead" and envision the desired outcome (the εἶδος προαιρετόν) and then "return" from there to utilize some means to achieve that end. In making a declarative statement (an ἀπόφανσις), we first have a pre-understanding of the possible predicate and then "return" to the subject matter to synthesize it with that predicate.

Heidegger derives this pattern of aheadness-and-return from Aristotle's notion of κίνησις, in which the *actuality* of a moving thing is its being-*possible-*for/unto-something. For Aristotle the being of a moving thing is its prolepsis of its goal, either its *functioning-unto*-its-completion (ἐν-έργ-εια) or its being *already in* its perfection (ἐν-τελ-έχεια: GA6, 2: 368.33–369.9). By looking ahead to what the thing is moving *toward*—whether by nature (acorn to oak tree) or by choice (this wood, cut and assembled for constructing a bookcase)—I discover what an acorn *is* or what a pile of wood in the carpenter shop *is for*. In these cases the "future" determines the "present," a rule that Heidegger took over in his interpretation of human temporality (SZ: 327.20–328.25).

Heidegger gathers these issues into his key term *Da-sein*, which should never, ever, be translated as being-here or being-there or being t/here. I choose to translate it as "ex-sistence" (hyphenated and misspelled to bring out its etymology). The word is made up of two elements:

1. **-sistence:** In Latin *sistere* is a causative verb, just as ἴστημι is in Greek. It does not mean "I stand" (by my own power, as it were) but "I am *made* to stand"—or with Heidegger, I am "*thrown* into standing."
2. **ex-:** I am thrown into standing (1) "ahead" of myself and (2) "out beyond" the persons and things I encounter. Into what?
    - As "ahead" of myself, I am thrown into myself *as possibility*.
    - As "out beyond," I am thrown into the open field of *possible meanings* that those persons and things can have.

"Ex-sistence" says two things about my structure: *Geworfenheit* and *Entwurf*, thrownness and openness, or taken together: thrown-open-ness. Structurally (i.e., in my ineluctable way-of-being as ex-sistence) I am a priori (structurally-existentially) the gap, the space, the clearing that makes (personal-existentiel) acts of discursive-synthetic meaning both possible and necessary.

For a while the early Heidegger called this existential thrown-openness "transcendence," understood as the ex-sistential-structural aheadness (always already beyond things and into their possible meanings) that makes possible all ex-sistentiel-intentional acts of taking-as. As he put it in 1927, transcendence is the *ratio essendi* of intentionality, and intentionality is the *ratio cognoscendi* of transcendence.[18] That is to say: transcendence as my structural aheadness-and-return (and thus ἀλήθεια-1) is what makes possible ex-sistentiel-personal acts of making sense of something (ἀλήθεια-2), acts in which I "reach ahead" to a possible meaning and "return" to synthesize that meaning (correctly or incorrectly) with the person or the thing I'm encountering. Such is Heidegger's early notion of transcendence, which, as we shall now see, he fills out in his later writings.

Second: What kind of "reduction" would be the proper procedure for discovering the appropriateness of ex-sistence?

For a moment let us allow Heidegger the words "transcendence" and "transcendental" even though he eventually transformed the terms by filling out their structure and meaning to include appropriateness. In a personal communication made to Professor Max Müller after World War II, Heidegger distinguished two meanings of "transcendental," namely, (1) *das Transzendentale*: "the transcendental"; and (2) *das Transzendenzhafte*: the transcendence-related.[19]

1. The adjective "transcendental" (*transzendental*) pertains to acts of passing beyond things to their possible meanings.
2. The adjective "transcendence-related" (*transzendenzhaft*) pertains to the kinetic structure of ex-sistence: the fact that it has always already—structurally and a priori—passed beyond *both* things *and* their possible meanings. "Transcendence-related" names the always-already operative appropriateness of ex-sistence to its existential condition of being-the-clearing (*Lichtung-sein*, GA15: 380.11f.)—and being, a priori, ἀλήθεια-1. That is, *tran-zendenzhaft* names ex-sistence's condition *as the clearing itself.*

As regards the relation of the two: the very structure of our being as *transzendenzhaft* (our *ratio essendi*: always being beyond things and in relation of their possible meanings) makes possible and necessary the structure of our knowing (*ratio cognoscendi*) as *transzendental.*

As we said, Heidegger's phenomenological in-duction leads our intentional focus *away* from the objects of intentionality and *forward* to the correlation between those objects and the possibilities that we are living into, possibilities that let those objects show up as having this or that meaning. And when fully unfolded, this in-duction also thematizes the particular meaning-giving context (the "world of meaning" organized around our aheadness in purposes, desires, etc.) wherein and whereby these specific things get their current significance.

But the further question is: What holds open (*offenhalt*) or sustains (*aussteht*) this meaning-giving context?

We have already seen the answer, namely, the fact that ex-sistence's way-of-being (its "essence") consists in its being a priori appropriated, that is,

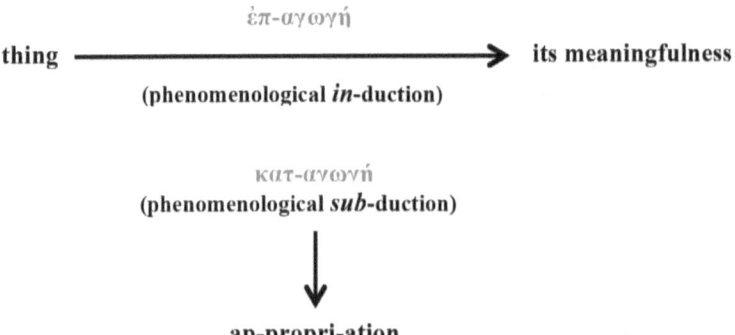

Figure 11.2

stretched-ahead (*erstreckt*) or drawn out (*angezogen, ausgetragen*) as the clearing, as the possibility of intelligibility. To thematically articulate that fact requires the phenomenologist to burrow *beneath* the horizontal-transcendental so as to reveal what makes it possible. In Greek such a leading of one's gaze "under" or "beneath" (κατά) one's transcendental aheadness in order to discover appropriation as what sustains and makes possible such transcendental aheadness would be called a καταγωγή—which in a rather lame and literal translation, we may call a phenomenological *sub*-duction as the complement of a phenomenological *in*-duction (see figure 11.2).

The phenomenological sub-duction is a *further* re-directing of one's philosophical gaze, but this time not away from things and "vertically" onto their possible meanings but rather away from the whole panoply of discursive meaningfulness (including whatever worlds constitute such meaningfulness) and onto ex-sistence's a priori appropriatedness as *das Lichten der Lichtung*, as opening up and holding open the clearing and thus making possible any and all such meaning-giving worlds.

For complete clarity on the matter we must note the distinction between (1) the *structures* of ex-sistence and (2) the subsequent *articulation* of those structures via the procedures of phenomenological method—that is, the distinction between

1. both the transcendental and the transcendence-related, taken together, as *structures* of ex-sistence
    and
2. the phenomenological procedures that *thematize* those structures:
    2.1 phenomenological *in*-duction as thematizing the *transzendental* structure

2.2 phenomenological *sub*-duction as thematizing the *transzendenzhaft* structure.

What the awkward and finally dispensable term καταγωγή ("sub-duction") refers to is Heidegger's radical recasting of the Husserlian transcendental reduction. As noted above, in his letter to Husserl (October 22, 1927) wrapping up his editing of the *Encyclopaedia Britannica* article, Heidegger wrote in opposition to any reduction to the transcendental ego: "Transcendental constitution is a central possibility of the *Existenz* of the factical self."[20] Ex-sistence as thrown ahead, and thus brought-into-its-own as the clearing, undoes any need for the transcendental ego and thus of a reduction thereto. Granted, Heidegger's response to Husserl in 1927 is an early and inchoate reference to appropriatedness as holding open the clearing. Nonetheless, it is the seed from which Heidegger's later articulation of *Ereignis* will spring, and it demarcates the definitive separation of Heideggerian from Husserlian phenomenology.

But one final objection: Didn't Heidegger eventually drop the term "transcendence" along with its partner in crime "transcendental"? Isn't that the gist of the *Kehre*, his famous "turn" in the 1930s? Doesn't the *Kehre* consist in Heidegger's move away from his earlier transcendental thinking to his later *seinsgeschichtlich*-thinking focused on *Es gibt Sein/Es schickt Sein*, the "giving" or "sending" of the clearing? Surely, one might object, the later Heidegger abandoned the notion of transcendence as what opens up and sustains the clearing, and turned instead to *Ereignis* as the *Es, das gibt*, the mysterious meta-existential power (heuristically called "being itself") that gives/sends the clearing and thus all forms of being.

But again: wrong on all counts.

In the first place, *Ereignis* is the later Heidegger's name for *Geworfenheit* as thrown-open-ness. This is borne out by the way he frequently and focally places thrownness and appropriatedness in apposition to each other:

1. Ex-sistence is "thrown, . . . that is to say, appropriated" (*geworfener . . . das heißt er-eignet*," GA65: 239.5).
2. "Ex-sistence is thrown, appropriated" ("*Das Dasein ist geworfen, ereignet*," GA65: 304.8).
3. Ex-sistence's taking over its thrownness ("*die Übernahme der Geworfenheit*" at SZ: 325.37) is equated with ex-sistence's taking over its being appropriated ("*die Über-nahme der Er-eignung*" at GA65: 322.7–8).[21]
4. Existence's readiness for ap-propri-ation is equated with resolutely assuming and becoming the thrownness it already is ("*die . . . Bereitschaft des Daseins für die Er-eignung, das Geworfenwerden*," GA65: 34.8–9).

5. The projectedness of ex-sistence as "thrown" is equated with the same projectedness as "belonging to ap-propri-ation" (*"als geworfen . . . zugehörig der Er-eignung,"* GA65: 252.23–25).
6. Or in a simple hendiadys that expresses one and the same phenomenon: *"Geworfenheit und Ereignis"* (GA9: 377, note d).

In fact, Heidegger scholarship would do well to drop the term *Ereignis* entirely, and to always use *Geworfenheit* in its place, thereby underscoring that *Faktizität* is the archi-existential that unifies the early and the later Heidegger.

In the second place, and in contrast to the widespread but erroneous understanding of the term, the *Kehre* in its *proper* sense is the oscillating sameness (*Gegenschwung*) of *Da-sein* and *Da-sein*, that is, the inseparability of (1) ex-sistence's sustaining of the clearing and (2) the clearing that is sustained (cf. GA65: 29.15 et passim; GA70: 126.18; GA75: 59.15; etc.; also GA26: 270.4–5).

Therefore, the *Kehre* in its proper sense is:

- not a move that Heidegger carried out in the 1930s, beginning with GA65, *Beiträge zur Philosophie* (cf. GA13: 149.29–30);
- not the change in how he thought through his fundamental question, beginning in the 1930s; that was what he called not the *Kehre* but the *Wendung* or *Wandel im Denken* (GA13: 149.21–22);
- not a change in the standpoint of SZ (GA13: 149.23);
- not a change in his fundamental question: "What accounts for the fact that there is significance at all?" (cf. GA9: 201.30–32);
- not a change in his *answer* to that fundamental question: ex-sistence as appropriated to being the Open (cf. GA9: 202.5–9); and therefore it is
- not a matter of "demoting" ex-sistence in relation to the Open (aka "Being Itself").

A further issue follows from the above but would require much more space to spell out in detail: all of the middle and later Heidegger can be folded back onto the earlier work up through December 1930, the point where he discovered the *intrinsic hiddenness* of the clearing (which is usually and wrongly called "the self-concealing of being"). Yes, there were plenty of new *formulations* after 1930—"ap-propri-ation" is one of them; the confused term *"Seinsgeschichte"* and the so-called givings of being are others—as well as some new topics (the nature of art, the analyses of poetry, and so on). But as I have argued elsewhere, these new formulations and topics can be more clearly and convincingly explained in terms of the early work and its less obscure lexicon.[22]

Let me conclude by saying two things about Steve Crowell's rich and clearly argued *Normativity and Phenomenology in Husserl and Heidegger*.

First, the book not only lays out programmatically the possibility of a renewed dialogue between Husserl and Heidegger but goes further and *enacts* that dialogue. And second: If read closely and with an eye to its presuppositions about method, it could liberate Heidegger scholarship from its obfuscating tropes, its fuzzy "methodology," and its slavish parroting of an exhausted Sein-ology. It could free up Heidegger scholarship for re-appropriating crucial but neglected elements of its phenomenological heritage and open the way to what Plato called τὸ πρᾶγμα αὐτό, the elusive "thing itself" that Heidegger spent a lifetime pursuing.[23]

NOTES

1. See, for example, Augustine, *De diversis quaestionibus octaginta tribus*, no. 46, "De ideis," and Thomas Aquinas, *Summa Theologiae* I, 15, 1. Much transformed, this is the case even in Hegel 1830/1969, §577 regarding the citation from Aristotle's *Metaphysics* XII 1072 b 18–30.

2. Respectively: "Zuhandenheit ist die ontologisch-kategoriale Bestimmung von Seiendem, wie es 'an sich' ist" (SZ: 71.37–38; the entire sentence is italicized in the original). "Das eigentümliche und selbstverstandliche 'An-sich' der nächsten 'Dinge' begegnet in dem sie gebrauchenden . . . Besorgen" (SZ: 74.29–31). My emphasis in both texts. See also ibid., 75.23–25; 87.19–23; 106.34–36; 118.3–5; etc.

3. Respectively *Metaphysics* XI 8, 1065a 24 and VI 4, 1028a 2. Cf. GA6, 2: 379.34–380.13.

4. For Husserl, see *Husserliana VI, Die Krisis der europäischen Wissenschaften und die transzendentale Phänomenologie*, ed. Walter Biemel (The Hague: Martinus Nijhoff, 1976), 169n1; ET *The Crisis of European Sciences and Transcendental Phenomenology* (Evanston, IL: Northwestern University Press, 1970), 166n. Perhaps correlation is already intimated by Aristotle: see *De anima* I 1, 402b15 and II 4, 415a20 ἀντικείμενα ("correlative objects").

5. Richard Capobianco, *Engaging Heidegger* (2010) and *Heidegger's Way of Being* (2014), both from Toronto University Press. See his review of Martin Heidegger's *Heraclitus* at *Notre Dame Philosophical Reviews*, April 23, 2019: https://ndpr.nd.edu/news/heraclitus-the-inception-of-occidental-thinking-and-logic-heraclituss-doctrine-of-the-logos/.

6. William J. Richardson, *Heidegger: Through Phenomenology to Thought*, 4th ed. (New York: Fordham University Press, 2003; 1st ed., 1963), 633.16–17; also 633n30.

7. For Plato, see Henri-Domenique Saffrey, "Ἀγεωμέτρητος μηδεὶς εἰσίτω. Une inscription légendaire," *Revue des Études Grecques* 81 (1968): 67–87. Regarding Heidegger, perhaps: ἀφαινομενολόγητος μηδεὶς εἰσίτω.

8. GA24: 29.15–9: "Fur uns bedeutet die phänomenologische Reduktion die Rückfiihrung des phänomenologischen Blickes von der wie immer bestimmten Erfassung des Seienden auf das Verstehen des Seins (Entwerfen auf die Weise seiner

Unverborgenheit) dieses Seienden." Re "understanding" in the translation above, see GA16: 424.21–2: "Verstehen, d.h. Entwerfen." See also GA20: 423.4–5.

9. *Philosophy and Phenomenological Research* 7, no. 4 (1947): 652.8–9.

10. Thomas Aquinas, *Scriptum super sententiis*, I, distinctio 3, quaestio 4, articulum 5, corpus.

11. Heidegger in Edmund Husserl, *Phänomenologische Psychologie: Vorlesungen Sommersemester 1925 (Husserliana* IX), ed. Walter Biemel (The Hague: Nijhoff, 1968), 261.8–9: "Das Ding gehört zur Wahrnehmung als ihr Wahrgenommenes." ET *Psychological and Transcendental Phenomenology, and the Confrontation with Heidegger* (Dordrecht, Boston, London: Kluwer Academic Publishers, 1997), 113.14–15.

12. Originally found in Husserl, *Phänomenologische Psychologie* (see previous note), 601.45–602.1; ET, 138.11–12: Heidegger's letter of October 22, 1927.

13. See *Summa Theologiae*, II–II, 83, 1, obj. 3: "secunda vero [operatio] est compositio et divisio, per quam scilicet apprehenditur aliquid esse vel non esse" (referencing *De anima* III 6, 430a27–28).

14. *De interpretatione* 5, 17a21 and 10, 19b5; *Metaphysics* VIII 3, 1043b30–31.

15. GA15: 380.6: "eine offene Weite zu durchgehen." Cf. GA14: 81.35 and 84.3–4; GA7: 19.12; etc.

16. For example, Thomas Aquinas, *Summa theologiae*, I, 75, 3, corpus, ad finem: "similiter unumquodque habet esse et operationem." Or in the opposite direction, "qualis modus essendi talis modus operandi": a thing's way of *being* determines its way of *acting*.

17. Argument by retorsion, i.e., περιτροπὴ τοῦ λόγου, "turning the argument [of the opponent against him]": Sextus Empiricus, Πυρρωνείων ὑποτυπώσεων/*Outlines of the Pyrrhonians,* II, 128 ad fin.

18. GA24: 91.20–22. On ratio cognoscendi, cf. Thomas Aquinas, "Commentum in tertium sententiarum ['De incarnatione Verbi'] Magistri Petri Lombardi," distinctio 14 ("Si anima Christi habuerit sapientiam parem cum Deo, et si omnia scit quae Deus"), quaestio 1, articulus 1 ("Utrum in Christo sit aliqua scientia creata"), quaestiuncula 5, solutio 4: "Ratio autem cognoscendi est forma rei inquantum est cognita, quia per eam fit cognitio in actu; unde sicut ex materia et forma est unum esse; ita *ratio cognoscendi* et res cognita sunt unum cognitum: et propter hoc utriusque, inquantum huiusmodi, est una cognitio secundum habitum et secundum actum," in Thomas Aquinas, *Opera omnia*, ed. Stanilaus Fretté and Paul Maré (Paris: Louis Vivès, 1873), IX, 215, column a, ad fin.

19. Max Müller, *Existenzphilosophie im geistigen Leben der Gegenwart.* Heidelberg: Kerle 1949, 73f.

20. See note 12 above.

21. Cf. GA94: 337.7–8: resolve as "ein Zurückwachsen in das Tragende der Geworfenheit."

22. *Making Sense of Heidegger: A Paradigm Shift* (London and New York: Rowman and Littlefield International, 2015).

23. Plato, "Seventh Letter" (ἐπιστολή Z), 341c7; *Protagoras*, 330d15.

Chapter 12

Heidegger's Philosophy of Science

Ingo Farin and Jeff Malpas

> Die Besinnung auf die Wissenschaft ist "wissenschaftlich" nicht möglich, sondern nur auf Grund und auf dem Weg eines anderen Wissens, das man seit alters her das philosophische nennt.[1]
>
> (Heidegger GA76: 166)

I

That Heidegger never "developed a systematic philosophy of science"[2] was, as Trish Glazebrook (2016) has pointed out, a common and long-held view. In the last decades, however, more and more Heidegger scholars, Glazebrook (2000) included,[3] have drawn attention to the centrality of science in Heidegger's philosophy.[4] Some Heidegger scholars even contend "that Heidegger not only made significant contributions to the philosophical understanding of science, but that philosophy of science was at the centre of his project and its development throughout his career" (Rouse 2005: 1).[5]

The real question today is, therefore, not *whether* Heidegger developed a philosophy of science, but rather, *what form* does his philosophy of science take. Heidegger's thinking of science cannot be set apart from his thinking of philosophy, so much so that one cannot understand Heidegger's conception of philosophy without a proper grasp of his thought on science, and neither can we understand his conception of science without a proper grasp of his thought on philosophy. The two tasks are, in fact, one and the same. On this basis, we must attribute to Heidegger a genuine philosophy of science, not as an "application" or particular "branch" or "region" of his philosophy, but as an integral part within the whole of his philosophical thinking.

In explicating Heidegger's thought on science from his philosophy and vice versa, we can also block what Foucault called the "blackmail" of the Enlightenment, that is, the presumption that one must answer whether one is "for" or "against" the "Enlightenment," or, in our case, science (2000: 312). In fact, reading Heidegger's philosophy of science exclusively with an eye on which of his texts "endorse" or "contradict" currently held views in science or philosophy of science misses Heidegger's philosophy of science altogether, as does the all-too-simplistic division into Heidegger's supposedly "constructive" and "deconstructive" accounts of science.[6]

No one who writes on philosophy and science today can ignore the way in which the "prestige and the enormous success of science" appears to have put in question "the raison d'être of philosophy," making it look like "a relic from the past," perhaps best to be abandoned and given up as a "vast mistake" (Putnam 2012: 40). On this way of thinking, truth is seen as exclusively residing in the sciences, and philosophy, along with the rest of the humanities, readily appears as an irrelevant and even pointless pursuit. Part of the significance of Heidegger's approach is that it directly contends with this view, showing how it ignores the intrinsic bounds or limits of science and of scientific truth. Those bounds are precisely what are brought to light through genuine philosophical thinking.

II

Throughout his career, Heidegger insists that philosophical thinking proper is *sui generis*, neither reducible nor comparable to other human endeavors. Philosophy is not a particular species of (scientific or positive) knowledge or a kind of worldview, let alone a peculiar religious outlook, or reducible to the expression of a creative mind (GA34: 115–16). Philosophy is original, something standing on its own and something ultimate (GA29/30: 3). As a consequence, philosophy must find its determination and explication only in and through itself, only in and through its own occurrence, on each occasion of its occurrence—it must determine and explicate itself from the place that belongs to it and only thus (GA27: 15). "There is no true philosophy," says Heidegger, "that could determine itself from anywhere than itself" (GA6.1: 4).

This means that "only in philosophizing is philosophy understood" (GA27: 380), and so both the task of philosophy and the criteria germane to that task, which are in a constant process of evaluation and reevaluation from within philosophy, cannot be adduced or assessed from outside—whether from the perspective of common sense, science, religion, politics, art, or whatever. When Heidegger claims, seemingly tautologically, that "philosophy is philosophizing" (GA29/30: 6) or that "philosophy philosophizes" (GA27: 380), he is staking out the strict autonomy, independence, and unsurpassable originality of philosophy.[7] This autonomy does not, however, entail any apartness or irrelevance: "Philosophy is something primordial that stands on its own, yet for this very reason it is not something isolated. Rather, as something that is ultimate and primary, it is already comprehensive of everything, so that any application of it comes too late and is a misunderstanding" (GA29/30: 35).

Heidegger often claims that "to be human already means to philosophize" (GA27: 3). But this does not mean that any and every thought had by a human being qualifies as philosophy. Heidegger's point is that philosophy is not a body of fixed beliefs or a predetermined set of questions—instead it is something that "happens" in human beings and is specific to them. It is what defines them *as* human,[8] inasmuch as it is through philosophizing that humans articulate, in "theoretical" language, what it means for them *to be-there* (to articulate their own Dasein) in the midst of all beings as a whole or the world at large. Heidegger holds that everyone has an implicit grasp of this through what he dubs the understanding of Being, *Seinsverständnis*, because everything that is, including human beings and the world they inhabit, is in Being—*alles Seiende ist im Sein*.[9]

The task of philosophy is to respond to what there is, namely, Dasein in conjunction with the world, and to explicate and clarify this self- and world-understanding—which is to say, to explicate and clarify the understanding of Being as such. Yet for all the emphasis on the question of Being, one must not mistake it for a semantic or abstruse speculation about the word "is," or lose sight of (1) Dasein and (2) the world or beings at large as the two basic poles that stand in question in philosophy. Heidegger addresses both Dasein and the world as necessary conditions for there to be anything in the first place, that is, his investigation is essentially transcendental and ontological (and also *topological*, as we say below), not psychological or cosmological. Nevertheless, in clarifying the structures of Dasein and world, philosophy helps to shape the identity and self-understanding of the human being within the totality of beings—and so, to adumbrate a key point in our analysis below—in its proper *place* within that totality. Indeed, philosophy would have no traction unless it could tap into the motivation to get clear about one's own self and the world at large (which is the ultimate horizon for human beings). This *human* interest is definitive of Heidegger's concept of philosophy.

In an early lecture from 1920, Heidegger argued that "the self" was the "*Urwirklichkeit*" [fundamental reality] as such, and that "all reality" [*alle Wirklichkeit*] received its "original sense" by way of the "care of the self" [*Bekümmerung des Selbst*] (GA59: 173). Even though the phrase "care of the self" is restricted only to Heidegger's early thinking, the focus on the self that is indicated by his use of that phrase remains a key element in *Being and Time*—something evident in the way the methodological strategy of the 1927 work centers on the "analytic of Dasein." The way the self remains at issue here reflects the inseparability of the questioning subject, and its concern for its own there-being, from what it questions, namely what it means for something to be within the world—within "the totality of all beings" (SZ: 87) (and the totality that is the world, within which beings are encountered, is the same world within which Dasein finds itself).

On this basis, philosophy itself appears as a form of self-clarification undertaken by that to which it is also directed, namely, the inquiring human subject. And while Heidegger is critical of the way in which the subject is taken up, for instance, in the idea of the Cartesian *cogito*, this criticism cannot be taken to imply a wholesale rejection of the focus on the question of human being as such. That criticism is instead directed at certain specific understandings of the human that is at work there—in the case of Cartesianism, against the idea of the human being as a disembodied entity apart from the world. Heidegger is committed to providing an alternative account of the human subject that takes human being to be inseparably bound to the world—that takes the being-in-the-world as the essence of human being.

Moreover, the nature of "being-in" at issue here (though this is not fully explicit in *Being and Time* itself) is precisely a *being-placed*—something that should already be evident from the thematization of the human in terms of *Da-sein*. It is thus that the analytic of Dasein can be seen, retrospectively, as a *topology*—a topology of human being that looks toward a topology of being. Inasmuch as it does indeed involve a topology of the human, so it also implicates what we might think of as a topology of the subject—but this is not a topology of the subject taken on its own or apart from the world (which is partly what it means for it to be a *topology*). Instead, Dasein is itself essentially determined by its being-placed in the world, which is to say that Dasein is itself dependent upon beings at large.

If we are to understand Dasein, Heidegger argues, then we must understand Dasein's relation to the world—its relation to beings as a whole (*das Seiende im Ganzen*). Dasein only exists to the extent that it is in the world—to exist is to be "in" the world. What is crucial here is the fundamental interdependence of Dasein and world, which can also be understood as the hermeneutical entailment of one in the other.[10] According to Heidegger, one must not posit the world here and Dasein there, as if they were two separate entities. Rather, Dasein is placed "within" the world, and in being-in-the-world it becomes itself and the world is lit up for it: "To selfhood belongs world; the world is essentially related to Dasein" (GA9: 157). There is no world, then, that is independent of Dasein, just as Dasein is not independent of the world—and this is so without entailing any form of subjectivization or idealization of the world.

The world is not made by Dasein; rather, both emerge together as part of a single complex structure. Yet this structure is not an immediately evident one—it does not simply present itself as an object of description or scientific investigation. Instead it must be retrieved from the concealment that follows from its fundamental, encompassing, and conditional character. Engrossed in its daily affairs and attending to the needs of the day, Dasein can "overlook" and thus miss its own self and the world that it inhabits. Philosophical insight is thus required to articulate and lift into consciousness the structure and intrinsic relatedness of Dasein, world, and Being. In the absence of such philosophical elucidation, there is the distinct possibility that what will occur is both loss of self (*Selbstverlorenheit*) (GA38: 51–70) and a loss of world,[11] issuing in what Heidegger calls homelessness, *Heimatlosigkeit*.[12] Given the tendency of the structure at issue here to its own concealment, such homelessness is an inevitable tendency of Dasein, of the human, and of the self. Philosophy is the antidote to this. It articulates the concealed sense of being a self "in" a world; it thus prepares the possibility of becoming at home with oneself and the world. In this way, the "care of the self" goes hand in hand with the "care" of all beings at large" (GA6.1: 427).

In arguing that Dasein is "in" the world, inhabiting and sojourning at a place (SZ: 73), and together with this, insisting on "being-in" as an irreducible ontological structure,[13] Heidegger commits himself to a fundamentally topological mode of thinking. It is a mode of thinking in which Dasein and world are drawn together in an essential interdependence, and that also gives full recognition to the spatial character of Dasein's being (see SZ: 76, 149).[14] If in traditional philosophy space is often taken as an a priori, then this is so because of the a priori topological structure, including the structure of spatiality, in which Dasein and the world are interrelated. Thus, Heidegger explicitly holds that "neither is space in the subject, nor is the world in space.... Rather, space is 'in' the world, inasmuch as what is constitutive for Dasein, being-in-the-world, has opened up space" (SZ: 149).

The account of Dasein's spatiality in *Being and Time* remains, however, incomplete, and it is only later that Heidegger provides a fuller explication of the essential spatiality of existence or the proper topology in which it is embedded. Thus, in the Nietzsche lectures, for instance, Heidegger argues that since Dasein is amid the entire ensemble of beings, it is necessarily "a local being" [*standörtlich Seiendes*], placed within its "locale" [*Ort*], from which finite place the whole of beings is apprehended, intended, or indeed, felt—although the whole is always and only given from such a local or particular perspective or "standpoint" (GA6.1: 340). Heidegger makes clear, in a more pronounced fashion than in *Being and Time*, that the very essence of the human being is to be placed—to be "there"—it is thus that the essence of the human is Da-sein: "The being of human being—and as far as we know, of human being *alone*—is grounded in Dasein; the there [*das Da*] is the sole possible locale [*Ort*] for the necessary location [*Standort*] of its being at any given time" (ibid.).

III

Having sketched the basic outline of Heidegger's thinking of philosophy, what of his thinking of science—how does it appear against this background? Central to his conception of science is the insistence that science cannot be understood as a totality of context free, timelessly true propositions. The reason behind this insistence is simple: like all human activities and endeavors, science is embedded in the world—it is something undertaken by Dasein in a space and a time; it emerges always in and at a place.

In *Being and Time* Heidegger writes:

> Science in general can be defined as the whole of a justificatory nexus of true propositions.[15] This definition is neither complete, nor does it get at the meaning of science. As ways in which human beings behave, the sciences have this being's (the human being's) kind of being. We define this being terminologically as *Dasein*. Scientific research is neither the sole nor the most immediate kind of being of this being that is possible. (SZ: 15)

This brief paragraph defines Heidegger's basic position throughout his career. Whatever the self-interpretation put forward by scientists and other philosophers of science, Heidegger grounds scientific theorizing in Dasein and the world (i.e., in the structure of being-in-the world) in the very place in which Dasein exists in the world amid beings at large. To the extent that scientific theorizing also manifests Dasein's own way of being, science and scientific projects have their own finitude (are capable of "death" as Haugeland [2000] puts it). Moreover, scientific theory or scientific research has an "authentic" or "inauthentic" mode, depending on whether it is mindful of its origin, its facticity, its inherently projective nature, and its proper bounds. Undeniably—and unsurprisingly—Heidegger pursues his interpretation of science and scientific research from an overarching *philosophical* perspective. Nonetheless, this does not involve simply passing judgment on science from on high. Rather, Heidegger attempts to understand the phenomenon of science from the ground up and doing so requires that he engage the sciences on their own terms as well.

The ontological genesis of the theoretical attitude underlying scientific work is a key element of Heidegger's analysis in *Being and Time*. Leaving to one side the "logical" construction of scientific theory, Heidegger focuses on the "existential concept of science," which thematizes science from the perspective of the theorizing human being, and according to which scientific theorizing is a specific "mode of being-in-the-world" (SZ: 472).

Heidegger claims that originally "circumspection" [*Umsicht*] within the environing world discloses what there is. Such circumspection, being prior to all theory and science, operates in the context of our ordinary, everyday engagements, concerns, and errands, all of which are embedded in the meaningful structures of references and assignments that constitute the world in which we always already exist (ibid.: 474). Circumspection has its own mode of reflection and corroboration, "deliberation" [*Überlegung*], which sheds light on details, hidden aspects, and deficiencies in what is "ready to hand" [*Zuhandenes*] (ibid: 475). *Deliberation* includes temporality, memory and anticipation, the "if-then" schema, causal inferences, and so on (ibid.: 475–76).[16] All of this is part of finding one's way around in the environing world. As such, it does not qualitatively change or transform Dasein's immersion in the world; rather, it entrenches Dasein even deeper in its environing world.

The circumspective disclosure of entities within the world is the necessary precondition on which all theorizing is based. The theoretical attitude thus takes whatever has been previously grasped by circumspection and deliberation and thematizes it within a new theoretical framework. This theoretical thematization abstracts from the characteristics usually ascribed to the thing in question, setting aside the significations that belong to the thing in its usual context of meaningfulness as ready-to-hand [*zuhanden*], and, instead, treating the thing as a merely present entity independent of its usual environing structure of signification, and so as present-at-hand [*vorhanden*]. To use Heidegger's own example, one may abstract from the circumspective considerations that pertain to the hammer as a ready-to-hand tool—its being too heavy or too light for the job to be done—in order to focus instead on the properties attributable to it—its weight or mass—as a mere physical object present-at-hand. Taken in this way as a mere object, the hammer can then be compared, in just this respect, with other objects—in terms, for instance, of some theorization of comparative weights or masses (and where the shift from weight to mass occurs there is also a further degree of abstraction)—all of which lies entirely outside the space of meaning in which the hammer was originally disclosed in circumspection.

This "shift" or "changeover" [*Umschlag*] from the original disclosure of something ready-to-hand to its theoretical thematization as something present-at-hand constitutes nothing less than a changeover in the ontological understanding or *Seinsverständnis* of the thing in question. While the ready-to-hand hammer has its customary location or "place" (*Platz*) in the workshop and is embedded in an entire work-world and work-processes, the merely present-at-hand physical object of such-and-such a weight or mass has no such world context anymore (SZ: 478). To this extent, the hammer loses its meaning as a tool within the world disclosed in circumspection. At the same time, Heidegger emphasizes that the hammer is now recontextualized and inserted into the context of a theoretical subject matter delineated by the research objectives of the science in which it has become thematic, say physics. It now functions as a mere example of an "entity with 'mass'" (ibid: 477). But it can do this only within this new theoretical framework upon which it is projected.

Once some general theory is in place, one can then gather "facts" about the theorized object, but there are "no bare facts" as such, outside the projection of a theory that provides the ontological matrix for objects present at hand to be observed (ibid: 479). Heidegger illustrates this with an illuminating reference to the genesis of mathematical physics:

> What is decisive for this development [of mathematical physics] lies neither in in its higher evaluation of the observation of "facts," nor in the "application" of mathematics in determining events of nature, but the *mathematical projection of nature itself*. This project discovers in advance something constantly objectively present (matter) and opens the horizon for the guiding perspective on its quantitatively definable constitutive moments (motion, force, location, and time). Only "in the light of" a nature thus projected can something like a "fact" be found and be taken as a point of departure for an experiment defined and regulated in terms of this project. (ibid.)

There is a surprisingly strong Kantian inflection here, underscored by Heidegger's emphatic insistence on the a priori character of the theoretically projected design of nature (which orients and binds the researcher ahead of the actually undertaken research [ibid.]). At the same time, it is evident that Heidegger also holds to a hermeneutical, and so interpretive construction of the projective character of scientific theory. These Kantian and hermeneutic elements indicate that if Heidegger is following phenomenology here, it is in a somewhat unorthodox form.

On the surface, Heidegger's understanding of the projective nature of science shows a certain family resemblance to the ways of thinking instantiated in Thomas Kuhn's *scientific paradigms* or Michel Foucault's *episteme*. Yet comparisons of this sort hide as much as they reveal. For instance, it would be wrong to read Heidegger as a precursor to neo-structuralism or an advocate of "irrational" worldviews dictating the change of scientific paradigms. Yet equally, Heidegger does not claim that science occupies some privileged ontological status—as he writes: "the existence of man is neither primarily nor solely determined by science" (GA27: 159). The theoretical turn toward a scientific interpretation of the world is not an inevitability, either ontologically or historically, and neither does it constitute some sort of bulwark against "barbarism," as some advocates like to believe (see ibid.: 161). Heidegger is not "for" or "against" science. Rather, he develops an account of science as a real possibility of Dasein, within the proper "bounds and limits" of science (*Grenzen and Schranken*) (ibid.: 157), which are often ignored in the philosophy of science, because they start from the "fact of science," instead of the condition of science in the prior circumventive disclosure of the world.

IV

Heidegger never ascribes truth, in an unqualified sense, to the findings of scientific theory. There are two distinct but interrelated lines of argument relevant here. One proceeds on a strictly philosophical plane; the other takes its departure from a critique of a crucial methodological presupposition in the sciences (as well as much of traditional philosophy and philosophy of science)—i.e., that truth ultimately rests in the proposition. To begin with the first, we must recall that Heidegger holds that science does not stand on its own but is parasitic on the prior disclosure of the world through circumspection within the environing world. So long as this pre-condition is not reflexively taken up into the concept of science and incorporated into the theory itself, science remains blind to its own origin—the being-in-the world structure of Dasein and world.

There are two points that Heidegger seems to have in mind here. First, the sciences are unable to "explain" or even make sense of their very own existence through the theoretical framework set up to "explain" whatever their designated subject matter is. For example, a physicist has no way to "explain" her "doing" science by relying on her physical theory about mass, energy, etc. (ibid.: 38).[17] Semantic facts, theories, and reference are not physical facts, but indispensable for physical theory.[18] Furthermore, as a theoretical "I," the scientist must abstract from his or her historical and situated "I," such that "doing" science is actually predicated on forgetting oneself as a historical person within the historical world.[19] Given that science cannot exist unless humans produce it, science runs up against a limit or bound, since it presupposes that which it cannot thematize. The elucidation of that limit, and so of that on which science depends, falls to philosophy (GA27: 157)—and so, whether or not science knows it, philosophy must be presupposed by science.

Second, in line with modern epistemological conceptions, Heidegger holds that "science is positive knowledge" (ibid.: 219) directed at a specific subject matter that is defined in relation to a specific scientific orientation. This means that any positive science is limited or bounded by what also constitutes and defines it—and indeed, any specific science is made possible only on the basis of this defining limitation. But this means that both in the specific case and in the case of science in general, the constituting limits or bounds of scientific inquiry cannot themselves be made the object of such inquiry—science must be blind to its own conditions (conditions that include the encompassing world at large). The narrowing of focus that is essential to science, and that allows scientific knowledge to develop through the concentrated focus on things under certain delimited projections, cannot be remedied by turning to some "global science" of all things. As Heidegger points out, "a science of all beings at large is essentially impossible" (ibid.: 219)—its impossibility lying precisely in the way in which such a turn would require the abandonment of the very projection of the delimitation and thematization of things on which science depends.

That which is the limit or bound of science cannot be made an object for science. Yet inasmuch as science is limited or bounded (and necessarily so), so the inquiry into the limits or bounds of science requires a form of inquiry that is other than that of science itself. And so, once again, we come back to philosophy. In understanding the limits or bounds of science we are indeed directed toward philosophy as "the other" of science (ibid.: 157). Seen from another perspective, we can say that the limit or bound of science is to be found in Dasein, in the world, in beings at large. And as it is these that are, by contrast, the proper objects of philosophy, then philosophy already thinks the limit and bound of science in its thinking of self, of world, and of beings at large. It is thus that Heidegger can write the provocative sentence: "Science does not think," and still claim that such an assessment is not "pejorative," but an "essential characterization" of science (GA8: 9). Here, to "think" (though Heidegger does not make it explicit) is to attend to limit or bound—we might say it is also to attend to place—and this is just what science does not and cannot do. Inasmuch as science is necessarily limited in this regard, then no matter its claims to universal truth, those claims can never be made good—scientific truth is "positive," at best partial and incomplete, always dependent upon the prior circumspective disclosure of the world.

V

Heidegger draws attention to the general problem that science has in attending to or addressing its own limits or bounds. But he also focuses on a more specific limit or bound—one that operates in relation to a commonplace assumption at work in both science and the philosophy of science, namely, the idea that scientific truth is primarily based in the proposition, or, as Heidegger himself puts it, that "the 'place' of truth is the proposition" (SZ: 284). Heidegger rejects the foundational role that is given to the proposition here.

Propositional truth, he argues, always depends upon a prior, direct, unmediated, and non-representational encounter or acquaintance with the object that the proposition is about. And inasmuch as this prior encounter or acquaintance is required by propositional truth, so it also marks the limit or bound of that idea. To see exactly how this is so, it is necessary to consider Heidegger's argument in more detail.

Heidegger differentiates between two propositional relations that are relevant here: the "predicative relation," in which a predicate is said of a subject (the proposition as such); and the "veritative relation," in which the propositional content (the predication) is attributed to the object in question (GA27: 52/53).[20] To use Heidegger's own example, the predication "This piece of chalk is white" is attributed to an object (i.e., the piece of chalk that is already discovered and encountered in the world)—for instance, by students who happen to find themselves vis-à-vis the piece of chalk in the lecture theater when they follow a teacher who uses the chalk to write on the blackboard. As such, the students are in direct contact with this piece of chalk in the lecture theater, and do not relate to it merely by way of a representation or idea in their heads that is then matched up with what is in the lecture theater. The piece of chalk is there in its being-discovered as one of the objects in the place that the students and teacher share; the piece of chalk is discovered as the same piece of chalk, albeit encountered from different standpoints, by the multiplicity of persons, students and teacher, collected together at the site that is the lecture theater. For Heidegger, truth resides in this *direct relation* to the "real thing," as the thing is discovered by human beings engaged in a situation, at a particular space and time, that is to say, as disclosed from a certain place (SZ: 289). Truth is grounded in the topological structure of being-in-the world—in the always already open region in which things are discovered as being thus and so (as being attractive, repellent, ready-to-hand, or neutral, etc.).

Of course, whatever has been discovered in this way can be expressed and articulated in a sentence or proposition, but the proposition is neither the primary nor the sole access to what is real or true. Least of all, is it the original "place" of truth. Indeed, cut off from the original site of truth, the proposition is reified as a mere "present-at-hand" entity, that somehow "corresponds" to another "present-at-hand" thing, without anyone being able to explain how a proposition could ever "correspond" to what is not one (ibid.: 297). Put differently, Heidegger's criticism of the conception of truth at issue here—truth as a matter of correspondence—amounts to the claim that the veritative relation of the proposition to the object is, on this conception, either entirely ignored or else is subordinated to the predicative synthesis. To ignore the veritative relation, however, is to construe the proposition as a strangely self-contained (and presumably "mental") entity apart from anything that it might be supposed to be "about"; to subordinate the veritative relation to the predicative synthesis would be to make the discovery of that which the proposition is supposedly about dependent upon the synthesis within the proposition—to make what is discovered secondary to what is predicated—and this, surely, is to reverse the proper order of things.

The idea that truth has its primary place in the proposition brings with it the idea of the proposition as the verbal expression of a representation or belief. Such representations are taken to be *internal* to the mind, and so as *private* and inaccessible to others, and yet as also the means by which the mind relates to the world that is *external* to it.[21] It is this view that Richard Rorty (1979) famously attacks, partly under Heidegger's influence (as well as that of Dewey), in *Philosophy and the Mirror of Nature*. Against such a view, Heidegger holds that the original access to things in the world is *directly* discovered, not *mediated* by so-called representations or ideas lodged in the private recesses of one's mind (SZ: 288–99). In contrast to the picture of such an internal/external divide, Heidegger asserts that Dasein is "always already 'outside' together with some being encountered in the world" (ibid.: 83), the original discovery of which, like the piece of chalk in the lecture theater, is what it means for something to be true. Truth in this sense is not private, but public, common, and not monological, or in Heidegger's words, truth is "in its essence something shared," and "not" like a "property" privately owned (GA27: 120). In the end, truth itself comes to be understood not propositionally, but topologically—as the original disclosedness of things. Truth is the prior opening that allows the worldly encounter that encompasses self and thing. It is thus that properly to understand the place of truth is to understand the primordial character of truth (truth as ἀλήθεια) as itself a mode of place, as "the openness" [*die Offenheit*] in which things show themselves to Dasein (GA9: 184). Because this sense of truth—this "openness"—is required by the sense of truth at work in propositional truth, but is apart from it, so it does indeed represent the limit or bound of propositional truth. And inasmuch as science remains always and only at the level of propositional truth, so truth as this "openness" remains outside of the purview of science even though it is required by it.[22]

VI

As we have seen, Heidegger provides a philosophical, onto-topological explication of the phenomenon of science and its intrinsic and ineluctable limits. However, observing the ongoing reality of scientific research in big research institutes and the university at his time, Heidegger also takes issue with what he considers the inauthentic and distorted mode of science. This kind of philosophical commentary consistently runs throughout Heidegger's entire oeuvre. As such, the critique is not "against" science but directed at "rehabilitating" the originality of science in the face of various dangers, such as its routinization and/or absorption into "business" (GA58: 20). Thus, in 1928–1929, when Heidegger diagnoses a "crisis of science" (GA27: 27), he insists that his intervention is meant to enable science to become fully and authentically "existent" in alignment with its "essence" (ibid.: 39) and to regain its "original stance" in society and the world at large (ibid.: 32). Heidegger's analysis of the "crisis" at issue in the 1928–1929 lecture is itself illuminating. He identifies three forms that this crisis takes.

First is a "crisis of the inner architectonic" or "crisis of the basic foundations" in several sciences (physics, biology, mathematics, theology, etc.) (ibid.: 35). Heidegger interprets this as a symptom of a deeper lack of clarity concerning the "essential nature" of science, in particular the inability of science reflexively to integrate the thought about its necessary topological conditions, as discussed above (ibid.: 37). Heidegger notes that the much-needed discussion about the essence of science, which would have to be informed by philosophy *and* science, has not come to pass (ibid.: 39). The reason is philosophy's failure to engage science on the one hand and the disinterest of science on the other, and the result is the perpetuation of science as essentially unquestioned (ibid.: 38).

Second, Heidegger diagnoses a crisis in regard to the very "position" or "stand" [*Stellung*] of science within "the whole of the historical-social existence" of man, or, more narrowly conceived, of one's own society (ibid.: 30–31). The point here is twofold: Heidegger observes that while the traditional connection linking science to the old ideals of (a humanist) education is irretrievably broken, there is no alternative conception forthcoming concerning how the "results of science" and, more broadly speaking, a "scientific culture" can issue into "a genuine culture for communities" (ibid.: 31). That is to say, freed from its submission to the old cultural ideals, science, on its own, is not able to project anything like a new cohesive blueprint for society at large, precisely because it has withdrawn from the truth of place that humans share in society. Left to its own devices, science contracts to a minimalist and purely instrumentalist position according to which, in its own self-understanding as well as in that of society at large, its social significance lies in its utility—in the "results" it yields. As such, science cannot inform or shape the broader cultural space. As Heidegger points out, the "results" of science are mere exterior products, divorced from the real work and ingenuity of scientific thinking; they are a rather superficial ersatz for a serious and central position of science within society at large. Despite its great visibility, then, science is not "valued" in itself, but only in terms of its subsequent "effects," which in turn tends to valorize applied science over basic scientific research (ibid.: 32–34).

Third, for Heidegger, the crisis of science is manifest in "the individual's relation to science" too (ibid.: 27). Recalling the post–World War I unrest among the academic youth, disaffected by the highly specialized, bureaucratized, and rigid ways of science and science teaching at the university, Heidegger reads this disaffection, and the immediate conditions to which it reacted, as indicative of a basic failure to project "the primary, original and essential content of science in a way that directly speaks to the existing individual" (ibid.: 28). Heidegger argues that this deficit, which he also notes as having persisted, cannot be "solved" by resorting to some romantic vision of "a revolution of science" aimed at liquidating "the academic science of old" (ibid.: 27). Instead, Heidegger argues for the need "to reform science from within" by articulating the very human dimension of science as an activity undertaken within the world and whose human and worldly dimension is essential to it. When this dimension is ignored and is not incorporated into the self-understanding that governs scientific practice, then the relation of the scientist to science is rendered both obscure and also problematic. As we would say today, science becomes just another job, measured and valued against the economic gain to be had from it—an outcome that is yet another manifestation of the general reduction of all things to mere utility, or of the near universal monetization of human existence that is now so commonplace.

Heidegger's much discussed but little understood address on "The Self-assertion of the German University" (GA16: 107–17) must be read as Heidegger's attempt to find a way out of the crisis of science. Yet whereas the earlier Heidegger had argued for a genuine dialogue between science and philosophy, in which both would be acknowledged in their distinctive natures and tasks, in the Rectoral Address Heidegger simply subordinates science to philosophy.[23] At the same time, he lays down, as if by personal fiat, an account of the concrete forms by which the limits of science are determined—the character of its embeddedness in the shared place, the πόλις, and the personal commitment to science as a form of life. But obviously philosophy cannot dictate the exact forms of such concretization—instead it must be achieved in a dialogue in which scientists, philosophers, and the public at large come together. What gives rise to the problem here is not, however, any topological commitment on Heidegger's part (since what is at issue is precisely not topology but its concretization); instead, it is the extremity of his commitment to the primacy of philosophy that leads to an over-exaggerated view of philosophy's capacity to dictate the very form in which science can and should be realized.[24]

VII

Following his departure from the Rectorate, Heidegger abandons the idea to impose his philosophical vison onto science. He continues, however, to reflect on the crisis of science, focusing, in the *Contributions to Philosophy* especially, on the "contemporary" shape of science (GA65: 144). In fact, Heidegger realizes that, given the splitting up of the scientific project into so many separate sciences and disciplines, it is untenable to hold on to the notion of a strict essence of science.[25] All the same, there are still shared characteristics that hold across the sciences that Heidegger looks to delineate.

First and foremost is the shift toward the operational and industrial organization of science, rationally administered in big institutions and universities, geared toward achieving "results" and "effects" for the purpose of the "domination and direction" of what is objectively represented. Ultimately, science is given over to the pursuit of harnessing, exploiting, and breeding of whatever resources there are (GA65: 148). Heidegger predicts that under the imperative of utility and control, "the humanities" will morph into "communication science" [*Zeitungswissenchaft*], whereas the natural sciences will turn into "machine science" (ibid.: 158). Needless to say, philosophy as traditionally understood will no longer find "a place" within the modern research industry (ibid.: 156).

It is in this context of the emergence of big corporate science and the imminent threat to philosophy in Nazi Germany that Heidegger resolutely denies that science is a kind of binding knowledge, *massgebendes Wissen* (ibid.: 141). Instead, Heidegger finds a fundamental "truthlessness" [*Wahrheitslosigkeit*] at the heart of science (ibid.: 143). Perhaps the most unsettling aspect of Heidegger's diagnosis is that the instrumentalization of science means that it is in principle compatible with any form of government, including authoritarian ones, for if the "truth" of science is identified with the "truth of propositions only," and the mere "results" and "effects" generated, nothing in science itself delimits what use is to be made of it in society.[26] But if science is just a tool, it cannot possibly lay claim to truth, let alone the whole of truth.

All of this informs Heidegger's conception of *Ge-stell* in the 1950s, as well as its precursor concept, *machination* or *Machenschaft* in the *Black Notebooks* of the 1930s and 1940s.[27] In particular, when Heidegger describes the essence of technology as *Ge-stell*, that is, the revealing of what is real in terms of setting upon it, ordering it, challenging it as a resource and standing-reserve, he specifically adds that it is ultimately modern science, in particular, modern physics that "prepares the way" for the essence of technology (GA7: 23). According to Heidegger, the "challenging gathering-together" already holds sway in physics (ibid.): "Because physics, indeed already as pure theory, sets nature up to exhibit itself as a coherence of forces calculable in advance, it orders its experiments precisely for the purpose of asking whether and how nature reports itself when set up in this way" (ibid.: 22). Generalizing, Heidegger holds that, as "theory of reality," modern science already "sets up" reality, enframing it and rendering it intelligible as standing-reserve for humans (GA7: 50). In the last analysis, Heidegger traces this back to an ever-accelerating trend in modernity, especially since Descartes—i.e., the concentration of all relations to reality through the representing subject, the *cogito*, which forms theories about seemingly objectively present things in the world, while forgetting that it itself is part of the world it represents. Already this objectification in modern philosophy and modern science has the character of setting-upon that Heidegger identifies as the essence of the *Gestell*.

Even though the emphasis, in this later account of modern science, is on the conjunction of science and technology, and on the underlying will to power that informs modernity, it is entirely consistent with Heidegger's earlier account of science in *Being and Time*, including the clear and unmistakable warning not to mistake scientific objectivity for what in truth reality *is*. That is to say, in inscribing modern science in modernity or *die Neuzeit*, Heidegger is careful not to identify the two,[28] nor is he losing sight of his specific argument that science is unable to reflect on its own limits, including the always presupposed but unthematic truth of that which humans encounter in the place they inhabit. Moreover, it is noteworthy that although Heidegger calls for a preparatory thinking that aims at "overcoming" modernity or even "metaphysics," Heidegger nowhere envisions anything like the "overcoming" of science or its replacement by something else. When Heidegger points to the possibility that "the world civilization that is just now beginning might one day overcome its technological-scientific-industrial character as the sole measure for man's world sojourn" (GA14: 75), it is clear that he takes issue with the exclusive orientation in all walks of life to expect the solution to all problems in more technology, more science, and more industrial output, which obviously does not imply anything like an "overcoming" of science as such.

VIII

As we have seen, science looms large in Heidegger's philosophy and there are two principal reasons for this. First, as described above, corporate science is one "of the essential phenomena of modernity."[29] As such, it increasingly determines and shapes the outlook and reality of our modern way of life, not only in Europe and America, but across the globe. Since Heidegger understands philosophy as the attempt to come to grips with what there is, and with what confronts us in our lives, an account of science is therefore absolutely necessary and indispensable.[30] Second, inasmuch as science itself purports to be the true "theory of reality,"[31] it is imperative that philosophy engages with it. This is all the more so if one holds, as Heidegger does, that truth, ἀλήθεια, is not only the preeminent theme in philosophy, but also constitutes the very basis of our relating to the world at large.

Heidegger's philosophy is not just peripherally concerned with science, but instead offers an account of the phenomenon of science as part of its very core. It not only provides a genealogy of scientific theory as it arises from out of our prior engagement with the world, but also shows up the inherent limits of science (i.e., its inability to reflexively incorporate into its own theory the necessary conditions of its being rooted in the openness of the world in which Dasein is situated). It is this situatedness, properly understood, that is the very space of truth or truth of space that Heidegger argues for in his topological theory of truth.[32] Based on this, Heidegger not only contests the claim that science as the putative "theory of reality" captures the whole truth of what there is,[33] but he also shows how, since modernity, the topological nature of human existence has been pushed to the sidelines for the sake of an ever-more-rigid subjectivism and a concomitant objectivism.[34] He shows a subjectivism in which being comes to mean, in the first instance, just the being of the theoretically or scientifically represented object as it stands before the contemplating subject, but in which being is eventually transformed so that it appears as nothing more than the being of what is produced, consumed, and transformed within the unbounded network of mobilities and flows that is so often taken to characterize the contemporary globalized world. In this way, Heidegger's thinking of science, though it includes a genuine philosophy of science, nevertheless extends beyond the usual confines of such a philosophy.[35] Heidegger's thinking of science is a thinking of philosophy, of the world, and of our own being. It is also therefore a thinking or rethinking of our contemporary situation within technological modernity—a thinking and rethinking of our own place.

NOTES

1. Translation: "Reflection on science is 'scientifically' not possible, but only on the ground and by way of another knowledge, which from times immemorial has been called philosophy."

2. J. J. Kockelmans, "The Era of the World-as-Picture," quoted in Glazebrook (2016: 337).

3. Glazebrook's (2000) work is notable for being perhaps the only serious book-length attempt to engage with Heidegger specifically on the issue of science and the philosophy of science.

4. The edited volume *Heidegger on Science* (Glazebrook 2012) contains some of the best scholarly articles on Heidegger's thought on science.

5. In the same vein, Trish Glazebrook suggested "to read Heidegger's thought as a philosophy of science" (2000: 13). Emblematic for the creative appropriation of Heidegger's thought for a philosophy of science is the work by John Haugeland—see Haugeland 2013.

6. While Caputo's argument for the "unity" of Heidegger's constructive and deconstructive views on science leaves behind the simplistic division, it still misses that Heidegger's constant philosophical aim is to draw the limits of science from the perspective of philosophy. See Caputo 2012.

7. Thus, in "What is Metaphysics?" Heidegger states that "philosophy can never be measured against the idea of science" (2004b: 122).

8. "The animal cannot philosophize; God does not need to philosophize. A God who philosophized would not be a God, because the essence of philosophy is to be a finite potentiality of a finite being" (GA27: 3).

9. See GA11: 14.

10. See GA6.1: 325. As Heidegger puts it in *Die Grundprobleme der Phänomenologie*, "world-understanding" always implies "understanding-of-oneself," and *vice versa* (GA58: 250).

11. Already in the early 1920s Heidegger argues against the "reification" of "life," because it brings about a "loss of self" and "world." See GA58: 188.

12. *"Brief über den 'Humanismus,'"* GA9: 339.

13. See especially Malpas 2006.

14. This remains so despite Heidegger's seeming attempt in *Sein und Zeit*, § 70, to argue for the secondary character of spatiality.

15. The German reads as follows: *Wissenschaft überhaupt kann als das Ganze eines Begründungszusammen-hanges wahrer Sätze bestimmt werden*. The emphasis here is on the justificatory nexus or system that underwrites the derivation of true propositions. In point of fact, Heidegger's reference here is Husserl's *Logical Investigation*, Vol. 1, translated by J. N. Findlay (London: Routledge, 1982), 16–19.

16. Heidegger's concept includes pretty much everything that Aristotle calls "experience." See *Metaphysics*, 980–981 (Aristotle 1985: 1552).

17. See also GA7: 59 and GA77: 36–37.

18. Putnam makes the same point: "[O]ne thing physics cannot do is account for its own possibility. If the only facts there are are indeed the facts of physics, then there cannot be semantical facts" (2002: 106).

19. On early Heidegger's criticism of theoretical and scientific disciplines as ahistorical and undermining an authentic life, see Farin 2016a.

20. See also GA3: 29.

21. John Locke thus characterizes the mind as much like a *camera obscura*—see Locke 1959: 211–12.

22. For more on the two senses of truth at issue here, see Malpas 2014.

23. We can see this when Heidegger, contradicting his own view in *Sein und Zeit*, asserts that "science is questioningly standing one's ground within the always concealed beings at large," or even makes science "the basic event" of Dasein (GA16: 110–11). This is in contradistinction to what Heidegger states in "Was ist Metaphysik?" where he holds that "metaphysics is the basic event in Dasein," and certainly not science, because science does not address the world at large and Dasein

(GA9: 122). In other words, in extending the definition of philosophy to science, Heidegger effectively makes science a philosophical discipline.

24. See also Farin and Malpas 2017.

25. "Thus there is never and nowhere anything like '*the*' science, as for example, there is 'art' and 'philosophy,' which are always in themselves essentially and fully what they are, when they *are* historical." Heidegger continues that "science is only a formal title" that no longer provides an essential definition of the innumerable disciplines and individual sciences (GA65: 145). On the "myth" of one science with "one voice" only, see Feyerabend 2011: xi.

26. Heidegger puts this in rather provocative terms: "Only genuine modern (i.e., 'liberal') science can be 'folkish science' ['*völkische Wissenschaft*']. Only on the basis of prioritizing method over subject matter and propositional truth over the truth of entities does modern science permit an adjustable shifting to various purposes, depending on need (executing decisive materialism and technicism in Bolshevism; deployment in the four-year plan; utilization for political education). In all of this science is everywhere *the same* and becomes, precisely with these various goals, basically and increasingly more uniform, i.e., more 'international'" (GA65: 148–49).

27. See Weston 2016.

28. Besides science, Heidegger lists technology, the aestheticization of art or the reduction of art to "experience," the emergence of "culture" and its organization around "values," and the flight of the gods as defining moments of modernity. See GA5: 75–76.

29. "Die Zeit des Weltbildes," 75.

30. Heidegger writes: "Science is one way, and a decisive one at that, in which everything that is presents itself to us. Therefore, we must say: the reality in which todays man keeps himself and moves about is in increasing measure co-determined by what is called the Western-European science" (*Wissenschaft und Besinnung*, 39).

31. *Wissenschaft und Besinnung*, 40.

32. "Western thinking in its beginning conceived this open region as τα ἀληέα, the unconcealed. If we translate ἀλήθεια as 'unconcealment' rather than 'truth,' this translation is not merely 'more literal'; it also contains the directive to rethink the ordinary concept of truth in the sense of the correctness of statements and to think it back to that still uncomprehended disclosedness and disclosure of beings" ("Vom Wesen der Wahrheit," in *Wegmarken*, 188–89).

33. *Wissenschaft und Besinnung*, 40.

34. See "Die Zeit des Weltbildes," 87–96, 98–100.

35. On the difficulty of a genuine Continental Philosophy of Science, see Babette Babbich, "'The Problem of Science' in Nietzsche and Heidegger," *Research Resources* 7, http://fordham.bepress.com/phil_research/7.

BIBLIOGRAPHY

All references to Heidegger's works are to the *Gesamtausgabe*, Frankfurt: Klostermann, 1975–.

Aristotle. 1985. *The Complete Works of Aristotle*, vol. II (Revised Oxford Translation). Edited by Jonathan Barnes. Princeton, NJ: Princeton University Press.

Babbich, B. 2019. "'The Problem of Science' in Nietzsche and Heidegger." *Research Resources* 7. https://fordham.bepress.com/phil_research/7/.

Caputo, J. D. 2012. "Heidegger's Philosophy of Science: The Two Essences of Science." In *Heidegger on Science*, edited by T. Glazebrook, 261–79. New York: State University of New York Press.

Farin, I. 2016a. "The Different Notions of History in Heidegger's Work." In *Hermeneutical Heidegger*, edited by Michael Bowler and Ingo Farin, 23–69. Evanston, IL: Northwestern University Press.

———. 2016b. "A Response to Sheehan's Attempted Paradigm Shift in Heidegger Studies." *Parrhesia* 26 (2016): 117–35.

———. 2018. "Reply to Prof Sheehan." *Parrhesia* 29: 234–40.

Farin, I., and J. Malpas. 2017. "On Overestimating Philosophy: Lessons from Heidegger's *Black Notebooks*." *Journal of Aesthetics and Phenomenology*, 4, no. 2: 183–95.

Feyerabend, P. 2011. *The Tyranny of Science*. Cambridge: Polity Press.

Foucault, M. 2000. *Essential Works of Foucault 1954–1984*, vol. 1. Edited by Paul Rabinow. London: Penguin.

Glazebrook, T. 2000. *Heidegger's Philosophy of Science*. New York: Fordham University Press.

———, ed. 2012. *Heidegger on Science*. New York: State University of New York Press.

———. 2016. "Science." In *The Bloomsbury Companion to Heidegger*, edited by F. Raffoul and E. S. Nelson, 337–44. London: Bloomsbury.

Haugeland, J. 2000. "Truth and Finitude: Heidegger's Transcendental Existentialism." In *Heidegger, Authenticity, and Modernity*, vol. 1, edited by Mark Wrathall and Jeff Malpas, 43–77. Cambridge, MA: MIT Press.

———. 2013. *Dasein: Disclosed*. Edited by Joseph Rouse. Cambridge, MA: Harvard University Press.

Husserl, E. 1982. *Logical Investigation*, vol. 1. Translated by J. N. Findlay. London: Routledge.

Locke, J. 1959. *An Essay Concerning Human Understanding*, Vol. 1. Complete and unabridged, collated and annotated by Campbell Fraser. New York: Dover Publications.

Malpas, J. 2006. *Heidegger's Topology: Being, Place, World*. Cambridge, MA: MIT Press.

———. 2014. "The Twofold Character of Truth: Heidegger, Davidson, Tugendhat." In *The Multidimensionality of Hermeneutic Phenomenology*, edited by Babette Babbich and Dimitri Ginev, 243–66. Dordrecht: Springer, 2014.

Putnam, H. 2002. "Are Values Made or Discovered?" In Putnam, *The Collapse of the Fact/Value Dichotomy*, 96–134. Cambridge, MA: Harvard University Press.

———. 2012. "Science and Philosophy." In Putnam, *Philosophy in an Age of Science: Physics, Mathematics, and Skepticism*, edited by Mario De Caro and David Macarthur, 40–50. Cambridge, MA: Harvard University Press.

Rorty, R. 1979. *Philosophy and the Mirror of Nature*. Oxford: Blackwell.
Rouse, J. 2005. "Heidegger on Science and Naturalism." *Division I Faculty Publications*. Paper 36. http://wesscholar.wesleyan.edu/div1facpubs/36.
Sheehan, T. 2015. *Making Sense of Heidegger: A Paradigm Shift*. London: Rowman & Littlefield.
———. 2018. "Which Heidegger? A Response to Ingo Farin." *Parrhesia* 29: 212–33.
Weston, N. 2016. "Thinking the Oblivion of Thinking: The Unfolding of *Machenschaft* and *Rechnung* in the Time of the *Black Notebooks*." In *Reading Heidegger's Black Notebooks 1931–1941*, edited by Ingo Farin and Jeff Malpas, 269–88. Cambridge, MA: MIT Press.

Index

ability-to-be (*Seinkönnen*): 30, 31, 102–3, 105–11, 114–16, 153–54, 158–59, 164, 223, 226–27, 229
agency: 7, 8, 79, 81–83, 86, 89, 99–101, 104, 107–16, 126–27, 1515–2, 218, 259
  prereflective: 21–22, 24, 27, 65, 104, 151–55, 162–64, 166–68, 187, 191
animal agency: 80–86, 89, 92–93, 245
answerability: 19, 21, 31–34, 37, 44, 93, 113, 178
anxiety (*Angst*): 4, 9, 38, 92, 94, 108–9, 126–27, 129, 139–41, 143, 224–32
Aristotle: 7, 19, 21, 25–26, 34–35, 54–55, 81, 83, 128–36, 140, 142, 151, 152, 155–62, 165, 167, 178–79
Augenblick, the: 19, 30, 31, 197
Augustine: 180, 260
authenticity: 2–4, 7, 31–32, 37, 71, 93, 100, 107–13, 116–19, 125–30, 133, 135–42, 176–82, 184, 197–200, 224–25, 230, 233–34, 282, 289

being-with: 28, 30, 130, 177, 179, 228, 230, 231
Brandom, Robert: 79–80, 82, 91, 95n13

Burch, Matthew: 7, 169n6, 207n26

care: 1, 8, 11, 17–18, 28–29, 33, 45n5, 47n30, 53, 86–87, 99, 107, 109–15, 118, 154, 172, 175–85, 187, 224, 226–27, 230
choice: 3, 33, 71, 120n9, 125–29, 133, 135–39, 141–43, 145–6n28, 146n33, 151, 156, 159, 270
circumspection: 27, 28, 153–54, 156–57, 161–68, 283–86
commitment: 26, 29, 37, 83, 89, 103, 105–11, 117, 118, 169n6, 175, 179, 187–88, 192, 194, 199–200, 290
concepts: 20, 23, 42, 44, 46n24, 83–85, 89–90, 164, 201, 244–45
concern: 28, 41, 130–31, 133, 135, 137, 140–41, 154, 224, 231, 263, 264
conscience: 4–5, 31–33, 36, 40, 42, 82–83, 108, 113, 178–80, 183–84, 196–99, 218, 226–33
constitutivism: 7, 99–119
conversation: 8, 171–85
  relevance in: 172, 174–75, 179–82, 184–85
cooperative principle: 171–74, 177, 179
Crowell, Steven: 6–9, 75n28, 79–80, 82–83, 86–89, 91–93, 99–100,

107–16, 128, 152, 155, 159, 166, 179–82, 188, 204, 213, 217–34, 248, 252–54, 259, 262–63, 274–75

Das Man (the one-self): 3, 31, 41, 92–93, 157, 176, 188, 197, 223–32
death: 4–5, 40, 49n63, 92, 130, 196–99, 226–28, 232, 264, 282
decisionism: 3–5, 7, 11, 31, 37, 99, 116, 125–29, 133, 135–36, 139, 142–43, 180, 188
deliberation: 3, 6–8, 17, 27, 81, 83, 90, 101, 144n10, 151–68, 169n6, 283
Derrida, Jacques: 82, 216
Descartes, Rene: 46n23, 234, 238, 292
destiny (*Geschick*): 40, 49n60
Dilthey, Wilhelm: 23, 45n12
discourse: 3, 8, 24–26, 30–32, 34, 42, 136, 157, 160–61, 172, 177–78, 226–28, 232
Dreyfus, Hubert: 1, 5, 47n32, 144n10, 154, 166, 225
Dreyfus, Hubert, and Rubin, Jane: 5, 126

embodiment: 25, 89, 91, 221–22
époche: 216, 222, 241, 247, 263–65; *see also* transcendental reduction
ethics: 4, 5, 115, 134, 180, 217, 259
eudaimonia: 131–33
exemplarity: 49n54, 59, 110, 117, 183, 188–89, 196–99, 201–3, 206n21

facticity: 22–24, 32–33, 36, 63, 109–15, 117–18, 226
Fermat, Pierre de: 234
Fink, Eugen: 213–16, 229, 233, 240
first–person: 9, 81, 92, 93, 104, 105, 110–12, 114, 117–18, 213, 217, 223–29
formal indication: 23, 27–28, 31, 32, 34, 35, 233, 235n6
formalization: 32, 213, 228, 230–34, 235n6
for-the-sake-of (*Umwillen*): 28, 31–36, 57–62, 65–66, 73n14, 73n16, 88–89, 135, 153–56, 158, 169n6, 224

form of life: 8, 102, 153, 158–61, 163–68, 290; *see also* ability-to-be; practical identity
Foucault, Michel: 10, 278, 284
foundationalism: 9, 69, 172, 207n29, 213, 217–19, 226, 229
Franklin, Benjamin: 171, 184, 185
freedom: 10, 31, 33, 36–37, 54–55, 57, 59–64, 69–71, 73n16, 81–83, 86–87, 94n3, 105, 113, 118, 125–27, 129, 138, 142–43, 177–78, 191, 205n11

God/gods: 39, 48n44, 179, 192–99, 203, 205n11, 206n16, 294n8, 295n28
the Good (*agathon*): 3–5, 8, 11, 114–15, 125, 129–37, 140–42, 156, 158–59, 172, 179–85, 192–95, 198–99, 218, 229
Grice, Paul: 8, 171–75, 177–79, 184
grounding (*Grund*): 33–37, 39–40, 43, 53–56, 59, 62–68, 71, 88, 213–14, 216, 225–26, 229–30
ground, taking over being a: 19, 35–37, 82, 92, 95, 227–30, 232
guilt: 4, 9, 32, 213, 226–34

Habermas, Jürgen: 3
Haugeland, John: 7, 96n20, 99, 101–3, 106–7, 109, 111, 117, 119, 282
Hegel, G. W. F.: 4, 17, 21, 31, 42, 44, 79, 83, 207n27, 213
Heraclitus: 39, 42–43, 178–79, 183
historicity: 213, 216, 233–34
Hume, David: 82
Husserl: 9–10, 18, 23, 24, 26, 45n1, 46n24, 62, 65, 74n23, 74n28, 88, 89, 213–22, 225, 229, 231, 233–34, 237–49, 251–55, 255n3, 256n10, 259–60, 262–64, 266–67

idle talk: 3, 178–79
inauthenticity: 3, 32, 37, 92–93, 95, 108, 111, 113, 118, 126–27, 129, 133, 137, 140–42, 177, 180, 223, 225, 227, 230–31, 282, 289; *see also* authenticity

instrumental rationality: 28–29, 130–34, 138–40, 154–56, 159–61, 165, 224

intentionality: 19–20, 54, 56, 62, 64–68, 72n8, 74n23, 74n28, 81, 86, 89, 91, 93, 106, 151, 153, 159, 161, 167–68, 176, 214, 219–26, 243, 245–48, 250–51, 266, 269–71

interest: 132, 176–78, 181, 185

interesting: 171, 174–76, 181, 185

interpretation: 9, 29–31, 153–54, 158, 161–66, 168, 176, 188–89, 198, 215, 244, 284

intuition: 18, 22–24, 26, 27, 30, 32, 37, 46n23, 55–56, 72n7, 160, 181, 191, 201, 219, 225, 260, 268–69

irrationalism: 2, 8, 17, 18, 29, 37, 45n1, 99, 189, 193, 284

judgment: 7, 8, 20–22, 24–26, 85, 87, 127–29, 135–38, 140–42, 145n26, 145n28, 146n33, 151–53, 155, 158–61, 164, 166, 188, 198, 207n22, 243–45

Kant: 6–7, 8, 19, 21, 23, 62, 79–93, 95n13, 95n18, 120n9, 125, 151, 152, 173, 180, 188, 190–99, 201–4, 229, 260, 284
 and the incorporation thesis: 81–83, 86, 92, 112–13, 120n9, 151

Katsafanas, Paul: 105

Korsgaard, Christine: 83, 85, 86, 100–1, 113, 155, 207n29

Kuhn, Thomas: 10, 284

Lance, Mark: 106

Lask, Emil: 20–23, 26, 29

legein, reason as: 18–19, 22–25, 29–30, 33–38, 40–44, 157; see also *logos*

Leibniz, Gottfried Wilhelm: 38, 48n51, 54, 55–56, 231

Levinas, Emmanuel: 3, 4, 88

logic: 19–25, 29, 30–31, 37, 39, 41, 43, 44, 80, 244

logos: 18, 19–22, 25–27, 32, 35–37, 39–40, 42–43, 156–57, 161; *see also legein*, reason as

Lotze, Hermann: 21

Löwith, Karl: 2

Marcuse, Herbert: 2

mathematics: 20, 46n23, 217, 230–31, 233–34, 244, 284, 289

meaning: 3, 4, 9, 18–31, 34, 37, 40–42, 44, 45n8, 57, 87, 89, 102, 139, 153, 163, 167, 185, 191, 213, 215–16, 218–19, 222, 228, 229, 233, 250–44, 260–72, 283

meaning, space of: 1, 6, 11, 36–38, 229, 283

meaninglessness: 5, 47n38, 109, 126, 140

measure: 1, 3, 10, 18, 21–22, 25–26, 34–38, 40–44, 87, 102–4, 109, 116, 218–20, 229, 265

metaphysics: 1, 17, 19, 38–39, 43–44, 53, 54, 81–82, 101, 194, 260–61, 264–65

metaphysics of presence: 216

mood (*befindlichkeit*; affect): 55, 60, 63–67, 75n28, 87, 94, 108, 176, 182, 193, 195–96, 226, 230, 232

Murdoch, Iris: 126–28

Nazism: 2–3, 291

neo-Kantianism: 21–23, 81, 243

Nietzsche: 79, 94, 125, 202

nihilism: 5, 11, 17, 38, 99, 108, 126–27, 129–30, 133, 135, 139–40, 143, 199

noein (*nous*), reason as: 18–19, 22–38, 40–41, 44, 46n23, 47n34, 156, 160, 228

normative pluralism: 114, 129, 134, 140, 143, 181, 190, 197–200, 207n29

normativity: 4–8, 11, 18–21, 25, 27–44, 79–92, 99–119, 159, 172, 181, 213, 217–23, 227, 229, 259

normativity, hypothetical: 99–103, 105–7, 109, 111, 119
normativity, categorical: 7, 99–101, 106, 107–111, 113, 115, 119, 125, 199
normativity, social: 4, 31, 61, 83, 92, 102–5, 174, 208, 223, 229, 231
normative force: 29, 33, 36–37, 80, 82, 84–85, 100, 103, 106–11, 113, 115, 168, 187, 213
norms as rules: 79, 83, 84, 87, 92, 104, 110–1, 117, 202, 218–20
norms, acting in light of: 4–6, 36–37, 79–94, 100–7, 110, 114–18, 129, 131, 141, 155, 187, 228–29
norms, first-personal: 104–5, 110–11, 114–19, 217, 223–39; *see also* self-responsibility
norms, second-personal: 29, 47n28, 104–5, 114–19, 198
norms, third-personal: 47n28, 81, 104–5, 114–19, 223–25, 227, 229; *see also* normativity, social

ontological difference: 19, 35, 54, 56, 108

Parmenides: 40
perception: 27, 30, 46n20, 47n34, 65, 67, 89–90, 156, 160, 165, 215, 219–22, 234, 246, 248
phenomenological method: 8–10, 19–30, 34, 38, 41, 44, 55, 65, 213–30, 233–34, 237–55, 256n10, 259–75, 284
phenomenological reduction: 10, 214–16, 240–22, 247–48, 251–53, 259–73; *see also* époche
philosophy of science: 10, 277–93
phronesis: 7, 104, 128–31, 134–39, 142–43, 144n10, 156, 160, 167, 228
Pippin: 4, 6, 79–80, 92, 94
Plato: 114, 161, 180, 183, 218, 229, 242, 262, 275

practices, social: 25, 27, 102–5, 153–54, 157–60, 164–68, 290; *see also* social normativity
practical identity: 8, 87, 93, 139, 155, 172, 182–84, 185n3, 188–90, 197, 199–202, 207n29; *see also* ability-to-be (*Seinkönnen*)
principle of sufficient reason: 38, 44, 53–56, 59
projection: 57–67, 69–70, 75, 87, 109, 169n10, 195, 201, 203, 267, 274
psychologism: 20–21

reason-giving: 3, 6, 25, 30, 32–33, 37, 39–40, 44, 178, 204, 218, 229
reflection: 21–23, 26, 60, 83, 85–86, 90, 95n14, 113, 151–52, 154–58, 161–63, 166–68, 213–16, 247
relativism: 2–5, 9–11, 17, 99
resoluteness: 2–5, 31, 130, 137–39, 179, 182, 263, 268, 273, 291
responsibility: 9, 83, 85, 86, 108–113, 117, 120n9, 172, 181–82, 185, 198, 200, 203, 213, 223, 229, 234, 259
reticence: 175, 178–79, 184–85
Ricoeur, Paul: 3–4

Sartre, Jean-Paul: 86, 125, 180, 207n29
self-expression: 118, 125–29, 136–38, 141–43, 204
selfhood: 58, 62, 72n9 & n10, 73n11, 83, 147n43, 190, 195, 198, 204, 280
self-understanding: 28–32, 47n34, 68, 81, 888–9, 117–18, 164, 183, 195–200, 214, 216, 222–23, 226–27, 229, 279, 289–90
self-reflection: 26, 75n28, 90, 113, 118, 151, 213–16, 247
self-responsibility: 9, 37, 83, 87, 95, 110–13, 117–18, 120n9, 198–200, 207n22, 213, 223, 228–29, 234; *see also* first-person norms

Scheler, Max: 180, 237–38, 241, 249
solicitude (*Fürsorge*): 28, 118, 177, 179, 182–85, 224, 263
speech acts: 90, 171, 175, 184

technology: 17, 38, 291–93
theory: 10, 17, 102, 216, 282–85, 293
thrownness: 57–59, 64–66, 71, 82, 87, 95, 113, 145, 176, 183, 198, 214, 227, 232, 267–68, 270, 272, 274
transcendental method: 9–10, 19–24, 29, 38, 54–71, 115, 116, 213–23, 226, 229, 233, 238–40, 248–52, 254–55, 259, 271–73, 279
transcendental subjectivity: 9, 53–71, 106, 214–15, 225, 247, 248, 250–54, 267
truth: 2–5, 19–26, 36–38, 43–44, 54–56, 67–69, 133, 173–74, 184, 268, 278, 285–88, 291–93, 295n32

Tugendhat, Ernst: 2–4, 127–28

understanding: 19, 22–23, 27–30, 42, 56, 59–70, 102, 151, 153, 163–67, 191, 214, 226, 243, 270, 279
unity of practical agency: 7–8, 19, 38–41, 63, 90, 187–204

validity (*Geltung*): 19, 21–22, 25, 243–44, 247, 250–53
Velleman, David: 99, 101, 188–90,199, 204n3–4, 205n5–7
Viète, François: 234
voluntarism: 86, 92, 94, 105–7; *see also* decisionism

wonder: 176, 179–81

Zahavi, Dan: 225

About the Authors

Matthew Burch is lecturer in philosophy at the University of Essex. He works on issues at the intersection of phenomenology, moral psychology, and the social sciences. He is a coeditor of *Normativity, Meaning, and the Promise of Phenomenology* (2019), and his work has appeared in multiple journals, including *Inquiry*, *The European Journal of Philosophy*, *The Journal of Applied Philosophy*, and *The International Journal of Law and Psychiatry*.

Steven Crowell is Joseph and Joanna Nazro Mullen Professor of Humanities and professor of philosophy at Rice University. In addition to numerous articles on figures and issues in the phenomenological tradition, he is the author of *Husserl, Heidegger, and the Space of Meaning: Paths Toward Transcendental Phenomenology* (2001) and *Normativity and Phenomenology in Husserl and Heidegger* (2013). Crowell also edited *The Cambridge Companion to Existentialism* (2012) and, with Jeff Malpas, *Transcendental Heidegger* (2007). He is currently coeditor, with Sonja Rinofner-Kreidl, of the journal *Husserl Studies* and is researching issues at the intersection of transcendental philosophy, metaphysics, and second-person phenomenology.

Daniel O. Dahlstrom, John R. Silber Professor of Philosophy at Boston University, has translated works by Mendelssohn, Schiller, Hegel, Feuerbach, Husserl, and Heidegger. He is author of *Heidegger's Concept of Truth* (2009), *The Heidegger Dictionary* (2013), *Identity, Authenticity, and Humility* (2017), and editor of *Kant and His Contemporaries II* (2018).

About the Authors

Chad Engelland is associate professor of philosophy and chair of the philosophy department at the University of Dallas. He is the author of several books, including *Ostension: Word Learning and the Embodied Mind* (2014), *Heidegger's Shadow: Kant, Husserl, and the Transcendental Turn* (2017), and *Phenomenology* (2020). His research on phenomenology has appeared in such journals as *Continental Philosophy Review*, *Journal of the British Society for Phenomenology*, *The Review of Metaphysics*, and *Journal of the American Philosophical Association*.

Ingo Farin is lecturer in philosophy at the University of Tasmania. He is currently working on Heidegger's concepts of the life-world, temporality, and history. He is also interested in the development of hermeneutical philosophy in the wake of historical thought in the nineteenth and twentieth centuries, particularly the historical constellation of Dilthey, Yorck von Wartenburg, Husserl, Heidegger, and Misch. Recently he has started an interdisciplinary project about the intersection of technology and landscape, with special reference to hydroelectric power stations in Tasmania.

Sacha Golob is senior lecturer in philosophy at King's College London, and the director of the Centre for Philosophy and the Visual Arts. He is the author of *Heidegger on Concepts, Freedom and Normativity* (2014) and coeditor of the forthcoming *Cambridge History of Moral Philosophy*. His work has appeared in multiple journals, including *Mind*, *European Journal of Philosophy*, *British Journal of the History of Philosophy*, and *Kantian Review*.

Burt Hopkins is a visiting researcher at the Institute of Philosophy, Czech Academy of Sciences, Prague. He is author of *The Origin of the Logic of Symbolic Mathematics: Edmund Husserl and Jacob Klein* (2011) and *Intentionality in Husserl and Heidegger: The Problem of the Original Method and Phenomenon of Phenomenology* (1993).

Jered Janes is a visiting assistant professor in the department of philosophy at Marquette University. He works primarily on issues in phenomenology, philosophy of mind, and philosophical pedagogy.

Patrick Londen received his PhD in philosophy from the University of California–Riverside. His work focuses on phenomenology, existentialism, and practical philosophy more generally in the post-Kantian European tradition. His dissertation is titled *Authenticity and Agency: Heidegger's Constitutivism*.

Sebastian Luft is professor of philosophy at Marquette University. He has published in the areas of phenomenology, classical German philosophy (including neo-Kantianism), and the philosophy of culture. He has edited a volume in the *Husserliana* series and has translated Husserl's text *First Philosophy* in the Husserliana—Collected Works series. He is the author of three monographs and numerous articles. Together with Andrea Staiti and Konstantin Pollok, he is editor in chief of the *Journal of Transcendental Philosophy*.

Jeff Malpas is distinguished professor of philosophy at University of Tasmania, Australia and the founding director of its Center for Applied Philosophy and Ethics. He is the author of more than twenty books, including *Heidegger's Topology: Being, Place, World* (2006) and *Dialogues with Davidson: Acting, Interpreting, Understanding* (2011).

Denis McManus is professor of philosophy at the University of Southampton. He is the author of *The Enchantment of Words: Wittgenstein's Tractatus Logico-Philosophicus* (2006) and *Heidegger and the Measure of Truth* (2012), and the editor of *Wittgenstein and Scepticism* (2004) and *Heidegger, Authenticity and the Self* (2015).

Irene McMullin is professor of philosophy at the University of Essex. She specializes in the existential phenomenological tradition, especially as it pertains to ethics. She is the author of *Time and the Shared World: Heidegger on Social Relations* (2013), and *Existential Flourishing: A Phenomenology of the Virtues* (2019). She is also a coeditor of *Normativity, Meaning, and the Promise of Phenomenology* (2019). Her work on Husserl, Heidegger, Arendt, and Sartre has appeared in journals such as the *European Journal of Philosophy*, *Continental Philosophy Review*, and *Philosophical Topics*.

Thomas Sheehan teaches philosophy and religion at Stanford University. His most recent book is *Making Sense of Heidegger: A Paradigm Shift*.

www.ingramcontent.com/pod-product-compliance
Lightning Source LLC
Chambersburg PA
CBHW031545300426
44111CB00006BA/182